Internet

TOP 100 Simplified®

Tips & Tricks

by Joe Kraynak

From
maranGraphics®
&

Wiley Publishing, Inc.

Internet: Top 100 Simplified® Tips & Tricks

Published by
Wiley Publishing, Inc.
111 River Street
Hoboken, NJ 07030-5774

Published simultaneously in Canada

maranGraphics, Inc.
5755 Coopers Avenue
Mississauga, Ontario, Canada
L4Z 1R9

Library of Congress Control Number: The Library of Congress Control number is available from the Library of Congress
ISBN: 0-7645-7474-4
Manufactured in the United States of America
10 9 8 7 6 5 4 3 2 1

1K/QW/QY/QU/IN

Trademark Acknowledgments

Important Numbers

For U.S. corporate orders, please call maranGraphics at 800-469-6616 or fax 905-890-9434.

For general information on our other products and services or to obtain technical support please contact our Customer Care Department within the U.S. at 800-762-2974, outside the U.S. at 317-572-3993 or fax 317-572-4002.

Permissions

maranGraphics
Certain designs, text and Illustrations by maranGraphics, Inc., used with maranGraphics' permission.

Wiley Publishing, Inc.

U.S. Corporate Sales

Contact maranGraphics at (800) 469-6616 or fax (905) 890-9434.

U.S. Trade Sales

Contact Wiley at (800) 762-2974 or fax (317) 572-4002.

CREDITS

Project Editor:
Timothy J. Borek

Acquisitions Editor:
Jody Lefevere

Product Development Manager:
Lindsay Sandman

Copy Editor:
Nancy Rapoport

Technical Editor:
Ethan Marcotte

Editorial Manager:
Robyn Siesky

Permissions Editor:
Laura Moss

Editorial Assistant:
Adrienne Porter

Screen Artist:
Jill Proll

Illustrator:
Ronda David-Burroughs

Manufacturing:
Allan Conley
Linda Cook
Paul Gilchrist
Jennifer Guynn

Book Design:
maranGraphics, Inc.

Production Coordinator:
Maridee Ennis

Layout:
Beth Brooks
Amanda Carter

Cover Design:
Anthony Bunyan

Proofreader:
Joanne Keaton

Quality Control:
John Greenough
Angel Perez
Robert Springer

Indexer:
Sherry Massey

Special Help:
Shelley Lea
Kimberly Skeel
David Mayhew

Vice President and Executive Group Publisher:
Richard Swadley

Vice President and Publisher:
Barry Pruett

Composition Director:
Debbie Stailey

ABOUT THE AUTHOR

Joe Kraynak has been writing and editing computer books and training manuals for over 15 years. Joe has a Master's degree in English and a Bachelor's degree in Philosophy and Creative Writing from Purdue University. Joe is dedicated to making computers and the Internet more easily accessible to the average user.

maranGraphics is a family-run business located near Toronto, Canada.

At **maranGraphics**, we believe in producing great computer books—one book at a time.

Each maranGraphics book uses the award-winning communication process that we have been developing over the last 28 years. Using this process, we organize screen shots and text in a way that makes it easy for you to learn new concepts and tasks.

We spend hours deciding the best way to perform each task, so you don't have to! Our clear, easy-to-follow screen shots and instructions walk you through each task from beginning to end.

We want to thank you for purchasing what we feel are the best computer books money can buy. We hope you enjoy using this book as much as we enjoyed creating it!

Sincerely,

The Maran Family

Please visit us on the Web at:

www.maran.com

HOW TO USE THIS BOOK

Internet: Top 100 Simplified Tips & Tricks includes the 100 most interesting and useful tasks you can perform online. This book reveals cool secrets and timesaving tricks guaranteed to make you more productive in using the Internet.

Who is this book for?

Are you a visual learner who already knows the basics of e-mail, Web surfing, and shopping online but would like to take your Internet experience to the next level? Then this is the book for you.

Conventions In This Book

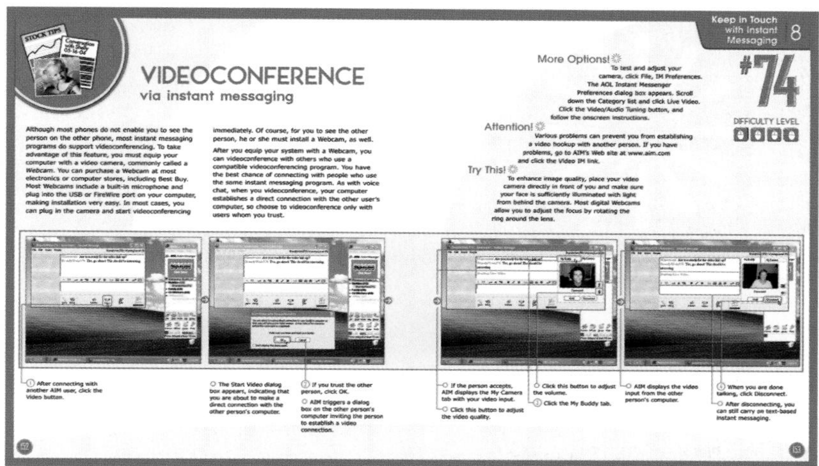
Keep in Touch with Instant Messaging 8

VIDEOCONFERENCE
via instant messaging

Although most phones do not enable you to see the person on the other phone, most instant messaging programs do support videoconferencing. To take advantage of this feature, you must equip your computer with a video camera, commonly called a *Webcam*. You can purchase a Webcam at most electronics or computer stores, including Best Buy. Most Webcams include a built-in microphone and plug into the USB or FireWire port on your computer, making installation very easy. In most cases, you can plug in the camera and start videoconferencing immediately. Of course, for you to see the other person, he or she must install a Webcam, as well.

After you equip your system with a Webcam, you can videoconference with others who use a compatible videoconferencing program. You have the best chance of connecting with people who use the same instant messaging program. As with voice chat, when you videoconference, your computer establishes a direct connection with the other user's computer, so choose to videoconference only with users whom you trust.

More Options!
To test and adjust your camera, click File, IM Preferences. The AOL Instant Messenger Preferences dialog box appears. Scroll down the Category list and click Live Video. Click the Video/Audio Tuning button, and follow the onscreen instructions.

Attention!
Various problems can prevent you from establishing a video hookup with another person. If you have problems, go to AIM's Web site at www.aim.com and click the Video IM link.

Try This!
To enhance image quality, place your video camera directly in front of you and make sure your face is sufficiently illuminated with light from behind the camera. Most digital Webcams allow you to adjust the focus by rotating the ring around the lens.

#74

DIFFICULTY LEVEL

1 After connecting with another AIM user, click the Video button.

The Start Video dialog box appears, indicating that you are about to make a direct connection with the other person's computer.

2 If you trust the other person, click OK.

AIM triggers a dialog box on the other person's computer inviting the person to establish a video connection.

If the person accepts, AIM displays the My Camera tab with your video input.

Click this button to adjust the video quality.

Click this button to adjust the volume.

3 Click the My Buddy tab.

AIM displays the video input from the other person's computer.

4 When you are done talking, click Disconnect.

After disconnecting, you can still carry on text-based instant messaging.

152 153

❶ Steps

This book walks you through each task using a step-by-step approach. Lines and "lassos" connect the screen shots to the step-by-step instructions to show you exactly how to perform each task.

❷ Tips

Fun and practical tips answer questions you have always wondered about. Plus, learn to do things on the Internet that you never thought were possible!

❸ Task Numbers

The task numbers, ranging from 1 to 100, indicate which self-contained lesson you are currently working on.

❹ Difficulty Levels

For quick reference, symbols mark the difficulty level of each task.

 Demonstrates a new spin on a common task

 Introduces a new skill or a new task

 Combines multiple skills requiring in-depth knowledge

 Requires extensive skill and may involve other technologies

TABLE OF CONTENTS

1 Boost Your Internet Connection Speed

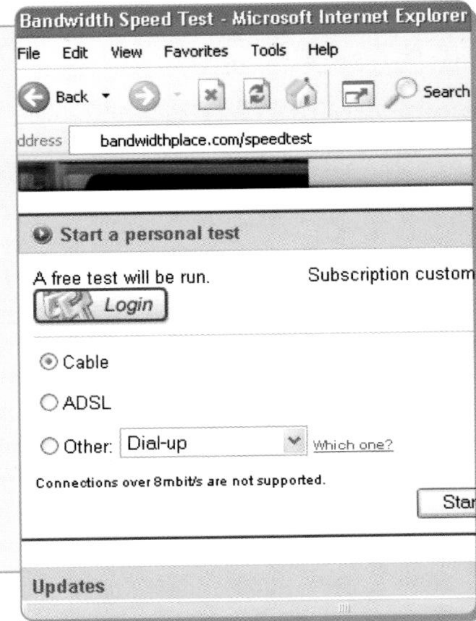

2 Customize Your Web Browser

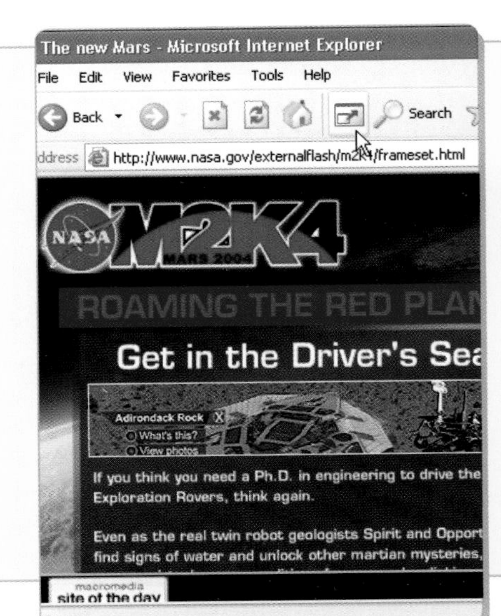

3 Accessorizing Your Web Browser

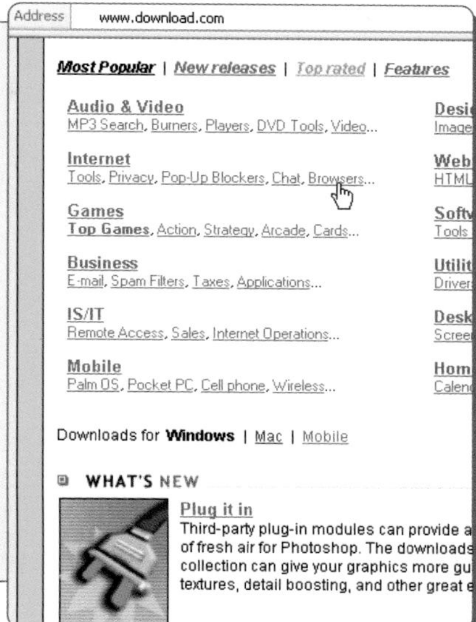

4 Power Browse in Private

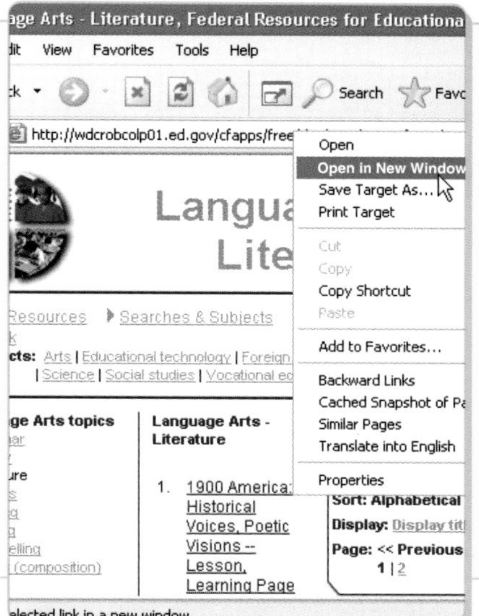

TABLE OF CONTENTS

5 Tap the Full Power of Google Searches

6 Maximize Your Success on eBay

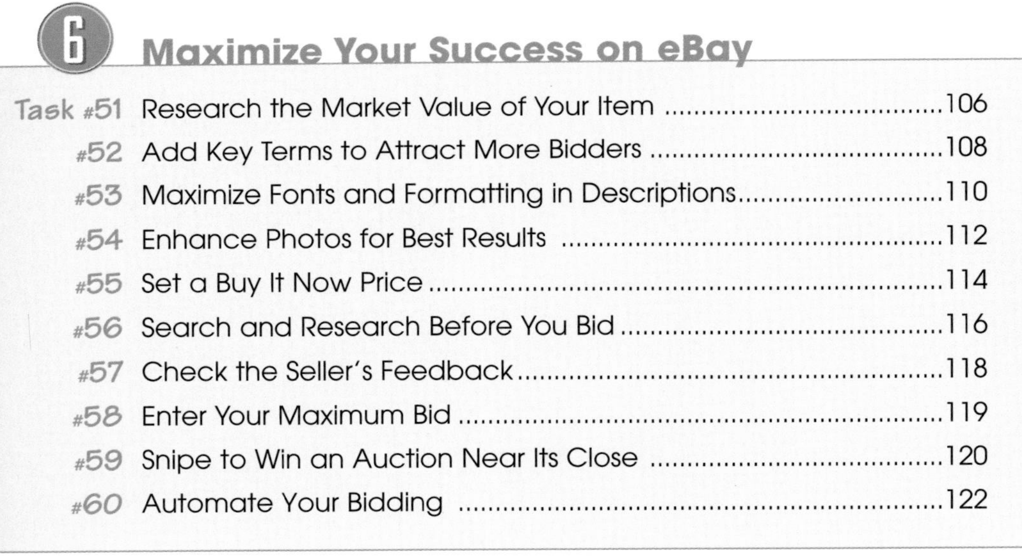

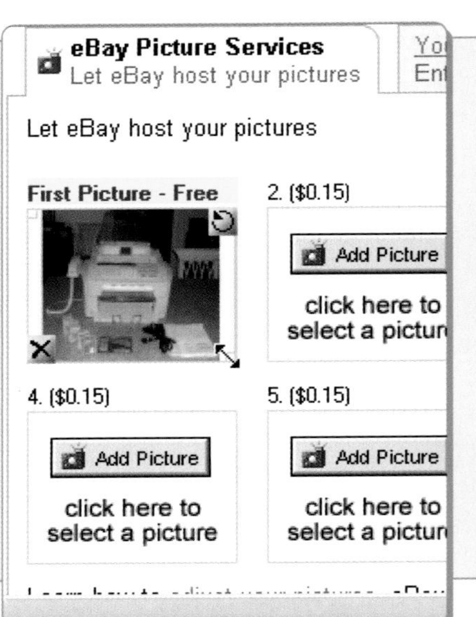

7 Master Your E-mail

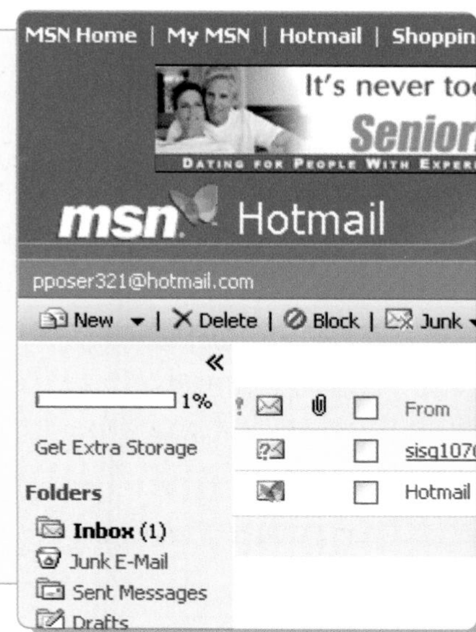

8 Keep in Touch with Instant Messaging

TABLE OF CONTENTS

9 Establish Your Web Presence with a Blog

BLOGGER
PUSH-BUTTON PUBLISHIN
CREATE YOUR OWN BLOG!
Blogger offers you instant communication power by letting you post your thoughts to the web whenever the urge strikes. Learn more about it. Or: Start Now!
WHAT'S UP
USA Today Iraqis enjoy new freedom of expression: "We suffered for years under Saddam Hussein, not being able to speak out,' says Omar Fadhil, 24, a dentist. 'Now, you can make your voice heard around the world.'" You said it Omar. That's pretty much our whole thing.

10 Protect Your System from Viruses and Crackers

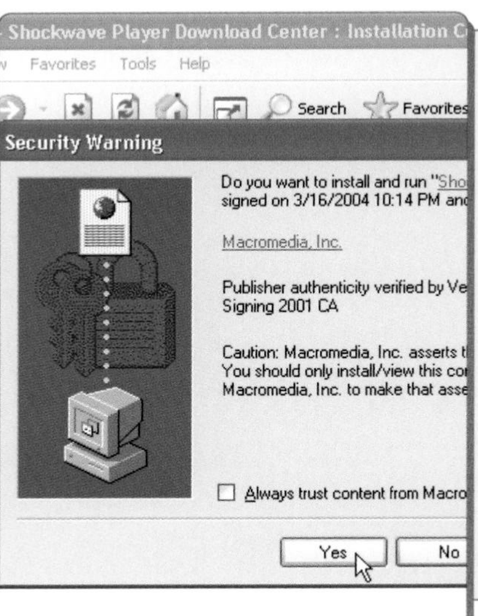

Boost Your Internet Connection Speed

Are you looking for ways to speed up your Internet connection without having to change providers and pay more for faster Internet access? Are you ready to rid your Web browser of those annoying and time-consuming pop-up ads? Do you want to surf the Web in a way that does not bog down your computer? This chapter provides the techniques and tips you need to maximize your Internet connection, streamline your browser, and take a shorter route to your favorite destinations on the Web.

With your computer, your Internet connection, and your Web browser, you have the tools you need to test your Internet connection speed, optimize your connection, tweak your browser to make it load pages faster, and download free utilities from the Web that can enhance your browsing experience as well as speed it up.

Even with a powerful computer, a broadband Internet connection, and the right browser settings, Web browsing can slow to a crawl if annoying ads keep popping up on your screen. You can download two utilities off the Internet and use them immediately to block pop-up ads and eliminate any spyware keeping track of your browsing habits. This chapter shows you where to find these utilities and how to use them.

This chapter also shows you how to optimize your hard drive storage and memory to improve the overall performance of your system to load pages faster. After you complete this chapter, you can begin cruising the Web at top speed!

TOP 100

Test your Internet CONNECTION SPEED

Internet service providers often advertise the top speed of their service, claiming that users can connect at 56 Kbps (kilobits per second) or 2 Mbps (megabits per second) or "up to 50 times faster than a standard dial-up connection." But what speed are you really experiencing and how does it compare to the advertised rate?

You can find out at any of several Web sites that offer tools for testing your Internet connection speed. These sites typically upload and download large files between the Web site and your computer and time how long it takes to upload and download large files to and from your computer in order to provide you with an accurate assessment of how fast your Internet connection really is at any time of the day or night.

You can expect to see your connection speed fluctuate throughout the day as more or fewer people go online to surf the Web, but if you notice that your Internet speed is always significantly slower than what your service provider advertised, you need to do some troubleshooting on your end and possibly contact your provider.

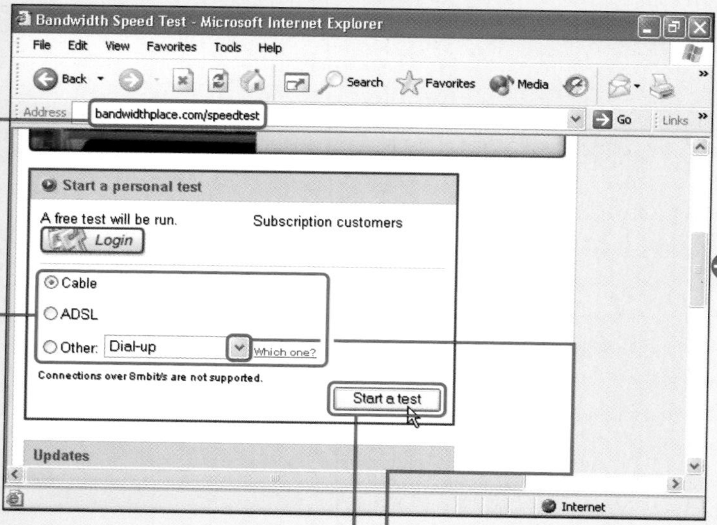

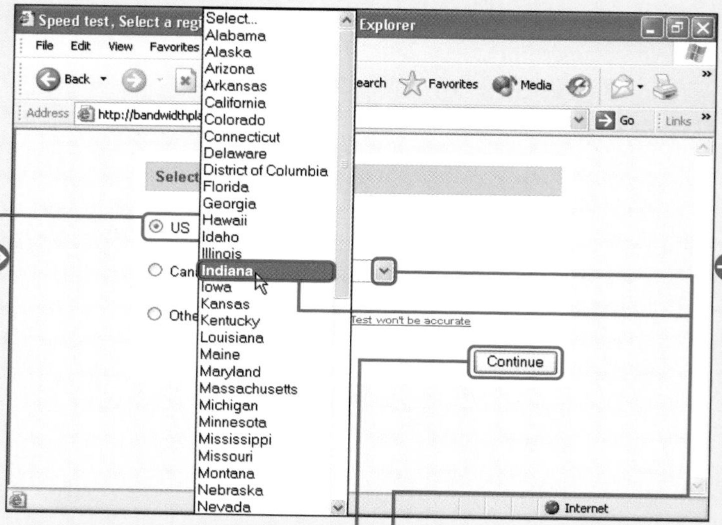

1 Type **bandwidthplace.com/speedtest/** and press Enter.

2 Scroll down and click your connection type.

- Additional connection types appear here.

3 Click Start a test.

- This screen prompts you to specify your geographical location.

4 Click your country.

5 Click here and select your state.

6 Click Continue.

DIFFICULTY LEVEL

Try This!

Test your speed in the morning, after you get home from work, and just before going to bed, and note any differences in connection speeds. Many people go online to check e-mail right after work, so you should notice a dip in the evening.

Did You Know?

Cable speeds vary greatly depending on how many of your neighbors are using the same service because customers in a given area share bandwidth.

Check It Out!

You can find many more sites on the Web where you can test your Internet connection speeds. Check out these sites:

www.dslreports.com/stest
us.mcafee.com/root/speedometer.asp
www.pcpitstop.com/internet/default.asp

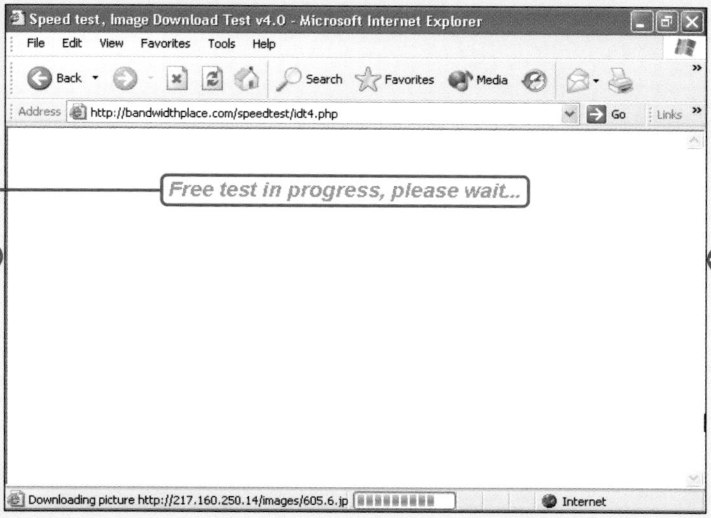

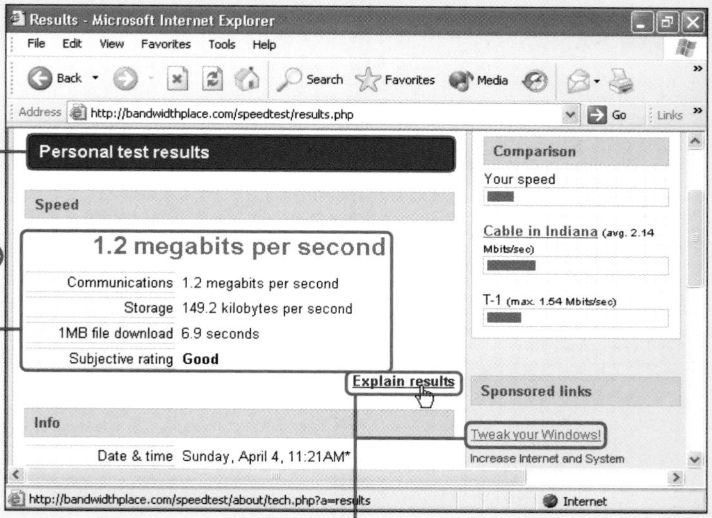

- As the test runs, this progress message appears.
- When the test is complete, personal test results appear.
- Your speed appears here.
- Click here for additional details.
- You can find tools for improving your connection speed.

Maximize the power of your BROWSER CACHE

As you surf the Web, your browser stores copies of the Web pages on your computer's hard drive in a temporary holding area, called the *cache*. When you revisit a page, the browser can call it up from the cache and update it rather than having to download the entire Web page again to your computer. Doing this helps pages load faster, because your computer's hard drive responds faster than the Internet.

You can increase the speed at which pages load by increasing the cache size, enabling your browser to store more pages for quick retrieval.

You can also change the cache settings to specify how often you want your browser to check for updates to any pages it has available in the cache. By having your browser check less often for updates, you can trim a little more off the time it takes to load a page. And when you start trimming a little time here and there, it soon adds up!

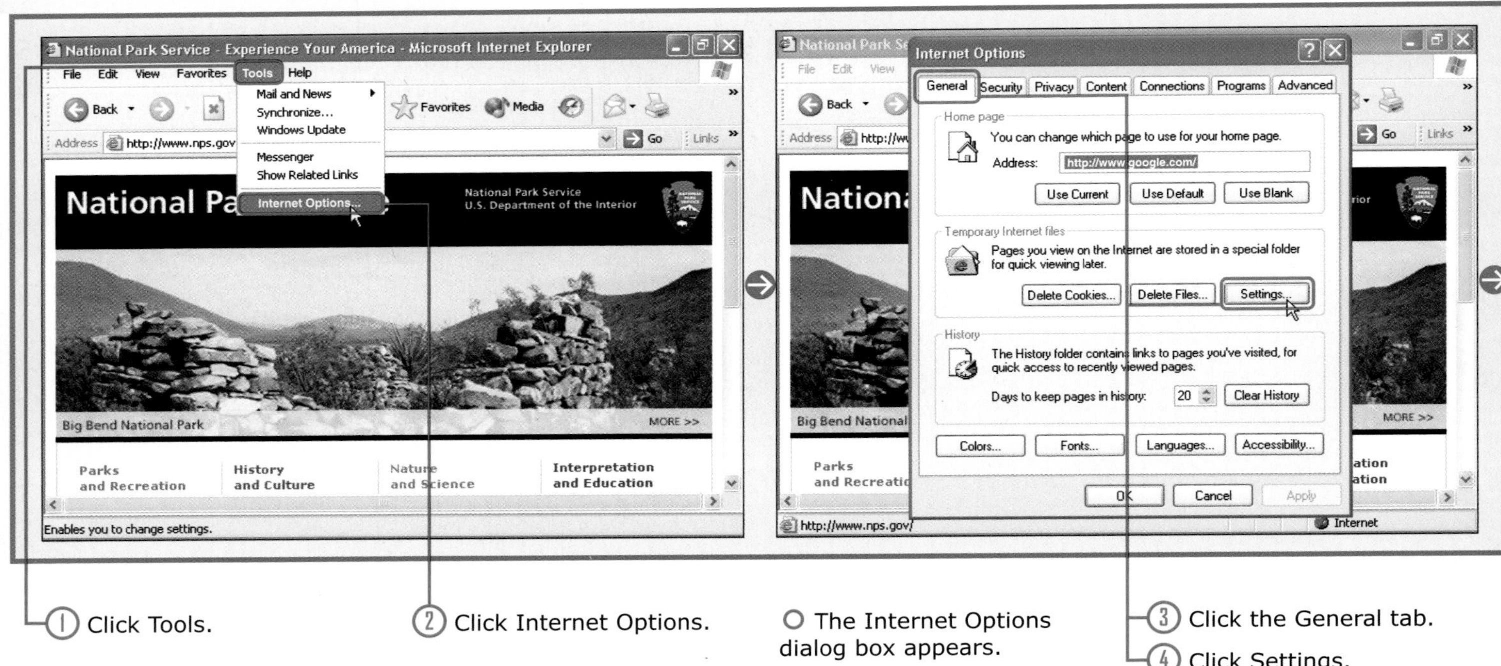

① Click Tools.

② Click Internet Options.

○ The Internet Options dialog box appears.

③ Click the General tab.

④ Click Settings.

Change It!

The cache is a folder on your computer's hard drive. If your computer has more than one hard drive, click Move Folder in the Settings dialog box, and move the folder to the drive that has the most available space.

DIFFICULTY LEVEL

Did You Know?

If you have your browser check less often for updates, you can always choose to check for update pages by clicking the Refresh button.

More Options!

Clear the cache occasionally to get rid of files for pages you rarely visit. Display the Internet Options dialog box, click the General tab, and click Delete Files.

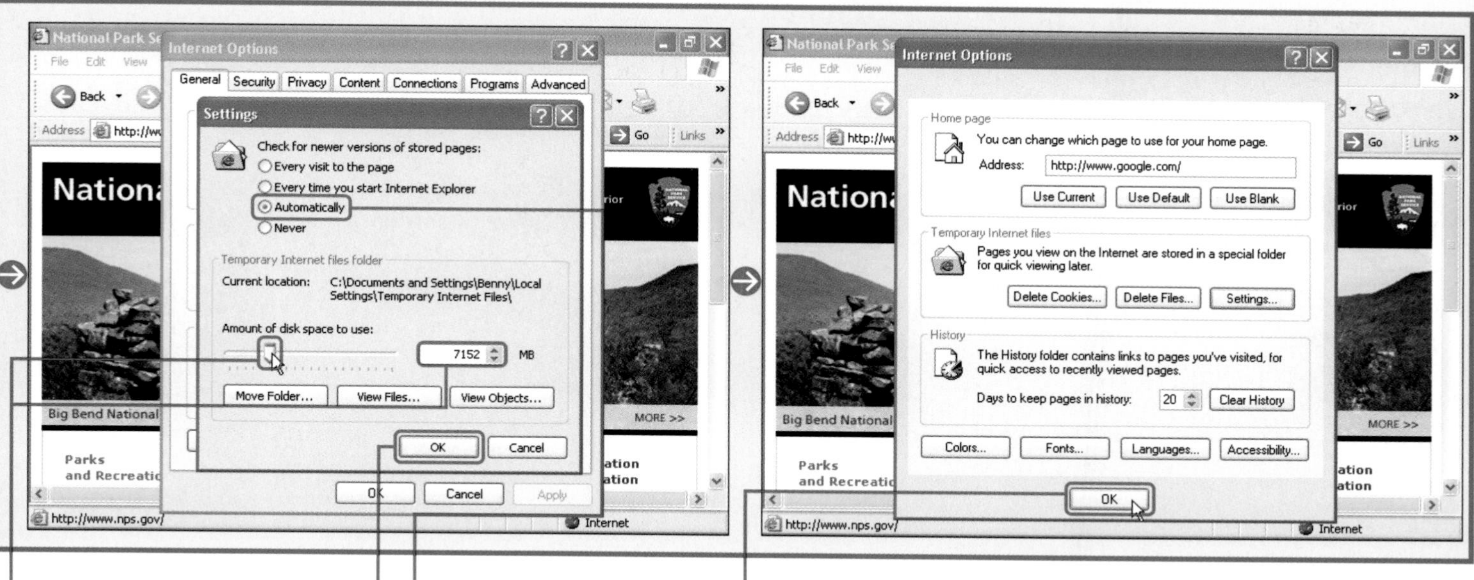

- The Settings dialog box appears.

5 Drag this slider to set the cache size.

- The cache size displays here.

6 Click Automatically to have Internet Explorer optimize caching for you.

Note: Although the Never setting results in faster browsing, it prevents Internet Explorer from checking for updated content.

7 Click OK.

- The Settings dialog box closes.

8 Click OK.

- Internet Explorer applies the changes.

Note: See task #8 and task #9 to optimize the performance of your computer's hard drive, where the cache is stored.

Optimize your dial-up MODEM SPEED

Most people assume that their modems are set up to transfer data over the Internet at the fastest rate possible, but that might not be the case. Settings that control the speed at which data can pass between the Internet and your computer might not be optimal for your modem. If your connection seems slow, you might benefit by checking and perhaps changing the *port speed* settings, which control the rate at which data passes through your computer's COM (communications) port.

Buffer settings can also affect the speed of a connection. A buffer stores data in memory, where the computer can access it more readily. In many cases, increasing the buffer size can help feed data at a more consistent rate to ensure that any data exchange proceeds smoothly without your modem having to wait to send or receive data. Generally, maximizing the buffer size increases speed, while decreasing it can help reduce communication errors, which can result in lost data. It is better to start high and then bump it down if you run into problems.

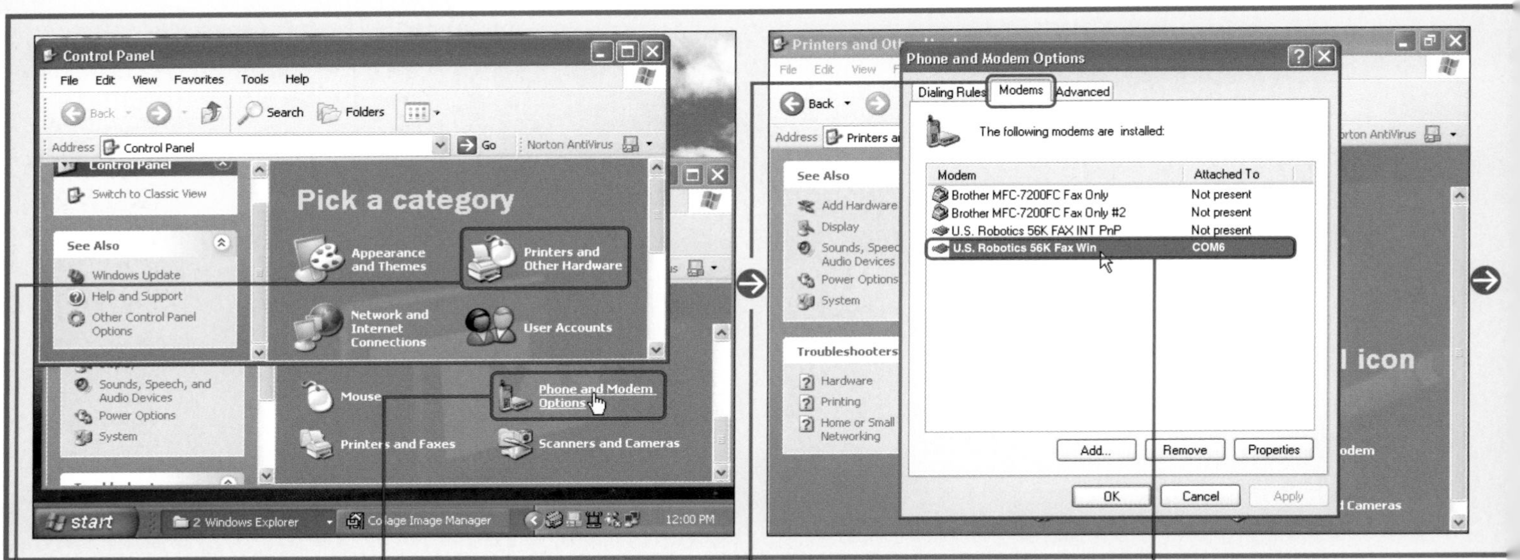

1. Open the Windows Control Panel.
2. Click the Printers and Other Hardware link.

- The Printers and Other Hardware screen appears.

3. Click the Phone and Modem Options link.

- The Phone and Modem Options dialog box appears.

4. Click the Modems tab.
5. Double-click the modem that you use to connect to the Internet.

Cross-Platform

These steps assume that your computer is running Windows XP. If it runs a different operating system, check its help system for details.

More Options!

In your modem's Properties dialog box, click the Advanced tab, click Advanced Port Settings, and select Use FIFO Buffers (☐ changes to ☑). Drag the slide controls to maximize the buffer sizes for optimal performance. If you experience intermittent connection problems, try decreasing the buffer settings.

Did You Know?

A 56 Kbps modem rarely connects at 56 Kbps. The limitations of data transfer over phone lines usually result in slower transfer rates, particularly when your computer is sending data, such as a request for a Web page. Speeds in a range of 33 Kbps to 53 Kbps are normal.

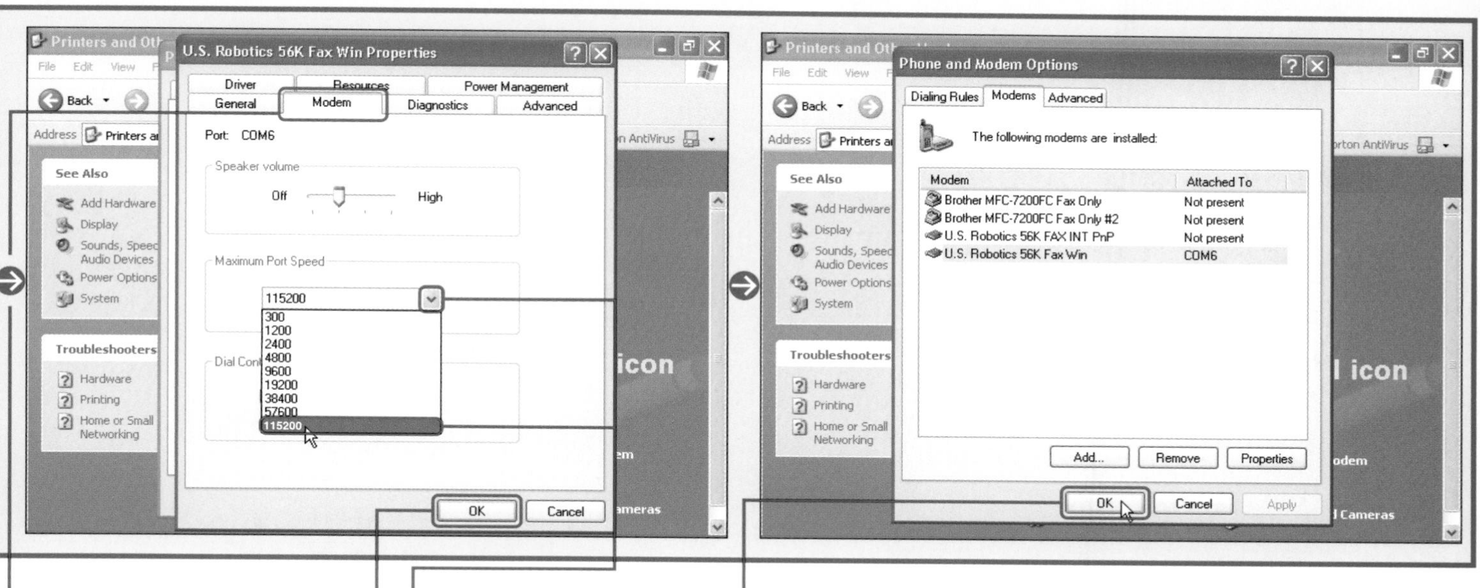

- The Properties dialog box appears.

6. Click the Modem tab.

7. Click here and select the highest setting.

8. Click OK.

- The Phone and Modem Options dialog box appears.

9. Click OK.

- The Phone and Modem Options dialog box saves your settings and closes.

Optimize your BROADBAND CONNECTION SPEED

Your computer's operating system contains settings that control the speed at which your system transmits and receives data over network connections. When you have a cable modem, satellite connection, DSL hookup, or other broadband Internet connection, your computer becomes part of a network, and the network settings that are built into your operating system govern that connection. Unfortunately, these settings are often optimized for Ethernet networks and dial-up modem connections, not broadband connections.

You can tweak the settings yourself or you can use a utility, as explained in task #5, that optimizes your operating system automatically. If you decide to try tweaking the settings yourself, you can find several Web sites that offer suggestions and instructions on which settings to change and how to change them. This task shows you how to navigate to one of the best Web sites devoted to optimizing broadband connections.

Each operating system uses different settings and stores them in different places, so the instructions differ depending on the operating system. SpeedGuide.net, highlighted here, focuses on various versions of the Windows operating system.

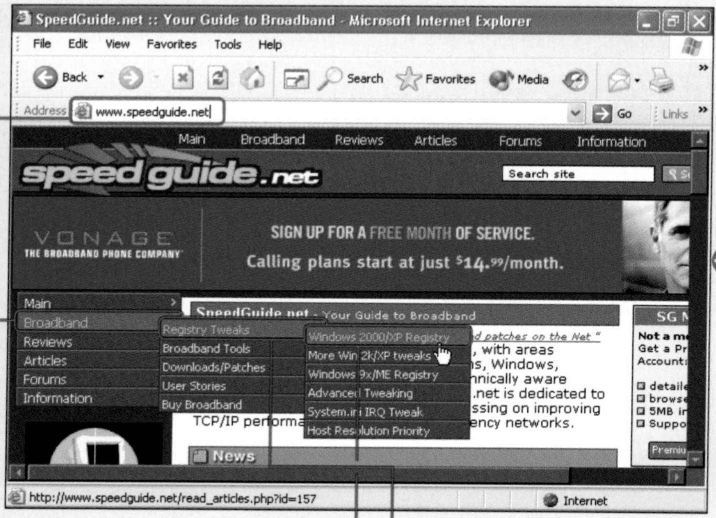

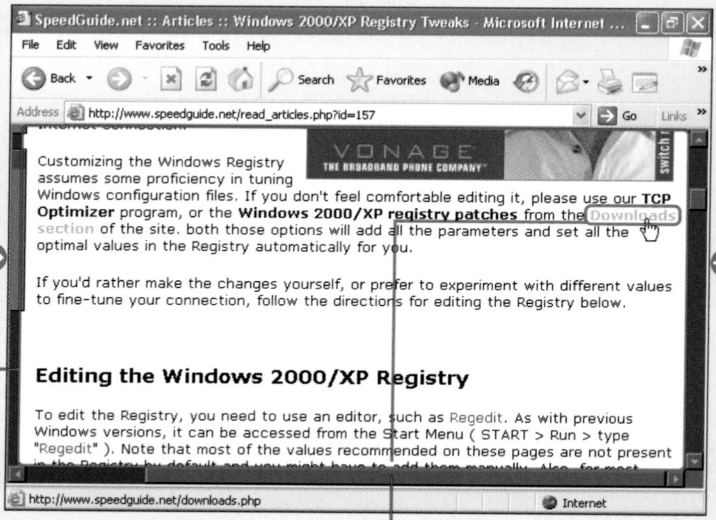

1. Type **www.speedguide.net** and press Enter.
2. Click Broadband.
3. Point to Registry Tweaks.
4. Click your operating system.

- Articles related to tweaking your operating system appear.

5. Click the link for downloading patches and tweaks.

Cross-Platform

A great place to learn more about Windows tweaks along with instructions on how to tweak Linux systems and Mac OS to optimize broadband connections is Cable-Modem.net at www.cable-modem.net.

Cross-Platform

Mac OS does not use a registry. It manages data transfer through its Open Transport Layer, but like Windows, it is optimized to work with Ethernet networks and dial-up modems, so consider tweaking it. You can find a utility for optimizing Mac OS broadband connections at www.sustworks.com.

Caution!

Errors in the Windows registry can cause serious problems in Windows, so tweak the registry only if you feel comfortable doing so and only after backing up your system and data.

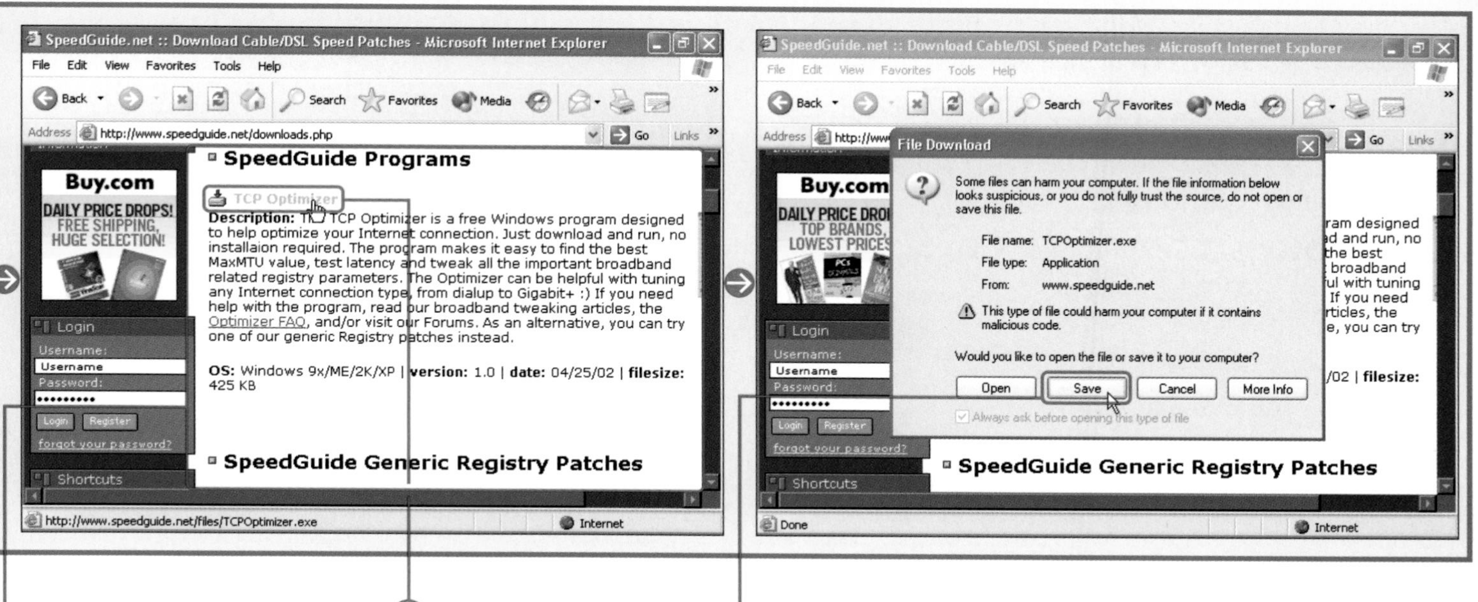

- The links and patches page appears.

6. Read about available tweaks and patches.

7. To download a tweak utility or patch, click its link.

- The File Download dialog box appears.

8. Click Save and save the file to your computer.

Note: Steps for installing and running patches and tweaks vary depending on the patch and on your operating system.

Improve connection speed with a WEB ACCELERATOR

You can speed up your Internet connection by using a Web accelerator. Two types of accelerators are available: *optimizers*, which are utilities that tweak your operating system settings for optimal performance, and *proxy servers*, which help your system load pages faster.

In this task, you learn how to install and use a shareware optimizer called TweakMaster to adjust the system settings in your computer that control data transfer. Many other such utilities are available, and you can find them simply by searching the Web for "web accelerator." TweakMaster is easy to use, and has delivered some positive results.

Other Web accelerators work on different principles. Some are utilities that run in the background on your computer and optimize caching by "learning" your browser habits and trying to anticipate which pages you might want next. Others are proxy services, such as NetZero Hi-Speed, that are designed to be more responsive to your requests for pages than the Web servers on which the original pages are stored.

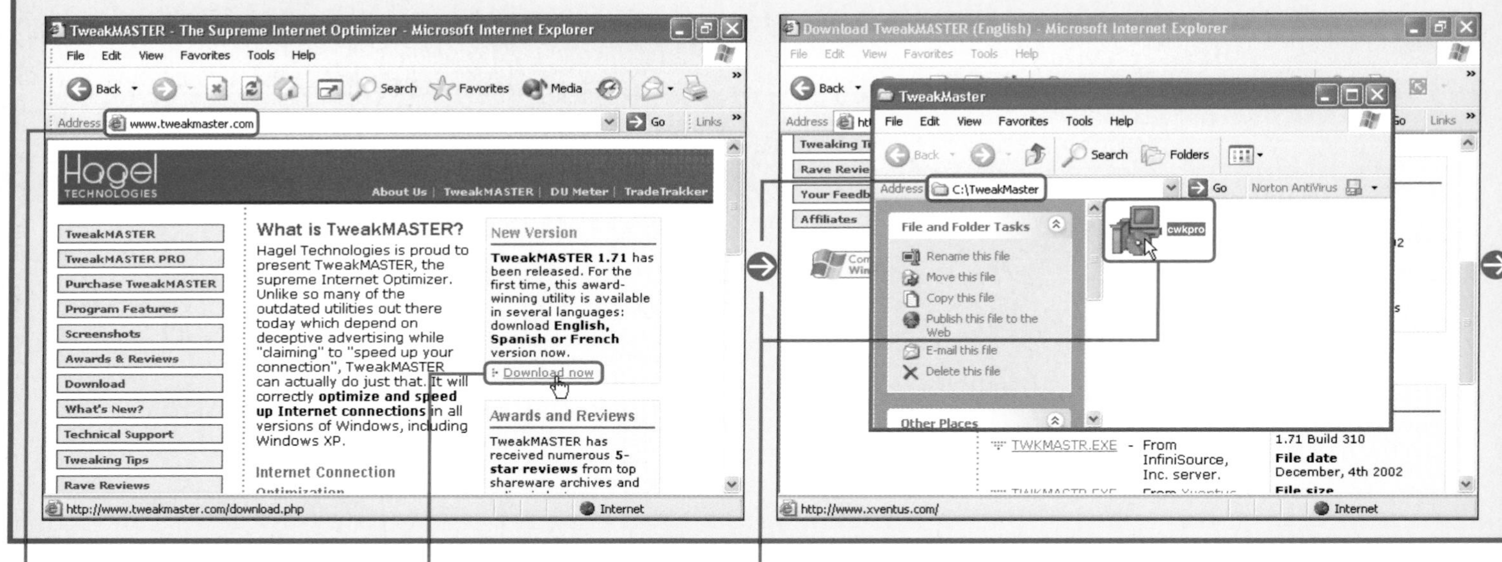

1. Type **www.tweakmaster.com** and press Enter.
2. Click "Download now" and download the TweakMaster installation file to a folder on your computer.
3. Open the folder that contains the TweakMaster installation file.
4. Double-click the TweakMaster installation file.

- Follow the onscreen instructions to install TweakMaster and run it.

DIFFICULTY LEVEL

Customize It!

The easiest way to optimize your Internet connection is to have TweakMaster's wizard make all of the system changes for you, but it might not make full use of your system's potential. Take note of the settings the wizard uses and then try different settings to see if you can obtain better results. You can run TweakMaster as often as you like to experiment with the settings.

Desktop Trick!

TweakMaster includes a clock synchronizer that can keep your system time current. On TweakMaster's opening screen, click the Clock Snyc link.

More Options!

TweakMaster also has a DNS (Domain Name Server) optimizer to help load the Web sites you visit most often faster. On TweakMaster's opening screen, click the DNS Accelerator link.

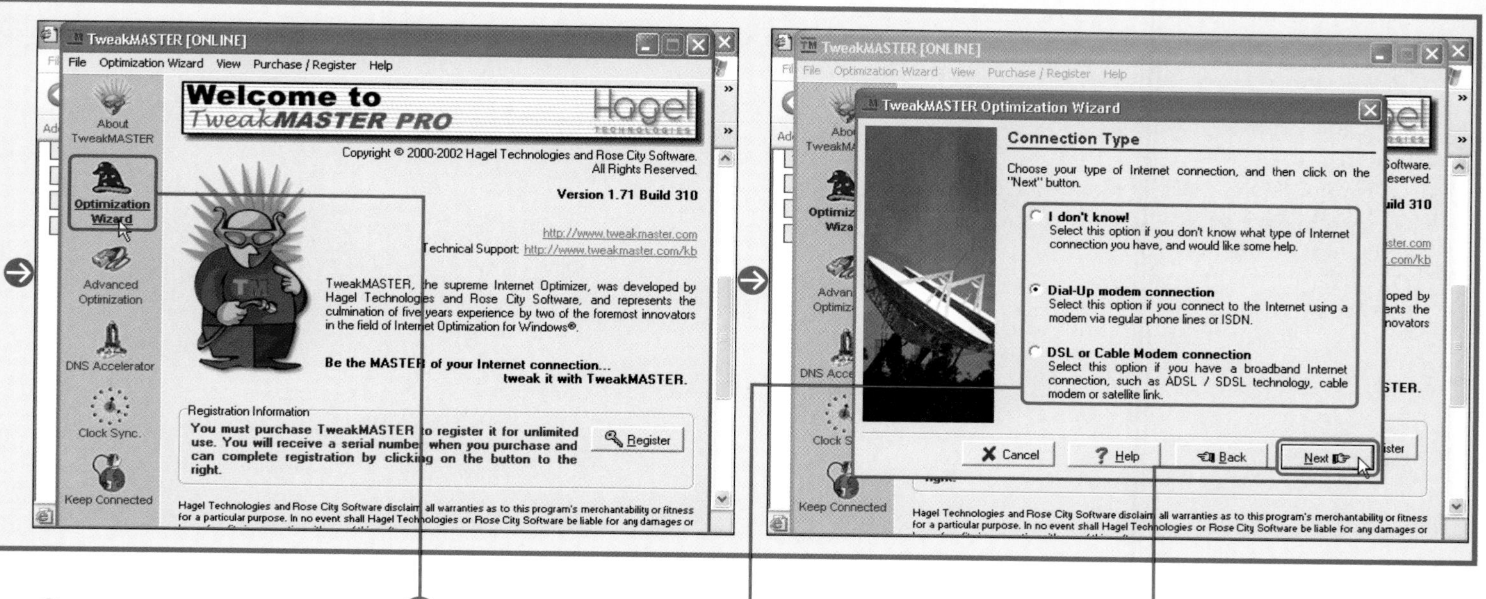

- TweakMaster's opening screen appears.

5 Click Optimization Wizard.

- The Optimization Wizard appears.

6 Click your Internet connection type.

7 Click Next.

- Follow the wizard's instructions to optimize your system.

Rid your computer of SPYWARE AND ADWARE

As you browse the Web, some Web sites install unsolicited software on your computer, often without your knowledge. In some cases, the software is *spyware*, like a *cookie*, that gathers information about your activity on the Internet. Sometimes, this can enhance your browsing experience by allowing a company or organization to offer information and products that might appeal to you, assuming, of course, you want these types of offers. Other software, commonly called *adware*, can generate annoying pop-up ads even when you visit a site that does not use pop-up ads.

Although you can acquire spyware and adware when browsing the Web, it often installs on your computer when you download and install other programs, such as games or shareware utilities.

Fortunately, you can download and use any of several very effective utilities — freeware, shareware, or commercial products — that can search your computer for commonly known spyware and adware and remove it from your system. This does not completely eliminate pop-up ads, so you also need to install a pop-up blocker, as instructed in task #7.

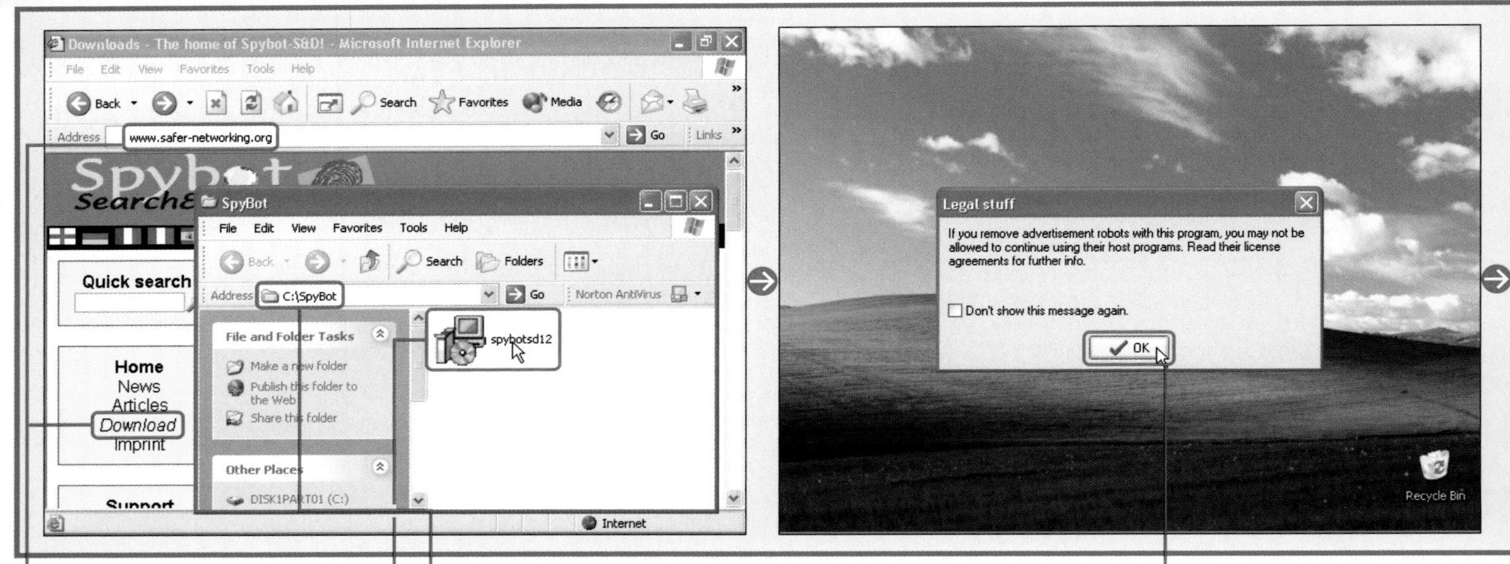

① Type **www.safer-networking.org** and press Enter.

② Click the Download link and download the Spybot installation file to a folder on your computer.

③ Open the folder that contains the Spybot installation file.

④ Double-click the Spybot installation file and follow the instructions to install and run Spybot.

○ The Legal Stuff dialog box appears.

⑤ Read the message and click OK.

DIFFICULTY LEVEL

Caution!

Some programs you download and install from the Web might come with spyware or adware that you must install in order to use the program. Uninstalling the required spyware or adware may prevent the program from running.

Did You Know?

Adware and spyware evolve constantly to avoid detection by Spybot and other similar programs, so make sure that you regularly update Spybot. On the opening screen, click the Search for updates button and follow the onscreen instructions to download the latest updates.

Remove It!

Spybot keeps a backup of any changes it makes, so you can undo changes. Click the Recovery button on Spybot's opening screen to learn more.

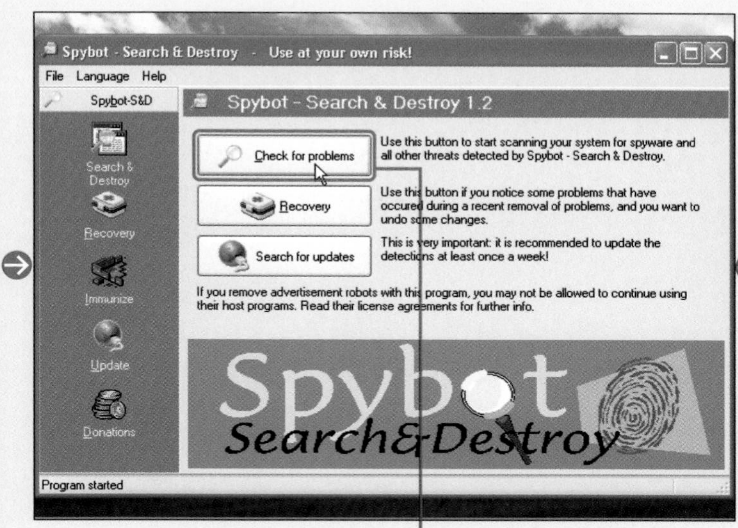

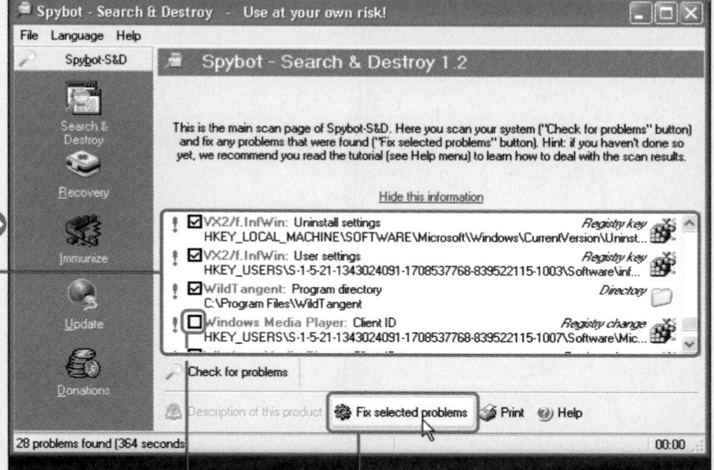

○ Spybot's opening screen appears.

6 Click Check for problems.

○ Spybot displays a list of any spyware or adware it finds.

7 Select the check box next to any software you do not want removed.

8 Click Fix selected problems.

Block annoying POP-UP ADS with 12Ghosts

Many Web sites earn money by selling advertising space or agreeing to support *pop-up ads* — windows or dialog boxes that automatically pop up on visitors' screens. When you visit some sites, as many as a half dozen pop-up ads may accost you, and some may display no noticeable controls for making them disappear.

Pop-up ads slow your Web browsing in two ways: They consume bandwidth and system resources that your computer could use to download the pages you really want to view, and they make you waste your time closing them. Some service providers help screen out some pop-up ads, but ads can bypass many of the systems used to block them.

Fortunately, you can install any of several utilities designed specifically to screen for pop-ups and block them before they reach your computer. These programs are not 100 percent effective, but they can help immensely. The utility recommended here is 12Ghosts Popup killer, a freeware program that is both effective and easy to use.

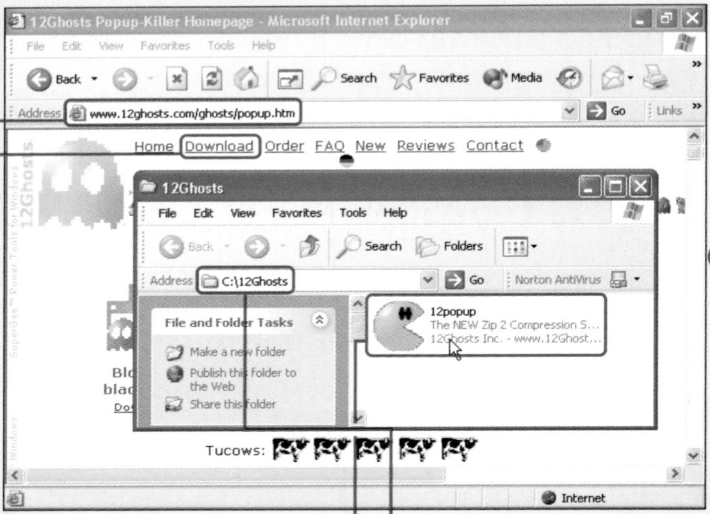

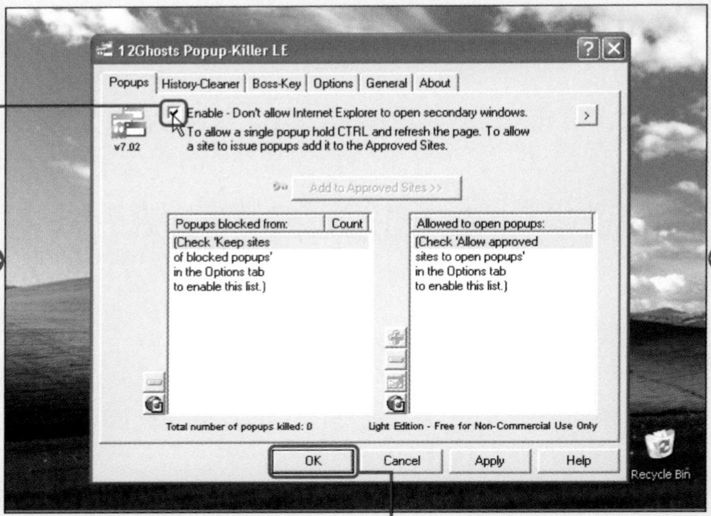

1. Type **www.12ghosts.com/ghosts/popup.htm**
2. Click the Download link and download the 12Ghosts installation file to a folder on your computer.
3. Open the folder that contains the 12Ghosts installation file.
4. Double-click the 12Ghosts installation file and follow the instructions to install and run 12Ghosts.

- The 12Ghosts Popup-Killer screen appears.

5. Click the Enable check box to enable or disable 12Ghosts.
6. Click OK.

Cross-Platform

12Ghosts is designed to be used only with Internet Explorer. If you use a different browser, plenty of other pop-up blockers are available, including STOPzilla and the Google Toolbar, discussed in task #46. Other Web browsers, including Netscape Navigator and Firefox feature integrated pop-up blocking.

Did You Know?

Many Web sites or e-mail messages have links that open a separate browser window. 12Ghosts treats this as a pop-up and prevents the window from appearing. If you click a link and you see the 12Ghost icon flash on your screen, you know it is blocking that site. Hold down the Ctrl key while clicking the link to open it.

More Options!

Some options, such as creating an approved-site list, are grayed out and unavailable in the freeware version, but are available in the Pro version, for a fee.

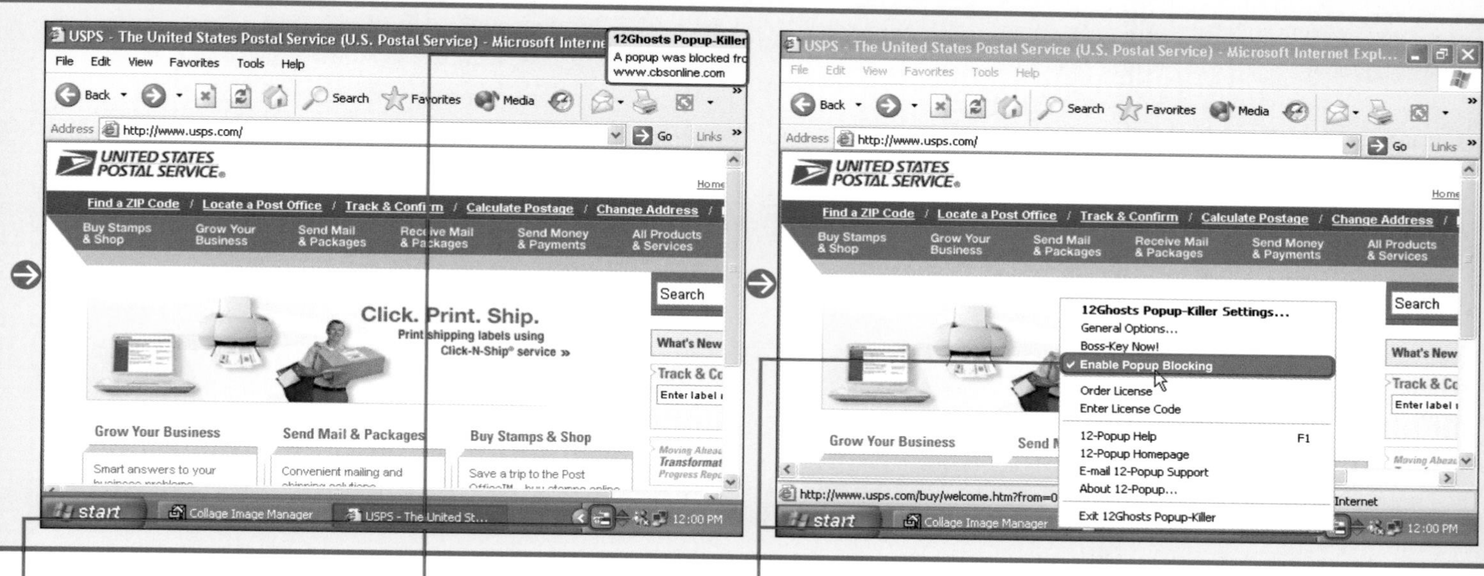

- With 12Ghosts enabled, its icon appears here.
- When 12Ghosts blocks a pop-up ad, it flashes this message.

7. Right-click the 12Ghosts icon.
8. Click Enable Popup Blocking.

- This toggles automated blocking on or off.

Optimize HARD DRIVE STORAGE

When focusing on Internet connection speeds, many people overlook the performance of their computers. When your computer opens pages, it opens the pages in memory and looks to the disk drive for any cached files it can pull up instead of downloading them from the Internet. If your hard drive is cluttered or the files on it are fragmented, that can affect the speed at which your browser loads pages.

To optimize hard drive performance, you generally need to do two things — clear old files off the disk to free up storage space, and then defragment the files on the disk to make sure each file is stored in a contiguous location and to prevent further fragmentation. You can delete files manually as you normally would or let your operating system's disk cleanup utility manage the cleanup for you. This task shows how to use the Windows Disk Cleanup feature to remove obsolete files. Task #9 shows you how to defragment files.

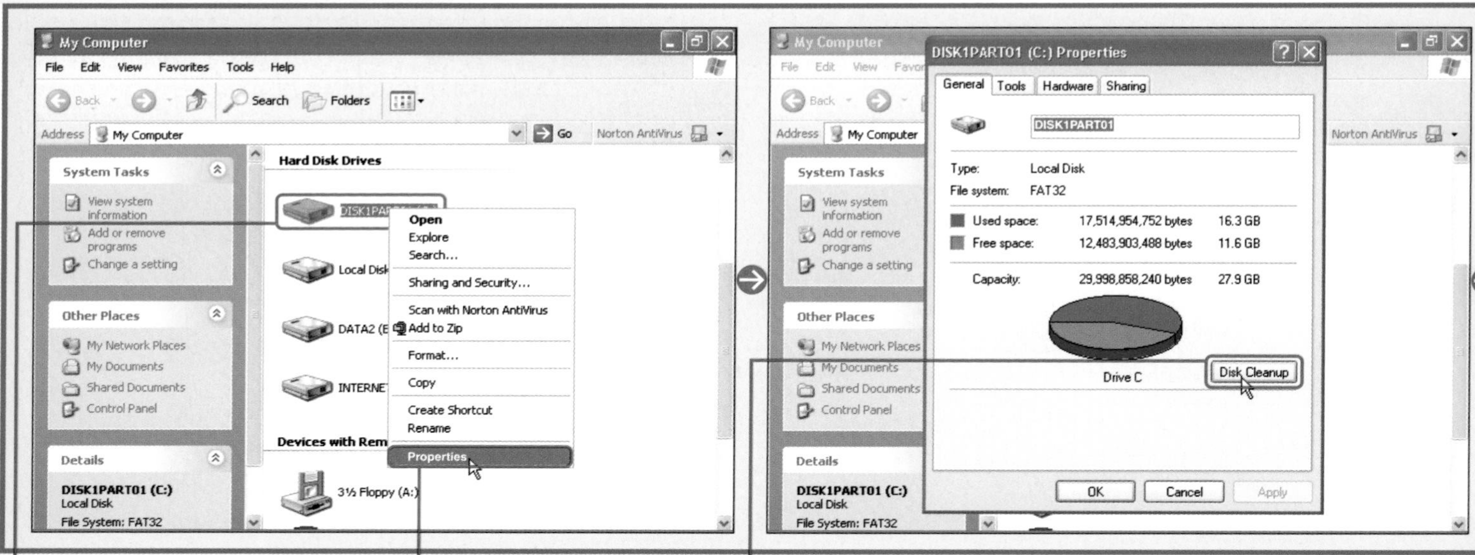

1. In My Computer, right-click the disk you want to optimize.
2. Click Properties.

- The Properties dialog box appears.

3. Click Disk Cleanup.

- Disk Cleanup inspects your hard drive for potential files to remove.

Note: This process may take a few minutes, depending on the size of the hard disk and the types of files it contains.

More Options!

The Disk Cleanup dialog box has a More Options tab that provides tools for removing installed programs, Windows components you no longer use, and old restore point data that can really clutter a drive.

Delete It!

E-mail can consume a great amount of space, especially if you have many e-mail messages that have attached files. While you are clearing files from your hard drive, clear out the various folders in your e-mail program, as well.

Caution!

Emptying the Recycle Bin can free up disk space, but it also permanently removes any files you might have accidentally deleted. Before you empty the Recycle Bin, check its contents.

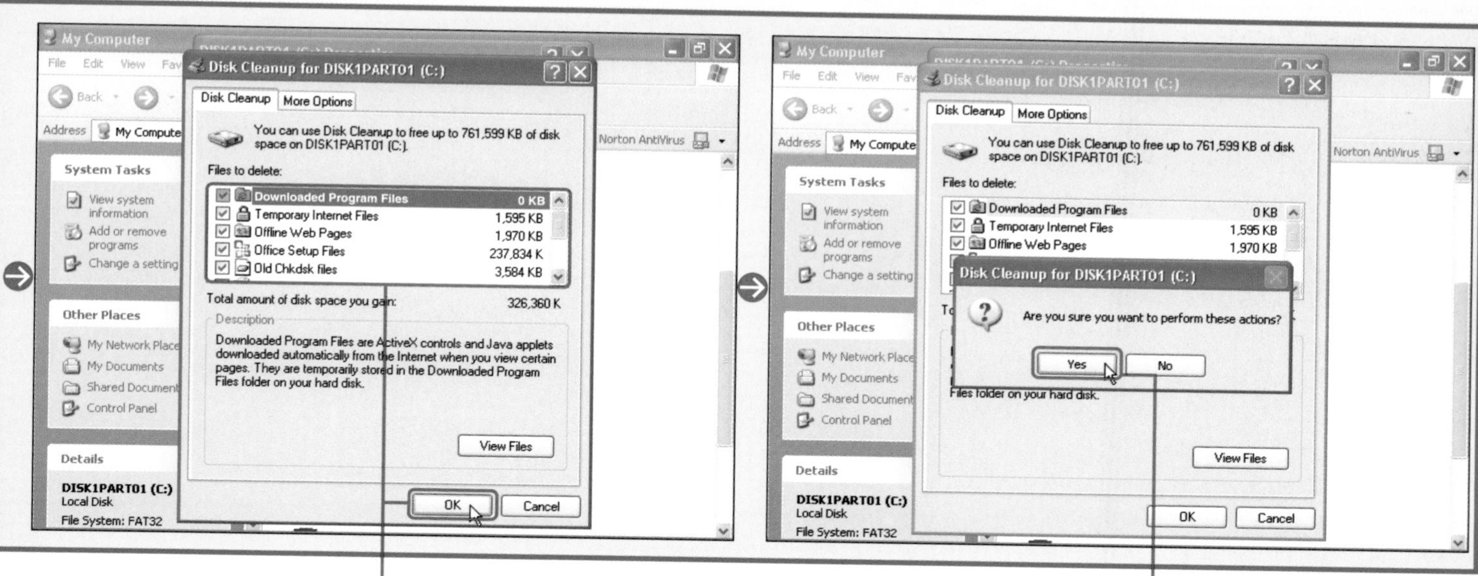

○ After Disk Cleanup inspects your hard drive, it displays the Disk Cleanup dialog box.

4 Click the check box next to each group of files you want removed.

5 Click OK.

○ The Disk Cleanup dialog box prompts you to confirm.

6 Click Yes.

Optimize HARD DRIVE PERFORMANCE

If you never delete any files on your computer, your computer stores every file in its own separate area on the hard drive. But when you delete a file and form an empty storage area, the next time you save a file, your computer stores part of it in the open area and stores any other parts of it that do not fit there somewhere else. Over time, your computer scatters parts of files all over the surface of the disk. The files are then *fragmented*, and the disk drive must work a little harder to read the files.

To keep your hard drive running at top speed and make it less likely that files will become corrupt, you can defragment the disk every so often. The process is fairly easy, as this task illustrates, but it is often very time-consuming, especially if you need to defragment a large number of files on a disk that has not been defragmented for some time. Consider initiating the process before you go to bed.

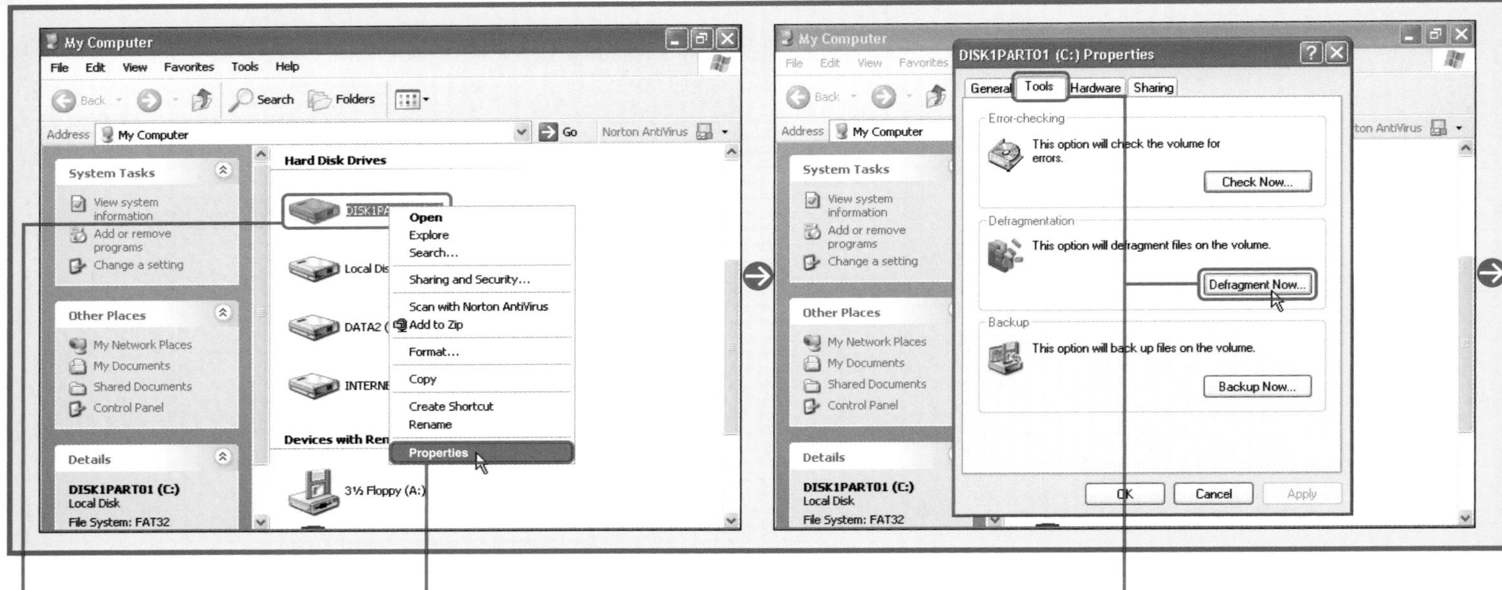

① In My Computer, right-click the disk you want to optimize.

② Click Properties.

○ The Properties dialog box appears.

③ Click the Tools tab.

④ Click Defragment Now.

Important!

Defragmentation works best if no other programs are running and if any power-saving features of your operating system are disabled. In Windows, right-click a blank area of the desktop, click Properties, and click the Screen Saver tab to access screen saver and power-saving settings.

Did You Know?

The more fragmented a disk already is, the more fragmented it will become. By defragmenting your disk regularly, you limit the fragmentation of any new files you save to the disk.

Did You Know?

When your computer's memory is full, it uses the hard drive for additional — *virtual* — memory. The faster your drive operates the faster virtual memory is!

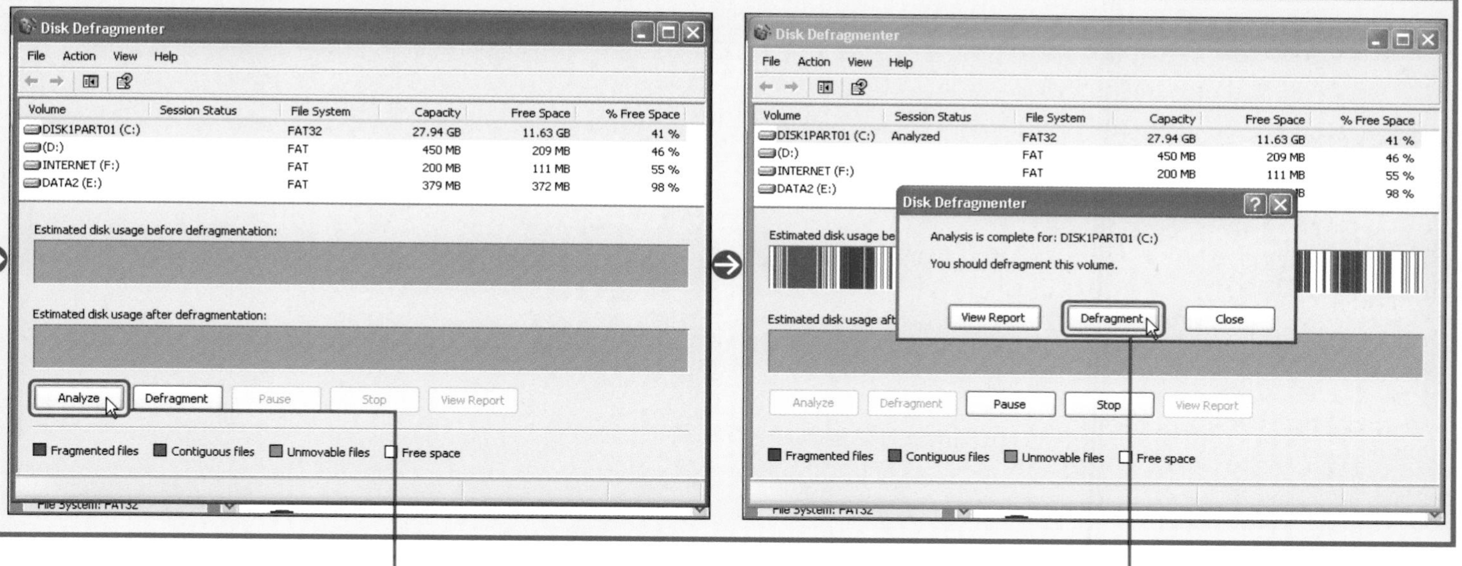

○ Disk Defragmenter appears.

5 Click Analyze.

○ Defragmenter analyzes the disk to determine if defragmenting is recommended.

6 If defragmenting is recommended, click Defragment.

○ Defragmenter starts defragmenting the files and displays a dialog box informing you when the

Give your memory a SPEED BOOST

Whenever you browse the Web or do just about anything else on your computer, files that you are viewing are stored in your computer's memory. If you have several programs running at the same time — either open where you can see them or running in the background — less memory is available for opening Web pages. And if no memory is available, your computer begins using the much slower hard drive for additional storage. This can significantly impact the speed at which pages load.

If you want to take advantage of every way possible to increase the speed at which your browser loads pages, look at your computer's memory. Shut down any programs that do not need to be running, and then determine which programs your computer is set up to run in the background. You might be surprised to find that many programs that are set up to run in the background do not need to be. Here, you learn how to free up memory in Windows.

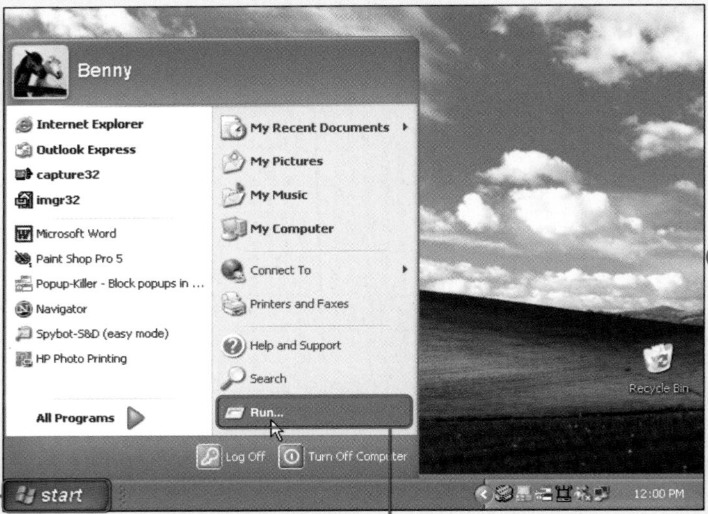

① Click the Start button.

② Click Run.

○ The Run dialog box appears.

③ Type **msconfig**.

④ Click OK.

DIFFICULTY LEVEL

Did You Know?

If you are unsure how much memory your computer has, right-click My Computer and click Properties. On the General tab, under Computer, you can find the processor type and speed and the amount of memory.

More Options!

Many programs do not completely remove themselves from your computer's memory when you close them. A memory optimizer utility, such as FreeRAM XP Pro, can help. You can download it from www.yourwaresolutions.com. Or simply shut down and restart your computer when it slows down.

Remove It!

You can return your system to the way it was at any time. Run the System Configuration Utility, click the General tab, and click Normal Startup. Click OK.

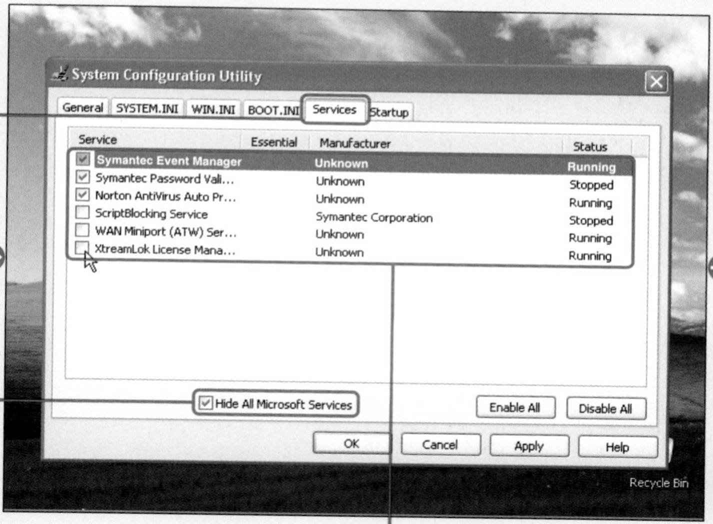

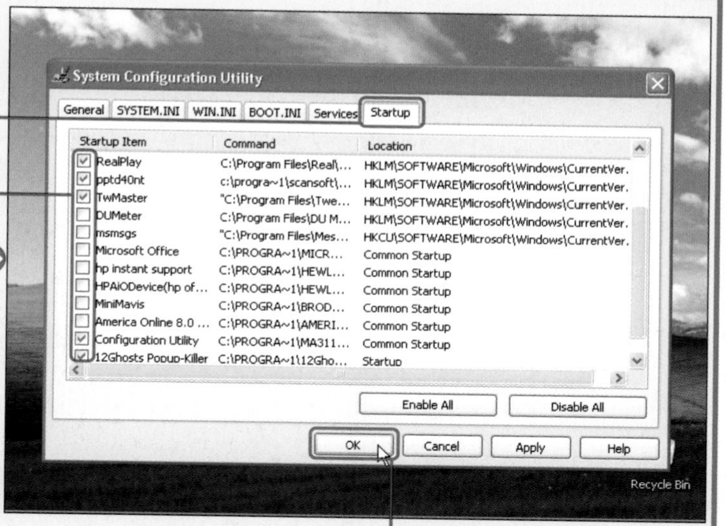

- The System Configuration Utility appears.

5 Click the Services tab.

6 Click the Hide All Microsoft Services option.

7 Click the check mark next to any service you do not want to run.

Note: Do not disable anti-virus software.

8 Click the Startup tab.

9 Click the check mark next to any program you do not want to run on startup.

10 Click OK and restart your computer.

- Your computer restarts without loading the programs you chose to omit from the startup.

Customize Your Web Browser

Your Web browser is like a television set for the Web, opening and displaying the sites you request as you enter Web page addresses or click links. And like a TV set, your browser offers settings that you can change to control its appearance and operation. In task #2, you accessed your browser settings to manipulate the cache, but you can change many other settings to reconfigure your browser's toolbars, specify which page loads on startup, control the size of the text that your browser displays, and even browse in full-screen mode.

By learning the options available in your browser and customizing its appearance and operation, you can increase the speed at which pages load, make your browser conform to the way you work, and display Web pages in a way that is easier for you to view them and more suitable for printing.

This chapter covers common settings that can enhance your Web-browsing experience but few users take the time to explore. Of course, these tasks do not cover all of the available options, so as you work through the tasks, be aware of other options that might appeal to you and feel free to experiment with them. Before you change a setting, note the original setting so you can change it back if the results are not what you had expected. After your Web browser has the look and feel you desire, you may never need to adjust the settings again.

TOP 100

Start faster with a BASIC HOME PAGE

Your browser may seem sluggish when you first start it if it loads a graphics-heavy home page or a page from a busy site that is typically slow. You can always press the Esc key if the page takes too long to load, but even that requires some time.

You can make your browser start more quickly by choosing not to load a home page on startup or to load a page that is more basic and usually loads quickly any time of the day.

Of course, if you always want to look at the same page whenever you start your browser — maybe your favorite news site or the weather page — you may keep that page as your home page. But if your browser is set up to load a page you rarely look at, consider loading nothing at all or something more basic, such as Google.

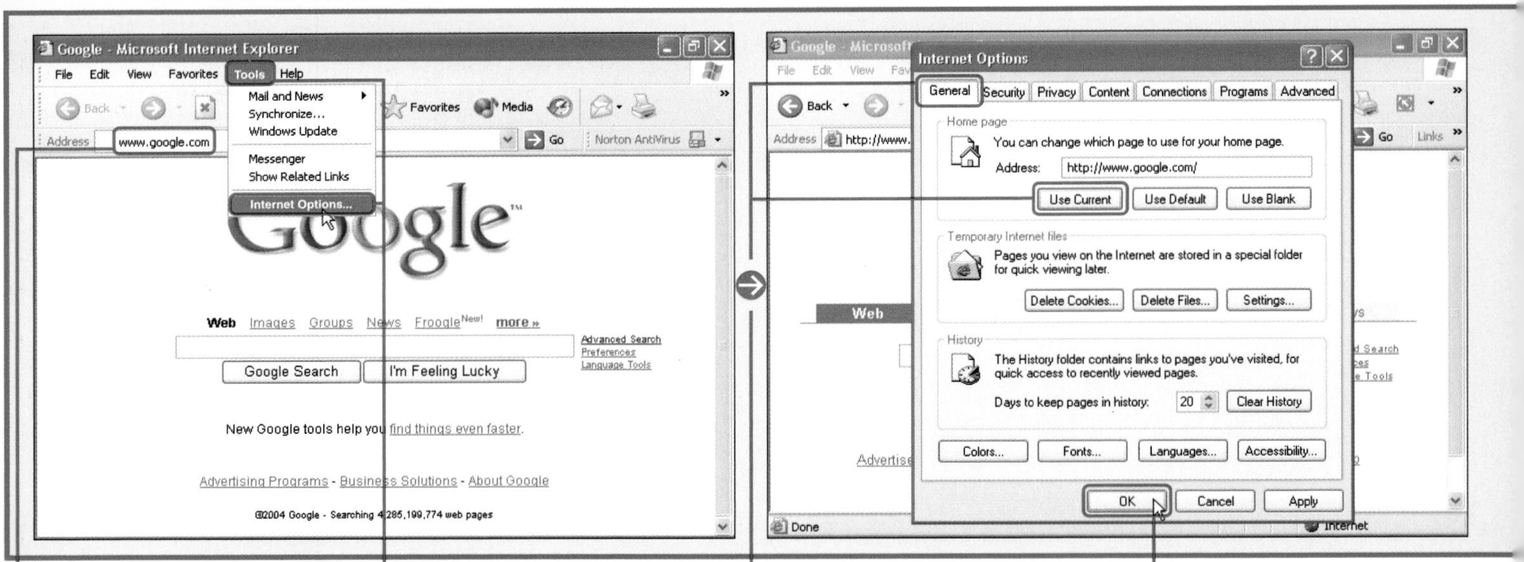

CHANGE OPENING WEB PAGE

1 Type the address of the Web page you want to use as your browser's opening page and press Enter.

- This example features the Google Web site.

2 Click Tools.

3 Click Internet Options.

- The Internet Options dialog box appears.

4 Click the General tab.

5 Click Use Current.

6 Click OK.

- The Internet Options dialog box saves your change and closes.

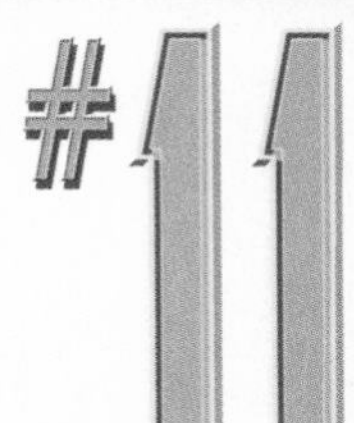

Remove It!

To go back to the default home page, open the Internet Options dialog box, click the General tab, and then click the Use Default button.

More Options!

You can have Internet Explorer automatically check for any available updates to it. Open the Internet Options dialog box, click the Advanced tab, and then click the Automatically Check for Internet Explorer Updates option (☐ changes to ☑). Internet Explorer checks for updates approximately once per month, so turning on this option does not have a significant effect on how fast Internet Explorer starts.

Caution!

Some sites employ so-called adware to automatically change your home page and prevent you from changing it back. Task #6 shows you how to get rid of adware.

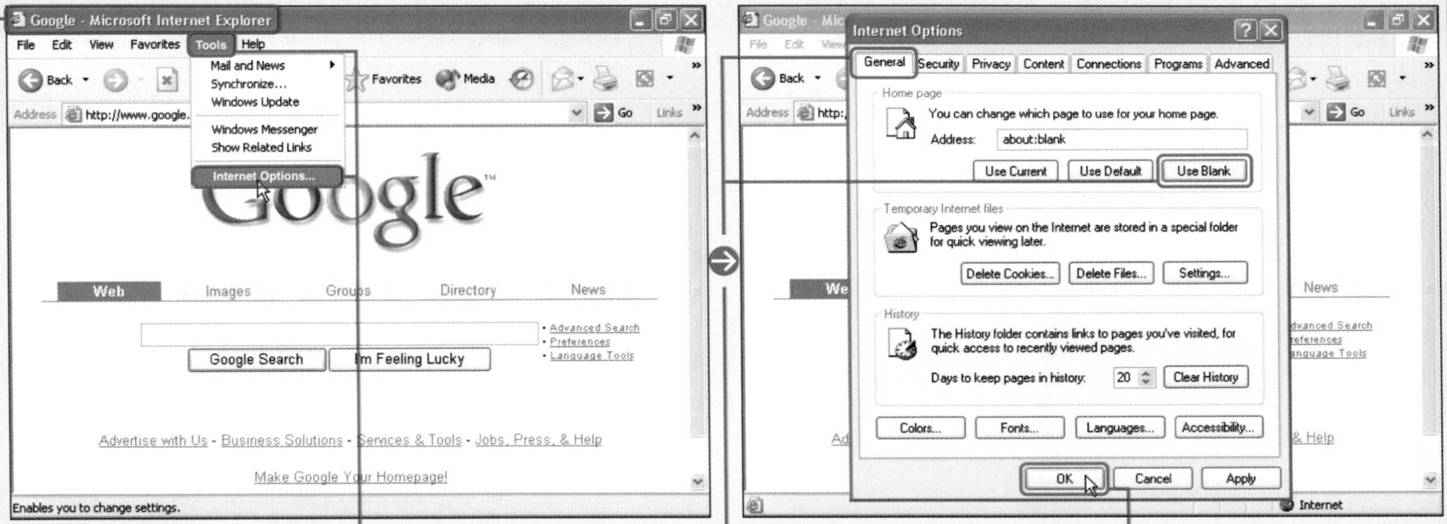

USE BLANK PAGE

1. Launch Internet Explorer.
2. Click Tools.
3. Click Internet Options.

- The Internet Options dialog box appears.

4. Click the General tab.
5. Click Use Blank.
6. Click OK.

- The Internet Options dialog box saves your change and closes.

Surf the Web faster GRAPHICS FREE

Large graphics, audio clips, video clips, and animations take the most time and system resources to download from the Internet. If you browse for research and are looking only for text, you can choose to load pages without the graphics and animations. When your browser opens a Web page that contains graphics, it displays all of the text and links but displays placeholders for the graphics. You can choose to view individual pictures as shown in the task.

Surfing the Web without its accompanying audio-visuals might not appeal to most people, but if you have a relatively slow dial-up connection, and you need some additional speed, this can provide a big boost. Even if you choose to keep pictures on and disable audio, animations, and videos, you can see an increase in speed for those pages that use these types of media.

In this task you learn how to disable sounds, video, animations, and pictures in Internet Explorer.

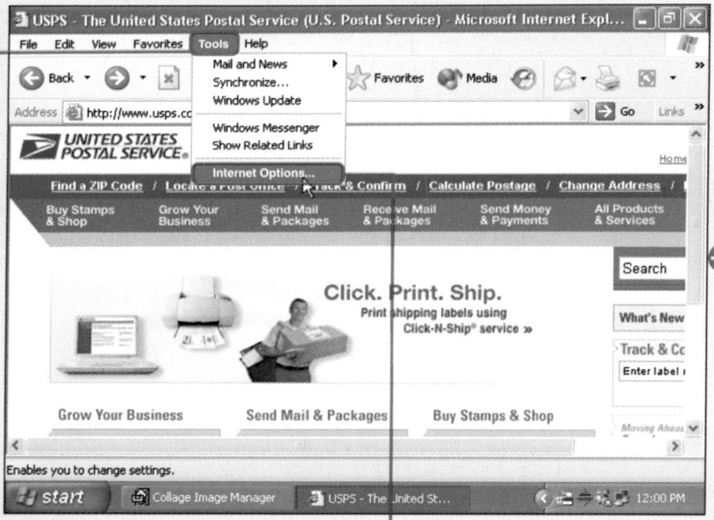

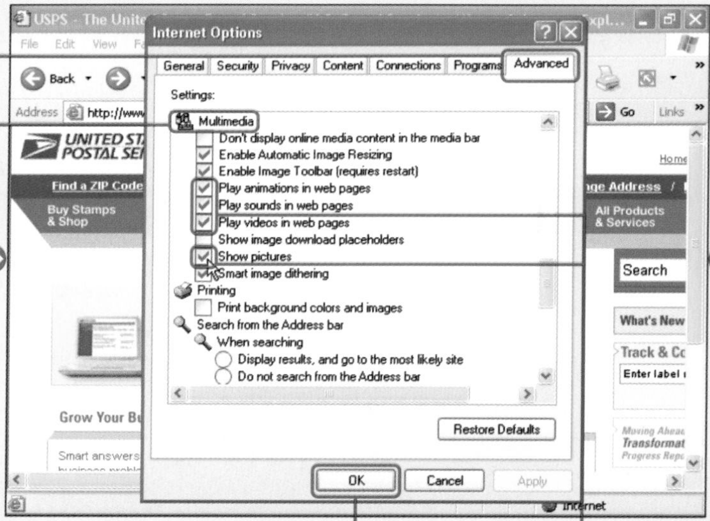

1. Click Tools.
2. Click Internet Options.

- The Internet Options dialog box appears.

3. Click the Advanced tab.
4. Scroll down to the Multimedia options.
5. Clear the check marks next to any media you want to disable.
6. Click OK.

#12

DIFFICULTY LEVEL

Remove It!

Anything you change in the Internet Options dialog box, you can change back. To change all options back to their original settings, open the Internet Options dialog box, click the Advanced tab, and click Restore Defaults.

More Options!

The Internet Options Advanced tab is packed with options that many users choose to ignore. Check them out. If the purpose of an option seems unclear, click the option's name, right-click it, and click What's This?

More Options!

Internet Explore 6 features an Enable Image Toolbar option. With this option on, whenever you rest the mouse pointer on an image, a toolbar pops up with buttons to save, print, or e-mail the image or open your My Pictures folder.

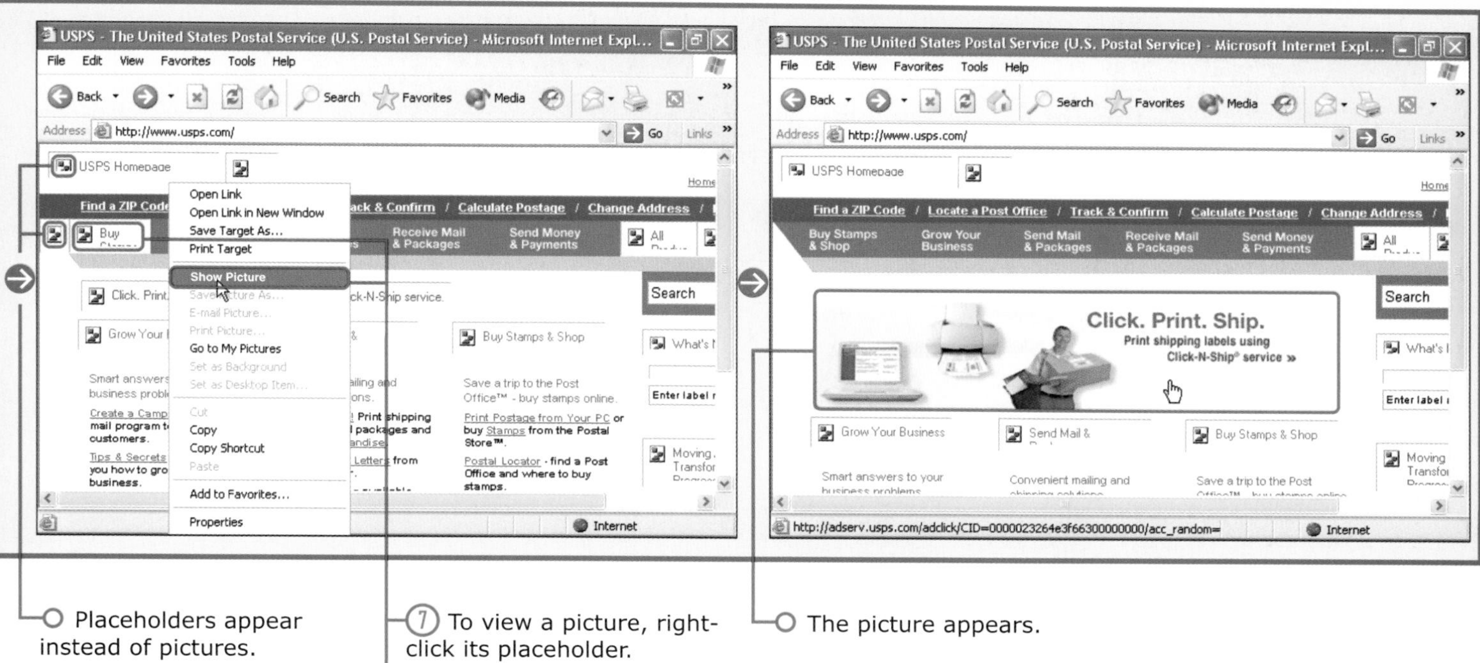

Placeholders appear instead of pictures.

7 To view a picture, right-click its placeholder.

8 Click Show Picture.

The picture appears.

Customize your BROWSER TOOLBAR

Your Web browser has a toolbar that typically provides buttons for moving back and forward, stopping a page from loading, refreshing a page, printing a page, displaying a history of pages you have visited, and more. You can customize the toolbar by adding or removing buttons, rearranging the buttons, changing their size, and choosing whether to display text labels for the buttons. You can even hide the toolbar to provide more room to display Web pages.

Internet Explorer gives you complete control over the toolbars, allowing you to remove, add, and rearrange buttons, and change the appearance of the buttons themselves. Other Web browsers typically allow you to show or hide toolbars and specify which buttons you want to appear on the toolbars, but some do not allow you to rearrange buttons or change their appearance.

This task shows you how to reconfigure the Internet Explorer toolbar.

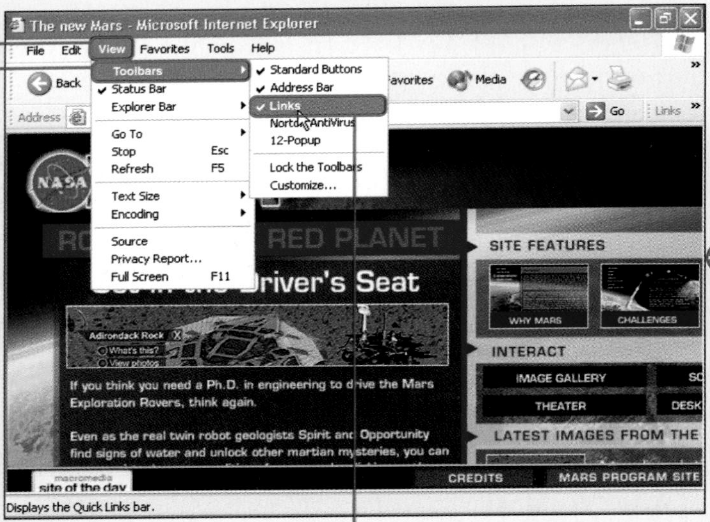

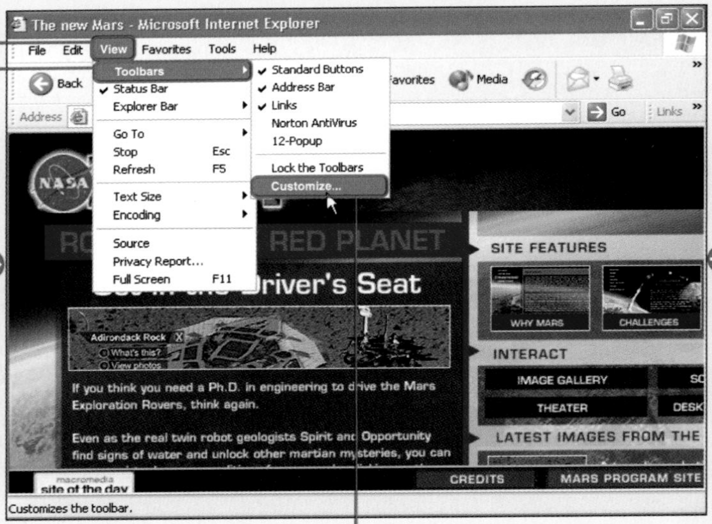

1. Click View.
2. Click Toolbars.
3. Click a toolbar's name to toggle it on or off.
4. Click View.
5. Click Toolbars.
6. Click Customize.

#13

DIFFICULTY LEVEL

Remove It!

To restore the toolbar to its original condition, display the Customize Toolbar dialog box and click the Reset button.

More Options

To move a toolbar, move the mouse pointer over the vertical stack of dots on the left end of the toolbar, so the mouse pointer turns into a double-headed arrow, and then drag the toolbar up or down. To resize the toolbar, drag left or right.

Try This!

You can lock the toolbars to prevent them from being changed. Right-click a blank area of any toolbar or the menu bar and click Lock the Toolbars. Repeat the step to unlock the toolbars.

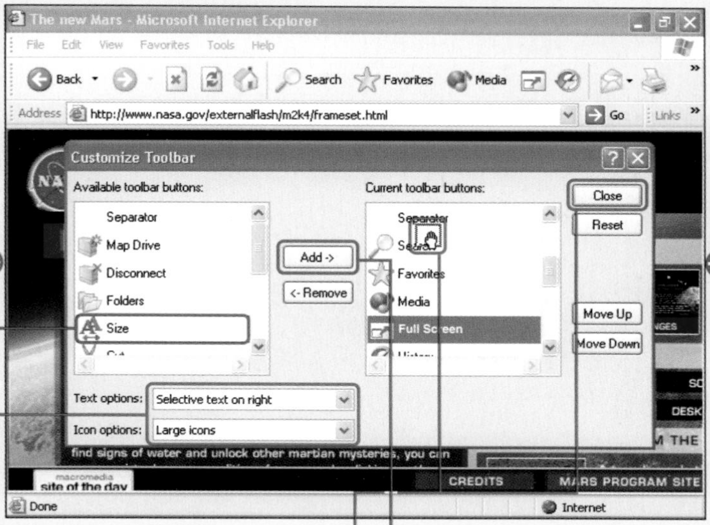

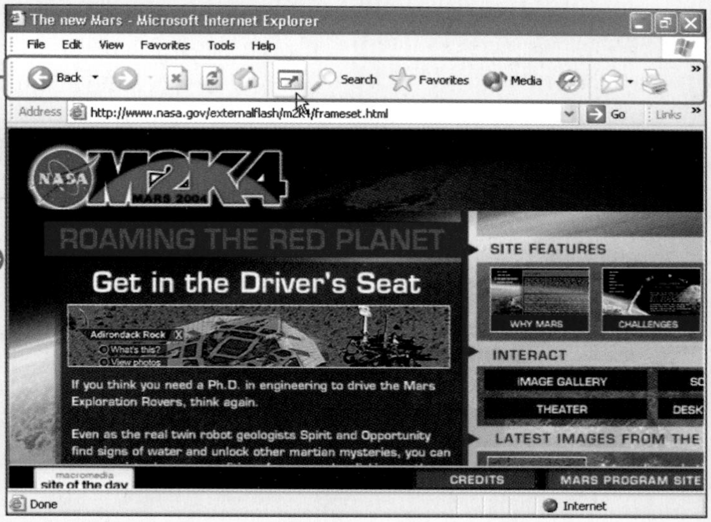

- The Customize Toolbar dialog box appears.

7. Select text and icon options here.
8. Click a button to add it to the toolbar.
9. Click Add.

- You can drag buttons up or down or use the Move Up or Move Down button to change their order.

10. Click Close.

- The toolbar reflects any changes you made.

ADD LINKS

to toolbars

DIFFICULTY LEVEL

Internet Explorer features a Links toolbar on which you can place links for your favorite Web sites and pages. The links appear as buttons on the toolbar, and you can open a page simply by clicking its button.

You can add buttons to the Links toolbar even if the toolbars are locked. If the toolbar is hidden, first bring it into view by following the steps in task #13.

Did You Know?

When you add a link to a toolbar, the browser places the link in a subfolder in its Favorites folder. To access Internet Explorer's Favorites folder, open the Favorites menu and click Organize Favorites.

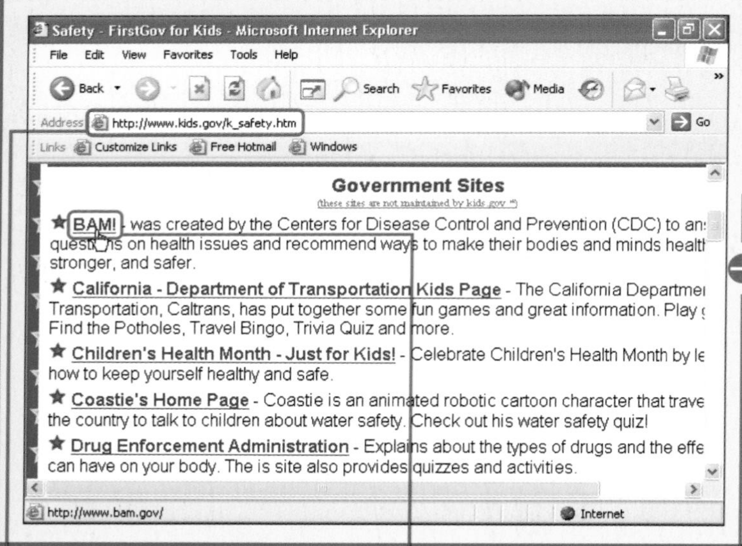

① Open the page that contains the link you want to add.

② Move the mouse pointer over the link.

③ Drag the link over the Links toolbar and drop it in place.

○ The I-beam pointer shows where the button will be added.

○ The link appears on the toolbar as a button.

Add an ADDRESS BAR to your taskbar

DIFFICULTY LEVEL

Most users run their Web browser first and then type the address of the page they want to view. However, you can save yourself a step by adding an Address bar to the Windows taskbar. When you type a Web page address in the bar and press Enter, Windows automatically runs your browser and opens the page.

In this task, you learn how to turn on the Address bar and use it to open pages in your Web browser.

Desktop Trick!

Drag the top of the taskbar up to make it larger. Right-click a blank area of the taskbar, click Properties, click Auto-hide the taskbar, and click OK. To bring it into view, move the mouse pointer to the edge of the screen where it is hiding.

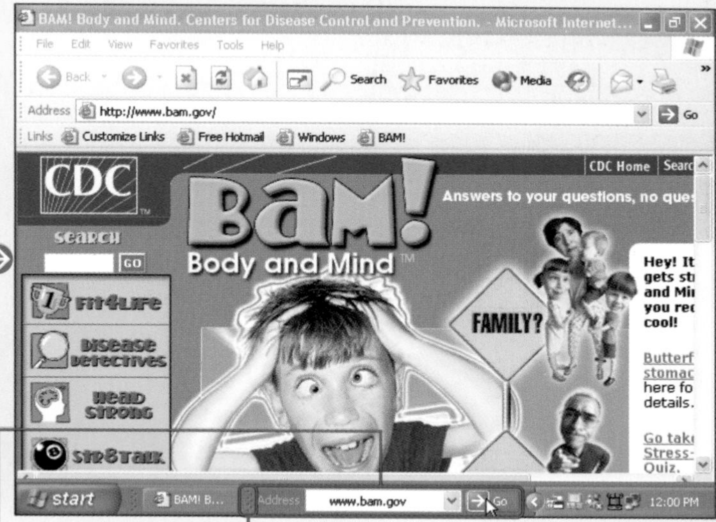

① Right-click a blank area of the taskbar.

② Click Toolbars.

③ Click Address.

- The Address Toolbar appears.
- You can drag here to make it bigger or smaller.

Mark your favorite sites for QUICK RETURN VISITS

The Web is a disorganized collection of more than 4 billion sites and pages that can be very difficult to successfully search and sort. So when you do happen to find sites that answer your questions and that you probably want to return to in the future, mark those sites. All browsers have a way of adding sites to a menu and/or toolbar, so you can quickly return to those sites later.

Netscape introduced the idea of bookmarking sites so users could easily return to them later. Internet Explorer refers to its bookmarks as Favorites, but they essentially do the same thing — they save the page's address (URL, uniform resource locator) and provide you with an entry to click to quickly return to the page. And if the page or a portion of it is stored in the cache, it loads even more quickly. Several techniques are available for bookmarking pages. This task shows you two quick techniques for adding Web sites to your Favorites menu.

If you have more than a dozen favorites, check the tips section to learn how to organize them.

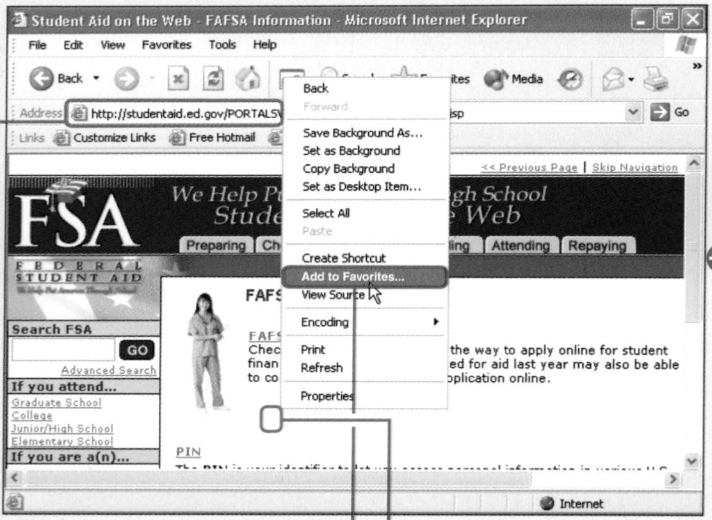

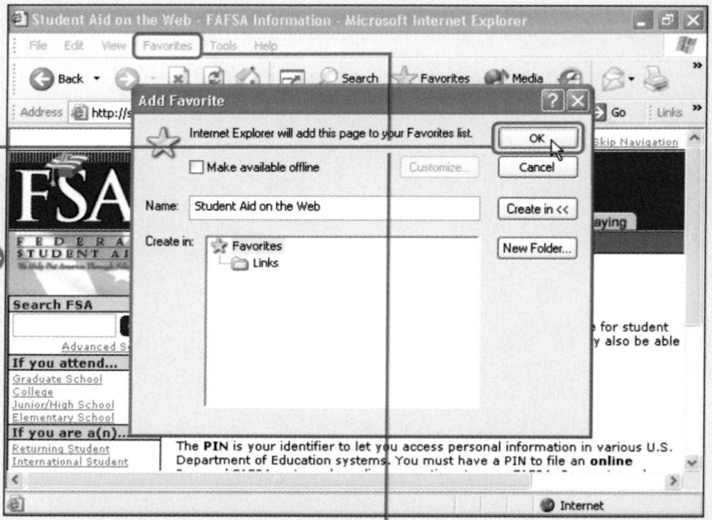

ADD CURRENT PAGE TO FAVORITES

1. Open a Web page you want to add to your Favorites menu.
2. Right-click a blank area of the page.
3. Click Add to Favorites.

- The Add Favorite dialog box appears.

4. Click OK.

- Internet Explorer adds the site to your Favorites menu.

DIFFICULTY LEVEL

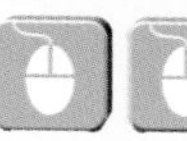   

Apply It!

If you have many favorites, store them in separate folders that appear as submenus on the Favorites menu. For example, you can create folders for News, Health, Family, Games, and so on. To create folders, open the Favorites menu, click Organize Favorites, and use the resulting dialog box to create folders and rearrange your favorites.

More Options!

You can rearrange your favorites by dragging them right on the Favorites menu. As you drag a favorite, a horizontal line appears, showing where it will be placed. Drag a favorite over a submenu of the Favorites menu, and the submenu opens so that you can drag the item onto the submenu.

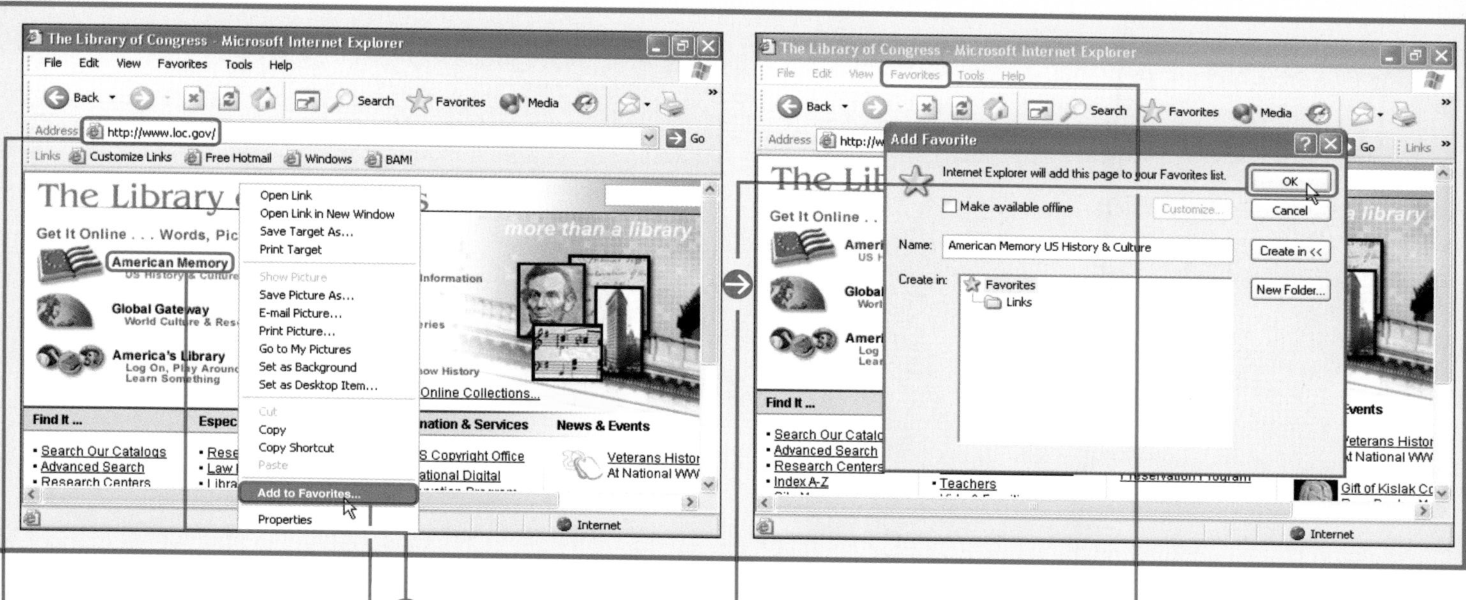

ADD LINKED PAGE TO FAVORITES

1. Open a Web page that contains a link you want to add to your Favorites menu.
2. Right-click the link.
3. Click Add to Favorites.

- The Add Favorite dialog box appears.

4. Click OK.

- The Add Favorite dialog box disappears and adds the linked site to the Favorites menu.

Display your FAVORITES AS A HOME PAGE

If you diligently mark the best pages you discover and organize them into separate folders, you have a custom directory of Web sites that can save you hours of time searching. You can now leverage the power of that collection by using it as your browser's home page. With your Favorites displayed as your home page, whenever you start your browser, you can quickly access the sites you visit most simply by clicking their links. And, whenever you want to view your favorites, you can click the Home button.

Internet Explorer stores favorites in a folder named Favorites. In order to use that folder as a home page, you must first convert it into an HTML file. Fortunately, Internet Explorer has an option that can perform the conversion for you. This task shows you how to export your Favorites folder to an HTML file and then refers you to task #11 for details on setting this new page as Internet Explorer's home page.

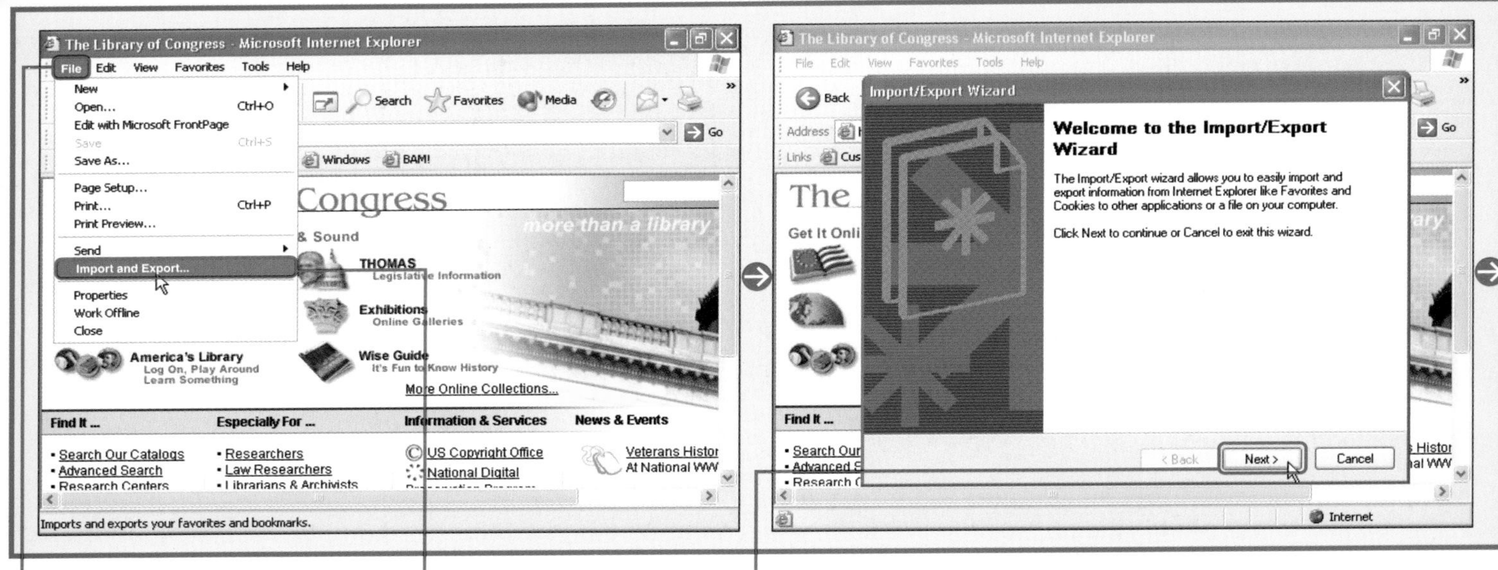

1. Click File.
2. Click Import and Export.

- The Import/Export Wizard appears.

3. Click Next and follow the wizard's instructions to export the Favorites folder to a file on your desktop.

Note: When asked where you want the file saved, click the Browse button, click Desktop, and click Save.

Cross-Platform

If you are using Netscape Navigator, use the Edit, Preferences command to set the home page, and click Choose File on the resulting screen. Navigator typically stores the Bookmarks file in C:\Program Files\Netscape\Netscape\defaults\profile\.

Attention!

When you add any new sites to the Favorites menu in Internet Explorer, those sites are not automatically added to the HTML file you exported. You must repeat the steps to create a new file.

More Options!

You can use Internet Explorer's File, Import and Export command to import a set of favorites as long as they are saved in an HTML file. Imported favorites appear on the Favorites menu.

- The bookmark file appears on the desktop.

4. Double-click the bookmark file.

- Your favorites appear as links on a Web page.

5. Click Tools.
6. Click Internet Options.

- The Internet Options dialog box appears.

Note: Refer to task #11 to make the current page your browser's home page.

Browse in FULL SCREEN MODE

When your Web browser displays all of its toolbars and its status bar, its controls can occupy much of the space that it could use to display Web pages. Of course, you can hide most of the toolbars, but the title bar and status bar still occupy valuable screen space. You also might want to keep the Standard Buttons bar onscreen, so you can use the Back and Forward buttons.

To give a Web page more screen space, consider switching to full-screen mode. In full-screen mode, your browser hides its title bar, status bar, and all toolbars except the Standard Buttons bar. It also displays the vertical scrollbar, so you can move up and down the page, and it displays window control buttons so you can return to the standard window display or close the window. This task shows you how to toggle back and forth between full-screen and normal view, so you can give more screen space to those pages that call for it.

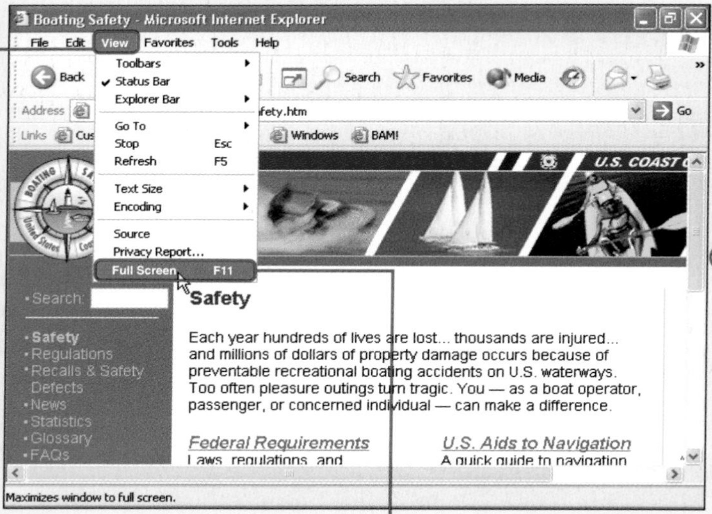

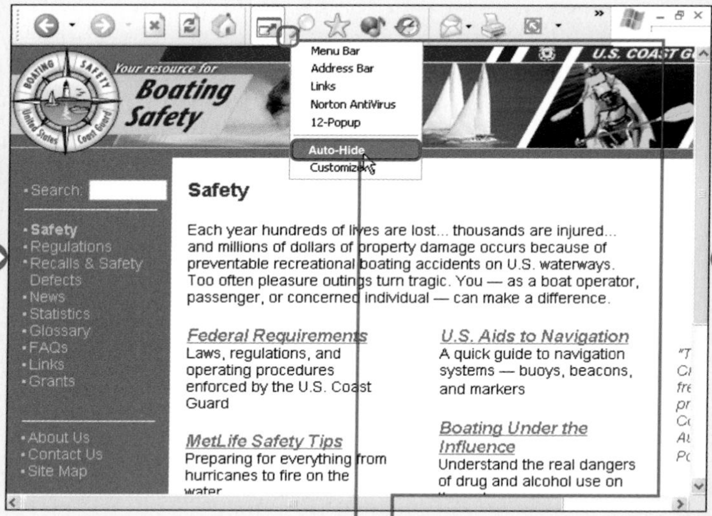

1. Click View.
2. Click Full Screen.

- Your browser changes to full-screen view.

3. For more screen space, right-click the Standard Button toolbar.
4. Click Auto Hide.

Cross-Platform

Netscape uses the same View, Full Screen command to change to full-screen mode but does not allow you to hide the toolbar at the top of the screen.

Try This!

Press F11 to toggle between normal and full-screen mode. Use Alt+left arrow and Alt+right arrow to move back and forth when the Standard Buttons toolbar is hidden.

Try This!

If you click the Search button () or Favorites button () in Internet Explorer, the Search or Favorites panel appears on the left side of the screen, but when you click the Web page, it hides itself. To bring it back into view, move your mouse pointer to the far left.

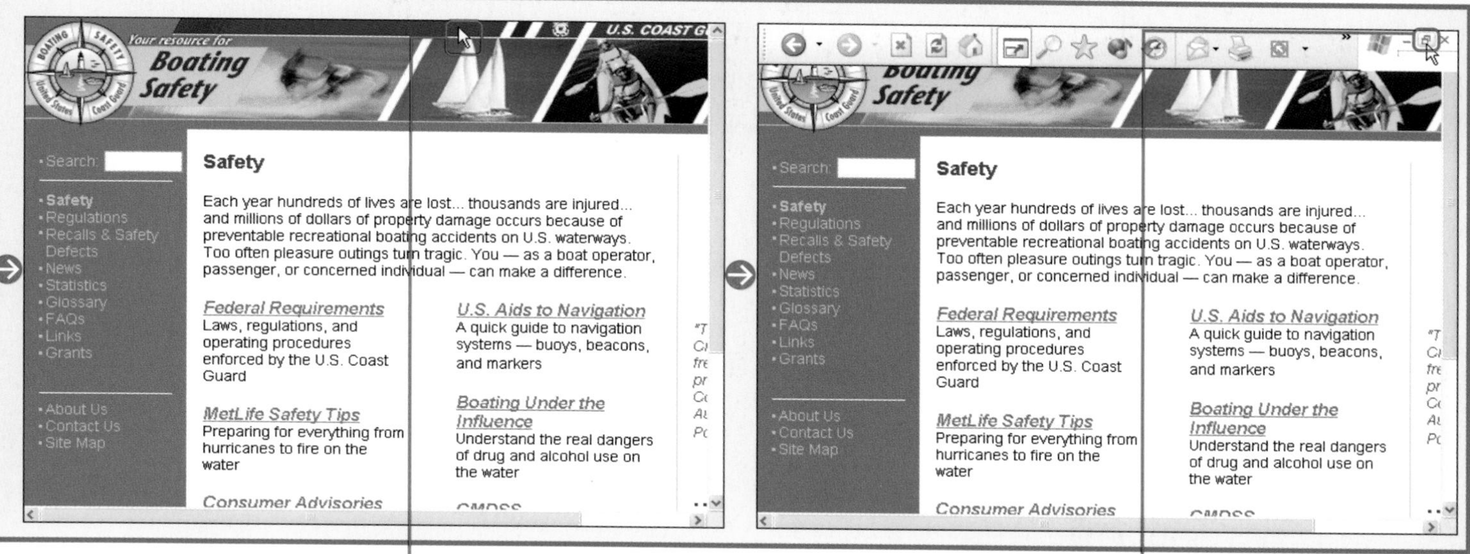

○ The Standard Button toolbar disappears.

5 Move the mouse pointer to the top of the screen.

○ The Standard Button toolbar reappears.

6 Click Restore to return to the normal browser display.

Increase or decrease

TEXT SIZE

DIFFICULTY LEVEL

Few users realize that their browser, not the Web page, typically controls the appearance of text. Most Web pages contain codes that specify the relative size of the text. For example, a Web page title might be coded as a title or heading, making it larger than the normal text that appears below the title. However, the Web browser interprets those codes according to its own settings and determines specifically how the text appears.

Of course, some pages use stylized graphics for some of their text, which a browser cannot control, and some pages use codes that lock in the size of certain blocks of text, but for the most part, your browser controls the size of the text.

By knowing how to change the text size, you can control how much information is displayed in your browser window and you can make text large enough for you to read. This task shows you how to increase or decrease text size in Internet Explorer.

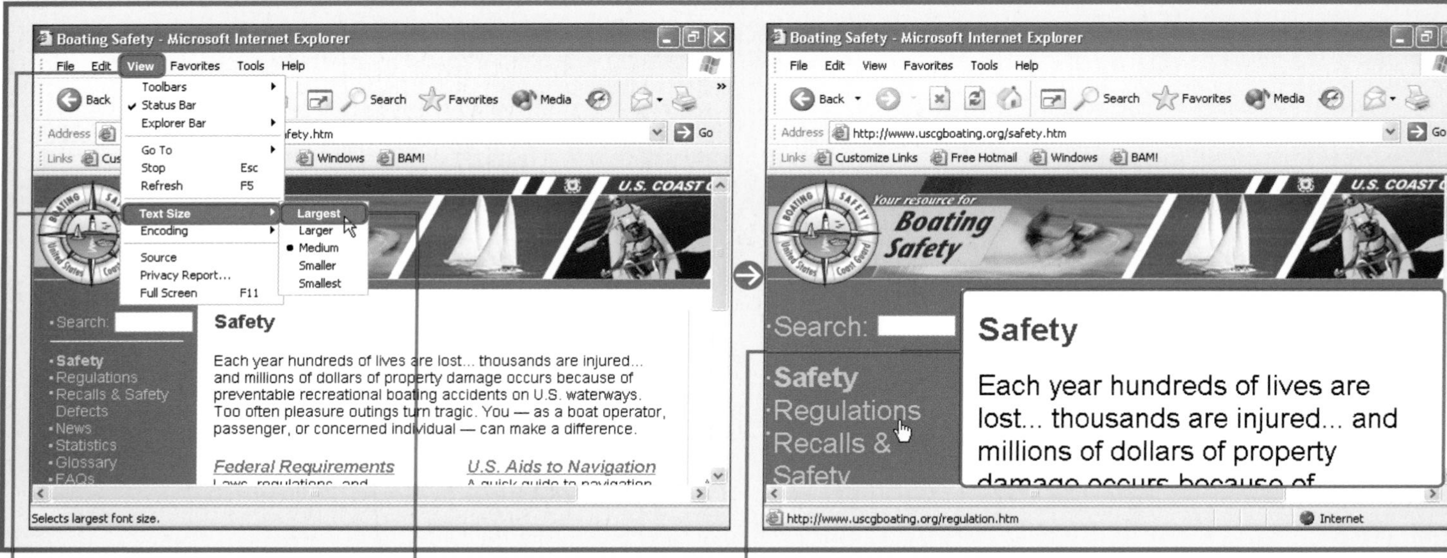

① Click View.

② Click Text Size.

③ Click the desired text size.

○ The page appears in the selected text size.

○ This screen shows the largest text size.

Control FONTS

A Web page's font settings typically overrule any font settings in your browser. In other words, if you open a Web page that uses a specific font, that font appears no matter what setting you entered in your browser.

However, many non-commercial sites on the Web do not use font codes, in which case the font settings in your browser have complete control over the appearance of any text on the page.

Did You Know?

You can employ user style sheets for even more control over the Web page display. For instructions on concerning user style sheets, visit one of the following sites:
cookiecrook.com/AIR/2003/train/userstyles.php
www.curlewcommunications.co.uk/c-style2.html
www.microsoft.com/enable/training/ie6/formatpage.aspx

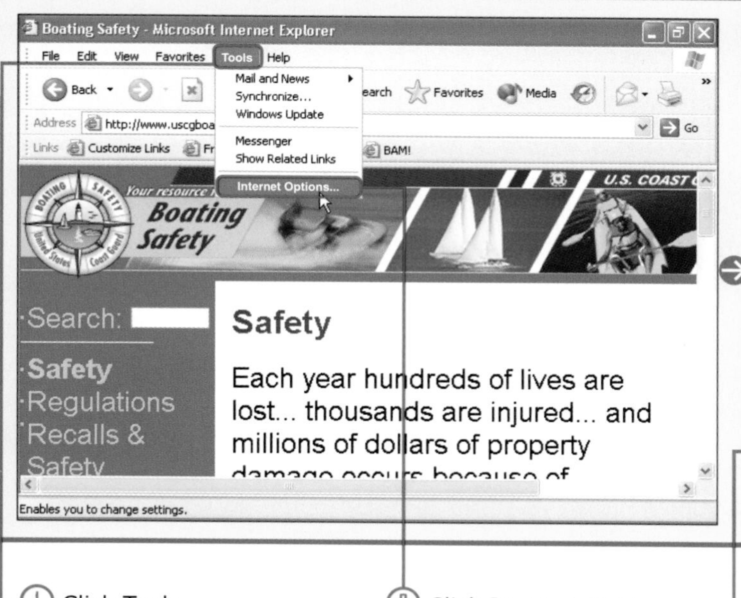

1. Click Tools.
2. Click Internet Options.

- The Internet Options dialog box appears.

3. Click Fonts.

- The Fonts dialog box appears.

4. Click the desired Web page font.
5. Click the desired plain text font.
6. Click OK.

- Internet Explorer applies your selections.

Accessorizing Your Web Browser

Web browsers are powerful programs for displaying a wide range of content on Web pages, including text, images, animations, and many types of built-in programming code. However, many unique types of media, such as audio and video clips and interactive presentations, that some sites feature require specialized programs. To play a QuickTime movie clip on your computer, for instance, you must install the QuickTime Player. With QuickTime Player installed, when you click a link for a QuickTime video clip, your browser downloads the video clip file and runs QuickTime Player, which proceeds to play the clip. These accessories, which people often refer to as *add-ons* or *plug-ins*, give your system the capabilities it needs to open otherwise inaccessible file types.

In many cases, if you click a link to play a file that your browser is incapable of opening, a dialog box pops up asking if you want to download the player needed to open it. You click the button to give your okay and then follow the onscreen instructions to download and install the player, and perhaps to register it. In some cases, however, a dialog box pops up indicating that your system cannot open the file. If this happens, you might need to search the Web for the required player and install it on your computer.

In this chapter, you learn how to search for popular Web browser plug-ins at Download.com and download them. You also learn where to find the most popular media players on the Web. By the end of this chapter, your system should be properly equipped to display or play almost every file you encounter on the Web.

TOP 100

Find BROWSER PLUG-INS at Download.com

Download.com acts as a distribution warehouse for a huge collection of *freeware* and *shareware* for Windows, Mac OS, and mobile operating systems. It features a wide range of software, including anti-virus utilities, screen savers, e-mail programs, and Web browsers, and it is one of the best places to track down Web-browser plug-ins and other accessories. Most of the software you can obtain at this site is shareware — you download and use the program for a free trial period, and if you continue using it, you pay the developer a fee to register. However, much of the software is freeware, which you do not need to pay for.

You can search the Download.com Web site for a specific program if you know its name or browse various software categories by operating system and category, such as audio/video or Internet. This task shows how to track down the collection of Windows Web browser plug-ins at Download.com and how to download a freeware plug-in for your computer. While you are browsing Download.com, consider looking for additional useful programs.

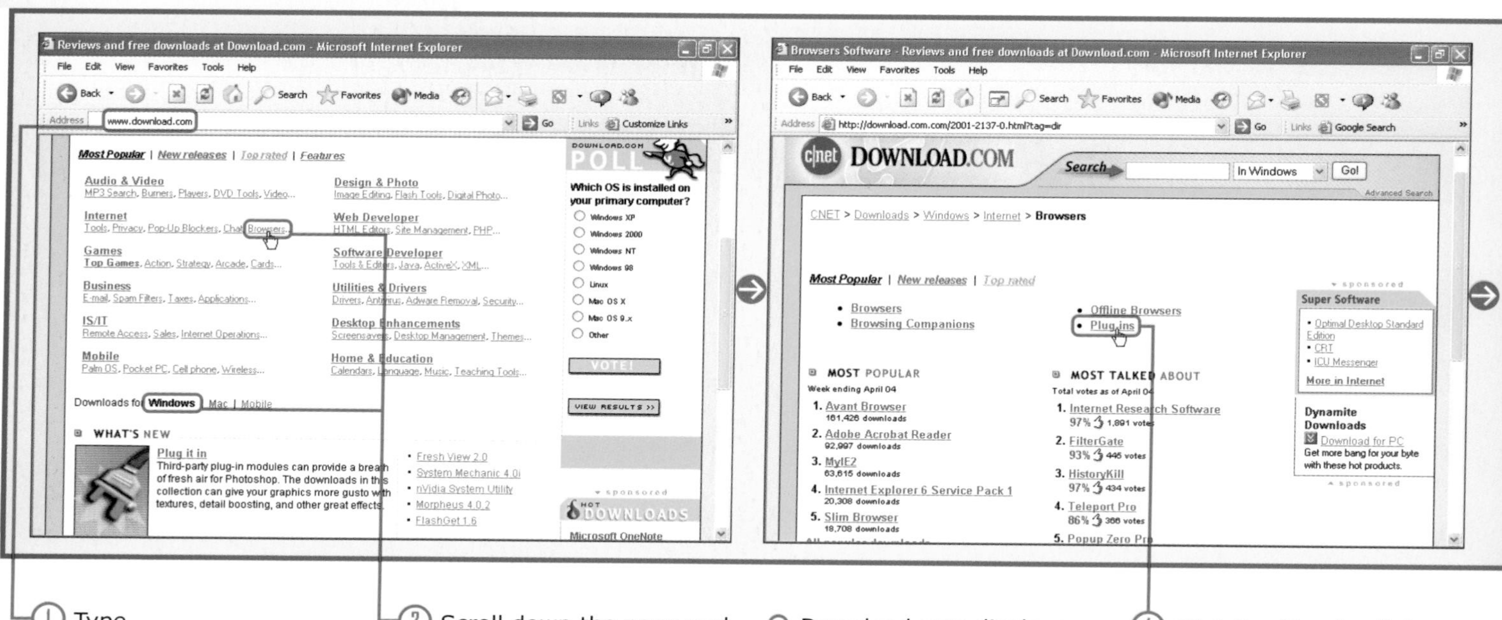

① Type **www.download.com** and press Enter.

② Scroll down the page and click the link for your operating system.

③ Click the Browsers link.

○ Download.com displays links to the most popular programs.

④ Click the Plug-ins link.

DIFFICULTY LEVEL

Did You Know?

After your browser saves the downloaded file, the Download Complete dialog box appears. Click the Open Folder button to open the folder in which you chose to save the file, and then double-click the file to install the program. This saves you from having to remember the location and name of the folder you used.

Check It Out!

Download.com is not the only shareware and freeware resource on the Web. Try these sites:

www.tucows.com
www.shareware.com
downloads-zdnet.com.com
cws.internet.com

Attention!

Shareware sites group their programs differently. One site might place a player in the plug-in category, where as another places the same program in the multimedia category. When searching for plug-ins, be flexible.

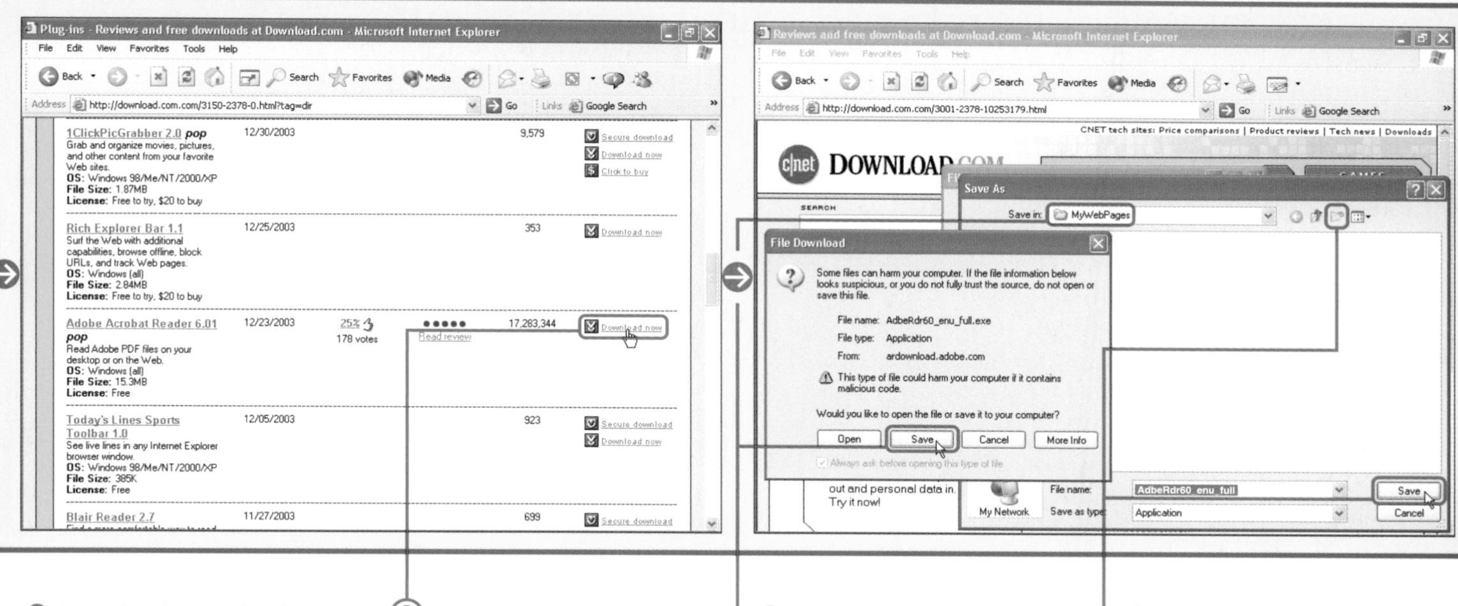

- Download.com displays links to dozens of browser plug-ins.

5 If you see a plug-in you want, click the Download now link

- The File Download dialog box appears.

6 Click Save.

- The Save As dialog box appears.

7 Navigate to the folder in which you want to save the file.

- You can click here to create a new folder.

8 Click Save.

- Your browser downloads and saves the file in the selected folder.

Extract COMPRESSED FILES with WinZip

To conserve storage space and transfer files more efficiently, many sites and individual users choose to compress files before storing or sending them. The compression option of choice is WinZip, a program that can both compress and extract compressed files. With WinZip, you can compress some files to nearly a tenth of their original size, and you can compress an entire folder full of files into a single zipped file, or Zip file.

Because many shareware programs are stored as zipped files and because many users rely on zipped files to shrink the size of e-mail attachments, WinZip is one of the most essential utilities for any Internet user. WinZip is a shareware program, so you can download it and use it for free for 21 days. After the trial period, you must pay a registration fee of $29 to continue using it.

This task shows you where you can obtain WinZip and then provides a brief demonstration showing just how easy it is to compress and decompress files.

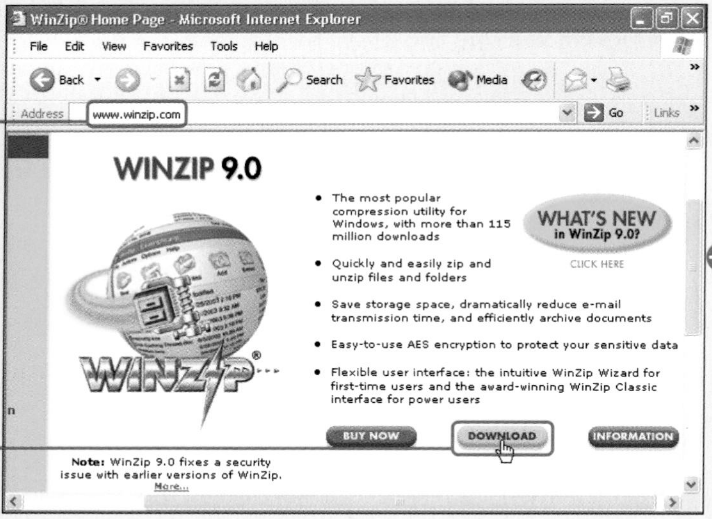

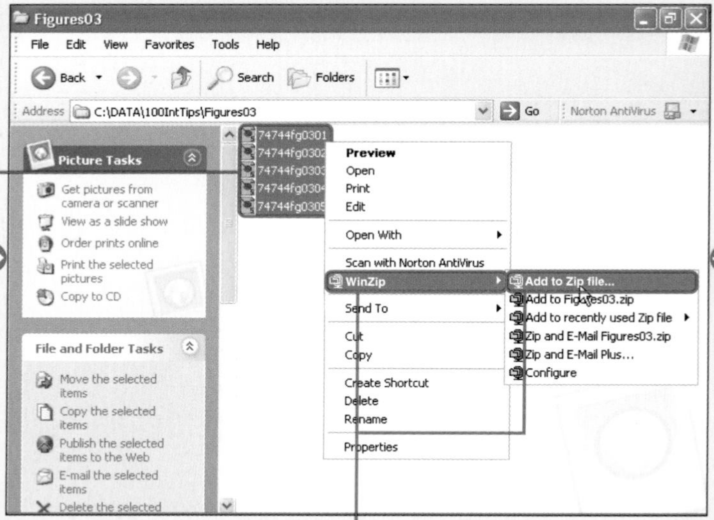

1. Type **www.winzip.com** and press Enter.
2. Click Download and follow the onscreen instructions to download and install WinZip.

Note: When installing WinZip, choose to run WinZip Classic to streamline its operation.

○ The installation routine installs WinZip on your computer.

3. To compress files, highlight the files you want to compress.
4. Right-click one of the selected files.
5. Click WinZip.
6. Click Add to Zip file.

DIFFICULTY LEVEL

More Options!

WinZip is a powerful program with options too numerous to cover here. With WinZip, you can choose to move, rather than copy, files to a Zip file; save the Zip file to a different folder; change the compression ratio; password-protect compressed files; and much more. Check out WinZip's help system for more information.

Try This!

If WinZip successfully associated itself with Zip files during installation, double-click a Zip file to extract its contents. This opens the WinZip window, and you can then click the Extract button ( ) to extract the files.

More Options!

To extract a single file from a Zip file, double-click the Zip file, right-click the file you want to extract, and then click Extract. To remove a file from a Zip file, right-click it and then click Delete.

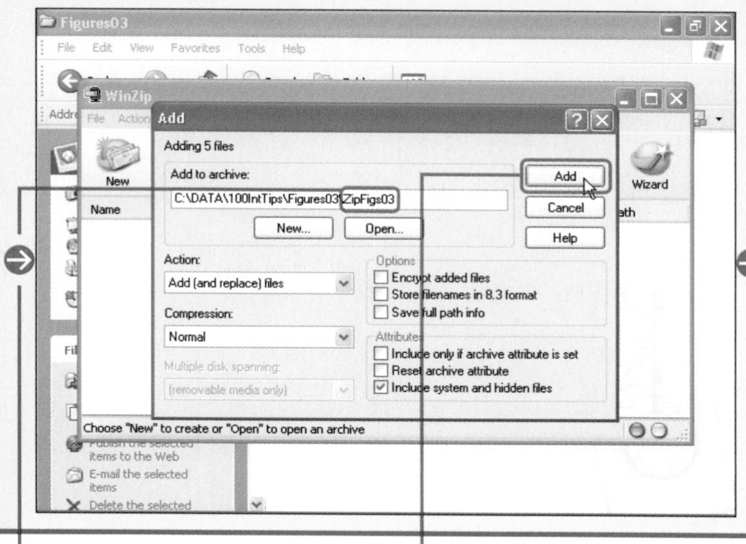

○ The Add dialog box appears.

⑦ Click at the end of the entry in the Add to archive box and type a name for your new Zip file.

⑧ Click Add.

○ WinZip compresses the selected files into a new Zip file and saves the file in the same folder that contains the original files.

⑨ To extract files from a Zip file, right-click the Zip file.

⑩ Click WinZip.

⑪ Click Extract to folder.

○ WinZip extracts the file or files from the Zip file and places them in the same folder that contains the Zip file.

Display PDF FILES with Adobe Reader

Many of the documents you encounter on the Web are not genuine Web pages but PDF files. PDF is a special document format that enables users to save their documents in a format that appears uniform on all computers and in any printouts. PDF files enable publishers to provide electronic versions of books and enable government agencies and businesses to distribute documents and forms that meet official guidelines. If you need an IRS tax form, for instance, you can download and print the PDF version in a form that is acceptable to the IRS using nearly any printer.

Adobe Systems, Incorporated developed the PDF format and develops the software for creating and reading PDF files. Adobe sells the PDF creation software, but it offers its reader, Adobe Reader, available to all users for free. This task shows you where to go to download the reader and what to expect when you display a PDF file in your browser.

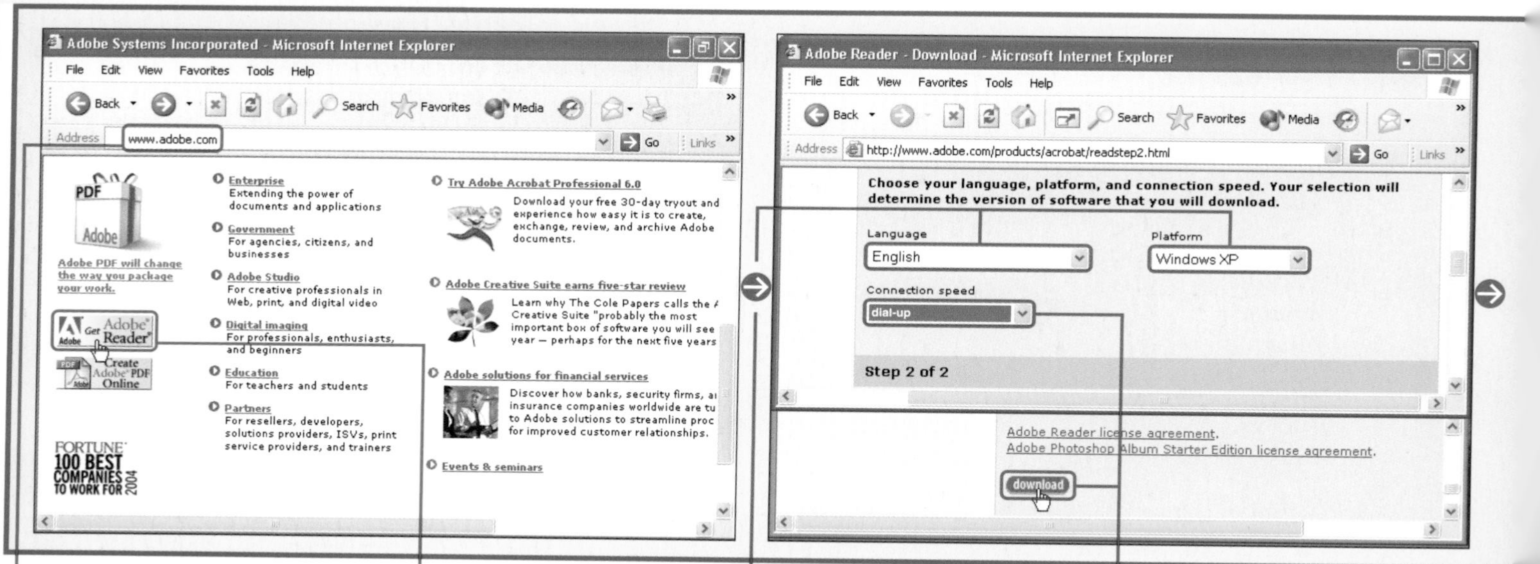

1. Type **www.adobe.com** and press Enter.
2. Scroll down the page and click the Get Adobe Reader icon.

- The Download Adobe Reader screen appears.

3. Click here and select your language.
4. Click here and select your operating system.
5. Click here and select your Internet connection type.
6. Scroll down the page, click the Download button, and download and install Adobe Reader.

More Options!

You can run Adobe Reader by selecting it from the Windows Start, All Programs menu. To update Adobe Reader, click Help, click Updates, and follow the onscreen instructions to download and install any available updates.

Did You Know?

In Adobe Reader, you can type your entries in the blanks and then print or e-mail the completed form, but Adobe Reader does not enable you to save the form with changes. To save completed forms, go to Download.com and download Adobe Acrobat, instead.

More Options!

If you have documents that you want to save in PDF format for distribution, you can create the PDF files online. Go to www.adobe.com and click the Create Adobe PDF Online icon. The service charges about $10 per month, and less if you subscribe for a full year.

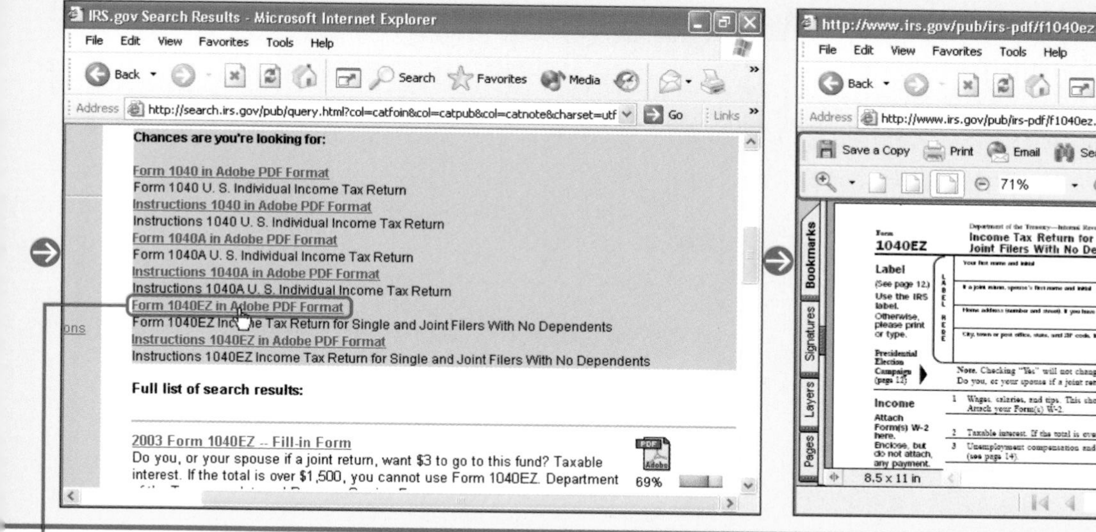

7 When you encounter a link for a PDF file, click the link.

○ Your browser runs Adobe Reader, displays its toolbar in the browser window, and displays the contents of the PDF file.

○ The Adobe Reader toolbar enables you to navigate the document.

Play audio and video clips with REALPLAYER

Your browser is well equipped to play most common digital audio that Webmasters embed in Web pages. If you have your speakers turned up, you might notice this capability when you visit a Web site that features background music or other audio. However, some types of audio files, particularly from companies that feature online radio stations or commercial music clips, store their audio files in a format that requires a special audio player.

One of the most popular players on the Internet is RealPlayer. In its early days, RealPlayer was RealAudio Player, and it played *streaming audio* over the Web. With streaming audio, the player acts like a radio, playing the audio as soon as it begins receiving data. Now, RealPlayer can handle both streaming audio and streaming video. Many Web sites that feature multimedia content, such as CNN, use RealPlayer technology, and if you want to access the audio or video content, you need the player. This task shows you how to download the free, basic version of RealPlayer.

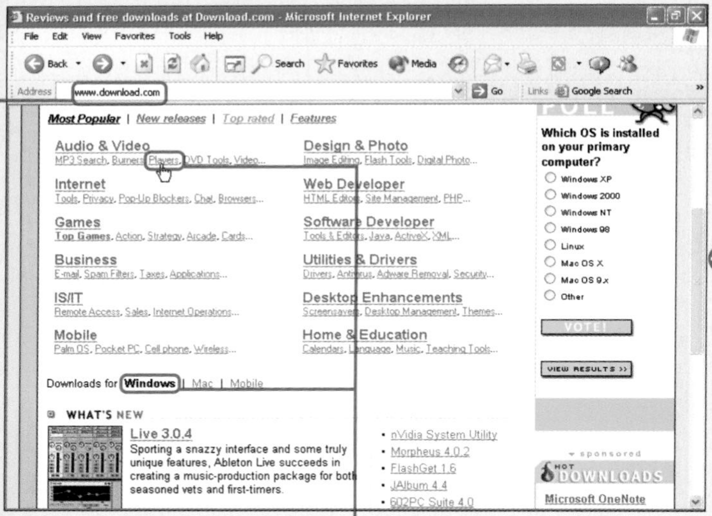

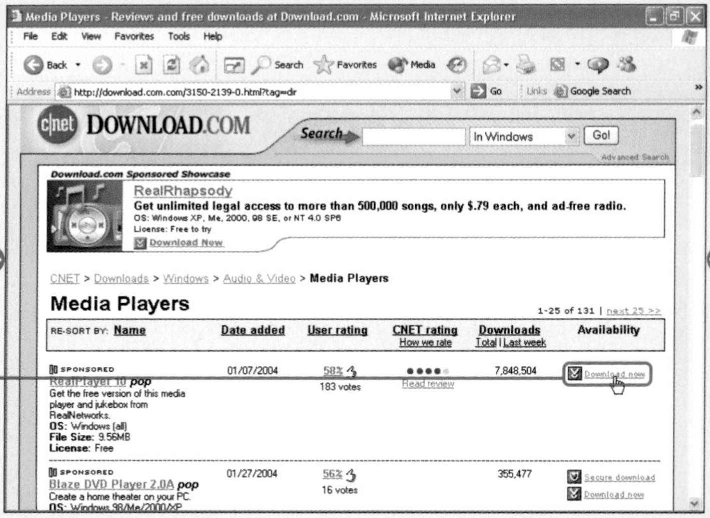

1. Type **www.download.com** and press Enter.
2. Scroll down the page and click the link for your operating system.
3. Click Players.

- Your browser displays links for audio and video players.

4. Click the Download now link for RealPlayer, and then follow the onscreen instructions to download and install the version of RealPlayer for your operating system.

Note: The download, installation, and registration process is fairly time-consuming.

- The RealPlayer shortcut appears on the desktop.

#24

DIFFICULTY LEVEL

Did You Know?

RealPlayer can play a wide range of multimedia formats, including QuickTime and Windows Media files. To have RealPlayer play these files, click its Tools menu, click Preferences, click the plus sign next to Content, and click Media Types. Select the check box next to each media type option (☐ changes to ☑) you want RealPlayer to play. Then, click OK.

Important!

Many audio and video clips that RealPlayer can play are not exactly free. You might click the link to play a clip and the site displays a dialog box indicating that you must subscribe to RealOne to access the selected media clip. You can then close the dialog box or choose to subscribe to the service. RealOne does offer some cool features.

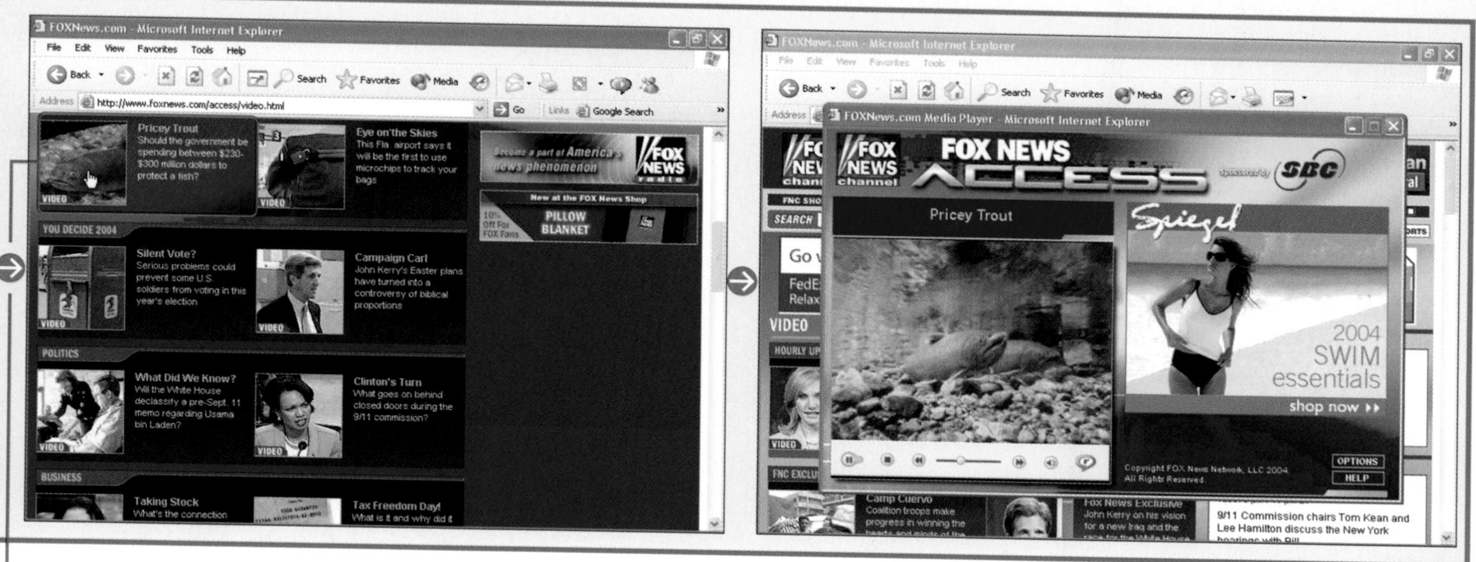

⑤ When you encounter a link or button to play a video clip, click the link or button.

○ If the link or button you clicked links to a RealAudio or RealVideo clip, RealPlayer runs and plays the clip.

Play audio clips with MUSICMATCH JUKEBOX

Musicmatch Jukebox is a free audio player that enables you to listen to a variety of online radio stations, play selected clips, download MP3 clips, *rip* tracks off CDs to store them as MP3 clips, and *burn* your own CDs. Ripping consists of converting tracks from a CD into files that you can store on your computer and transfer to an MP3 player. Burning consists of transferring MP3 files or other audio file types to a recordable CD.

Musicmatch Jukebox can play many audio file types that your browser cannot, including MP3, MPU, Windows Media, and Shoutcast files. It can also play WAV files, which most browsers can play. When you click a link to a file of one of these types, your browser launches Musicmatch Jukebox, which then plays the audio clip. You can also run Musicmatch Jukebox as you run any program on your computer, and use it to tune into radio stations, download music clips, and even create your own custom music CDs.

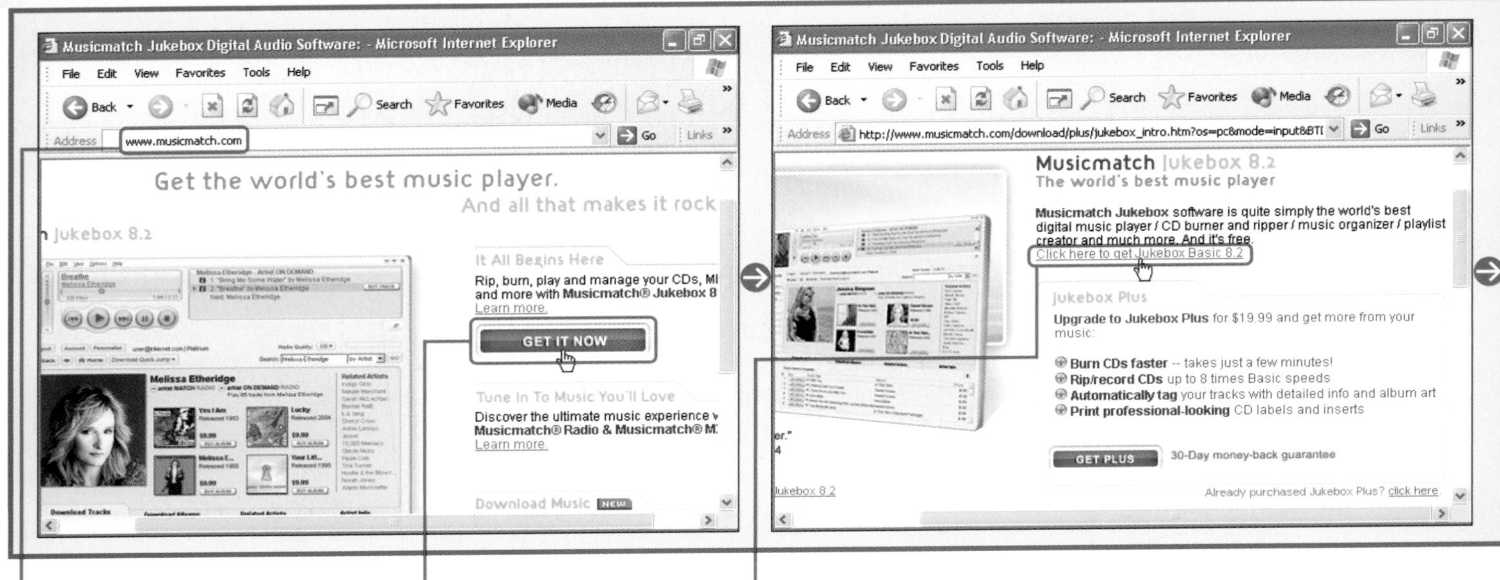

1. Type **www.musicmatch.com** and press Enter.
2. Click GET IT NOW.

- Your browser displays the page for downloading Musicmatch Jukebox.

3. Click the link and follow the onscreen instructions to download and install Musicmatch Jukebox.

- Musicmatch Jukebox is installed on your computer and you can run it as you run any other program.

Try This!

To search for MP3 audio clips and other audio file types, type **www.altavista.com** into your browser's Address bar and press Enter. Click the MP3/Audio tab. Enter a search word or words, select the type of audio file formats you want (☐ changes to ☑), and click the FIND button. AltaVista can help you track down video clips, as well.

#25

DIFFICULTY LEVEL

More Options!

To listen to music while you browse, tune in to an Internet radio station. Run Musicmatch Jukebox and click the Radio button. Click Radio Quick Jump, click Radio Stations, and click the type of music you like. Musicmatch Jukebox starts playing the station. Many stations require a subscription to Musicmatch MX.

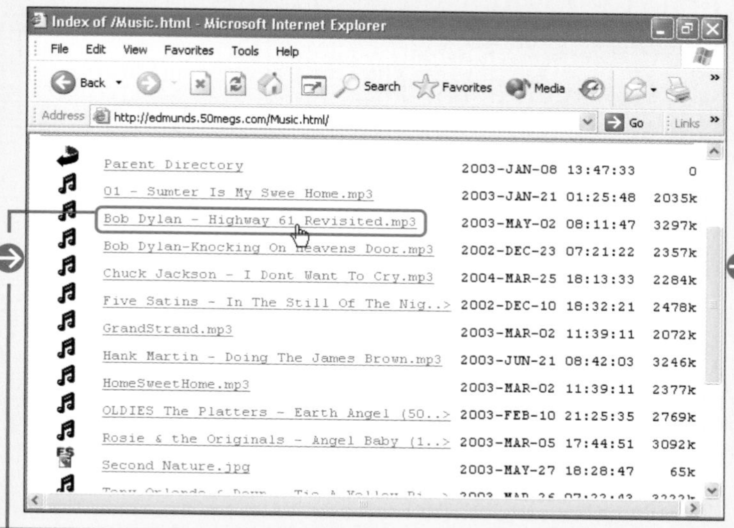

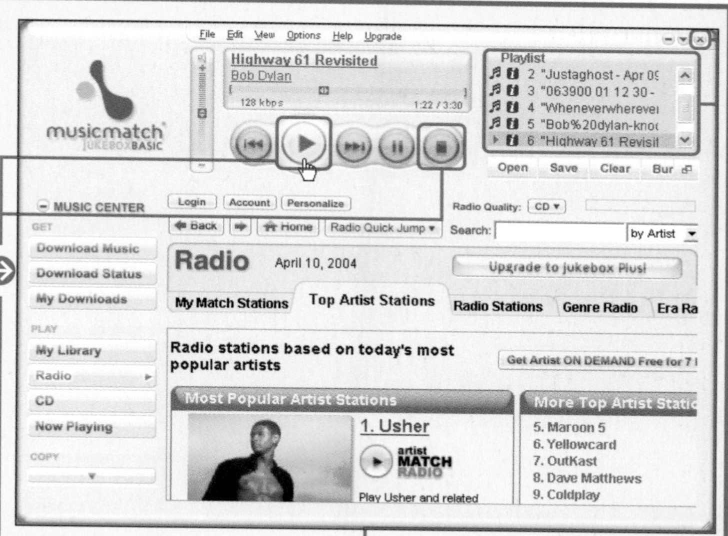

4 When you encounter a link for an MP3 or WAV audio clip you want to play, click the link.

○ Your browser downloads the audio clip, and runs Musicmatch Jukebox, which plays the clip.

5 Click the Play button to replay the clip.

6 Click the Stop button to stop the clip.

7 Click the Close button to exit.

○ If you downloaded more than one track, you can click here to select the desired track.

Play video clips with QUICKTIME PLAYER

Most video clips you encounter on the Web are in RealVideo, QuickTime, or Windows Media format. If you installed RealPlayer, your computer already has a player capable of playing all three media files types. However, some users find that they prefer using the QuickTime player or the Windows Media Player, so they use RealPlayer only for RealAudio and RealVideo files. If you want to see what these different players have to offer, consider installing all three players and letting each play the files it was designed to play.

QuickTime Player displays one of the least cluttered interfaces of any of the popular video players. QuickTime video clips often play right inside a Web page instead of in a separate window, making QuickTime seem like a more integral part of your Web experience. In this task, you learn how to download the QuickTime player, and you see it in action as it plays a video clip.

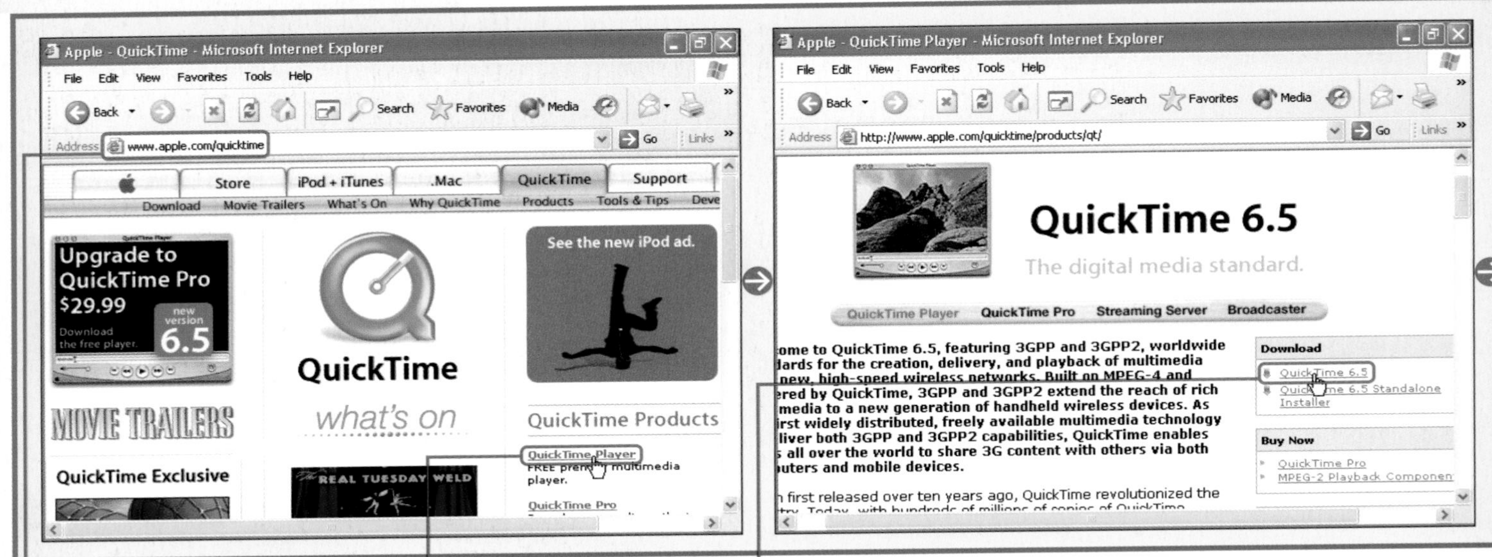

1 Type **www.apple.com/quicktime** and press Enter.

2 Click the QuickTime Player link.

- Your browser displays the QuickTime Player download page.

3 Click the QuickTime link and follow the onscreen instructions to download and install QuickTime Player.

- The installation routine installs the QuickTime Player on your computer, and you can run it as you run any other installed program.

#26

DIFFICULTY LEVEL

Try This!

Run QuickTime Player as a standalone application, so it opens its own window. When it opens, it displays an image and the message, "Click here for more content." Click the image to open the Web page that has video links related to that image. Click the "Click here for more content" link to open a Web page with links for playing additional video clips.

More Options!

To customize QuickTime Player, display its window, click Edit, click Preferences, and then click QuickTime Preferences. The QuickTime Settings dialog box that appears provides options for playing movies immediately, saving movies in your browser's cache, enabling kiosk mode, and adding a QuickTime system tray icon.

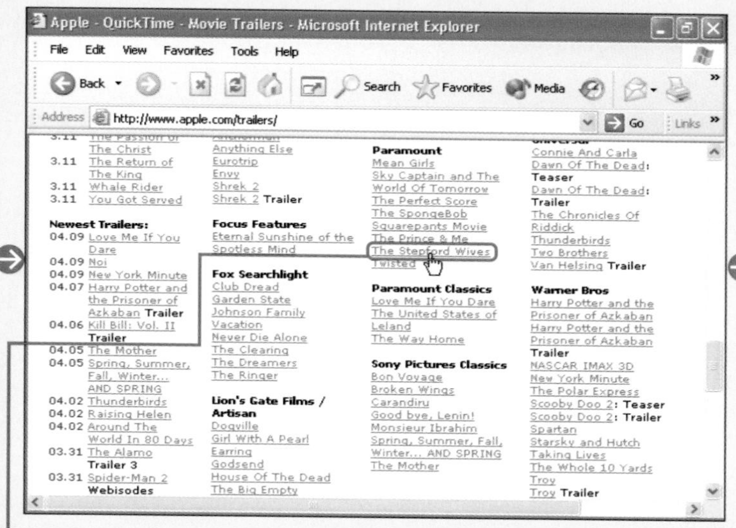

④ When you encounter a link for a QuickTime movie or video clip that you want to watch, click the link.

Note: Many Web sites display a generic video link. When you click the link, the site displays options for the type of player you want to use.

○ Your browser runs QuickTime and plays the selected movie or video clip in a viewing area on the Web page or in a separate QuickTime Player window.

○ Click here and drag the slider to adjust the volume.

○ Click here to pause or play the video.

Play video clips with WINDOWS MEDIA PLAYER

If you have a PC running Windows, you probably have a version of Windows Media Player installed on it. Windows Media Player is a full-service multimedia application similar to Musicmatch Jukebox. It can play audio and video clips and CDs, copy tracks from CDs, burn CDs, and tune into Internet radio stations. In addition, you can click the Media button in Internet Explorer's Standard Buttons toolbar for quick access to the player and any available media. Like QuickTime video, Windows Media Player can play video clips right on a Web page, making it seem more of an integral part of your Web-browsing experience.

If your computer does not have Windows Media Player installed or does not have the latest version of it, this task shows you how to download it and what you can expect to see when it runs on your computer. If Windows Media Player is installed but the installation of another player prevents it from playing Windows Media files, skip to task #30 to learn how to reset the file associations.

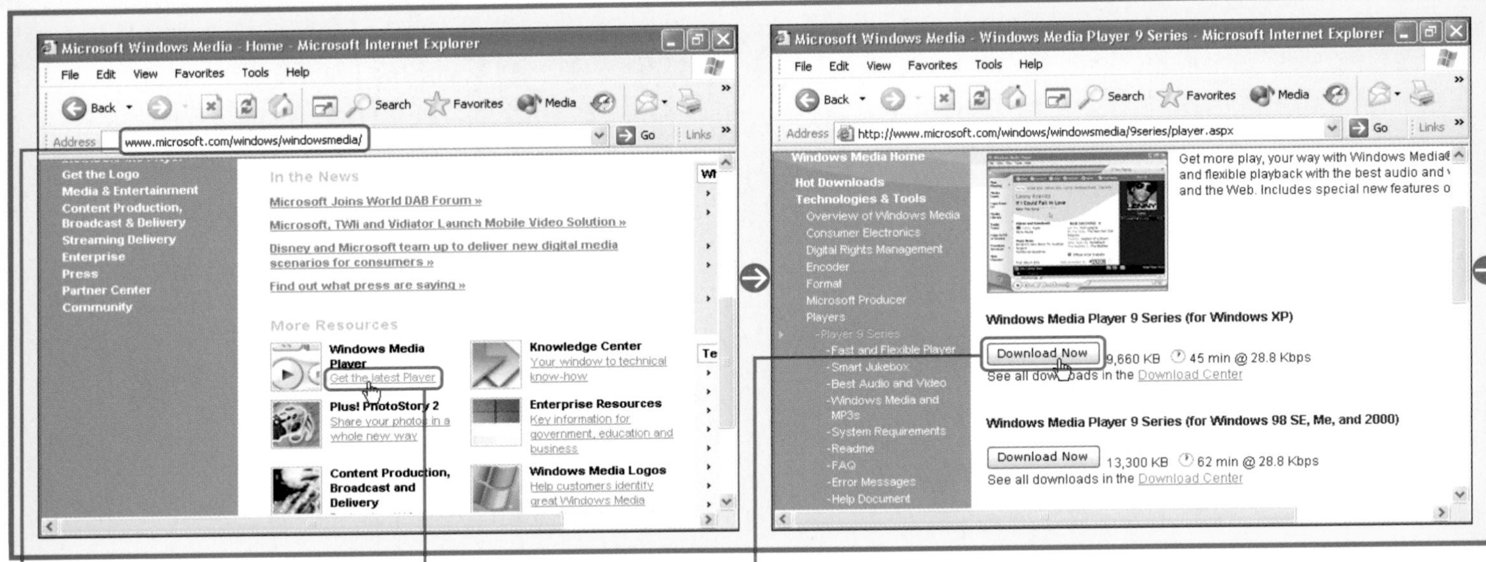

① Type **www.microsoft.com/windows/windowsmedia/** and press Enter.

② Scroll down the page and click the icon for downloading Windows Media Player.

○ The Windows Media Download Center appears.

③ Click Download Now, and then download and install Media Player on your computer.

Note: Make sure you select the correct version of Windows Media Player for your version of Windows.

More Options!

The Windows Media Player window initially hides its menu bar to make it look more like an onscreen game pad. To display the menu bar, move the mouse pointer slightly above the top of the Windows Media Player window. Click Tools, Options to view settings for customizing the player.

More Options!

Instead of playing movies in the Media bar, you can make Media Player play them in a separate window. In Internet Explorer, click the Media button to display the Media bar. Near the bottom of the Media bar, click Media Options, click Settings, and click "Play web media in the bar" (☐ changes to ☑).

Try This!

Windows Media Player 9 comes with its own taskbar toolbar. Right-click a blank area of the taskbar, click Toolbars, and click Windows Media Player.

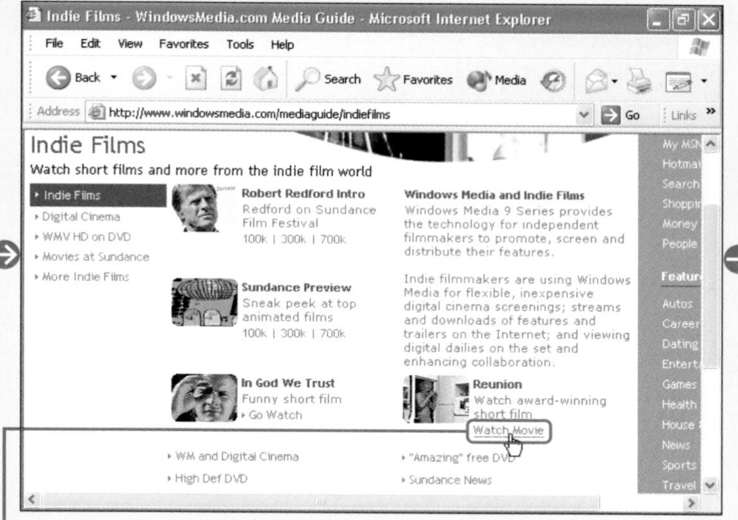

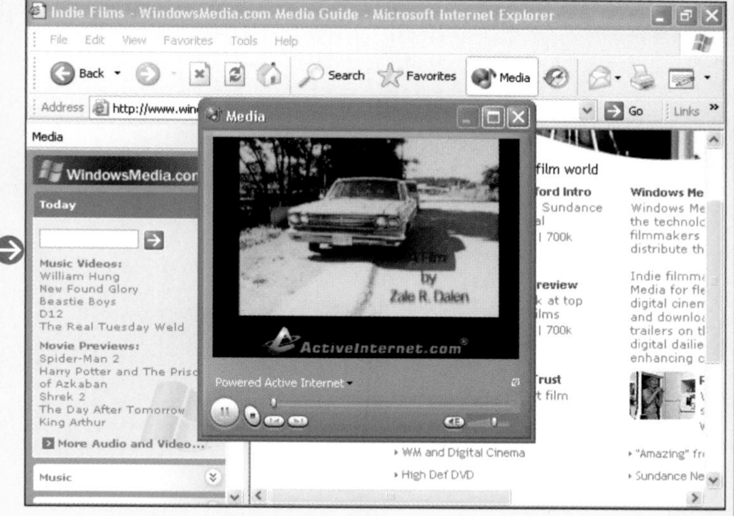

④ When you encounter a link for a Windows Media clip, click the link.

Note: If you insert an audio CD into your computer's CD-ROM drive, Windows Media Player starts playing the CD.

○ Your browser downloads the linked video clip and runs Windows Media Player, which plays the clip.

Play multimedia SHOCKWAVE ANIMATIONS

Shockwave is a browser add-on that plays interactive multimedia games, presentations, and demonstrations that programmers developed using Macromedia Director. A Shockwave presentation typically looks like a movie, complete with sound, video, and animation. In addition, many Shockwave programs are interactive, allowing users to play games online, tour three-dimensional objects, and take interactive tutorials online. For example, at a *Lord of the Rings* Web site, you can create your own warrior using an interactive Shockwave application.

Many sites that feature Shockwave media provide visitors a choice of using the Shockwave-enabled version. If you have a dial-up modem connection, you might want to opt for the non-Shockwave version. If you click the link for the Shockwave version and you have not yet installed Shockwave, a dialog box typically pops up asking if you want to install it. If you choose to install Shockwave, you can proceed to the download site. If this option is unavailable, you can download the Shockwave player from the Macromedia Web site, as shown here.

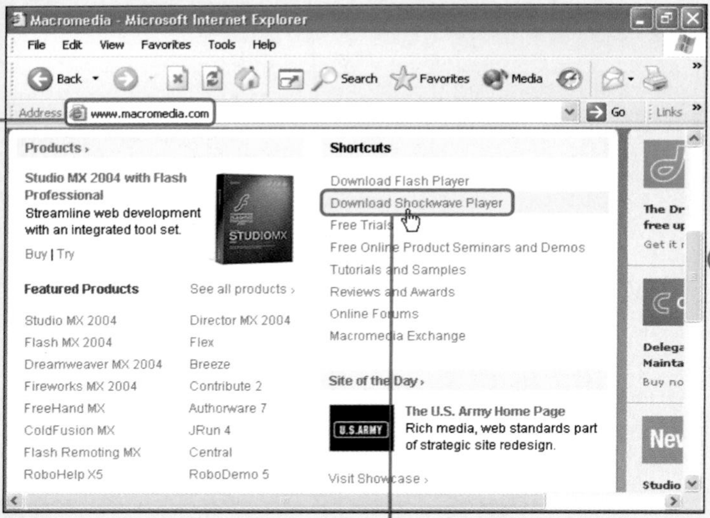

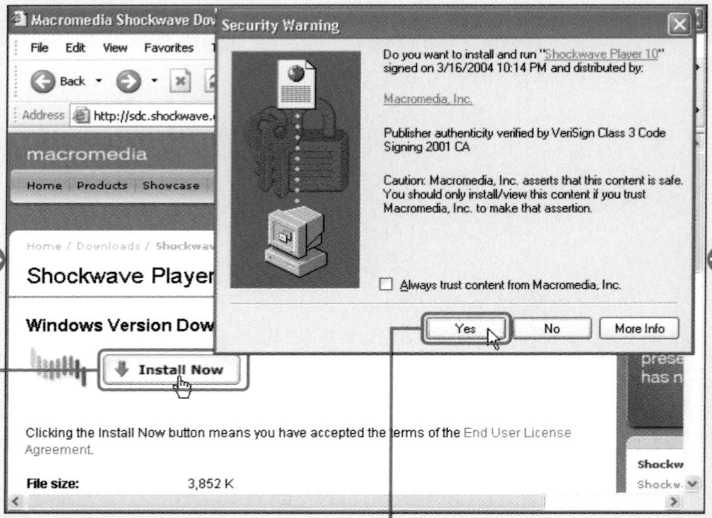

1. Type **www.macromedia.com** and press Enter.
2. Under Shortcuts, click the Download Shockwave Player link.

- Your browser displays the Shockwave Player Download Center.

3. Click Install Now.

- The Security Warning dialog box appears, asking you to confirm the installation.

4. Click Yes.

- The Shockwave player installs itself on your computer and displays a message indicating that it installed successfully.

#28

DIFFICULTY LEVEL

Did You Know?

Shockwave does not run as a standalone application on your computer; it relies on your Web browser for a display area. In Internet Explorer, Shockwave is an ActiveX control that actually becomes an integral part of Internet Explorer.

Try This!

You can view Internet Explorer's ActiveX controls. Click Tools, Internet Options. On the General tab, click the Settings button and then click the View Objects button. To update an ActiveX control, right-click it and click Update.

Check It Out!

Some of the most dynamic online games owe their existence to Shockwave. To check out some commercial games, go to www.shockwave.com. These games can take some time to download, even over a broadband connection.

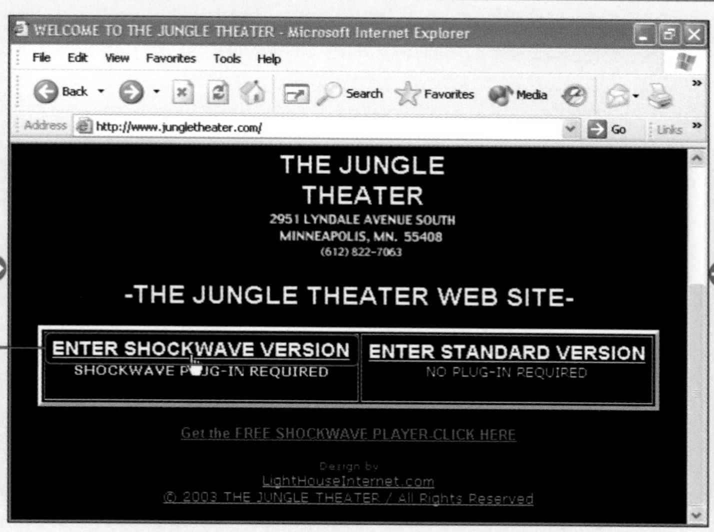

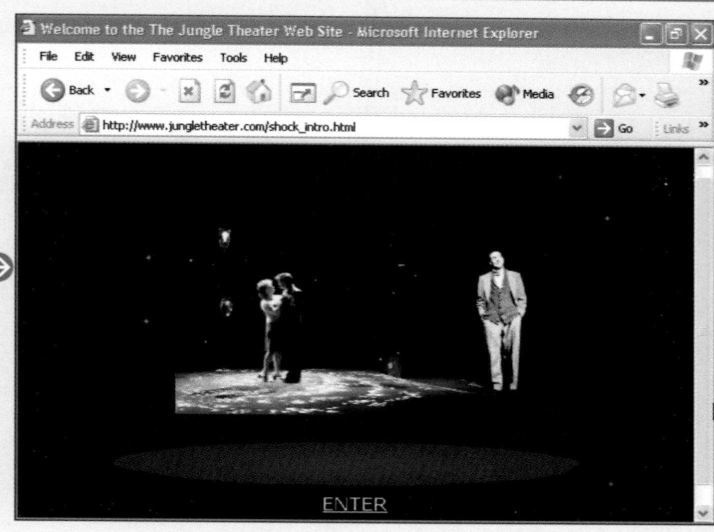

5 If you visit a Web site that offers a Shockwave version of the site, click the link for the Shockwave version.

○ Your browser plays the Shockwave site in the same window where it displays Web pages.

Play multimedia FLASH ANIMATIONS

Macromedia, developer of the Shockwave Player also has a Flash player designed to play smaller Web applications that load faster. Flash animations typically serve up high-impact, interactive animations, online advertisements, and short- to medium-length animations. Like Shockwave, the Flash player is a relatively small ActiveX control or plug-in that becomes an integral part of your browser. Many new computers, including those running Mac OS X and Windows XP, and several Web browsers have the Flash player installed, so chances are you already have it.

With the Flash player installed, a Flash file that you click a link to plays right inside the browser window or pops up in a separate browser window. Like Shockwave animations, Flash animations are dynamic, typically three-dimensional, and interactive. You can download and install the Flash ActiveX control or plug-in at the same Macromedia site from which you downloaded the Shockwave add-on. Even if your computer already has the Flash player, you can take these steps to update it.

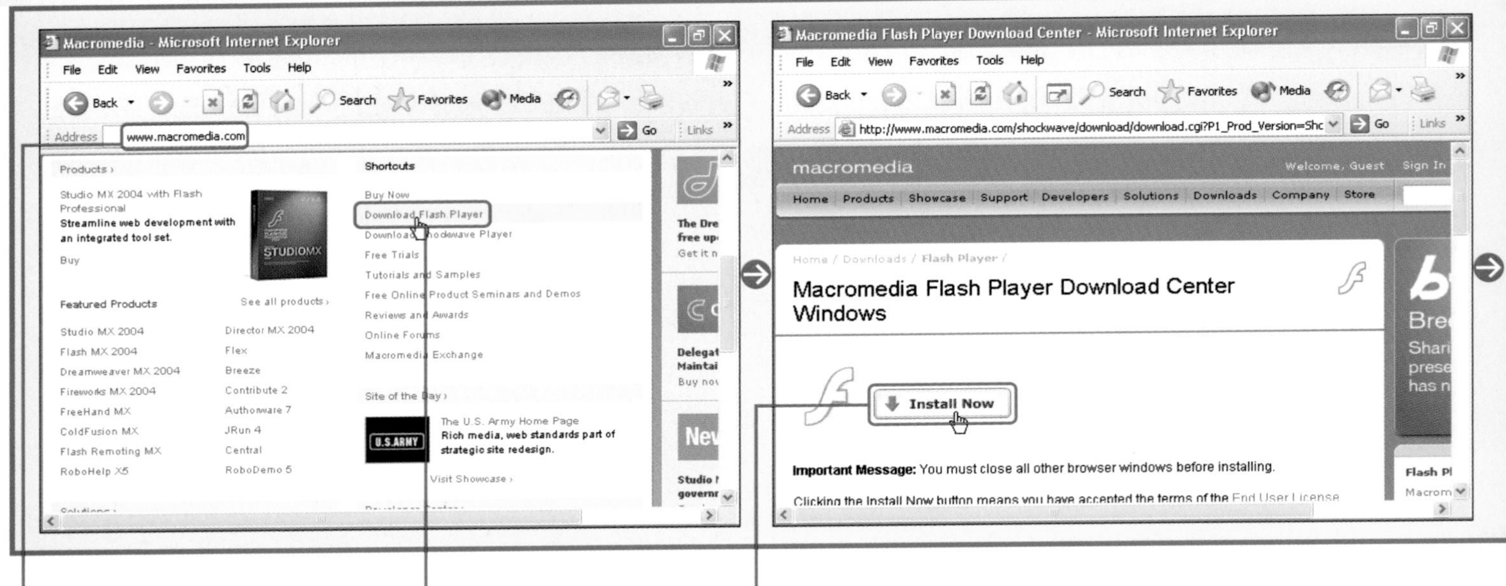

① Type **www.macromedia.com** and press Enter.

② Under Shortcuts, click the Download Flash Player link.

○ Your browser displays the Flash Player Download Center.

③ Click Install Now.

○ The Flash player installs itself on your computer and displays a message indicating that the installation succeeded.

DIFFICULTY LEVEL

Did You Know?

Flash does not run as a standalone application on your computer; it relies on your Web browser for a display area. In Internet Explorer, the Flash player is an ActiveX control that actually becomes an integral part of Internet Explorer.

Test It!

In your browser, type **www.google.com** and press Enter. Search for "sample flash animations" and then click a link for one of the sites that appears. Click a link for one of the samples and see how your browser plays it.

Remove It!

To access other Macromedia players or uninstallers for the players you have, use your Web browser to open www.macromedia.com/shockwave/download/alternates/ and then click the link for the desired player or uninstaller.

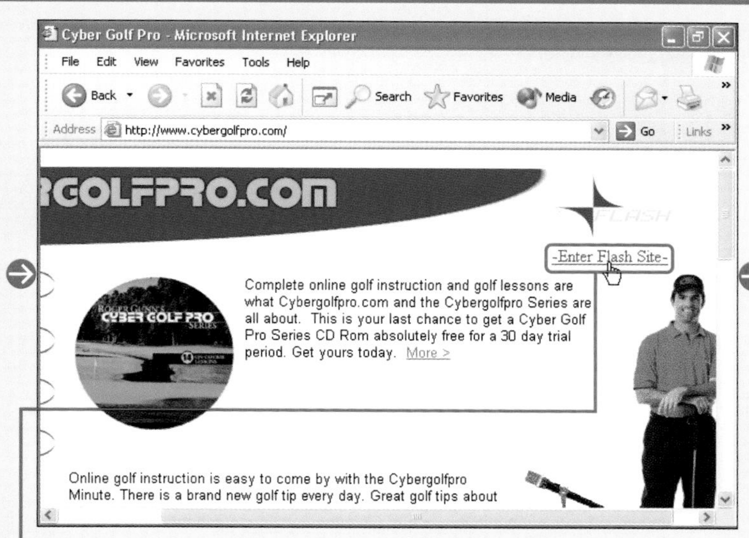

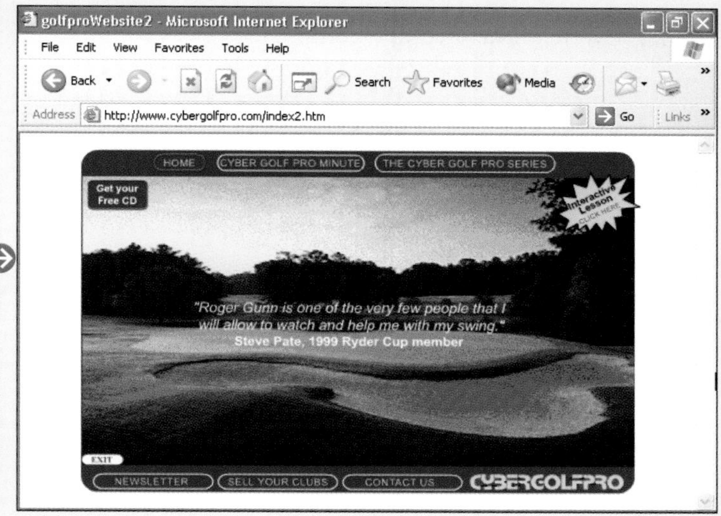

4. If you visit a Web site that offers a Flash version of the site, click the link for the Flash version.

- Your browser plays the Flash site in the same window where it displays Web pages or in a separate browser window.

ASSOCIATE FILE TYPES

with the desired player

Almost every file on your computer has a two- or three-character filename extension that indicates its file format. Microsoft Word documents, for example, end in .doc and WinZip filenames end in .zip. Your operating system uses the filename extensions both to identify file formats and to choose the right program to run when you double-click a file. If you installed RealPlayer in task #24, for instance, and you double-click a file whose name ends in .ra or .rv, your operating system automatically runs RealPlayer, which opens and plays the file.

Sometimes, when you install a plug-in or player, it does not associate itself with a file type that you want it to play or it associates itself with a file type that you want a different program to play. In such cases, you can adjust the filename associations yourself. Often, you can set associations by changing the player's options. If a player's options do not include filename associations, you can reset the associations in your operating system. This task shows you how to change filename associations in Windows.

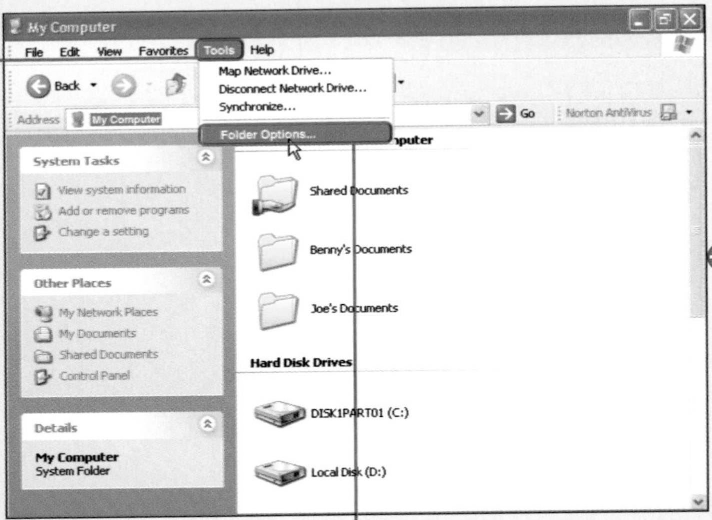

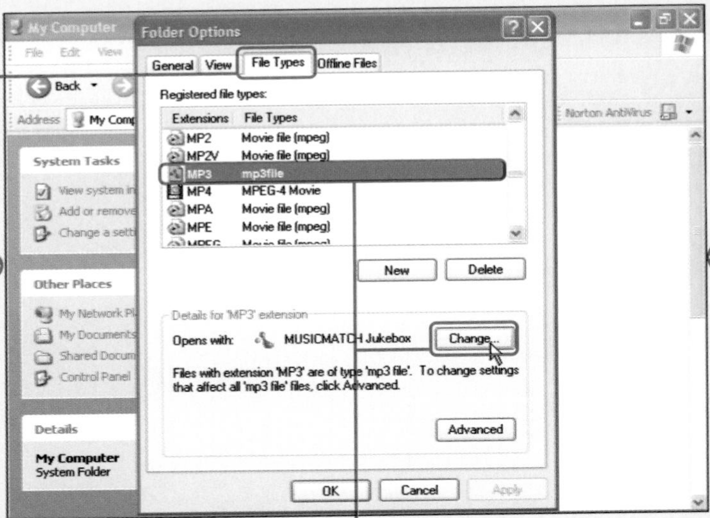

1. In the My Computer window, click Tools.
2. Click Folder Options.

- The Folder Options dialog box appears.

3. Click the File Types tab.
4. Scroll down the list of Registered file types and click the file type that you want to associate with a different program.
5. Click the Change button.

DIFFICULTY LEVEL

More Options!

In the Open With dialog box, you can choose the option for selecting a program installed on your computer to play the file or you can click the option to locate an appropriate program on the Internet to download and install.

Try This!

If you change a filename association and run into problems, try deleting the filename association and then double-clicking a file of the type you want to open. A dialog box appears asking if you want to pick a program from the list or search for a player on the Web. After you choose a player, your operating system automatically sets up the file association for you.

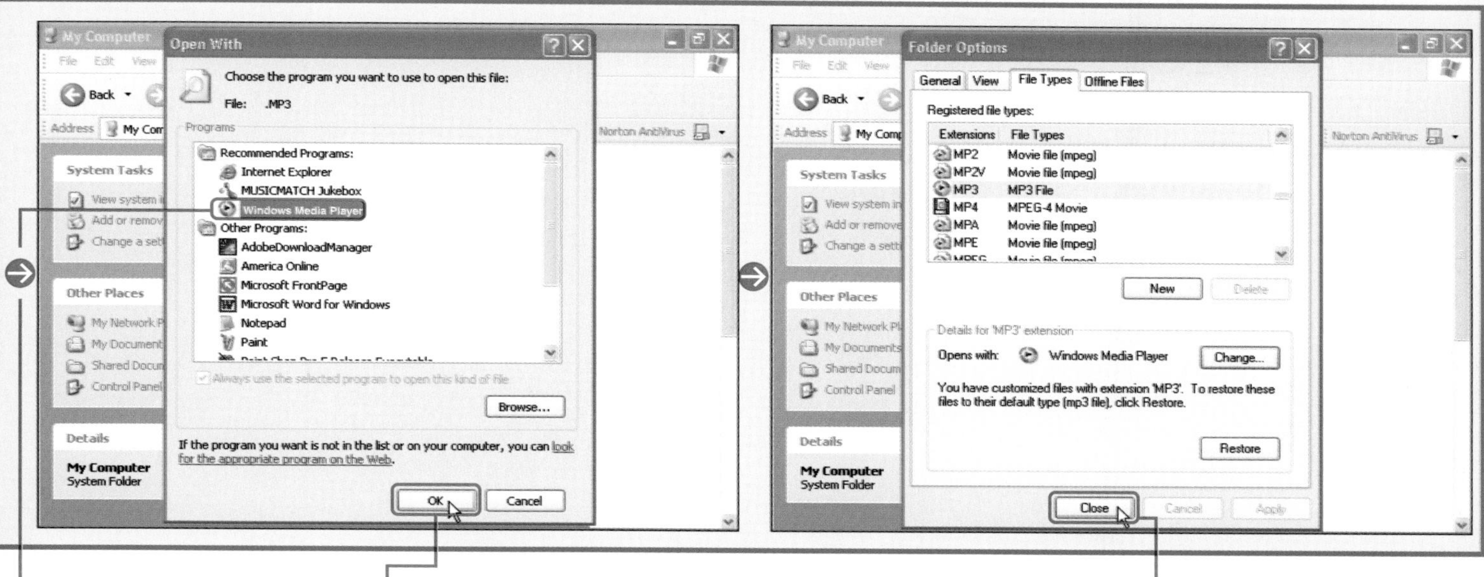

- The Open With dialog box appears, displaying a list of installed programs.

6 Click the program you want to use to open the selected file type.

Note: Not all programs can play all file types. Consider selecting a recommended program, at the top of the list.

7 Click OK.

- You return to the Folder Options dialog box.
- The program you selected is now in charge of playing files with this filename extension.

8 Click the Close button.

- Windows saves the change and closes the Folder Options dialog box.

Power Browse in Private

Chapters 2 and 3 show you how to optimize the speed of your Internet connection and customize your browser to enhance its appearance and operation. Both of these enhancements can make browsing the Web more enjoyable and efficient. Two additional components can have a strong influence on your efficiency and enjoyment of the Web — the techniques you use to browse Web sites and your ability to browse in private.

If you are accustomed to surfing the Web by typing site addresses, clicking links, and using the Back and Forward buttons, a few timesaving keystrokes and mouse maneuvers can help you browse more efficiently. You can also learn some tricks to avoid the tracking mechanisms that many sites use to collect information about you and your browsing habits.

In this chapter, you learn how to browse the Web in multiple windows, so you can quickly return to your original point of departure. You also learn how to browse in kiosk mode and use mouse and keyboard shortcuts to navigate pages rather than relying on the toolbars and address bars. And you learn how to have your browser automatically retrieve your favorite Web pages so you can read the pages offline at your convenience.

For those who are concerned about Web sites tracking and recording their browsing habits, the tasks at the end of this chapter show you various techniques to evade tracking on the Web. With the techniques you learn in this chapter, you can browse more efficiently and more privately.

TOP 100

Browse in MULTIPLE WINDOWS

One of the most inefficient ways to browse the Web is to browse in a single window. You might perform a search that generates a dozen or more links, so you click one of the links and follow a trail to a page that might not even have what you were looking for. Then, you must click the Back button several times to return to your search results or jump back using a history list.

A much more efficient approach is to explore a link in a separate window, leaving the search results window untouched. This enables you to follow a long trail of links and then close the window to quickly return to your search results. Of course, you can use this technique from any page to which you wish to return. For instance, at a news site, you might open the link for an article in a separate window and then close the window when you are done reading the article.

This task shows several methods of opening and using multiple windows.

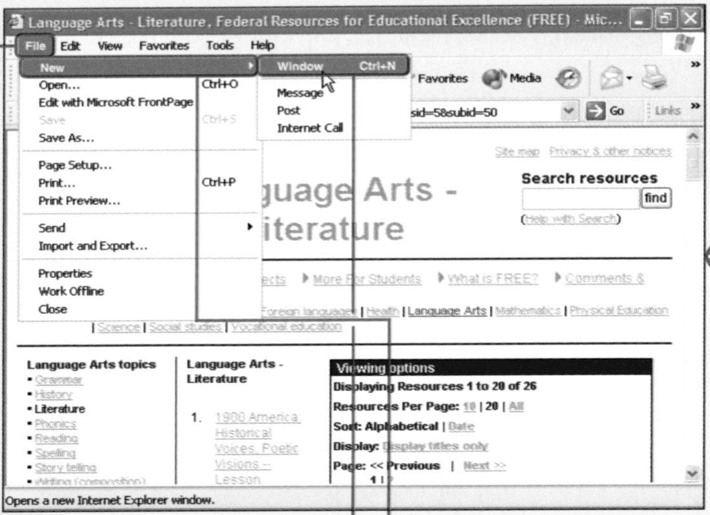

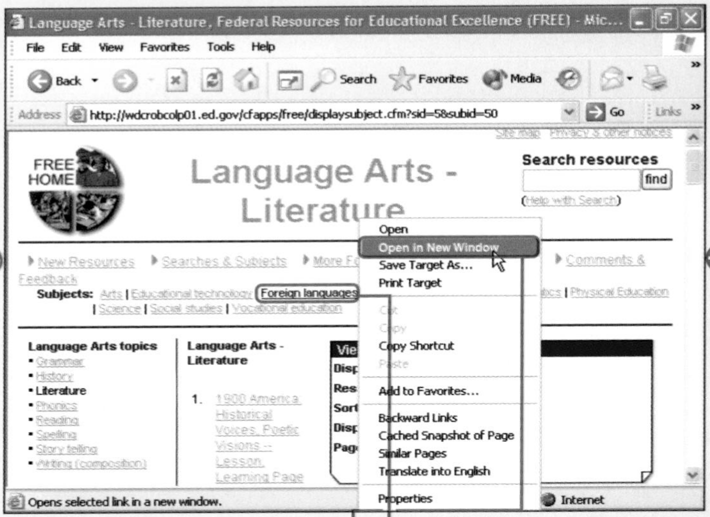

1. Click File.
2. Click New.
3. Click Window.

○ Your browser opens a new window displaying the same Web page.

4. Right-click a link.
5. Click Open in New Window.

Try This!

To print a page that a link points to, right-click the link and click Print Target. To copy a link, right-click the link and click Copy Shortcut. You can then right-click inside the Address bar or in a document and click Paste to paste the link.

Caution!

Every window you open consumes some of your computer's system resources, so if your computer seems sluggish, close any windows that you no longer need.

Attention

Most Web browser, including Netscape Navigator, Safari, and OmniWeb feature tabbed browsing, which enables you to open two or more pages in a single window. To switch to a page, you click its tab.

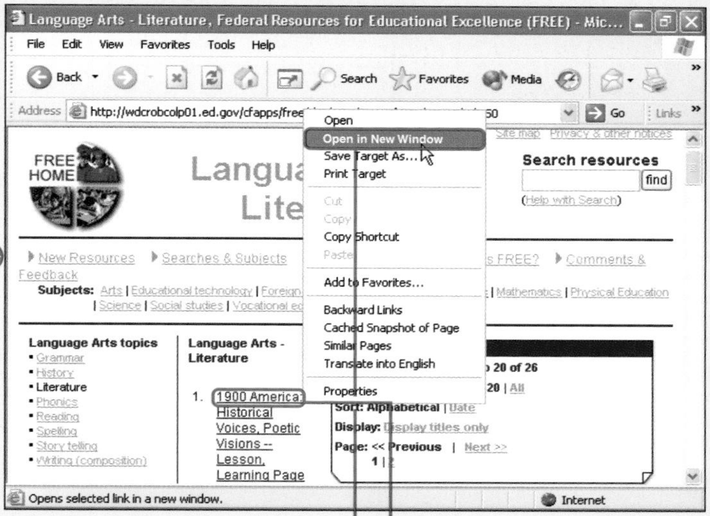

- Your browser opens the linked page in a separate window.

6. Click links to explore other pages or sites.
7. When you are done exploring, click the Close button.

- The window closes, returning you to the previous window.

8. Right-click another link you want to explore.
9. Click Open in New Window.

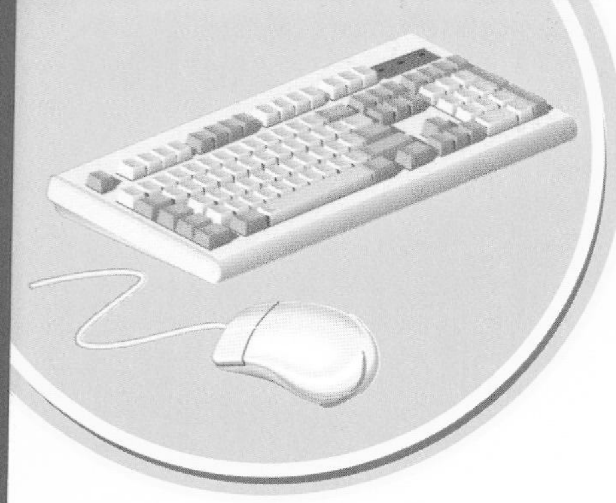

Browse in KIOSK MODE

Task #18 shows you how to browse in full-screen mode, with or without the Standard Buttons toolbar. Few users know that they can browse in another full-screen mode, called *kiosk mode*, which frees up additional screen space. Kiosk mode hides not only the browser toolbars and status bar, but also the Windows taskbar, providing a true full-screen mode. The only browser control you see in kiosk mode is the vertical scrollbar.

Kiosk mode is the ultimate power-browsing mode, delivering Web pages without browser controls or other screen distractions. Kiosk mode challenges your ability to navigate without toolbars, using only keyboard shortcuts and right-click mouse maneuvers. This task shows you how to run Internet Explorer in kiosk mode and survive without the toolbars and menu options. In the next task, you learn additional keyboard shortcuts that can save you time in whatever mode you choose to browse. After you try kiosk mode, you might decide to use it exclusively.

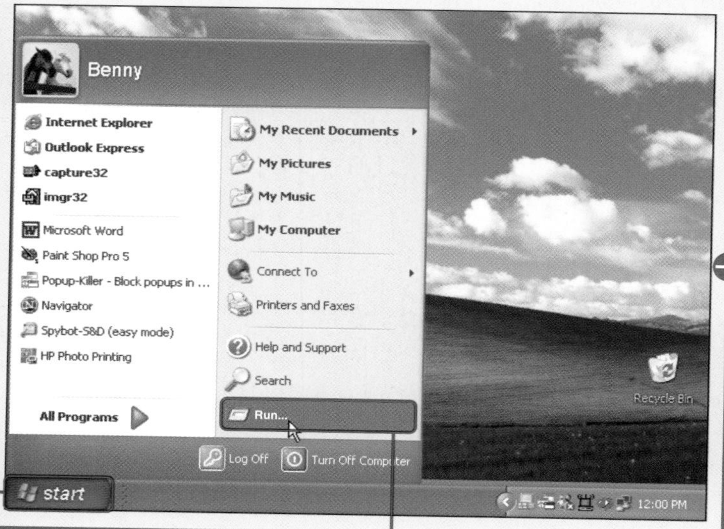

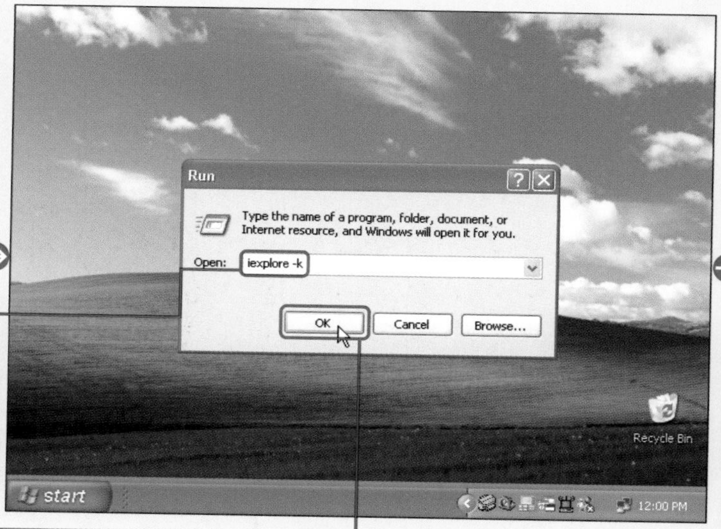

1. Click Start.
2. Click Run.

- The Run dialog box appears.

3. Type **iexplore –k**.

- You can follow the command with a URL to open a specific page; for example, iexplore –k http://www.cnn.com opens CNN's home page in kiosk mode.

4. Click OK.

Remove It!

Kiosk mode provides no menus or buttons to control the window or exit Internet Explorer. To exit out of kiosk mode, press Alt+F4.

Did You Know?

With the Windows taskbar hidden, to change to a different program, hold down the Alt key and press Tab repeatedly until the desired application is selected, and then release Alt. To display the taskbar and open the Start menu, press Ctrl+Esc or the Windows logo key, if your keyboard has one.

Desktop Trick!

If you like kiosk mode, create a shortcut for it. Right-click a blank area of the desktop, click New, and click Shortcut. Type **"C:\Program Files\Internet Explorer\iexplore.exe" –k**. Click Next, type a name for the shortcut, and then click Finish.

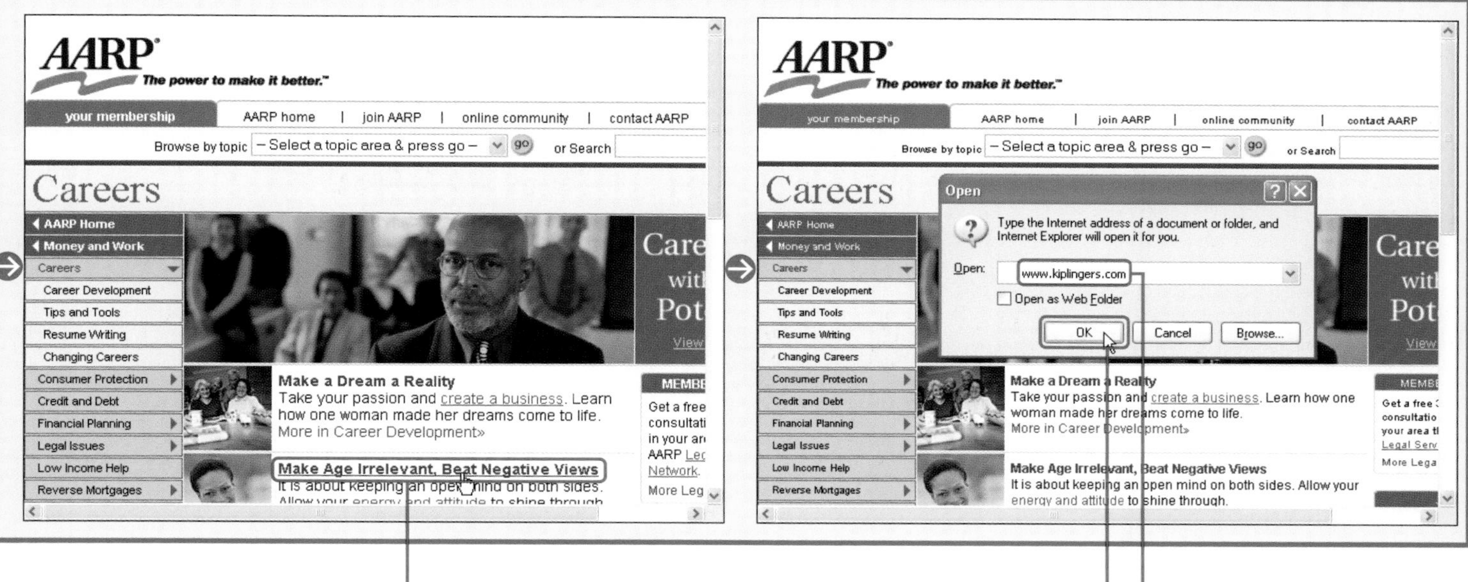

- Internet Explorer runs in kiosk mode.
- You can click links to navigate.

5. To open a specific page, press Ctrl+O.

- The Open dialog box appears.

6. Type the address of the page you want to view.
7. Click OK.

Make the most of MOUSE AND KEYBOARD SHORTCUTS

The preferred mode of travel on the Web is the mouse. You simply point and click to move from one page to the next. The browser controls and features make the mouse even more powerful, enabling you to move back and forth and access additional navigational tools. You can click various buttons in the Standard Buttons toolbar to view a history of pages you have visited, to view a list of Favorites, or even display a Search pane. When browsing the Web, however, going up to the toolbars to navigate takes additional time. Learning a few mouse maneuvers and keystrokes, you can cruise the Web much more efficiently.

Dozens of mouse and keyboard shortcuts are available to enhance the way you browse and optimize the speed at which you surf. This task highlights some of the more efficient and useful shortcuts, but you can find more in your browser's help system. These steps illustrate mouse maneuvers you can use. The tips section focuses on keyboard shortcuts.

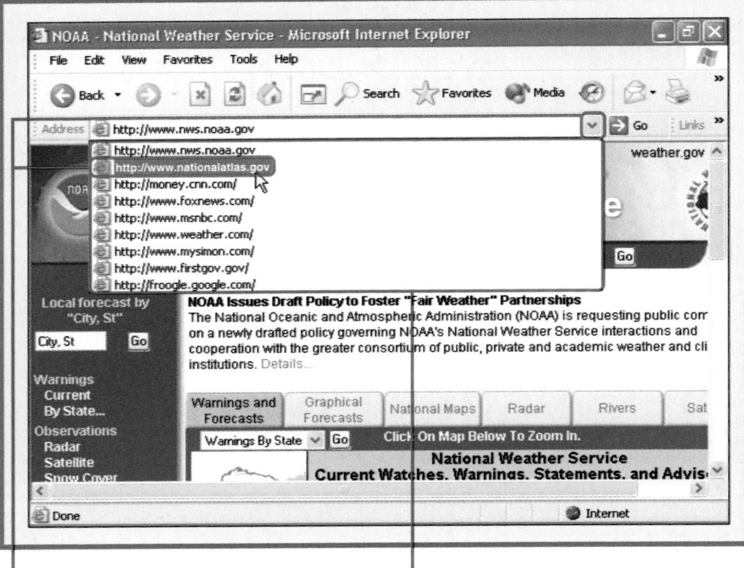

VIEW A RECENTLY VISITED SITE

① Click here and click the address of a page you recently visited.

○ Addresses of sites you recently visited appear.

○ Your browser loads the selected Web page.

VIEW NEXT AND PREVIOUS WEB PAGES

① Right-click a blank area of the current page.

② Click Back to return to the previous page.

③ Click Forward to return to the next page.

More Options!

Web browsers typically feature many shortcut keystrokes for navigating Web pages. Here are some of the more popular keystrokes: Esc stops loading a page. F5 or Ctrl+R refreshes a page. F11 toggles between full screen and normal window size. Alt+Home opens your home page. Backspace or Alt+left arrow displays the previous page. Alt+right arrow moves forward to the next page, if you backed up from the page. Alt+D moves the cursor to the Address bar. Ctrl+F lets you search for text on this page. Ctrl+N opens a new window. Ctrl+W closes the current window. Ctrl+P prints the page. PgUp and PgDn scroll one screen up or down.

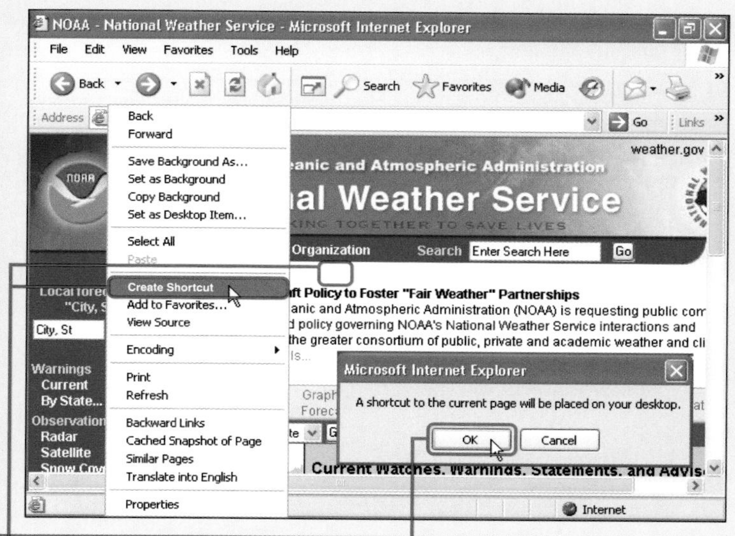

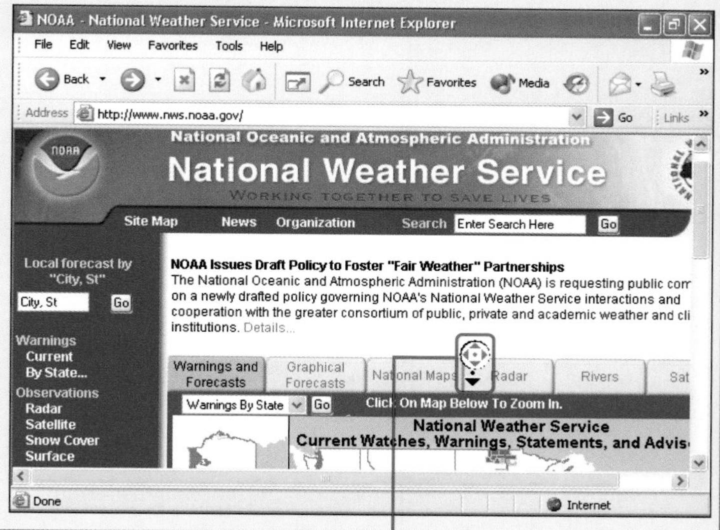

CREATE A SHORTCUT

① Right-click a blank area of the page.

② Click Create Shortcut.

③ Click OK.

○ Internet Explorer places a shortcut to the page on the Windows desktop.

SCROLL UP AND DOWN

① If you have a mouse with a wheel, click the wheel.

○ The scroll icon appears.

② Roll the mouse backward to scroll down or forward to scroll up.

ENABLE AUTO-COMPLETE

for Web page addresses

Internet Explorer's AutoComplete feature can help you type Web page addresses more quickly. With AutoComplete enabled, you click in the Address bar and start typing. As you type, Internet Explorer completes the entry based on addresses you had previously typed in. Usually, you need to type only five or six characters, and your browser "guesses" the rest. If the guess is correct, press Enter. If it is incorrect, just continue typing the correct address, and then press Enter.

More Options!

AutoComplete not only completes your entry for you, but it also opens the Address drop-down list, which displays a list of URLs that match a portion of what you typed. You can click a URL to open its page.

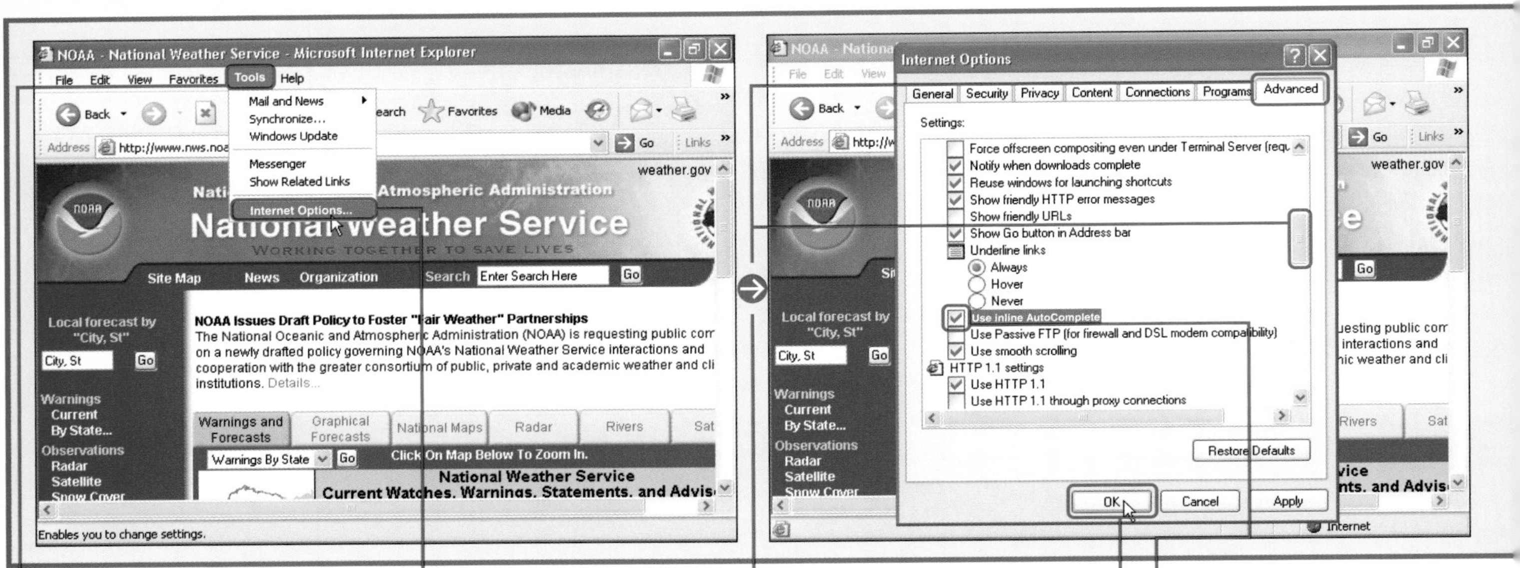

1. Click Tools.
2. Click Internet Options.

- The Internet Options dialog box appears.

3. Click the Advanced tab.
4. Scroll down to the bottom of the Browsing options.
5. Click Use inline AutoComplete.
6. Click OK.

- The Internet Options dialog box saves your change and closes.

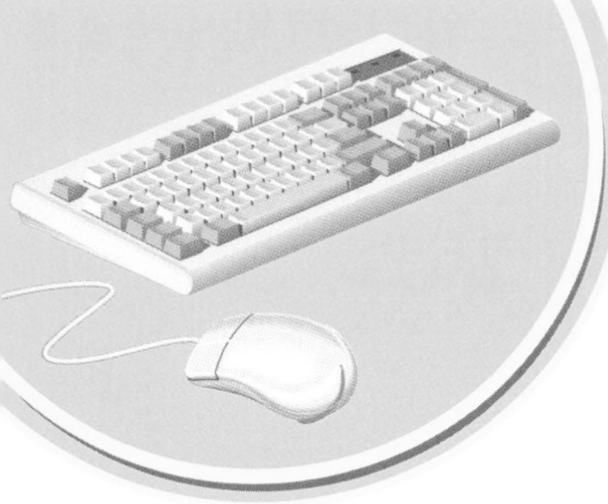

Get a DAILY TIP

Internet Explorer features a tip of the day, each of which can help you learn how to browse the Web faster and more efficiently.

When you turn on the tip of the day, it remains on until you turn it off, so every time you run your browser, a new tip appears. This task shows you how to display the tip of the day and read several additional tips, and turn off the feature.

More Options!

Most Web browsers, including Netscape Navigator, provide keyboard shortcuts and other features for browsing more efficiently. If you use a browser other than Internet Explorer, check its Help menu for tips, tricks, and new features.

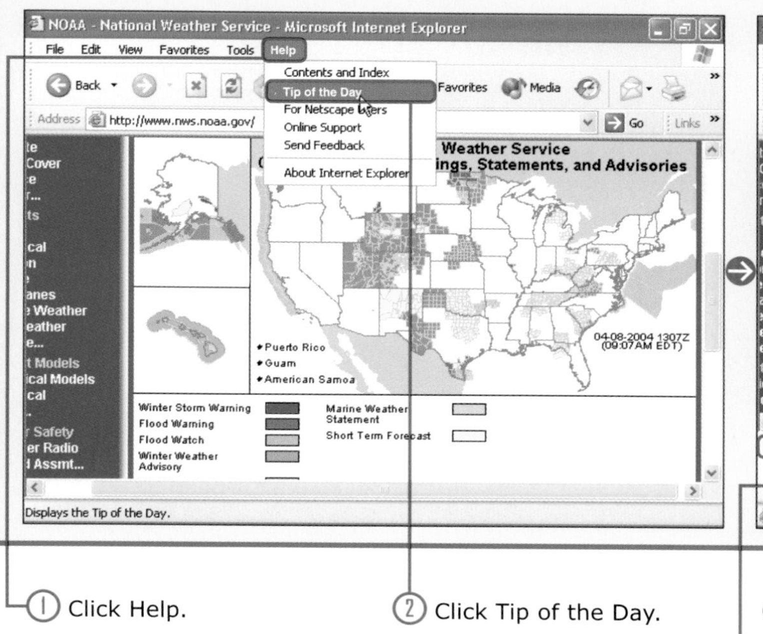

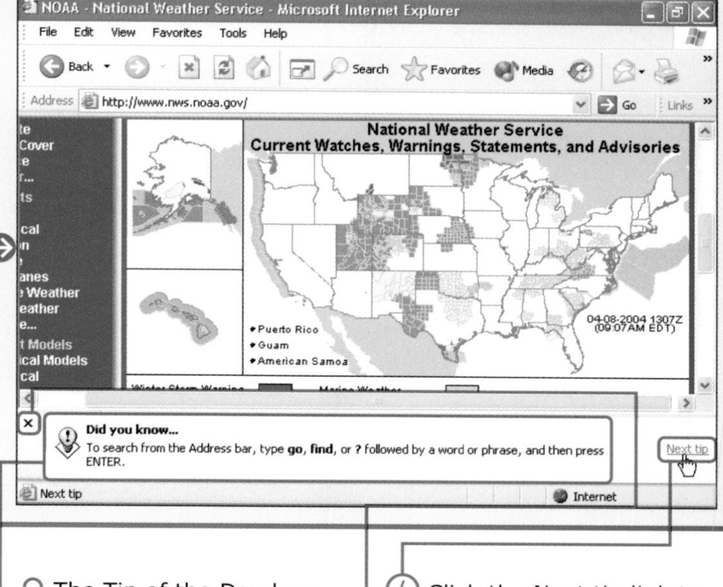

1. Click Help.
2. Click Tip of the Day.

- The Tip of the Day bar appears.

3. Read the tip.
4. Click the Next tip link to display another tip.
5. Click Close.

- The Tip of the Day bar disappears.

Save time with SITE SUBSCRIPTIONS

Your browser can surf the Web for you, gathering pages from your favorite Web sites and delivering them to your computer while you sleep or during the day while you are at work. It can then store the pages on your computer's hard drive and quickly load them later. You do not even need to connect to the Internet to view them later! Simply browse the pages offline.

You can do this in your Web browser by setting up site subscriptions. In Internet Explorer, you can set up a site subscription for offline viewing whenever you choose to add a site to your Favorites menu. You specify a Web site or page you want to subscribe to and can even have your browser download linked pages, so you do not have to go online to view them. You can have pages downloaded at a specified time automatically or whenever you enter the command to have your pages *synchronized* with fresh pages on the Web. Your browser can connect to the Internet at the specified time and acquire the subscribed pages for offline viewing.

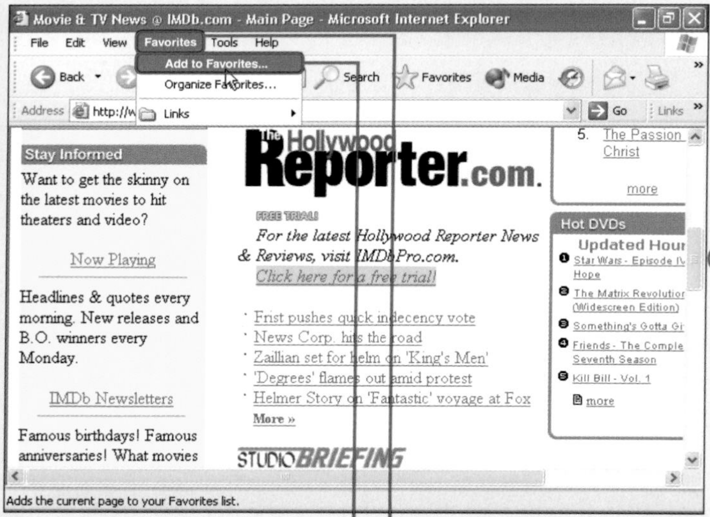

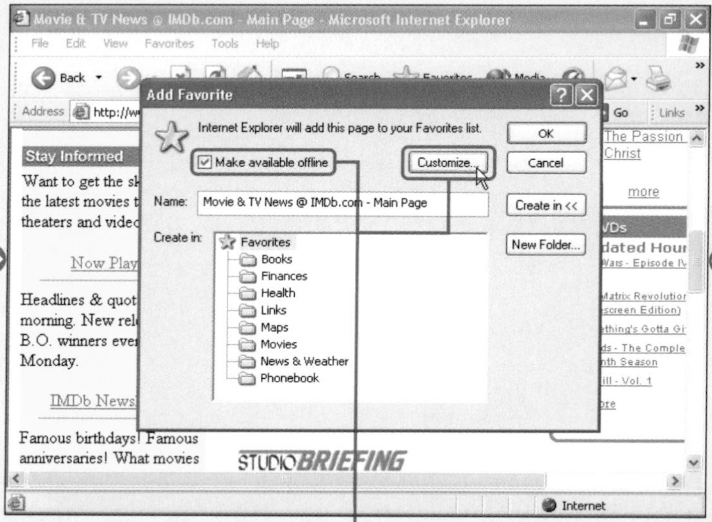

1 Open the Web site you want to subscribe to.

2 Click Favorites.

3 Click Add to Favorites.

- The Add Favorite dialog box appears.

4 Click Make available offline.

5 Click Customize.

DIFFICULTY LEVEL

Important!

If you choose not to schedule synchronization, synchronize your pages before going offline. Click Tools and click Synchronize. If you do schedule synchronizations, make sure your computer is on and can connect at the specified time.

Test It!

When you are ready to view your pages offline, open Internet Explorer's File menu and click Work Offline. Then, click Favorites and click the name of a subscribed page to try loading it. To go back online, click File and click Work Online.

Important!

Going offline does not necessarily disconnect your computer from the Internet. You usually need to open the Internet Connection dialog box and choose to disconnect or hang up. Alternatively, you can disconnect and then choose Work Offline in your browser.

CONTINUED

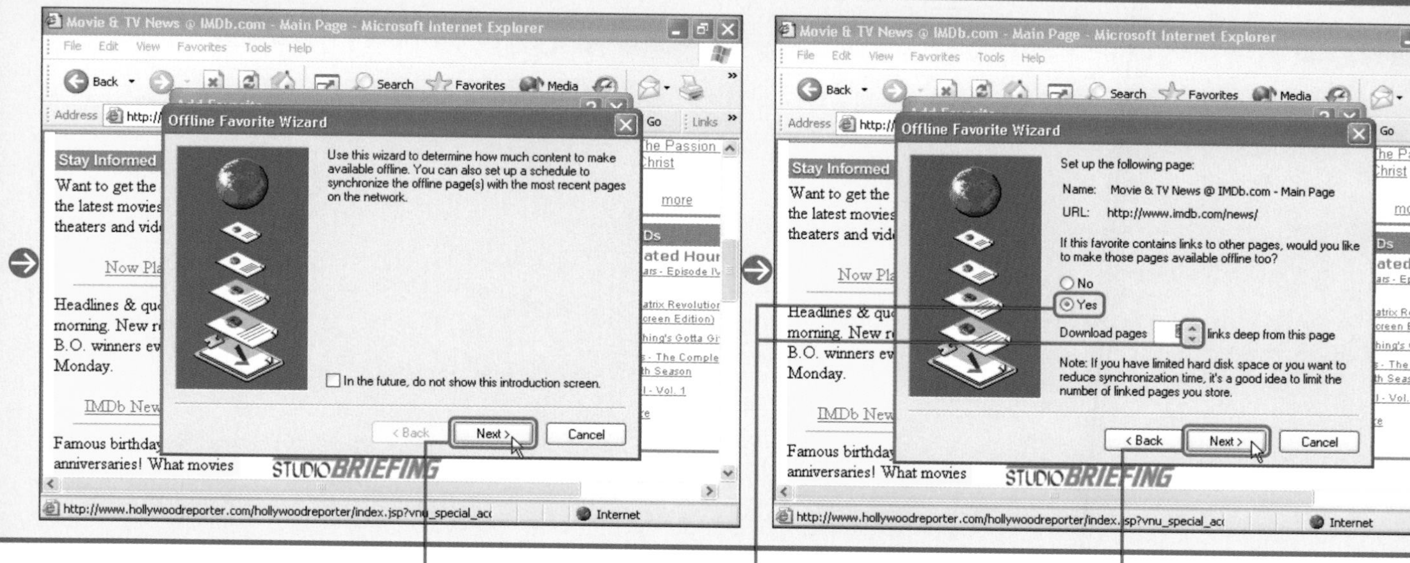

○ The Offline Favorite Wizard appears.

6 Click Next.

○ The second Offline Wizard page appears.

○ To download linked pages, click Yes.

7 Click here to set the number of levels deep you want to download.

Note: Avoid going more than one level deep, especially if you have a dial-up modem connection. Some pages link to dozens of additional pages.

8 Click Next.

Save time with SITE SUBSCRIPTIONS

The first time you choose to set up a site subscription, the Offline Favorite Wizard dialog box shown in the first figure below, displays only two options: one to update content only when you choose Synchronize from the Tools menu and the other to create a new schedule. If you choose to schedule downloads, click the option to create a new schedule. The next time you choose to mark a site as a favorite and make it available offline, a third option appears, allowing you to use an existing schedule. Selecting this option allows you to schedule all downloads at the same time.

If you have a cable modem or other Internet connection that remains connected to the Internet at all times, Internet Explorer runs at the specified time and downloads the page or pages for you. If you have a dial-up modem connection, the Offline Favorite Wizard provides an option that enables Internet Explore to automatically establish an Internet connection at the specified time.

CONTINUED

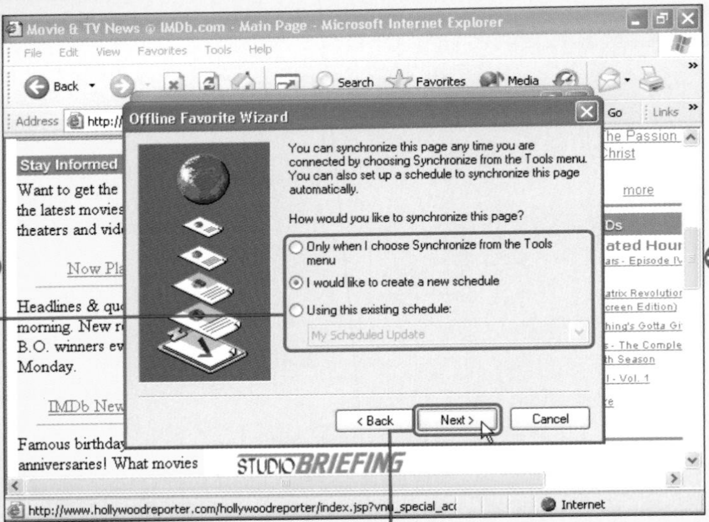

9 Click an option to choose to synchronize manually or on schedule.

10 Click Next.

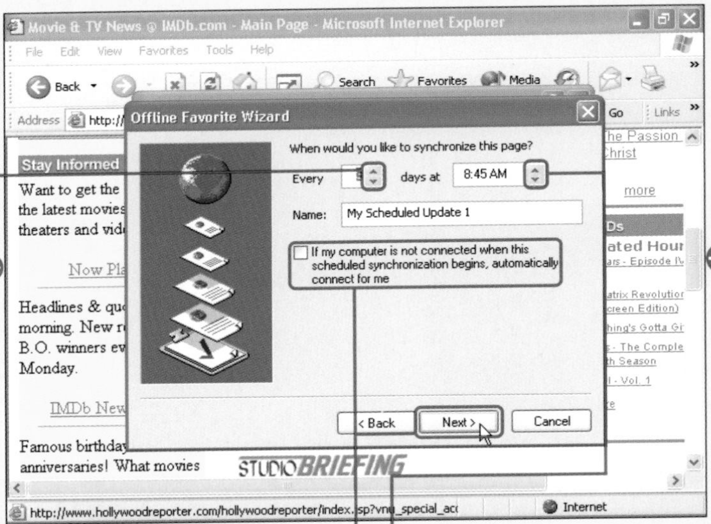

○ If you chose to create a new schedule, you can type a specific time. If you chose to synchronize manually or using an existing schedule, skip to step 14.

11 Click here to set the frequency of downloads.

12 Click here to set the time you want Internet Explorer to download the pages.

○ Click here to connect automatically if needed.

13 Click Next.

More Options!

If you already have sites on your Favorites menu, you can make them available for offline viewing as well. You can do this by clicking Favorites and then clicking Organize Favorites. To display the dialog box shown here. Click the site you want available offline, click the Make available offline option (☐ changes to ☑), and click Properties to specify your preferences.

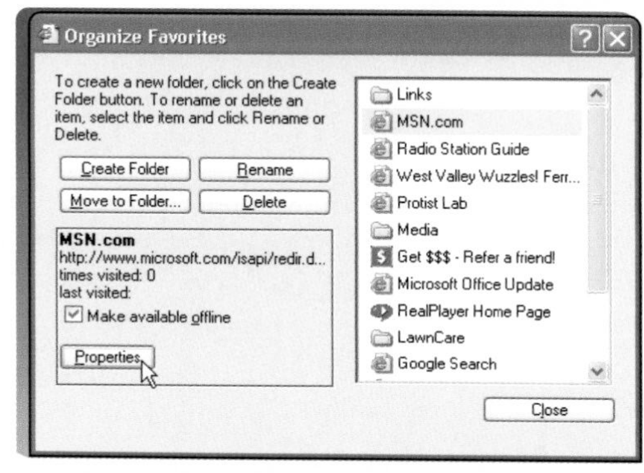

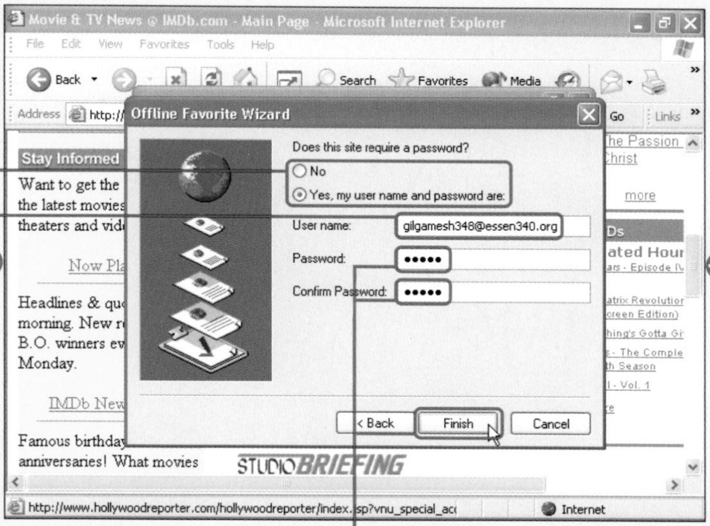

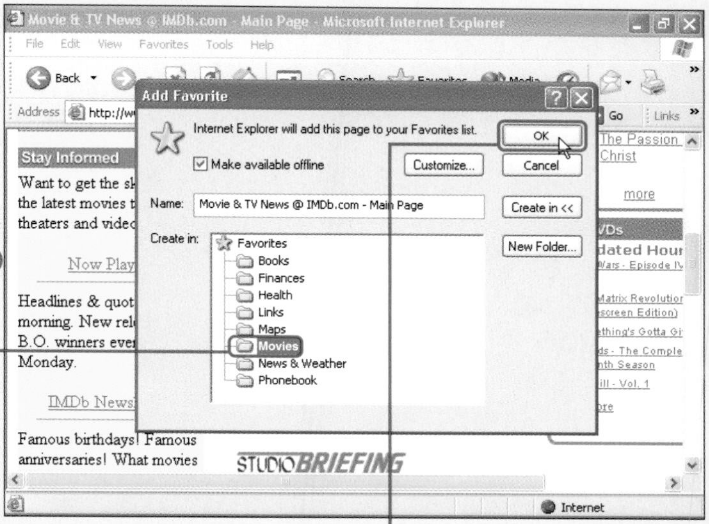

- The next wizard page appears.

14. Specify if the site requires a password.

- If the site requires a password, type your username.

- If the site requires a password, type your password.

- If the site requires a password, type your password again.

15. Click Finish.

- The wizard closes to bring you back to the Add Favorite dialog box.

16. Click the folder in which you want the favorite placed.

17. Click OK.

- Internet Explorer saves your settings and can now download the page or pages at the specified time.

Find out what COOKIES ARE TRACKING

When you visit a site, it often sends a small file, called a *cookie*, to your computer that assigns your computer an identification number. The site can then check this cookie whenever you visit to determine who you are and what you have done at the site. If you chose to purchase some products, for instance, and then left the site without paying, when you return to the site, it "remembers" what you chose to buy, and you can then complete the transaction.

In many cases, cookies enhance your Web browsing experience by helping Web sites deliver content that is tailored to your specific needs. However, cookies can be used to enable a site to record your movements on the site without your knowledge.

In task #28 and task #29, you learn how to delete cookies and prevent your browser from accepting them. However, before you delete the cookies, you might want to see which sites are sending you cookies, so you can gauge any threat to your privacy. This task shows you how.

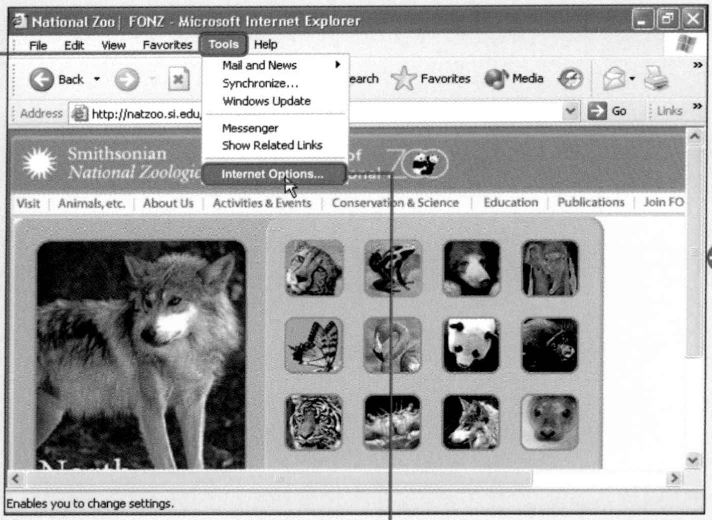

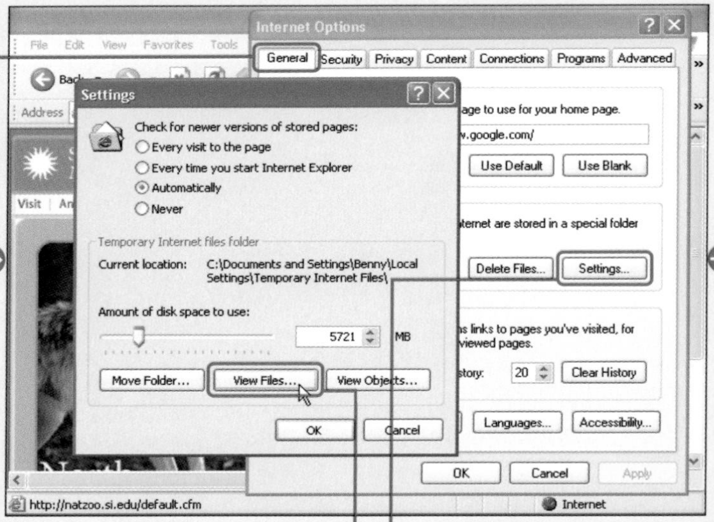

① Click Tools.

② Click Internet Options.

○ The Internet Options dialog box appears.

③ Click the General tab.

④ Click Settings.

⑤ Click View Files.

Try This!

To find out when a site placed a cookie on your computer and when the site last modified the cookie, right-click the cookie and click Properties. The Properties dialog box appears, displaying the date and time the site created the cookie and most recently accessed it and modified it.

Did You Know?

When a site places a cookie on your computer, that site is usually the only site capable of accessing and using the information stored in that cookie.

Did You Know?

Rarely does a cookie contain personal information, such as a credit card number or your name, but cookies are able to store this information.

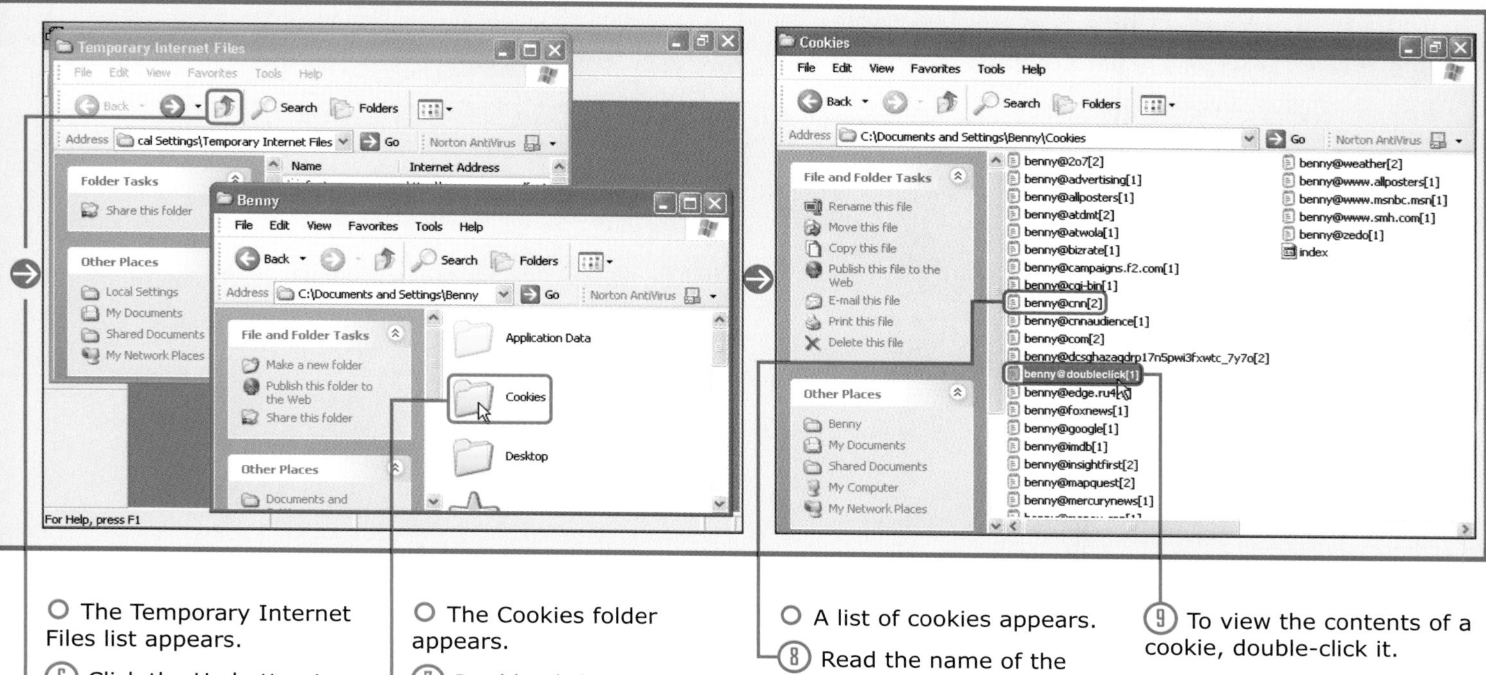

- The Temporary Internet Files list appears.

6 Click the Up button two times.

- The Cookies folder appears.

7 Double-click the Cookies folder.

- A list of cookies appears.

8 Read the name of the site that sent the cookie.

9 To view the contents of a cookie, double-click it.

- The contents of a cookie, typically an ID number, appears in your system's text editor.

DELETE COOKIES

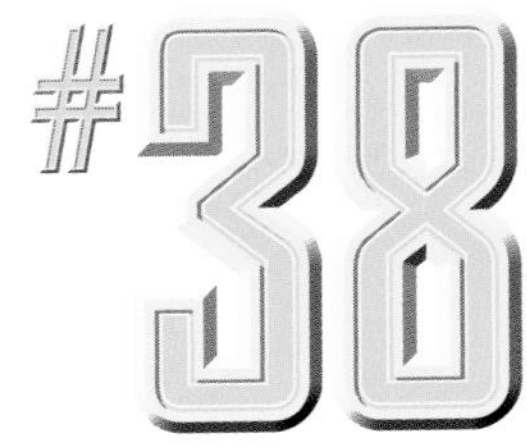

Cookies typically enhance Web browsing, so keeping them on your computer rarely threatens your privacy. If, in task #37, you saw a cookie from a site that you do not want to track your movements, you can right-click the cookie and click Delete.

If you want to rid your computer of any and all cookies stored on it, your browser can help find and remove them. This task shows you how to delete cookies in Internet Explorer.

Did You Know?

Did you know that your browser limits the number of cookies any one site can give you to 20 and the total number of cookies to 300? Find out more facts about cookies at www.cookiecentral.com. Don't miss the cookie FAQ, which features additional cookie trivia.

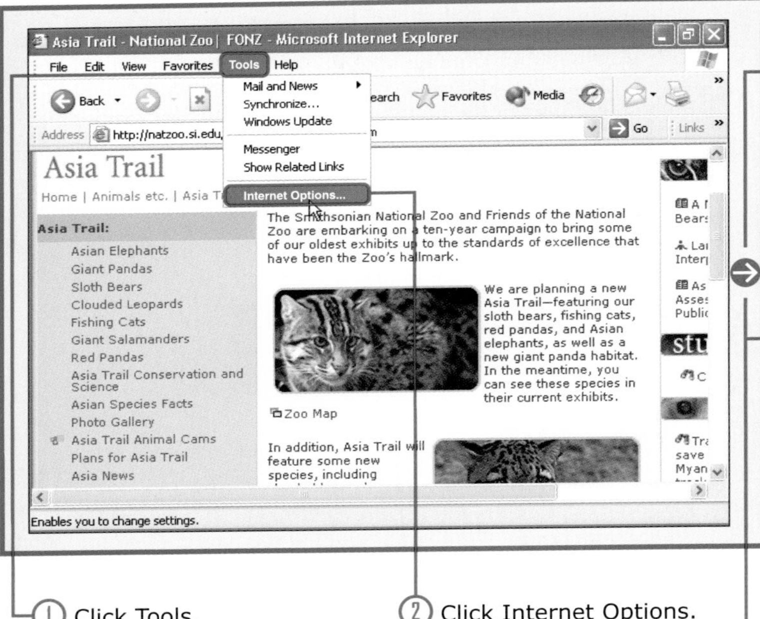

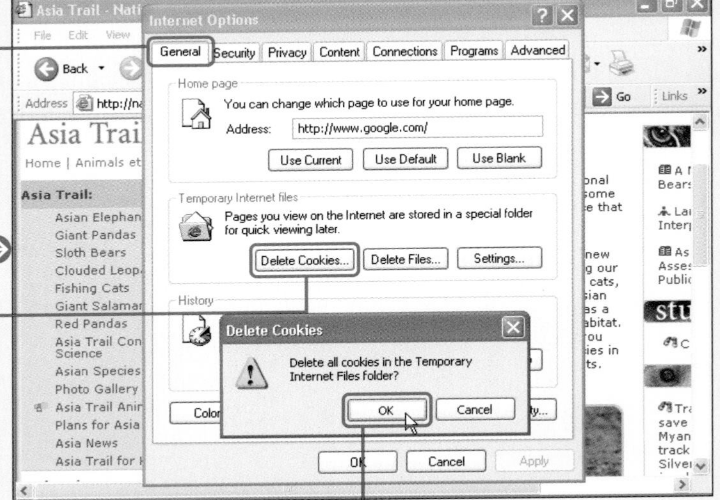

1. Click Tools.
2. Click Internet Options.

- The Internet Options dialog box appears.

3. Click the General Tab.
4. Click Delete Cookies.

- Internet Explorer prompts you to confirm.

5. Click OK.

- Internet Explorer removes all cookies from its folders and subfolders.

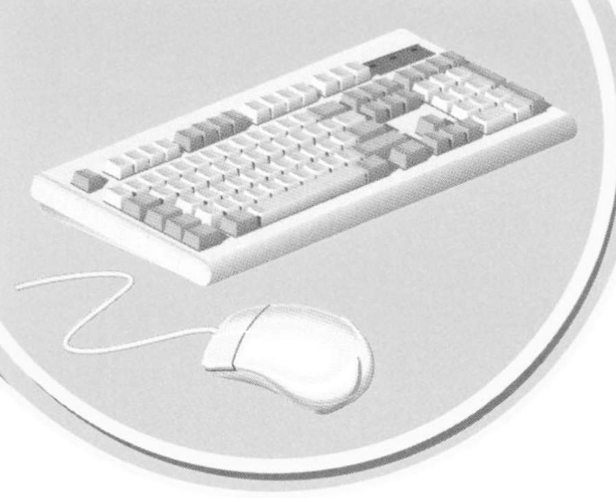

BLOCK COOKIES

DIFFICULTY LEVEL

If you are concerned about a site tracking your movements, you can instruct your browser not to let sites place cookies on your computer or read them from your computer.

Keep in mind, however, that if you choose to completely disable cookies, you cannot shop online at many sites or customize sites to deliver specific content. Without cookies, the site cannot identify you.

Most browsers provide several settings for controlling cookie access without completely disabling cookies. Internet Explorer, for instance, features six cookie security levels ranging from Accept All Cookies to Block All Cookies.

More Options!

Click the Advanced button to override Internet Explorer's automatic cookie handling feature. You can then choose to accept all first-party cookies, block all third-party cookies, and accept session cookies — so you can use a site during the current session without having the site identify you in the future.

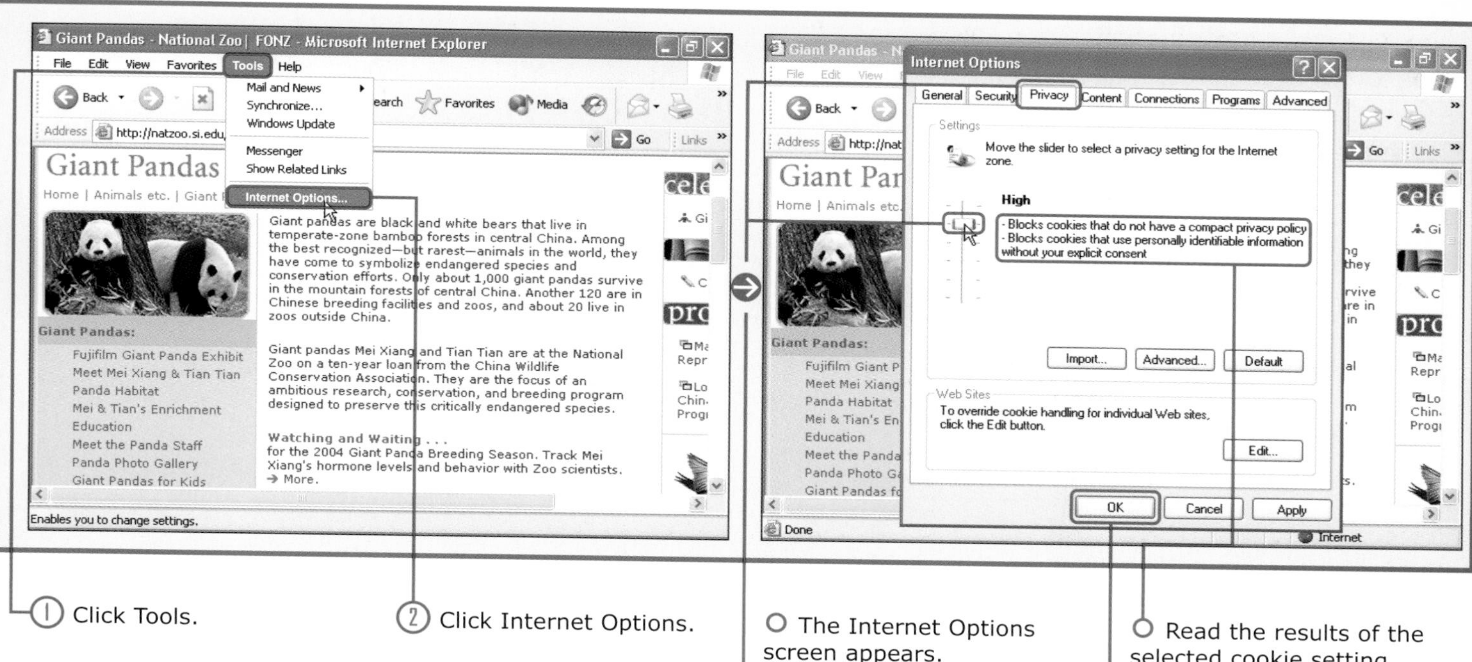

1. Click Tools.
2. Click Internet Options.

- The Internet Options screen appears.

3. Click the Privacy tab.
4. Drag the slider to the desired cookies setting.

- Read the results of the selected cookie setting.

5. Click OK.

- Internet Explorer saves the cookie setting.

Browse INCOGNITO

Every computer that connects to the Web has an IP address that may be used to track any activity initiated from that computer. So, even if you completely disable cookies, Web sites can track and record your activity on the Web.

If this concerns you, you can choose to browse the Web anonymously. Several available services allow you to browse the Web using a special *proxy server* that acts as a go-between. The proxy server keeps your computer's ID number hidden by downloading Web pages for you and then delivering them to your computer anonymously.

Most of these services do charge a fee because of the cost involved in running and maintaining the servers. Cost typically varies according to how much you use the service. Primedius WebTunnel, covered in this task, for example, has several packages that range in price from free for 3–6 megabytes (MB) per day to $250 annually for 500MB per day. WebTunnel's premium packages also feature no-spam, private e-mail; a history cleaner; a pop-up blocker; and additional privacy tools.

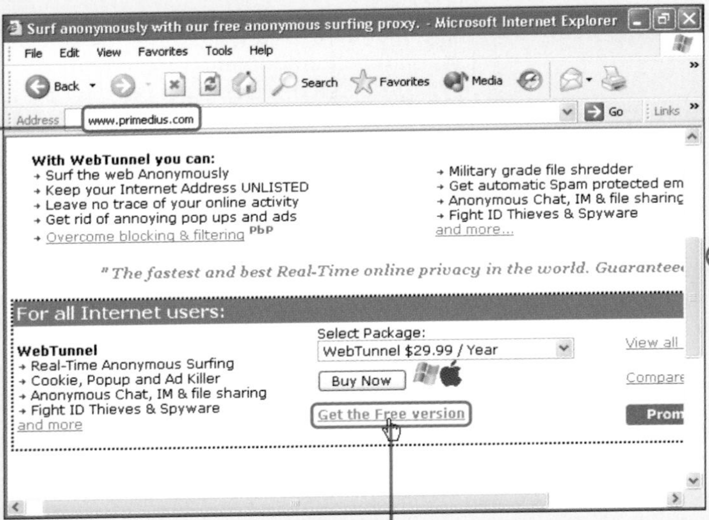

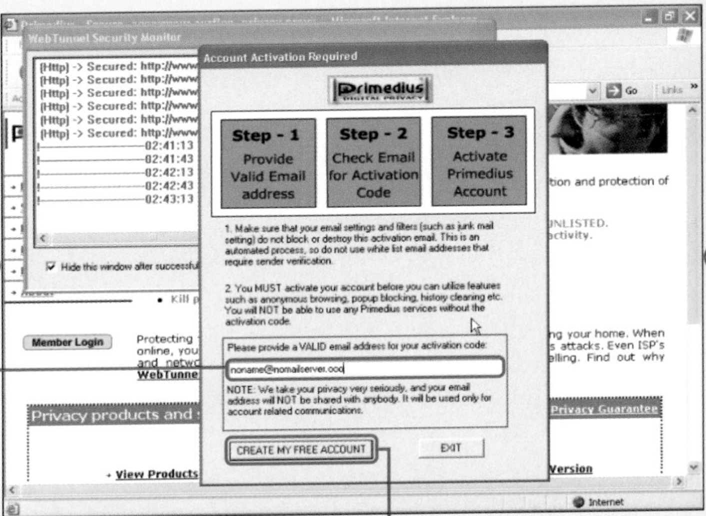

1. Type **www.primedius.com** and press Enter.
2. Click Get the Free version and follow the onscreen instructions to download, install, and run WebTunnel.

- When you first run WebTunnel, it prompts you to type your e-mail address to activate it.

3. Type your e-mail address.
4. Click GET MY FREE ACCOUNT and follow the onscreen and e-mail instructions to activate your account.

DIFFICULTY LEVEL

More Options!

To access options for downloading WebTunnel updates, upgrading your service, configuring WebTunnel, closing all browser windows, and more, right-click WebTunnel's icon in the system tray.

Check It Out!

WebTunnel is not the only service that allows anonymous browsing. Anonymizer, which you can find at www.anonymizer.com, also features anonymous Web browsing and has a privacy toolbar you can test for free. Or try Bypass Proxy Server at www.bypass.cc.

Remove It!

You can uninstall WebTunnel at any time by clicking Start, All Programs, Primedius, Uninstall.

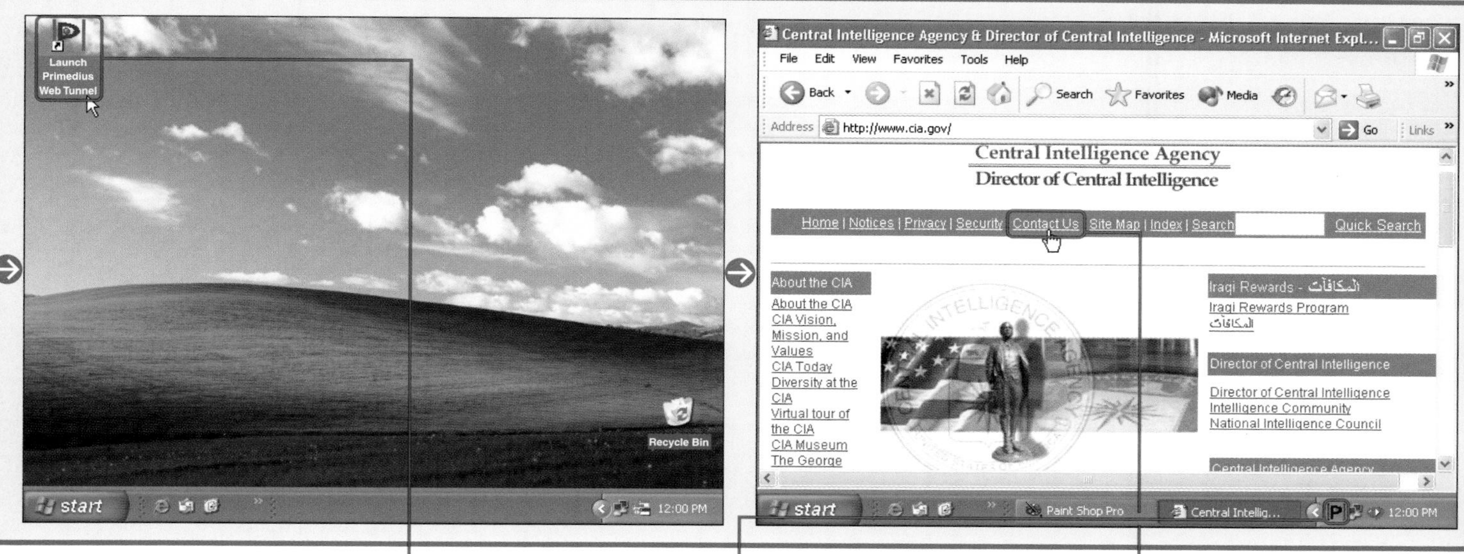

○ After you activate your account, an icon for WebTunnel appears on the desktop.

⑤ Double-click the Launch Primedius WebTunnel shortcut.

○ WebTunnel runs in the background. Its icon appears in the system tray.

○ You can browse the Web as you normally do, but now you browse anonymously.

Tap the Full Power of Google Searches

Google is the top search site on the Web, indexing more than 4 billion Web documents and providing millions of users with the tools they need to track down specific information, advice, products, services, and other resources.

If you are like most users, however, you tap only a fraction of Google's full potential. You might open Google's home page, type in a search word or phrase, click the Search button, and then explore the links that Google displays. But a general Google search like this often returns millions of links and buries the best sites under a heap of thousands. By learning to refine your searches and exploit the full power of Google's many tools, you can make your searches much more effective.

This chapter shows you how to use Google's advanced search tools to narrow your search, focus on specific topics, and use Google's Directory in tandem with its search engine to track down the best sites on the Web. You also learn how to add Google buttons to your browser, install and use Google's toolbar, access Google's news room, obtain maps and driving directions, find bargains on products and services, and make Google a more integral part of your Web browsing experience.

TOP 100

REFINE
your Google search

A standard Google search typically returns a list of more than a million sites that match the search word or phrase. For example, a search for "Caribbean cruise" returns nearly 3.5 million links. The order in which Google displays the results is automatically determined based on more than 100 different factors that Google does not disclose. However, many Web site creators employ tricks to achieve artificially higher ratings. In other words, the first site listed is not always the best or the one that you would find most useful.

If you enter a search word or phrase and see that Google has found more than a million links to sites that fit your description, consider refining your search to narrow the list of sites. Google provides an option that enables you to search only the list of sites that it returned as a result of your first search. For example, if Google returns 3.5 million sites for "Caribbean cruise," you can search only those sites for "luxury Cancun" or "family bargain" to narrow the search.

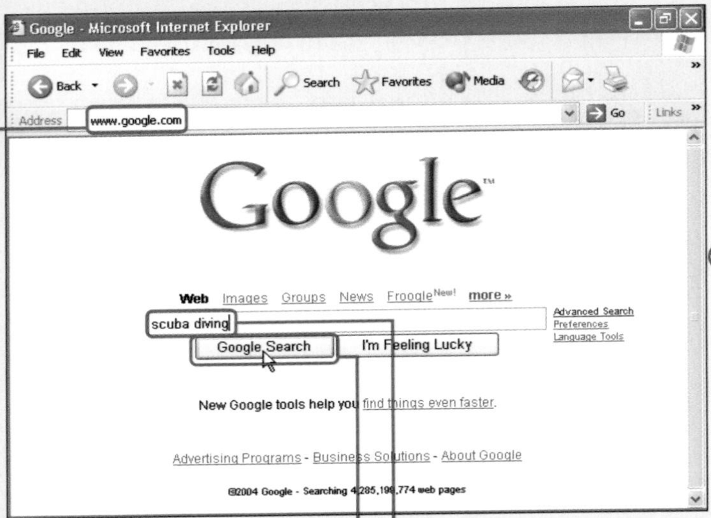

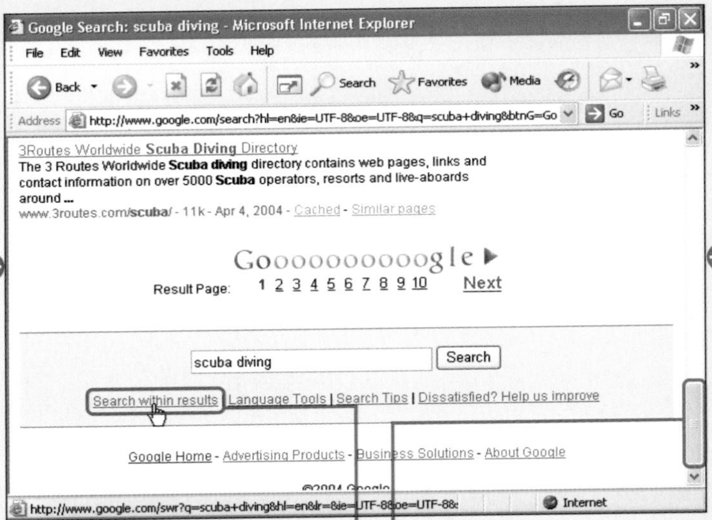

1. Type **www.google.com** and press Enter.
2. Type your search word or phrase.
3. Click Google Search.

- Google displays links to sites that match your search description.

4. Scroll down to the bottom of the page.
5. Click the Search within results link.

#41

Try This!

Enter your search phrase in quotation marks to find only those sites that mention your search phrase exactly as you have typed it. *"Caribbean cruise"* returns about 500,000 sites compared with 3.5 million when searched without quotations marks. The phrase "budget Caribbean cruise" returns about 50 sites.

DIFFICULTY LEVEL

Check It Out!

Precede your search with **allintitle:** to have Google search only for those pages that have all the words you specify in their title. For example, type **allintitle: tennis techniques** to view links to only those pages that have the words "tennis" and "techniques" in their titles.

More Options!

For more options and information about Google search operators, go to www.google.com/help/operators.html.

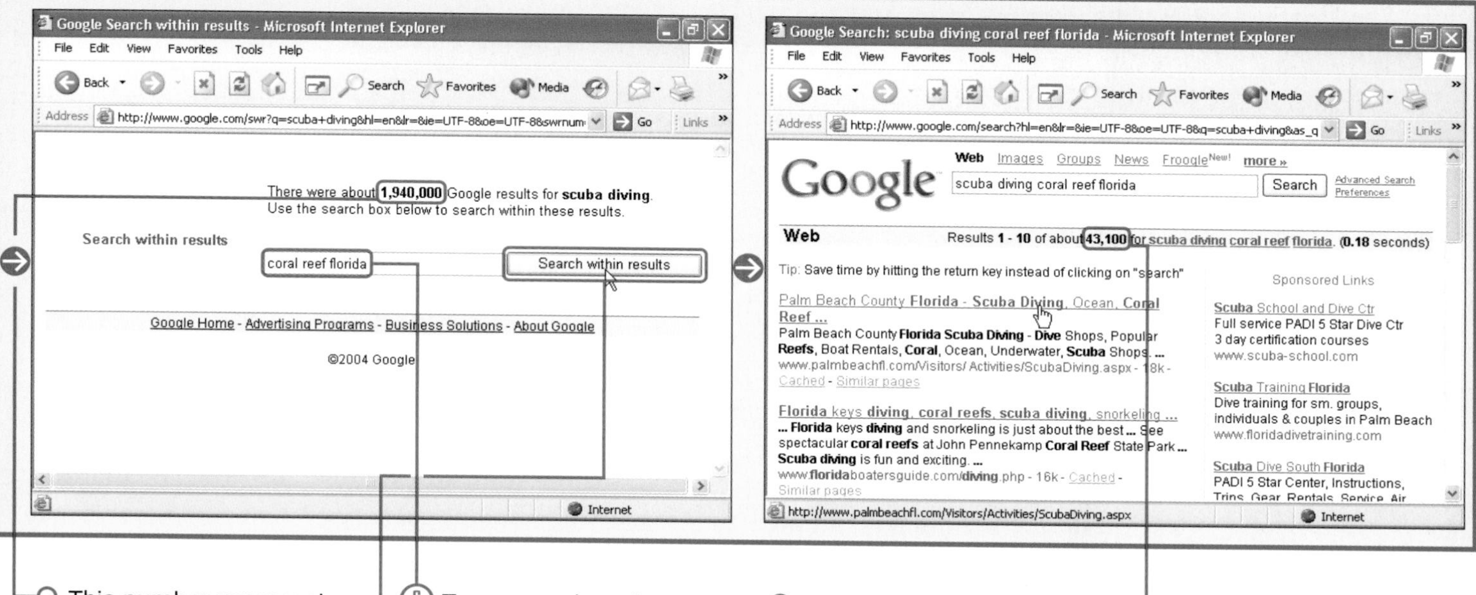

This number represents how many links your original search returned.

⑥ Type a word or phrase that narrows the search.

⑦ Click Search within results.

Google displays links that match new search instructions.

Google returns fewer links after a refined search.

Select your Google SEARCH PREFERENCES

By default, Google displays search results of all pages, regardless of language, and uses moderate content filtering to screen out any sites that might be inappropriate for children. Unless you specify otherwise, Google displays ten links at a time and displays them in the same browser window that you use to perform your search. The settings for these options work behind the scenes to control the way Google displays search results.

Most users leave Google's default settings as they are, either because they do not realize that they can change the settings or because they are satisfied with the way Google displays the search results. However, you can make your searches much more targeted by changing some of these preferences. For example, by choosing to have only those pages that appear in a specific language displayed, you automatically screen out dozens of other languages from your search. If children are using Google to search for sites, turning on SafeSearch Filtering screens out most sites that feature offensive content. Here you learn how to enter your preferences.

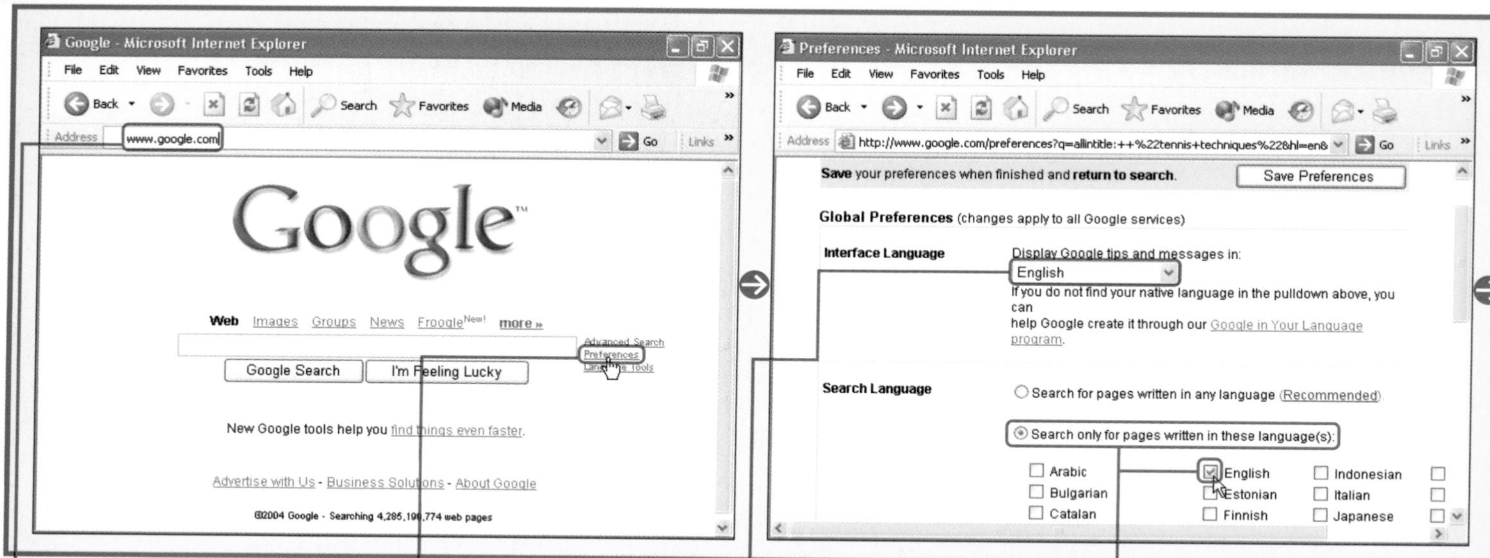

1. Type **www.google.com** and press Enter.
2. Click the Preferences link.

- Google's Preferences screen appears.

3. Click here and select the language in which you prefer to have results displayed.
4. Click here to screen out pages in other languages.
5. Click the check box next to each language to include in the search results.

DIFFICULTY LEVEL

Attention!

In order to have Google save your preferences, you must enable cookies in your Web browser. See task #39 for details.

Test It!

After entering your preferences, try a Google Search that you know will test the settings you entered.

Did You Know?

If strict SafeSearch Filtering fails to prevent an obscene site from turning up in a Google search, report the site to safesearch@google.com and Google will investigate it.

Did You Know?

If you share your computer with others and use Windows profiles to sign on, Google search preferences apply only to the user who is currently signed on. Each user must enter his or her own Google search preferences.

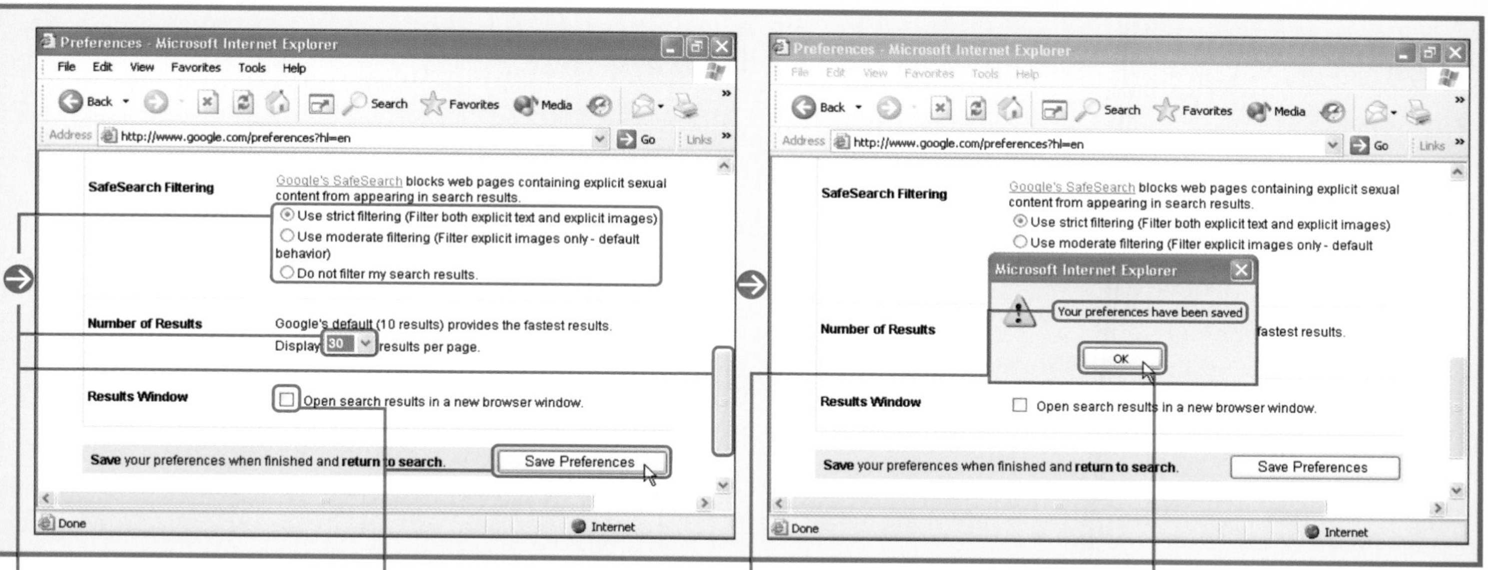

6 Scroll down the page.

7 Click the desired SafeSearch Filtering option.

8 Click here and select the number of results you want Google to display.

9 Click here to have search results displayed in a separate window.

10 Click Save Preferences.

○ Google informs you that it has saved your preferences.

11 Click OK.

Zero In with Google's ADVANCED SEARCH

By design, Google's basic search returns the most hits possible. It searches anywhere on a page for the word or words you entered and displays links to any pages that have any or all of those words. The number of links returned typically exceeds the needs of any user and often prevents users from finding links to the best sites in a particular category.

Fortunately, Google features an Advanced Search page that can help you focus your search and ignore many of the lesser sites. You can use the Advanced Search options, for example, to search only for those pages that have your search word or words in their page title, or search only for pages that Webmasters have updated in the last three months.

This task shows you how to access Google's Advanced Search page and use many of the more useful options for narrowing your search. You can also pick up some additional tips and suggestions for making your searches more focused.

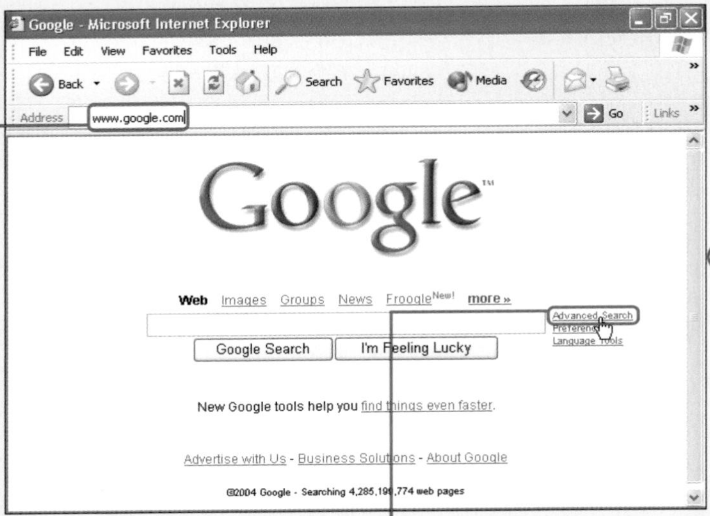

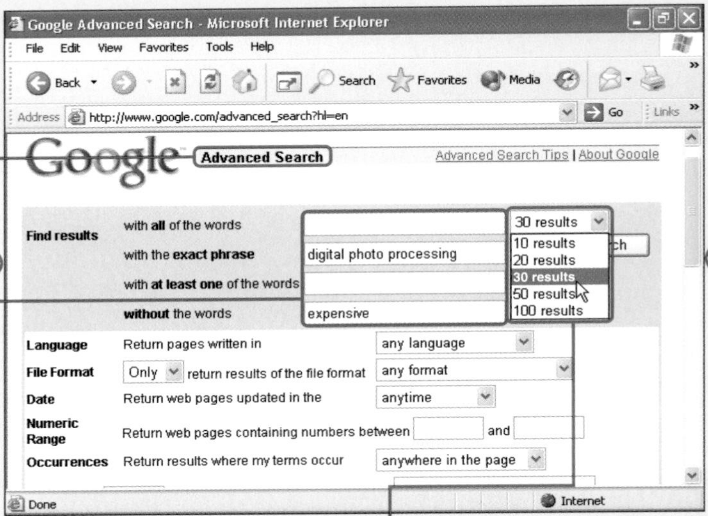

① Type **www.google.com** and press Enter.

② Click the Advanced Search link.

○ The Advanced Search Page appears.

③ Type your search word or words in one or more of the Find results boxes.

④ Click here and select the desired number of links to display per page.

DIFFICULTY LEVEL

More Options!

Scroll down the Advanced Search page to find options for searching Froogle, Google's shopping directory; searching for pages that are similar to other pages you know of; or search specific topics, such as government sites.

Try This!

You can have Google include synonyms in the search by typing **~** before search terms. For example, **~exercise ~health** returns results for fitness, nutrition, and bodybuilding, as well. However, this does broaden the search providing more results.

More Options!

For more advanced search tips, open the Advanced Search Page and click the Advanced Search Tips link in the upper-right corner. Google explains search tips that apply to all Web search tools and tips that apply only to Google.

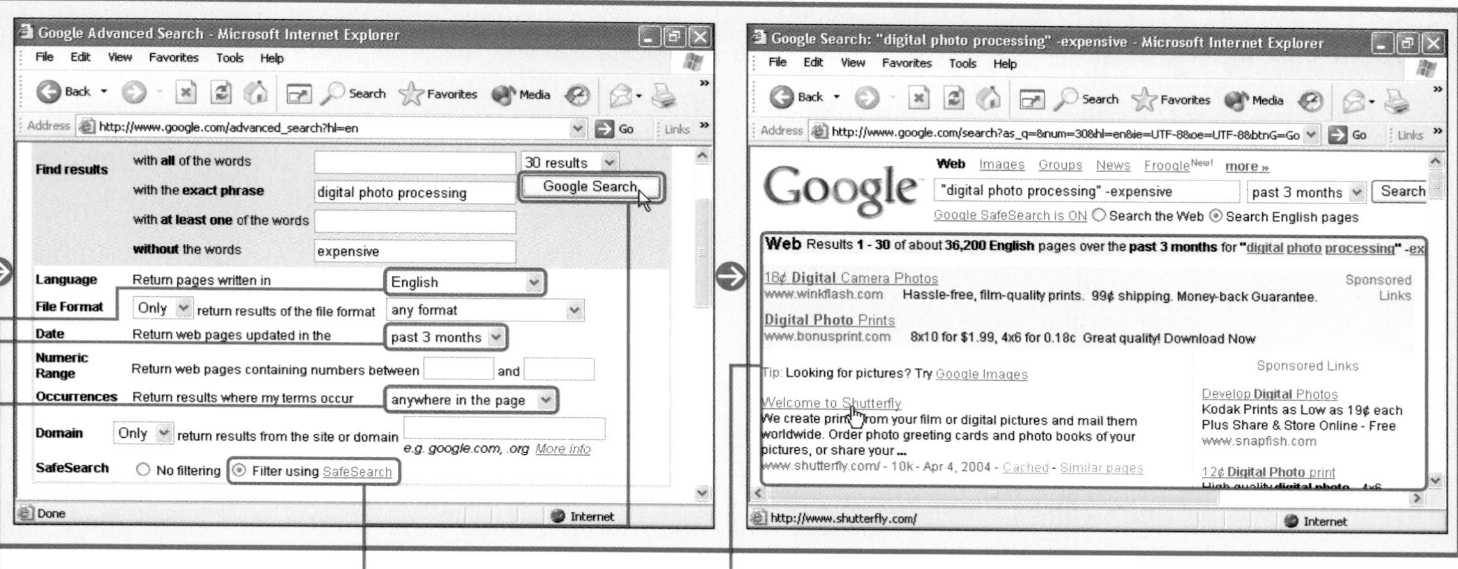

5 Click here and select the desired language.

6 Click here and select the desired page update range.

7 Click here and select where you want Google to look for the words you entered.

8 Click here to have Results filtered.

9 Click Google Search.

- Google displays links to pages that match your search instructions.

Browse the GOOGLE DIRECTORY

Because Google opens with its search page, many users overlook the outstanding Google Directory, which groups Web sites by category. In many cases, you can find better sites by following a trail of links in the directory rather than by searching for a specific site. Instead of searching Google for "Internet movie databases," which results in more than 3 million hits, you can go to the Google Directory, click Movies, click Databases, and find the top 13 movie databases on the Web.

You can also use the directory to narrow your search. To do this, go to the Google Directory and follow the trail of links to the desired category. Then, you choose to search only in the selected category and enter your search word or words as you normally do. Google searches only the items listed in the directory or subdirectory.

This task shows you how to access the Google Directory and follow a trail of links to the desired site.

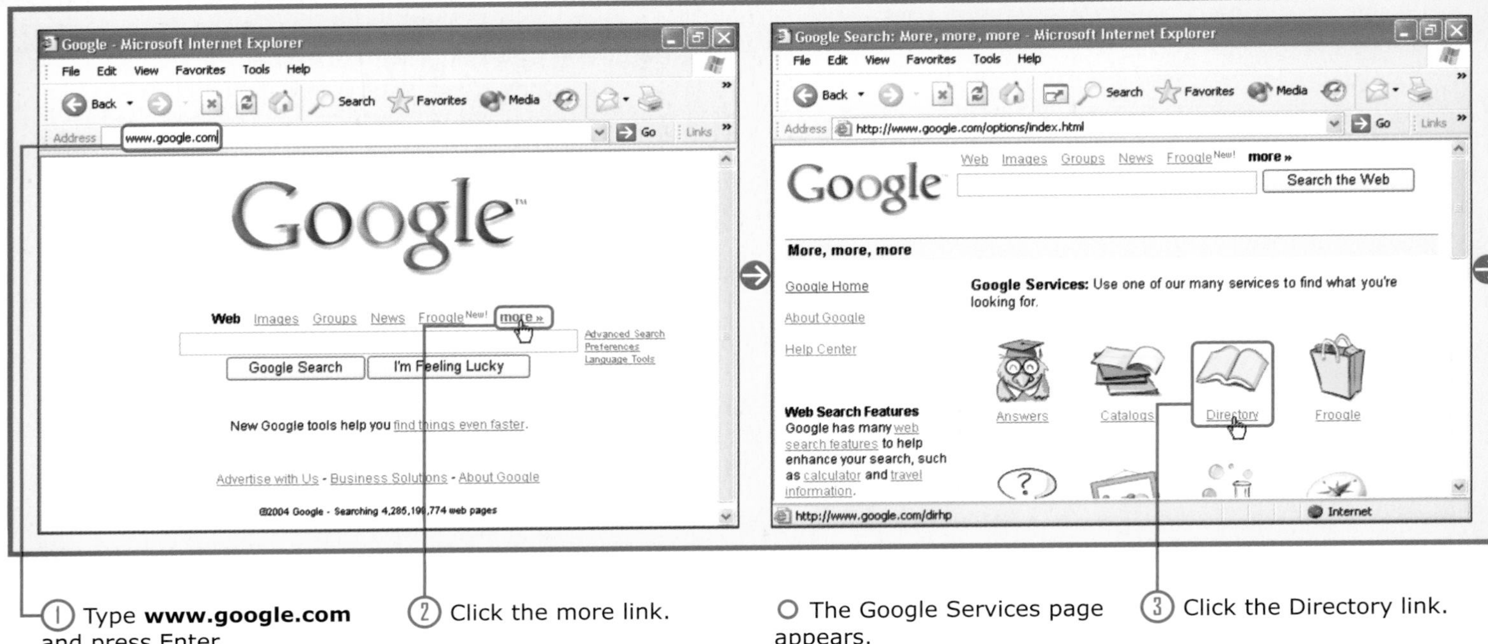

① Type **www.google.com** and press Enter.

② Click the more link.

○ The Google Services page appears.

③ Click the Directory link.

DIFFICULTY LEVEL

Did You Know?

The Google Web Directory starts with sites selected and rated by volunteers as part of the Open Directory project. Google then uses its Page Rank technology to determine the relative importance of a page. When you display a list of links in the directory, a green bar next to each link indicates its relative importance. You can access the Open Directory at dmoz.org.

More Options!

When Google displays the links in a particular category, it displays one or more related categories just above the list of links. Click a related category to view additional sites that might be related to what you are searching for.

Try This!

Above the list of Web sites, click the "View in alphabetical order" link to arrange the sites by name from A to Z.

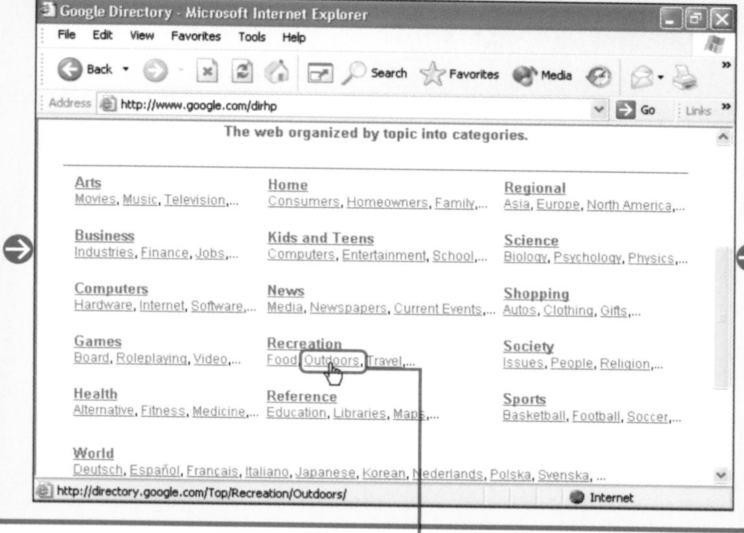

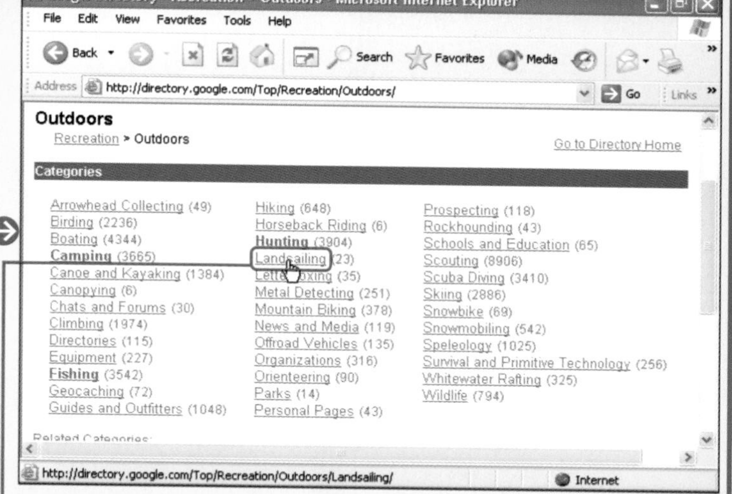

○ Google's main categories appear.

④ Click the link for the desired category or subcategory.

○ A list of additional subcategories appears.

⑤ Click the link for the desired subcategory.

○ Google displays links to additional subcategories or sites within the selected subcategory. Follow the trail of links to the desired site.

Add GOOGLE BUTTONS to your browser

One way to begin integrating Google into your Web browsing is to make Google your browser's home page, as suggested in task #11. Another way is to add Google buttons to your browser's toolbar. These buttons offer quick access to the most popular Google features without requiring you to access Google's site first.

Google provides two buttons you can add to your browser's toolbar: Google Search and Google.com. The Google Search button calls up a box in which you can enter your search words. You can also highlight a word or phrase on a Web page and click Google Search to run a Google search using the selected word or phrase. Google.com takes you directly to Google's opening search page, where you can perform a search as you normally do.

When using Internet Explorer to browse the Web, you can add the buttons to the Links toolbar, as this task shows.

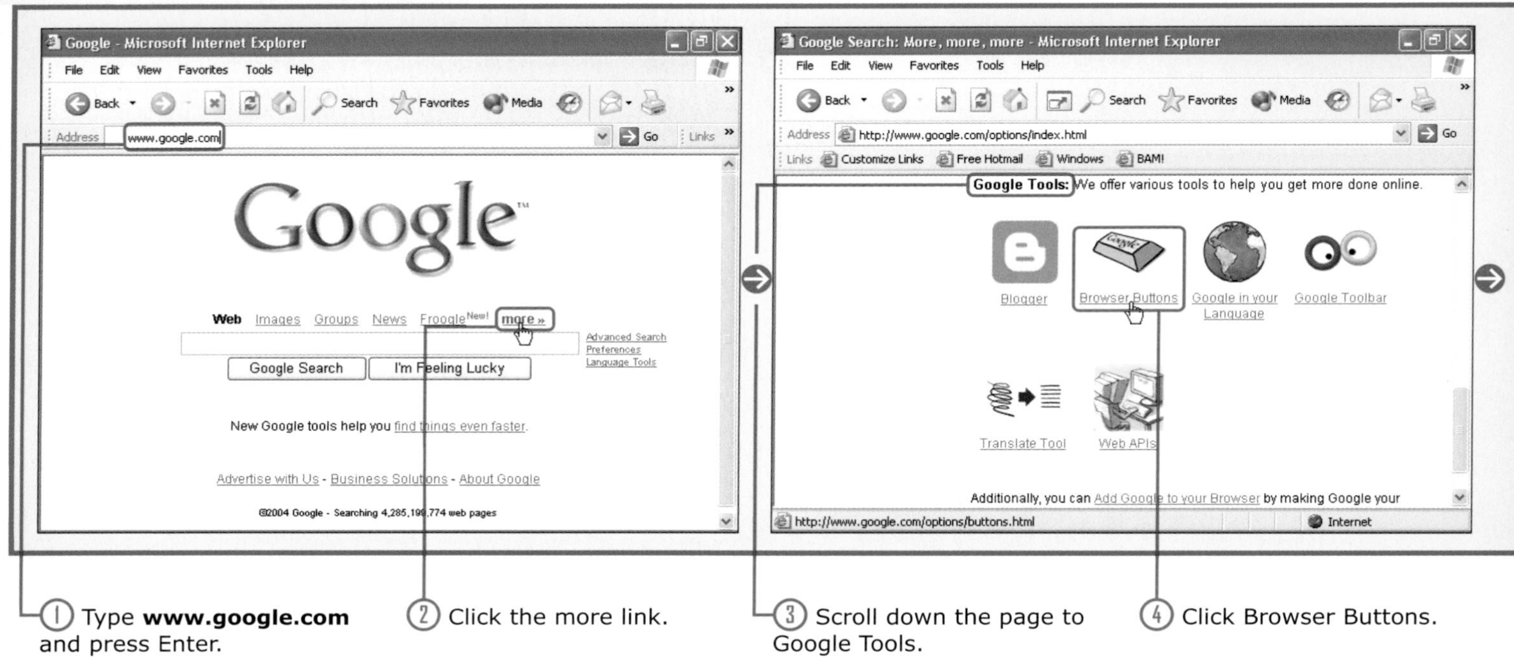

1. Type **www.google.com** and press Enter.
2. Click the more link.
3. Scroll down the page to Google Tools.
4. Click Browser Buttons.

DIFFICULTY LEVEL

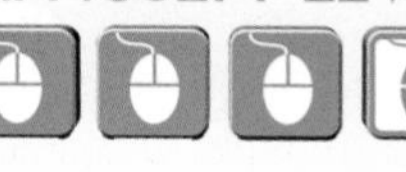

Attention!

When you attempt to add the Google Search button, a dialog box might pop up indicating that the object you are adding may be unsafe. The button is safe to add, so click OK.

Attention!

If the Google buttons do not function with your operating system and/or Web browser, use Google's toolbar, as explained in the next task.

More Options!

Many search sites, including Yahoo! and Alta Vista, have their own browser toolbars. In addition, you can find and download a selection of browser toolbars at Download.com, as explained in task #21. Some of these toolbars, such as 550 Access Toolbar, enable you to search several sites with a single search entry.

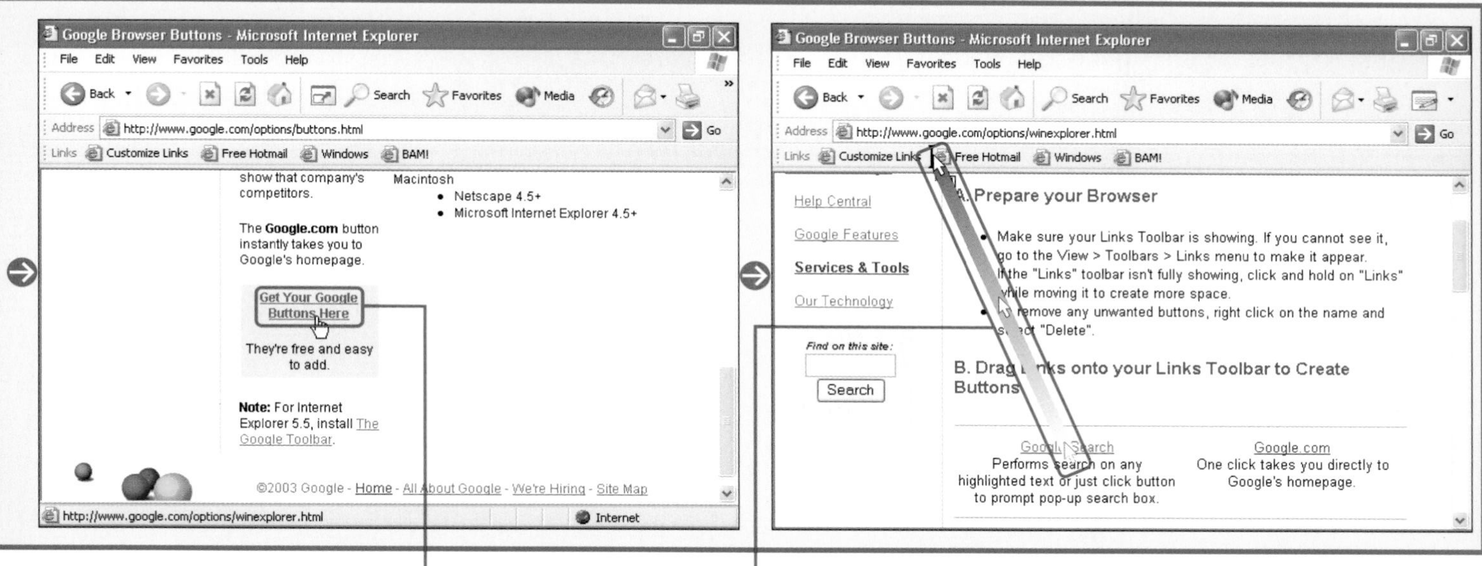

- The Browser Buttons page appears.

5 Click the Get Your Google Buttons Here link.

- Google's Browser Buttons links appear.

6 Drag the desired browser button up to the Links toolbar and drop it in place.

- The selected button appears on your browser's toolbar.

Install and use the GOOGLE TOOLBAR

You can install the Google Toolbar to add it to your browser. This toolbar equips Internet Explorer with a powerful set of tools for exploring the Web and focusing Google's search results. It also provides options that allow you to vote for or against sites you visit, rank pages, highlight key words in a document, and much more. In addition, if you are running Internet Explorer 5.5 or later, the toolbar comes complete with a pop-up blocker that can prevent most unsolicited Web ads from appearing in separate windows on your screen.

The Google Toolbar is completely free. You download it as you would download any software, run the installation routine, and then begin using it immediately. The toolbar appears just below your other toolbars, and you can choose to hide it at any time or uninstall it if you decide that you no longer want it.

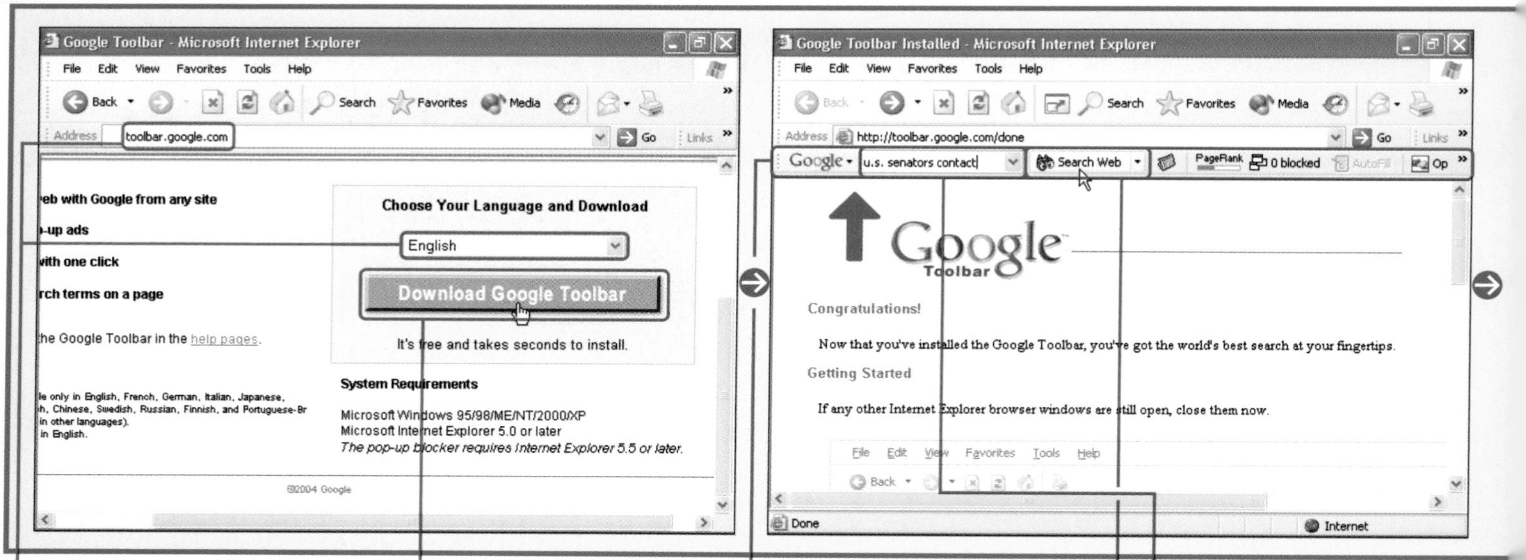

1. Type **toolbar.google.com** and press Enter.
2. Click here and select the desired language.
3. Click Download Google Toolbar, and follow the onscreen instructions to download and install it.
4. Run Internet Explorer.
   - The Google Toolbar appears.
5. To search Google, type your search word or words.
6. Click Search Web.

DIFFICULTY LEVEL

More Options!

The Google button, on the left end of the toolbar, opens a menu that contains links to special Google Searches along with an Options command. Click Options to customize the toolbar. The AutoFill button opens a form you can fill out with personal information. When you open a form on a Web page, you can click AutoFill to have Google fill out the form for you.

Try This!

To hide any toolbar in Internet Explorer, right-click the blank area of any toolbar or the menu bar and click the name of the toolbar you want to hide.

Remove It!

To uninstall the Google Toolbar software, click the Google button, click Help, and click Uninstall.

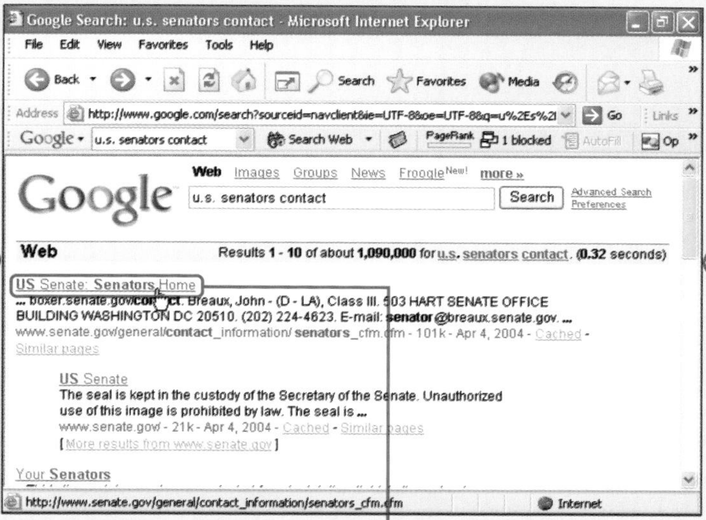

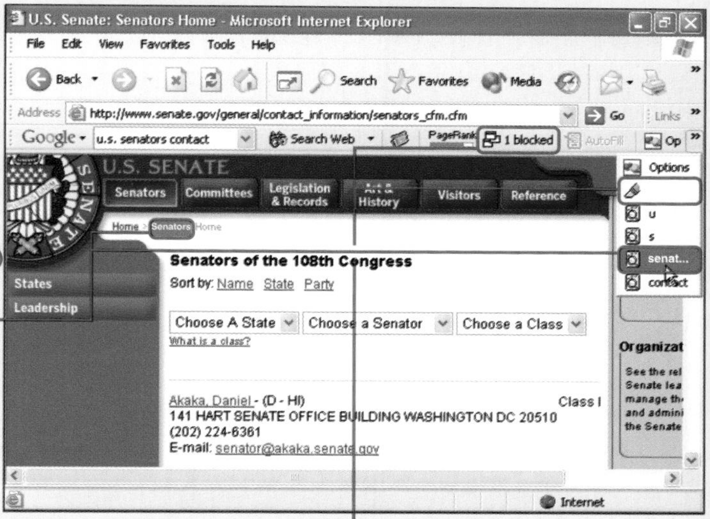

- Google displays its search page and links to pages that match your search word or words.

7. Click the link to the desired page.

8. Click the one of the search words you typed.

- Google highlights the word in the document.

9. Click the word again to highlight its next occurrence.

10. Click the Highlight button to highlight all occurrences of every search word.

- If Google's pop-up blocker blocks a site, it notifies you here.

FIND ADDRESSES
and maps

DIFFICULTY LEVEL

Google is one of the smartest search tools on the Web. If you enter a street address into Google's Search box and click Google Search, it automatically assumes that you want directions to the location and/or information about what's available in the area. Google displays links to Yahoo! Maps or MapQuest for a map to the area and displays a list of links for schools, businesses, restaurants, hotels, and other places of interest.

In this task, you learn how to use Google's Address Search feature to research an area of interest by address. When typing addresses, avoid abbreviating state names, such as IN or HI or ME because Google might consider them to be simple words, such as *the* and *an,* that it does not include in searches.

Google also has a local search tool in development. To access it, go to Google's home page, click the "more" link, and then click Google Local. Type in your search word or words and an address to specify the location, and then click Google Search.

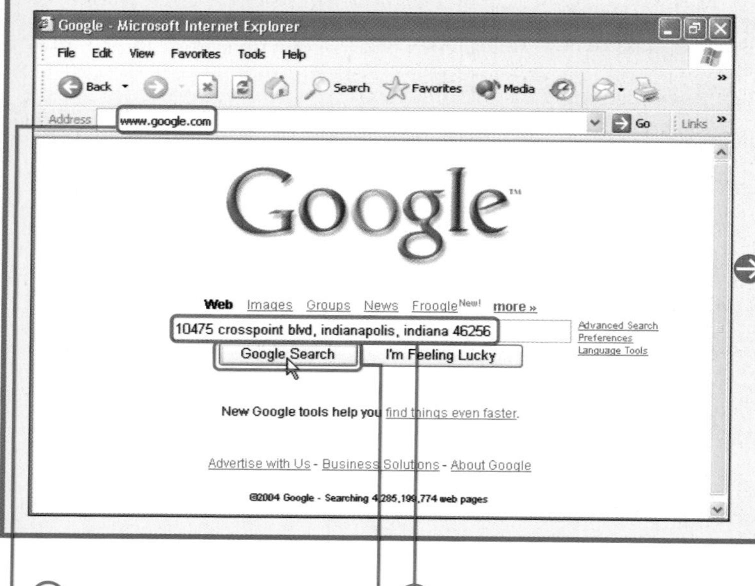

① Type **www.google.com** and press Enter.

② Type the address of the desired location.

③ Click Google Search.

○ Google displays links that relate to the area of the address you typed.

④ Click one of the map links to view a map of the area.

⑤ Click the link for a site or resource in the same locale.

TRANSLATE FOREIGN LANGUAGE Web sites

DIFFICULTY LEVEL

Unless you specify that Google show links to only those pages written in a particular language, Google's search results often contain pages from all over the world in many different languages. If you know the language, you can click the link and proceed to read the page. If you do not know the language, Google might be able to translate it for you, at least well enough so that you can obtain a basic understanding of it. This task shows you how to have Google translate a page. Keep in mind that Google cannot translate any text that is set up as a graphic image on a page.

For more powerful foreign language translation tools, go to Google's home page and click Language Tools. Here, you can search foreign sites, have specific Web pages translated for you, or even type a phrase in one language and have Google translate it for you into the language of your choice! The Language Tools page also provides links to the various Google search sites around the world.

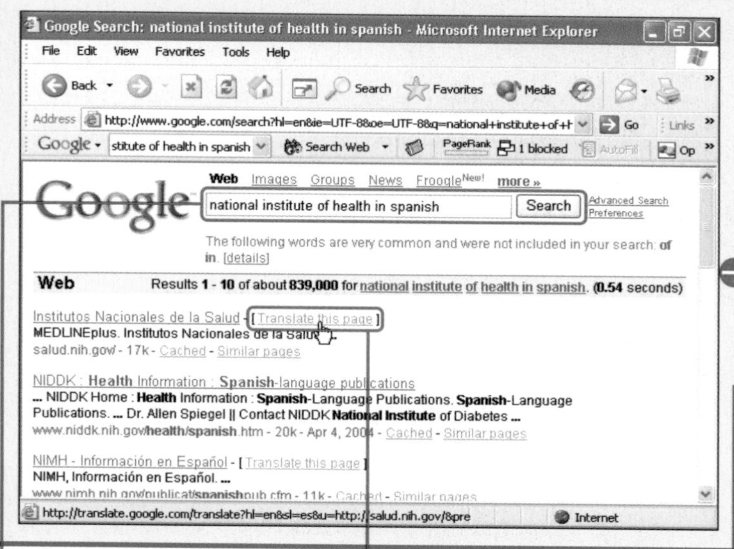

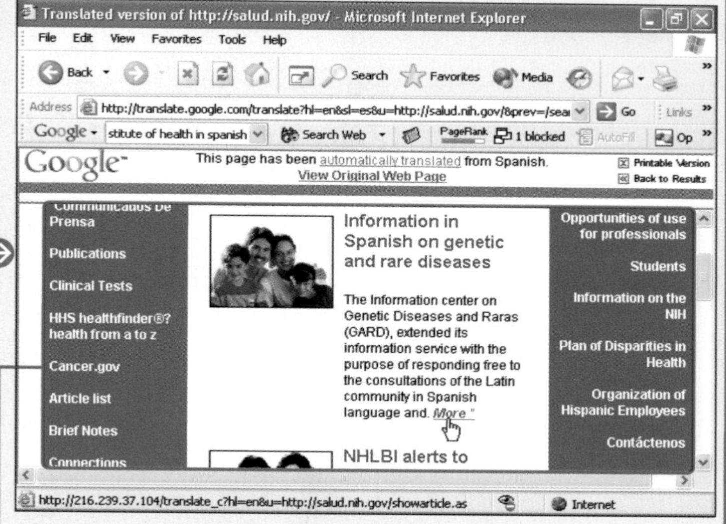

1. Perform a search with Google as you normally do.

Note: See tasks #41, #42, and #43 to improve your Google search efficiency.

- If the search returns links to pages in a foreign language, the Translate this page link appears.

2. Click Translate this page.

- Google translates the page as best as it can.

Search GOOGLE NEWS

Some of the more popular places on the Web are news sites, such as Fox News, MSNBC, and CBS. Google has its own news site at news.google.com that gathers news from thousands of sources all over the world and displays it on a single page that you can read for free. And the great thing is that almost every story has links to several different sources, so you can view the stories from various perspectives and access commentary from a number of experts.

Google News covers several news categories: World, U.S., Business, Science & Technology, Sports, Entertainment, and Health. Just click the button for the desired category to view summaries of several of the top stories along with links to other news sources.

Google News also provides a search tool that focuses on news sources, so if you are looking for a news story, you do not need to sift through general search results to find the information you need.

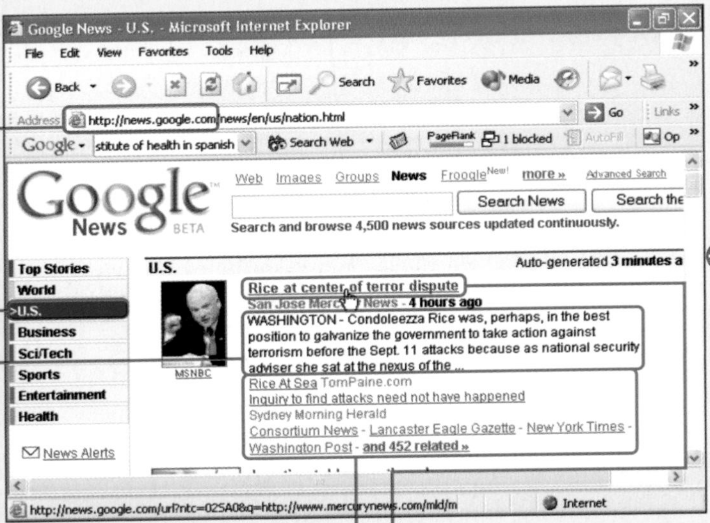

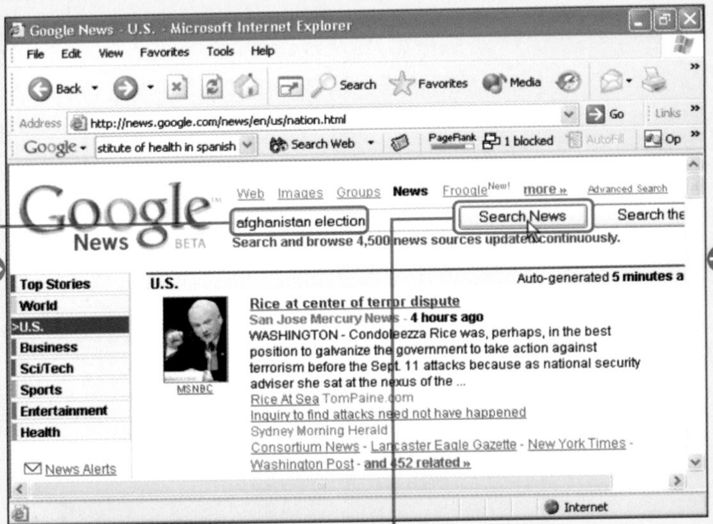

1. Type **news.google.com** and press Enter.
2. Click the link for the desired news category.
3. Read the summary.
4. Click the story's link to read the entire story.

- Google News displays links to other sources of information concerning this story.

5. To search the news, type your search word or words here.
6. Click Search News.

Customize It!

Click News Alerts on the Google News opening page to display a form for requesting e-mail notification about specific news topics from Google. Type a subject, type your e-mail address, and choose whether to be notified once a day or as the news happens. Then, click Create News Alert. You can also use this feature to follow your favorite sports team and check the latest scores.

More Options!

Many users set their favorite news and information page as their home page, so they can keep up on late-breaking news when they run their browsers. To make Google News your home page, go to news.google.com and click Make Google News Your Home Page.

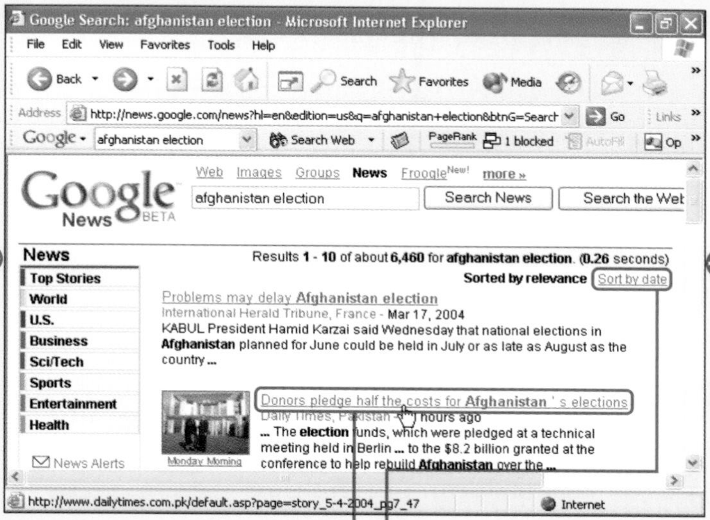

- Google displays links to the stories that match your search word or words.
- Articles are sorted by relevance.
- To sort articles by date, click Sort by date.
- Click the link for a related news source.
- Google opens the document from the selected news source and displays it in your browser.
- To return to Google News, click the Back button.

SAVE MONEY

shopping with Froogle

Froogle is Google's searchable online shopping directory that enables you to search for specific products and services. With Froogle you can save money by narrowing your search to a range of prices. Froogle is most useful for tracking down the lowest prices for a specific item, such as a DVD or video game, but it can help you find a wide range of products and services.

The same search rules apply to Froogle as apply to Google. If you type a general search phrase, the search typically returns far too many results to be useful. Although Froogle opens with a basic search page, consider using the Advanced Search for a more targeted selection, as shown in this task.

Froogle does not charge merchants for better placement or receive compensation if you choose to order a product you find through Froogle. After you find a product at a price that appeals to you, you click the link to connect to the merchant's site and then deal directly with the merchant to order the product or service.

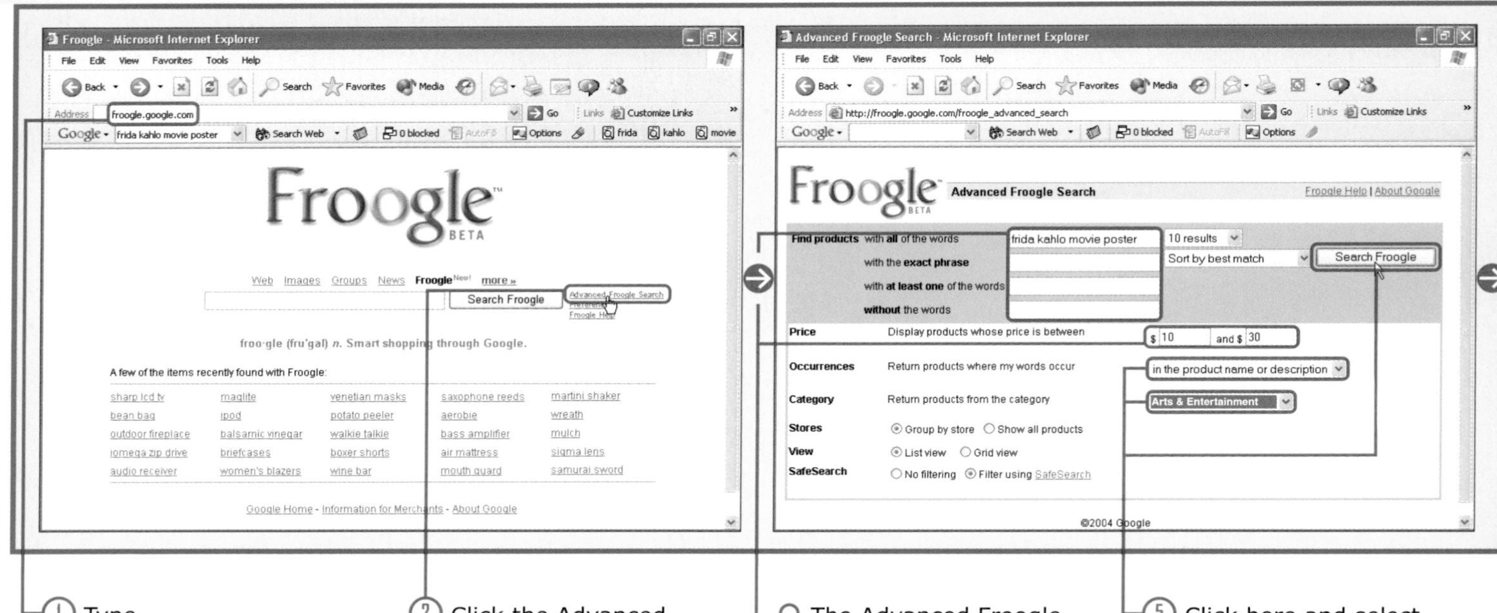

1. Type **froogle.google.com** and press Enter.
2. Click the Advanced Froogle Search link.

- The Advanced Froogle Search screen appears.

3. Type your search word or words in the Find products boxes.
4. Type the desired price range.
5. Click here and select where you want Froogle to look for the search word or words you typed.
6. Click here and select the desired shopping category.
7. Click Search Froogle.

DIFFICULTY LEVEL

More Options!

Google has a huge collection of catalogs. To access a store's catalog, go to www.google.com, click the "more" link, click the "Catalogs" link, and follow the trail of links to the desired catalog. A store's catalog consists of scanned catalog pages, which do not support online ordering.

Did You Know?

If you have a business and want to know if your products or services are listed on Froogle, do a search and see. If your product is not listed, you can submit a data feed to Froogle with a complete list of products and services. Click "Information for Merchants" at the bottom of the Froogle screen for more information.

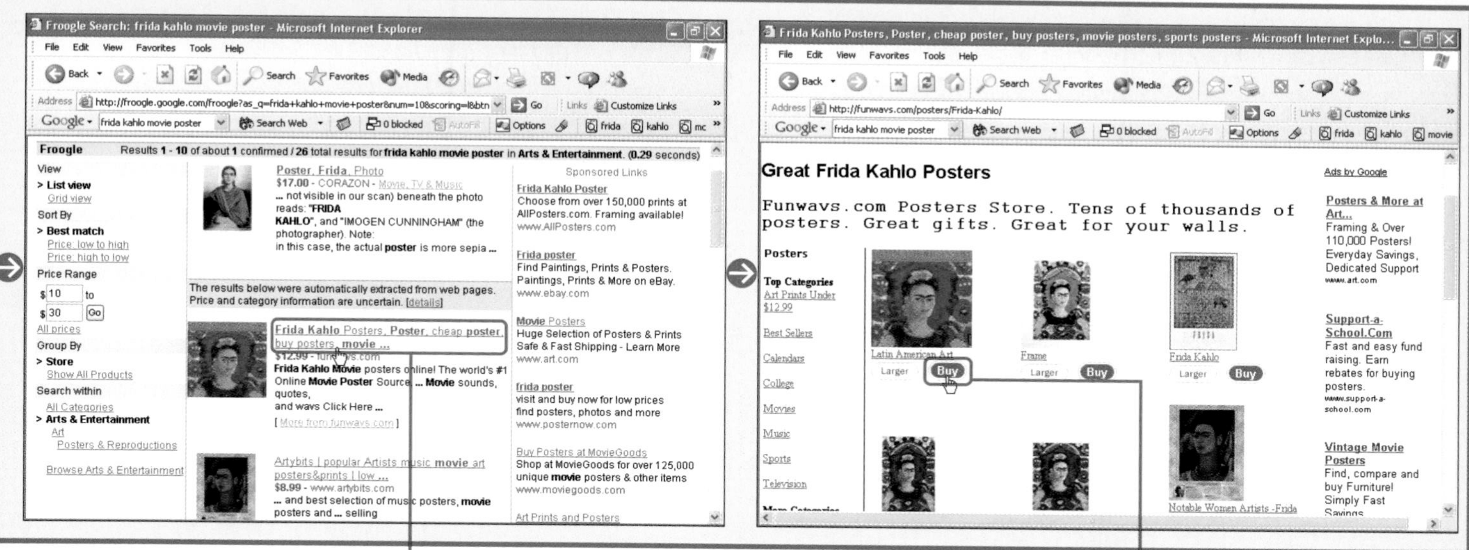

- Froogle displays items that match your search word or words.

8 Click the desired item.

- The merchant's Web site opens and displays the selected item.

- If desired, click the link for ordering the item online.

Maximize Your Success on eBay

If you buy or sell on eBay, you already know the basics of how to list an item for auction, place a bid, pay for items when you win a bid, and arrange for shipping or pickup. However, you might feel as though you are still a novice and that other buyers and sellers have an edge. Some people you know seem to get higher bids for the items they sell. Others seem to pay less for the items they buy. Some people even make a pretty good living buying and selling on eBay. What are their secrets?

This chapter provides ten tips to help you become a more savvy eBay user — five tips that can help you get more for the items you sell and five tips that can help you win auctions with lower bids. Here you learn how to research products and prices to make sure that you don't sell items for less than market value or buy items for more than they are worth. You learn how to present a product in a way that commands a higher price and attracts more bidders to drive up the price. And you learn how to automate your bidding and bid near an auction's close to buy an item right out from under the current high bid in an auction's final seconds. The tips and tricks you learn in this chapter give you the edge on eBay.

TOP 100

Research the MARKET VALUE of your item

Many people who buy items on eBay research the price of similar items that were auctioned in the past before they place a bid, so they know how much an item is worth. As a seller, you should know what your item is worth, as well. This enables you to set a realistic opening bid that attracts potential buyers and ensures that you receive a fair price for your item. Research can also help you determine whether trying to sell an item is even worth your time and money. For example, if you check out the auctions and see that 25 inkjet printers of the same make and model number you want to auction are going for $5 or less, you might want to reconsider listing it.

Fortunately, you can do much of your market research at eBay, simply by checking out the current auctions. Listings of similar items can give you an idea of the opening bid price, the popularity of the item, a general idea of what it might cost to ship the item, and the types of details to include in your description.

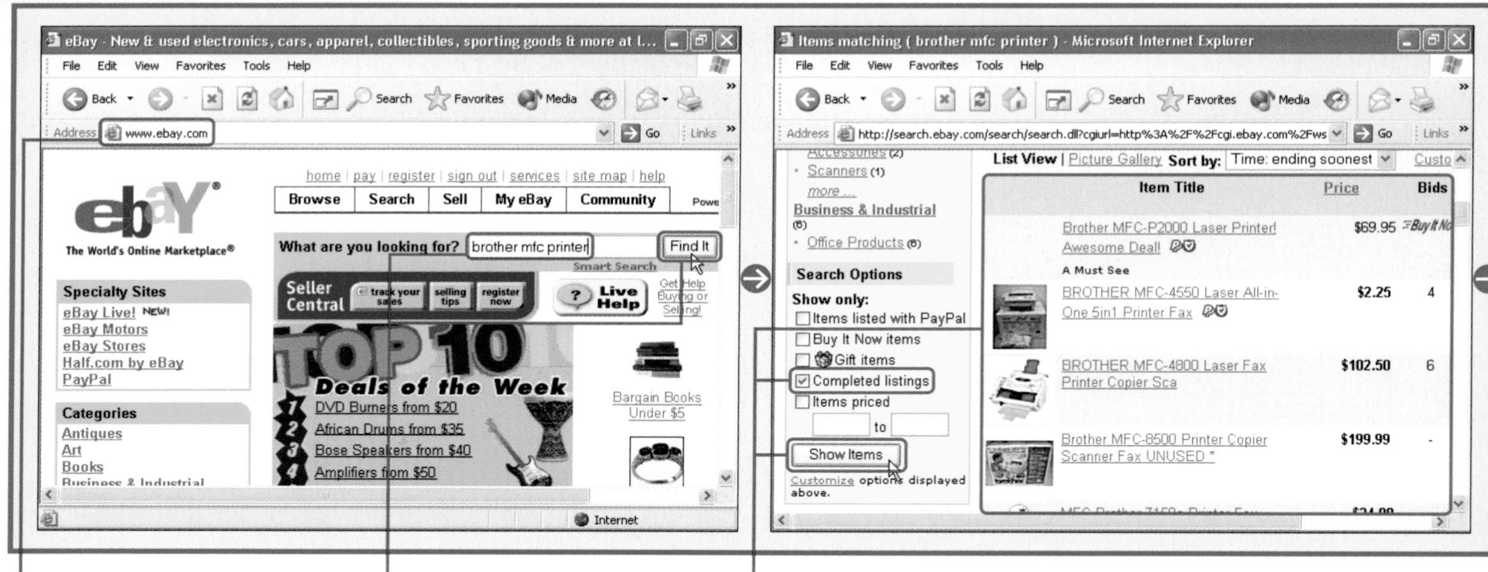

1. Type **www.ebay.com** and press Enter.
2. Type a description of the item you want to sell.
3. Click Find It.

- eBay displays a list of any items matching the description you entered.

4. Scroll down the page and click Completed listings.
5. Click the Show Items button.

Note: If you are not yet signed in, eBay prompts you to enter your eBay user ID and password. Type your user ID and password and click the Sign In button.

DIFFICULTY LEVEL

More Options!

Expand your research to other areas of the Internet, especially if you are selling something that might be rare, such as a coin or stamp collection or an antiquity. If you are unsure about what such an item might be worth, consider having it appraised before listing it on eBay.

Did You Know?

Scroll down to the bottom of a listing to obtain a general idea of how much it costs to ship the item. Usually the buyer pays the shipping fees, but you should list an estimate. Click the services link, which appears at the top of each eBay page, and click the Shipping Center link for additional details and access to shipping cost calculators.

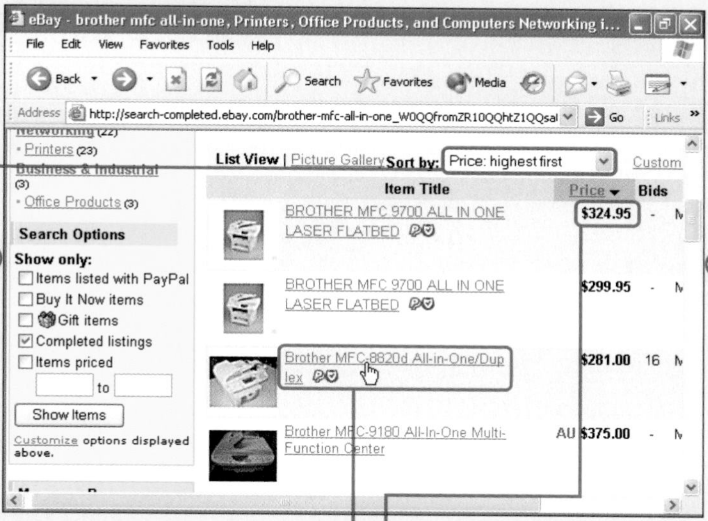

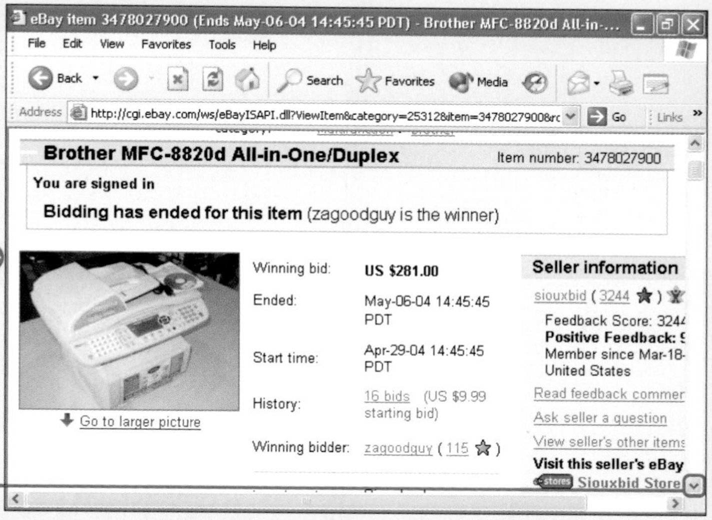

- eBay displays a list of items matching your description that have sold on eBay.

6. Click here and select Price: highest first.

- eBay sorts the list of items placing the highest priced item first.

7. Click an item that is comparable to the item you want to sell.

- eBay displays the item's listing, including any photos and description of the item.

8. Scroll down the page and examine the listing carefully, taking note of the categories in which the seller listed the item, its description, and any pictures.

Note: You can learn a great deal by examining successful listings.

Add KEY TERMS to attract more bidders

When prospective buyers search for items on eBay, they use the key terms that describe, most precisely, the item or items they are interested in purchasing. As a seller, you have 55 characters to use in the title of your listing, so include as many descriptive key terms as possible. Spend some time thinking about what a potential buyer might type when looking for the item you are selling. Use as many of those 55 characters as possible, and do not waste any characters on punctuation marks, articles (such as "the" or "an") or marketing jargon, such as "amazing" or "real bargain," which potential buyers rarely use in a search phrase.

If you already listed an item with a title that is less descriptive than it can be, you can go back to your item and change its title, as shown in this task. You can also change the item's description and picture at any time during the auction. However, you cannot change your opening bid price after someone has placed a bid or within 12 hours of the auction's close.

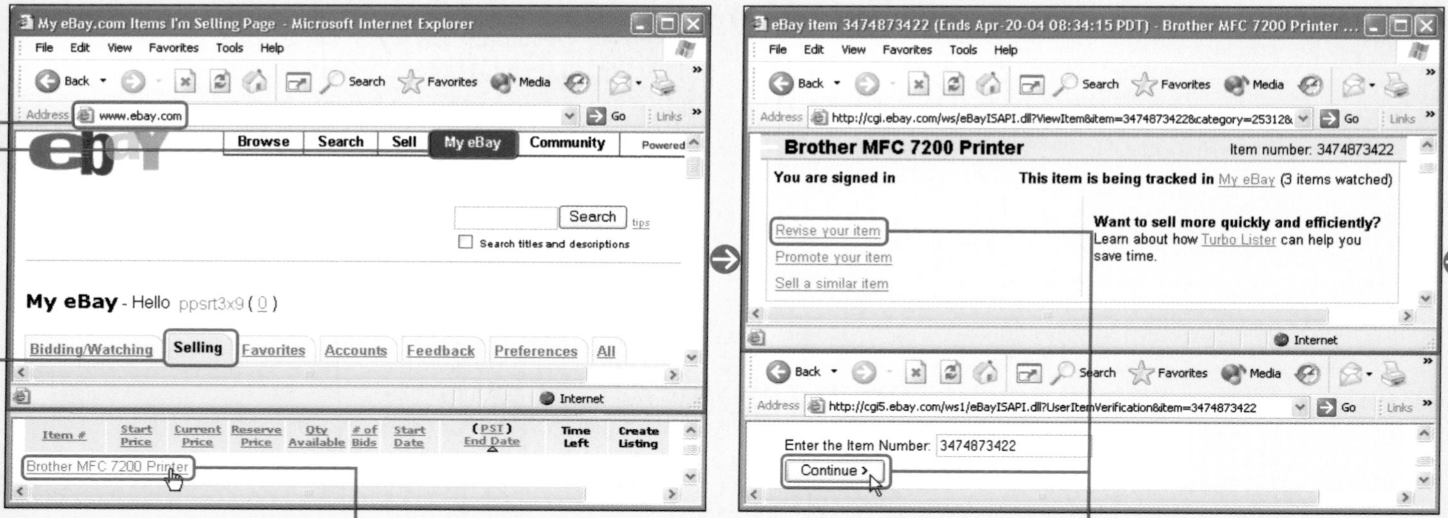

1. Log in to eBay, as you normally do.
2. Click My eBay.
3. Click the Selling tab.

- eBay displays a list of any items you are currently auctioning.

4. Click the item you want to change.

- eBay displays the listing for the item.

5. Click the Revise your item link.
6. Click Continue.

DIFFICULTY LEVEL

Caution!

Check your title and description for any typographical or spelling errors. Many savvy buyers use common typos in their searches to track down items that other buyers might not find when they spell the search terms correctly. The savvy buyer can then enter a low bid knowing that he or she might be the only one bidding on the item.

Did You Know?

If you are selling a popular brand name item, include the brand name in your title. Many prospective buyers search for items by brand. However, according to eBay rules, you cannot use a competitor brand name in the title or description to artificially steer buyers to the item you are selling.

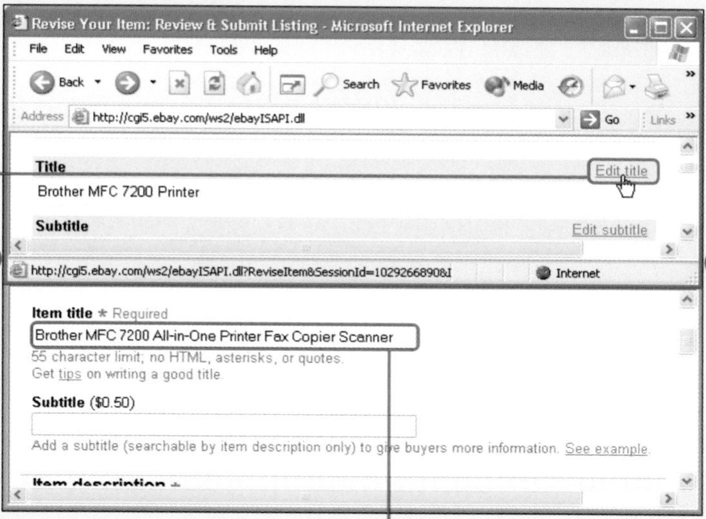

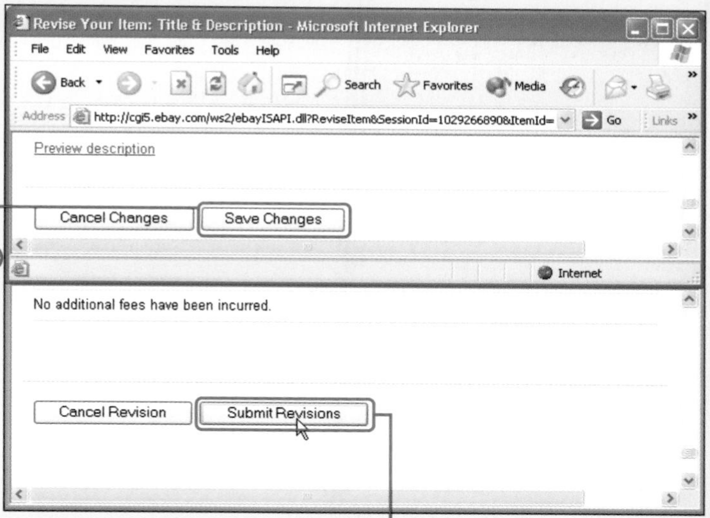

- The Revise Your Item: Review & Submit Listing Screen appears.

7. Click the Edit title link.

8. Type your changes in the Item title box, using as many of the 55 allotted characters as possible, and being as descriptive as possible.

9. Scroll down the page and click the Save Changes button.

- eBay saves your changes and returns you to the Revise Your Item: Review & Submit Listing Screen.

10. Click the Submit Revisions button.

Maximize FONTS AND FORMATTING in descriptions

Most advertisers and merchants know that a product commands a higher price when its appearance appeals to a buyer. On eBay, the same holds true. An attractive listing has a better chance of drawing more bidders and higher bids than an ad that looks shoddy. When composing your ad, be aware of all of the options available for controlling its format or appearance. eBay does offer an HTML option for high-end users to create their own mini-Web-page listings, but even if you choose to use the more basic, text-based editor, eBay offers formatting tools to enhance the appearance of the text. You can, and should, take advantage of them.

When composing a description, keep in mind that few buyers on eBay spend much time reading descriptions in depth, so place any strong selling points early in the description and use fonts and formatting to call attention to them. Sometimes, simply bolding a key term can help inspire a prospective buyer to place a bid. Here, you learn how to use fonts and formatting to your advantage.

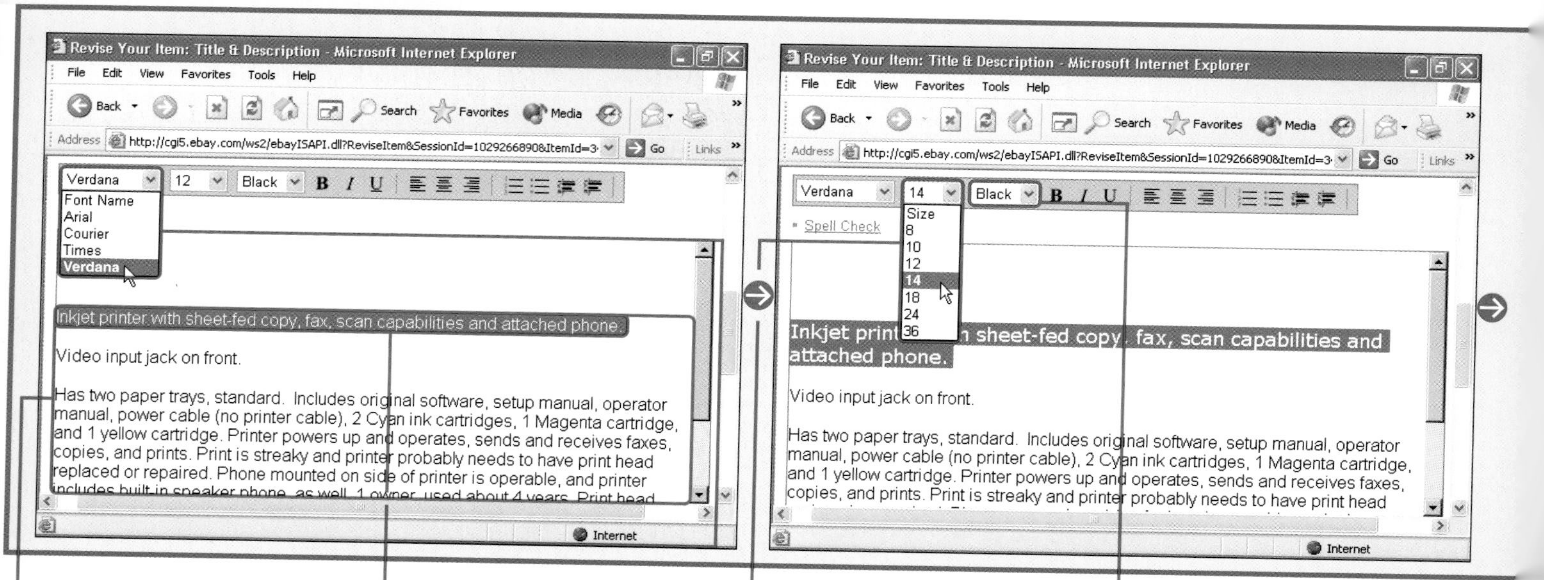

1. Compose your description as you normally do.

Note: If you already placed an ad, you can choose to revise it. See task #52 for more information.

2. Highlight one or more words whose formatting you want to change.
3. Click here and select a font.

- The highlighted text appears in the selected font.

4. Click here and select the desired font size.

- The highlighted text appears in the selected font size.

5. Click here and select the desired font color.

DIFFICULTY LEVEL

More Options!

Click the Spell Check link above the description area to have eBay check the spelling in the description and help you find the correct spelling.

Try This!

The description area acts like a word processor, allowing you to drag selected text to move it, Ctrl+drag text to copy it, and use shortcut keys, such as Ctrl+B to boldface selected text or Ctrl+I to italicize it. You can also right-click selected text to display a context menu of options.

More Options!

The screen that appears when you choose to add or edit a description features additional options for adding a background and specifying the layout of photos and text on a page.

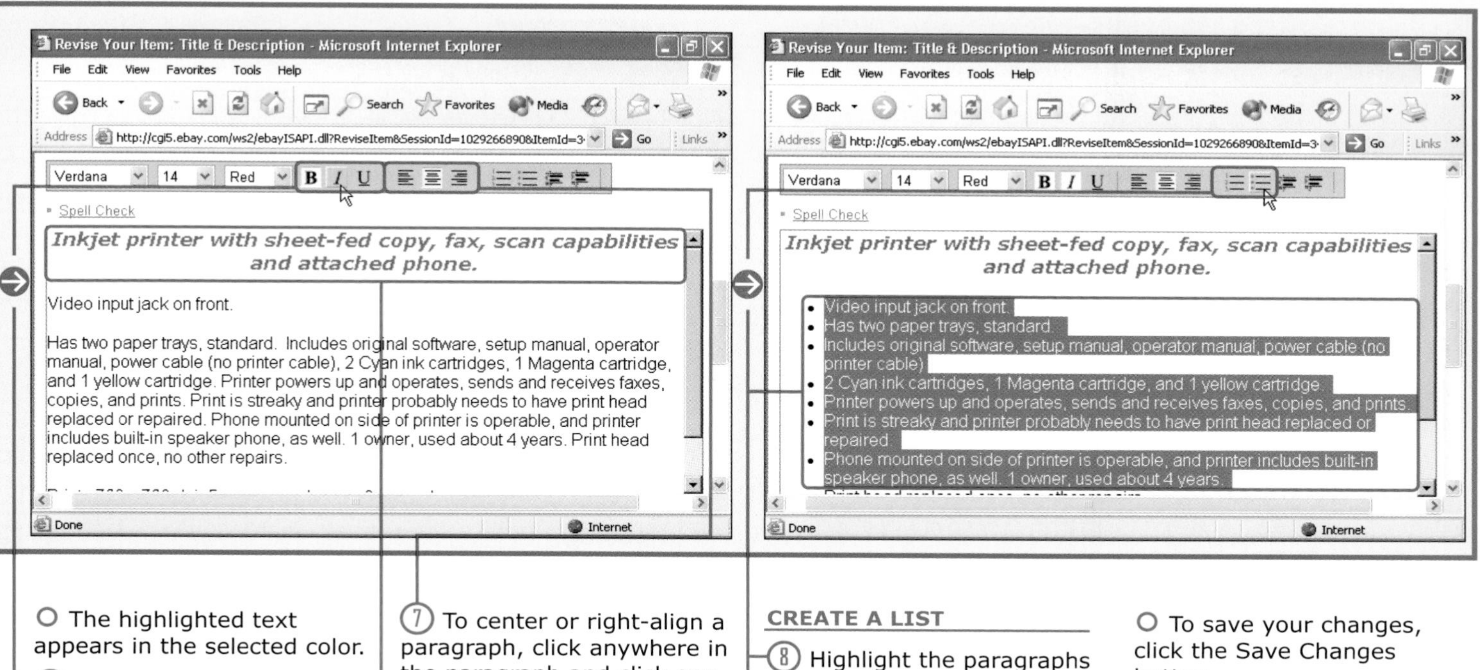

- The highlighted text appears in the selected color.

6. To add bold, italic, and/or underlining, click one or more of these text enhancement buttons.

- Clicking a text enhancement button toggles the enhancement on or off.

7. To center or right-align a paragraph, click anywhere in the paragraph and click one of these text alignment buttons.

- The text appears left, centered, or right-aligned.

CREATE A LIST

8. Highlight the paragraphs you want to convert into a list.

9. Click the Numbered Bullets or Standard Bullets button to create the list.

- To save your changes, click the Save Changes button.

- eBay updates your auction listing.

ENHANCE PHOTOS

for best results

A seller on eBay made a business of buying items at very low prices and then re-listing them using much better photos to command higher bids. A quality photo can attract more bidders and higher bids.

Of course, composition has a great deal of influence on the effectiveness of a photo. If you take a photo of an antique vase that is sitting in a box of junk, the photo looks trashy and probably does not have the desired effect. If you polish the vase and set it on a fancy tablecloth with an attractive background, the photo projects a rich ambience that can drive the bidding.

After you take a picture, you can enhance it to further improve its effectiveness. Most digital cameras and scanners come with photo enhancement software for adjusting a photo's brightness, contrast, and color balance. In addition, you can save the photo in a format that makes the digital image file smaller, so it loads faster on prospective bidders' computers.

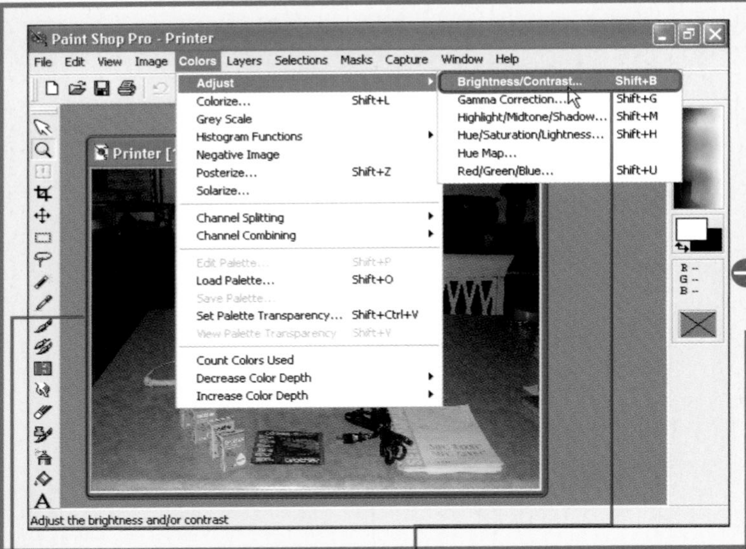

ADJUST BRIGHTNESS AND CONTRAST

① Open the photo of your item in a digital image editing program.

○ This example features JASC Paint Shop Pro.

② Select the command to adjust the brightness and contrast.

Note: The commands for adjusting brightness and contrast vary.

○ The brightness and contrast controls appear.

③ Drag the slider to increase or decrease the brightness.

④ Drag the slider to increase or decrease the contrast.

⑤ Click OK.

○ The program applies the changes to the photo.

DIFFICULTY LEVEL

More Options!

For a slight fee, you can add more photos to your listing. In many cases, a single photo is enough, but if you are selling an item that most people want to view from different perspectives, consider paying the small fee.

Did You Know?

Most digital cameras take photos that result in image files that can be as large as several megabytes. Many shoppers on eBay have dial-up modem connections that can take several minutes to load a single digital photo. Try to limit the size of your images to a couple hundred kilobytes.

Attention!

Although you can enhance a photo to improve its appearance, start with a quality photo. If the photo is out of focus, no digital imaging program can make it look crisp and clear.

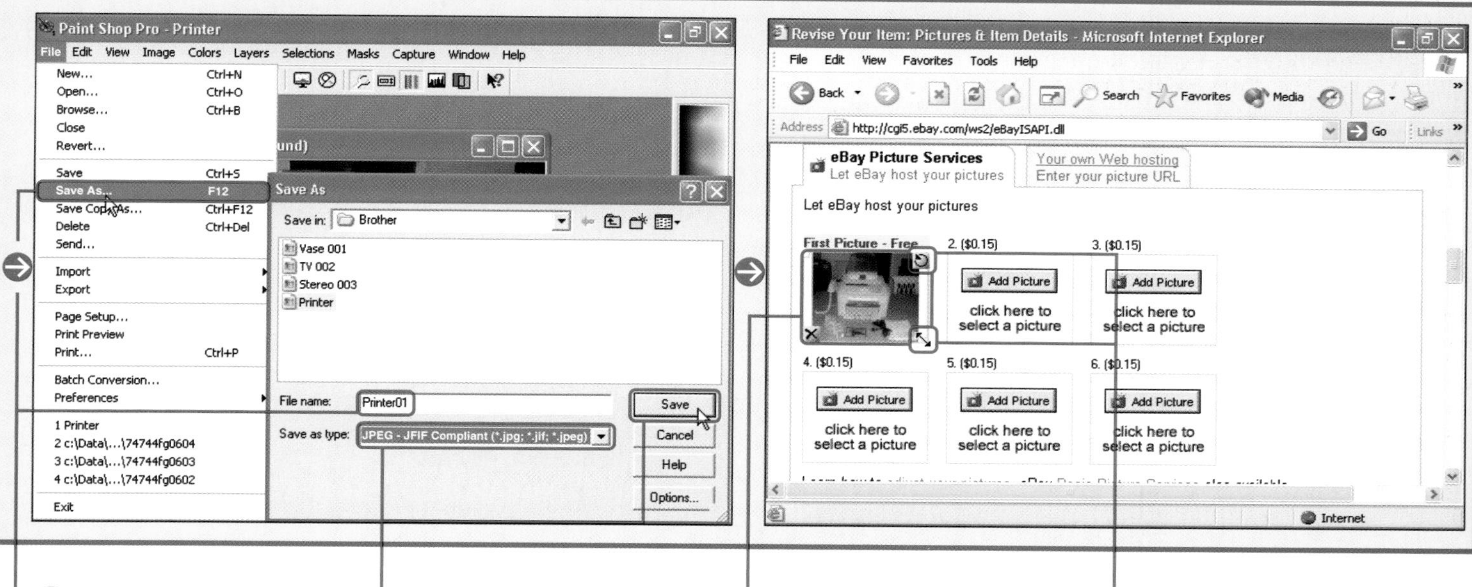

6. Click File and select Save As.
   - The Save As dialog box appears.
7. Type a new name for the image.
8. Click here and select JPEG to reduce the size of the image file.
9. Click Save.
   - The Save As dialog box closes, and the program saves your file.

ROTATE AND CROP AND IMAGE

- When you add or edit your listing in eBay, you can rotate or crop an image.

10. Click the image you want to rotate or crop.
11. To rotate an image 90 degrees clockwise, click here.
12. To crop an image, drag the corner toward the center.
13. Scroll down the page and click Save Changes.

Set a BUY IT NOW price

Many eBay shoppers prefer to avoid the bidding wars. They want a no-haggle transaction in which they obtain a particular product at a fair price. For these shoppers, eBay offers a Buy It Now option. The seller sets a satisfactory Buy It Now price, for which the shopper can choose to purchase the product immediately, before the bidding starts. It costs the seller five cents to set a Buy It Now price.

Of course, if you have a rare collectible, setting a Buy It Now price that is lower than what you could obtain through an auction may not be the best strategy. But if you are selling products that typically sell in a given price range, setting a Buy It Now price can often help you clear items out of your inventory and free up more time for auctioning additional items. If you browse eBay auctions, you notice that many sellers list Buy It Now prices; the reason is that the Buy It Now price works.

You can set a Buy It Now price when you first list an item, or you can add it later, as long as no one has bid on the item.

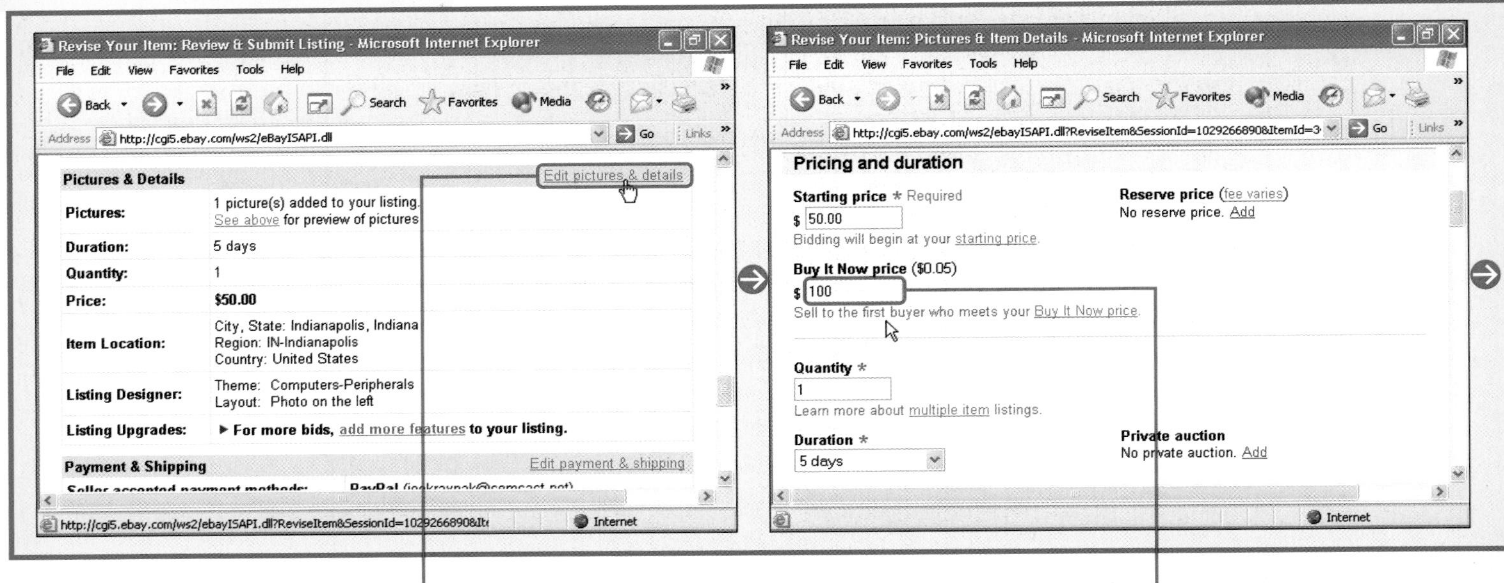

○ When you enter or edit a listing, you can set a Buy It Now price.

① If you are editing a listing, click the Edit pictures & details link.

○ The Revise Your Item: Pictures & Item Details page appears.

② Type the desired price here.

Attention!

To add the Buy It Now option, you must have a seller's rating of 10 or more or verify your ID online, for a slight fee. To achieve a seller's rating of 10, you must be an active seller with positive feedback from buyers. To verify your ID, eBay prompts you to enter some financial and identification information, which it cross-references with information in other business databases. Until you verify your ID, no Buy It Now price box appears.

Remove It!

The Buy It Now option automatically disappears when someone enters the first bid. To remove a Buy It Now price before the first bid, repeat the steps here to delete the entry in the Buy It Now price box and then click Save Changes.

Did You Know?

A reserve price is a hidden price below which bids are rejected. Many buyers avoid bidding on higher-priced items that have a reserve price.

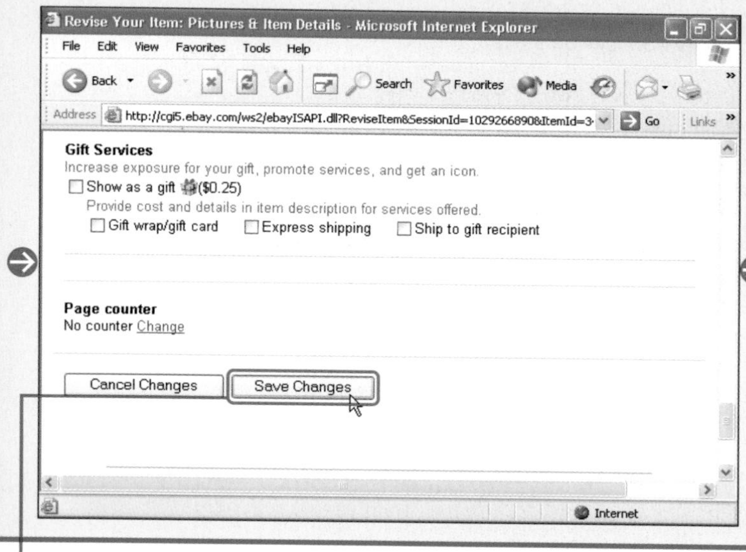

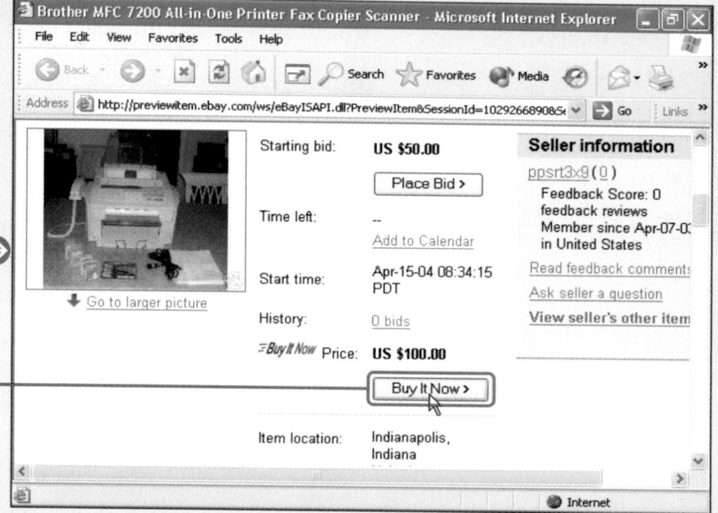

3 Scroll down the page and click here to save your changes.

When a shopper views your listing, he or she can now click the Buy It Now option.

Search and RESEARCH before you bid

On eBay, knowledge is power. A seller who knows the market value of an item has a distinct advantage over a less informed buyer, and vice versa. In fact, some sellers on eBay make a pretty good living buying items at discount retail stores and selling them for a modest markup on eBay. As a buyer, if you know the market value of a particular item, you can enter a bid just under the cost of what a local merchant might charge and usually win the bid.

Before you bid for an item on eBay, do your research. This task shows you how to research auctions on eBay to determine the market value of similar or identical items. However, you can, and often should, expand your research to other Internet resources, including online stores, specialty shops, and even other online auction sites. For collectibles and antiques, you might need to consult with an expert to determine a reasonable bid.

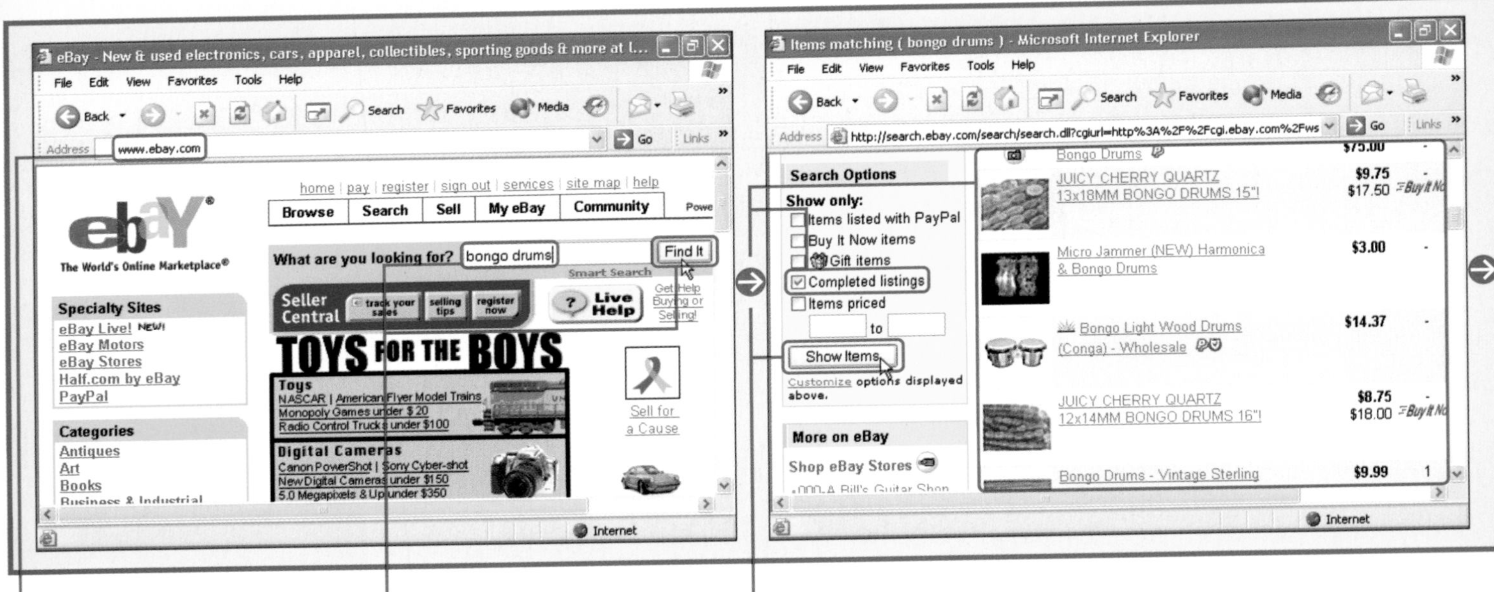

① Type **www.ebay.com** and press Enter.

② Type a description of the item you want to buy.

③ Click Find It.

○ eBay displays a list of any items matching the description you entered.

④ Scroll down the page and click Completed listings.

⑤ Click the Show Items button.

Note: If you are not yet signed in, eBay prompts you to enter your username and password. Type your user ID and password and click the Sign In button.

DIFFICULTY LEVEL

More Options!

Compare prices carefully. Some items come bundled with hundreds of dollars of extras and sell for only slightly more than the same item sold separately. Does one of the items include a warranty? Is it in better condition?

Try This!

When you search for specific auction items, try searching in different categories and using common misspellings in your search. Sometimes, you can find a bargain just because somebody misspelled a key word in the item's title or description.

More Options!

Research not only completed listings but also items currently on the auction block and near the auction close — bidding heats up near the close.

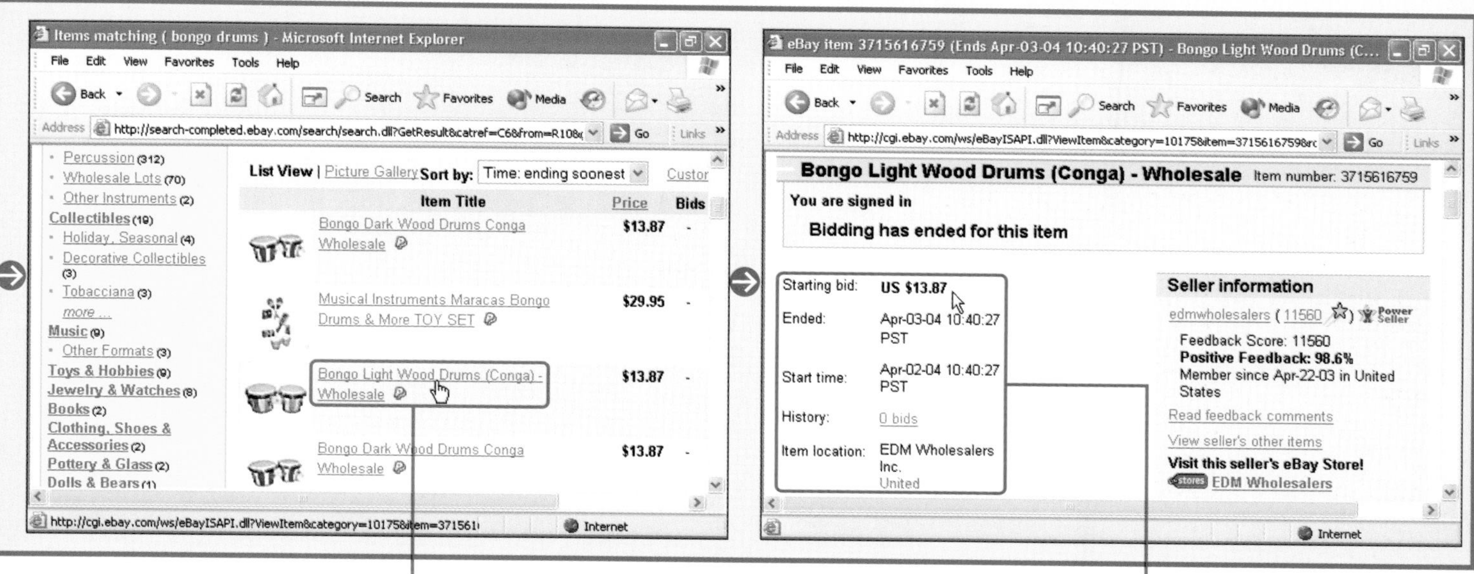

○ eBay displays a list of items matching your description that have sold on eBay.

⑥ Click an item that is comparable to the item you want to purchase.

○ eBay displays the item's listing, including its description and the winning bid.

⑦ Scroll down the page and examine the listing carefully, taking note of the winning bid, the description and condition of the item, and its shipping cost.

Check the SELLER'S FEEDBACK

DIFFICULTY LEVEL

Most eBay buyers and sellers are honest, responsible people who like to continue doing business on eBay. In order to remain in good standing with buyers and with the eBay service, sellers need to establish a solid reputation for honesty, reliability, and responsiveness. Because of this, most sellers are motivated to please the buyer.

However, not all sellers succeed at pleasing their customers. Some bend the truth about their products, delay shipping, or even try to cancel the transaction when you win the bid. You can avoid many bad experiences on eBay by researching the seller's feedback and dealing only with sellers who have a history of positive transactions.

Fortunately, eBay makes it easy to check a seller's rating before you place a bid. The rating shows the number of positive, neutral, and negative ratings the seller received and provides an option for viewing specific comments from buyers. After learning that a seller has a good reputation, you can bid with confidence.

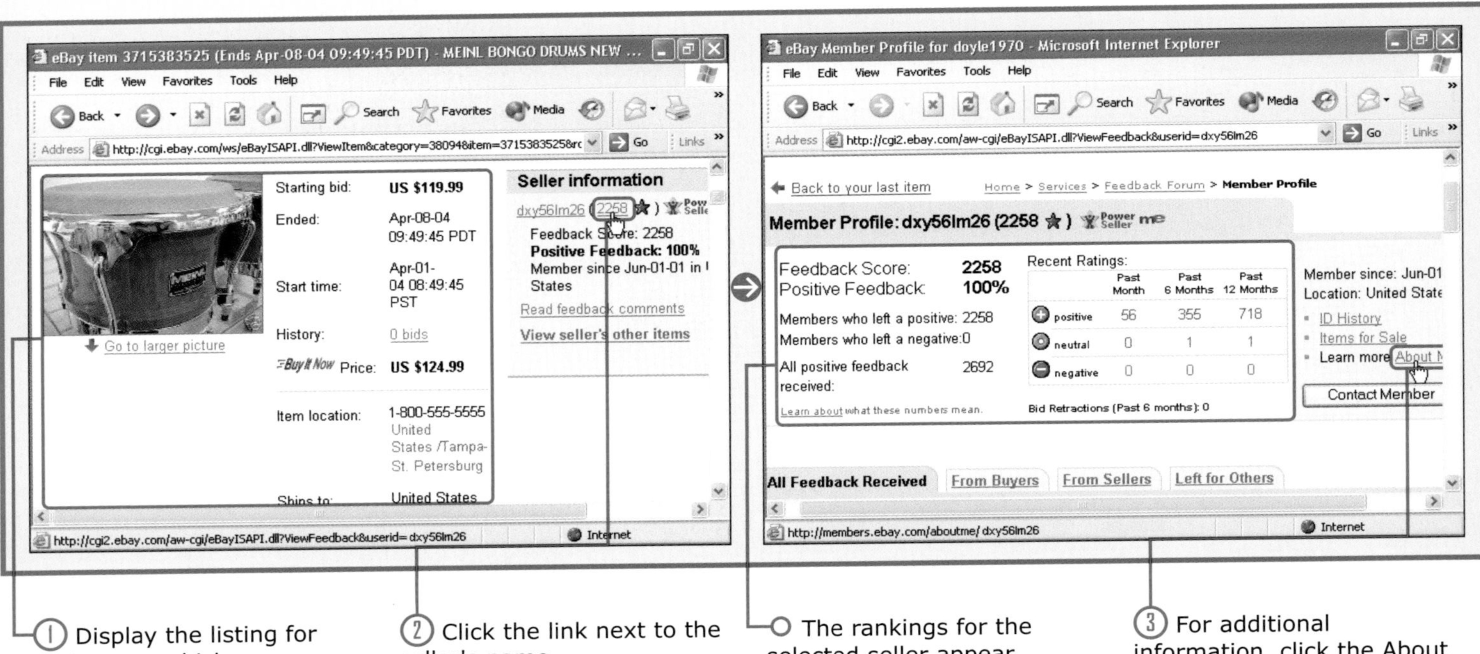

① Display the listing for an item on which you are interested in bidding.

② Click the link next to the seller's name.

○ The rankings for the selected seller appear.

③ For additional information, click the About Me link.

○ eBay displays additional buyers' comments.

Enter your MAXIMUM BID

DIFFICULTY LEVEL

Buyers often lose an auction by bidding low and then failing to follow the auction. As the bidding progresses, usually near the auction close, another buyer enters a bid a few pennies higher and wins the item fairly easily.

If you really want to win an auction, and you prefer not to follow the auction closely, consider clicking the Buy It Now link, if available, to purchase the item outright, or type your maximum bid as your opening bid. When you type your maximum bid, eBay's proxy bidding automatically enters bids for you, outbidding previous bids, until you win the auction or someone bids a price that exceeds your maximum bid.

Entering your maximum bid does not guarantee that you win the auction, but it does give you the best possible chance. And, if you stick with that maximum bid, it prevents you from getting caught up in a bidding war that results in your paying more for an item than what it is worth.

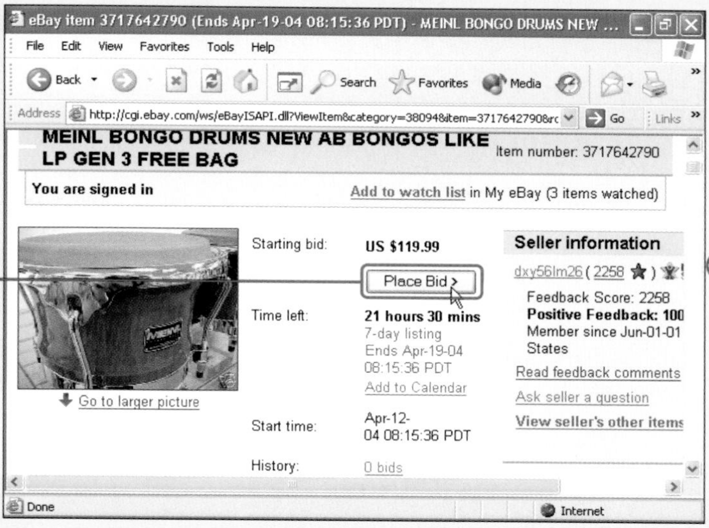

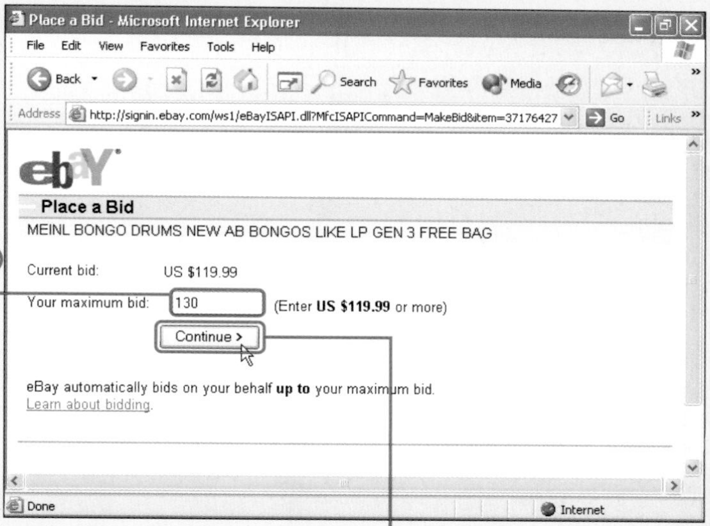

1. When you see an item you want, click the Place Bid button.

- The Place a Bid page appears.

2. Type the maximum amount you are willing to pay for this item.

3. Click Continue.

- eBay's proxy bidding incrementally increases your bids until you win the auction or the bidding exceeds your maximum bid.

SNIPE

to win an auction near its close

Potential buyers like to get a feel for the bidding to see what others are willing to pay before they enter a bid. Many successful buyers wait until the last few seconds of an auction and try to outbid the high bidder by a dollar or less just before the auction closes. This strategy, called *sniping*, is perfectly acceptable on eBay. Of course, sniping does not guarantee that you win the auction. In fact, if several bidders try the same tactic near the auction close, you can lose an item that you might have been willing to bid a little higher to win.

To snipe successfully, follow an auction closely, especially about 10 minutes or so before the auction's close. Refresh the page every minute or so to see if any new bids have come in and to get a feel for the auction's progress. If an auction draws several bids, expect the bidding to heat up in the final minute or so, and then enter your bid as close to the auction's close as possible. This task shows you how.

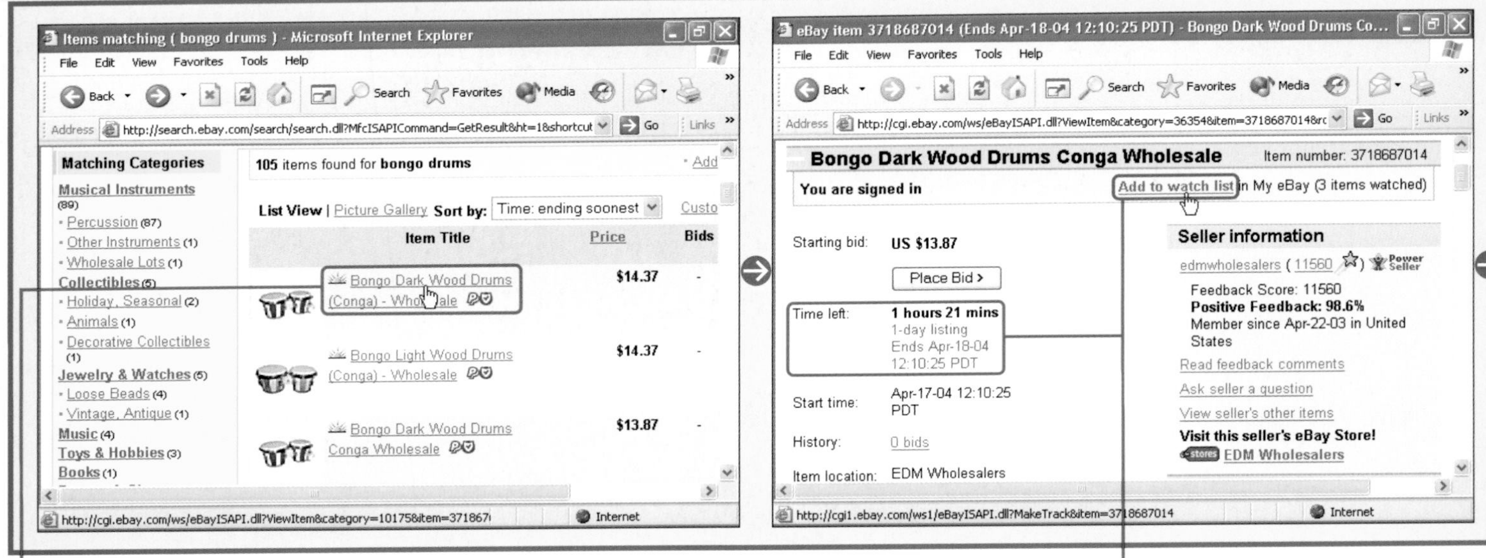

① When you find an item you want to bid on, click its link.

○ eBay displays the item's listing.

② Take note of the auction's closing time.

③ Click the Add to watch list link.

Attention!

The time it takes eBay to receive your bid depends on your connection speed and how busy the eBay server is. If you have a dial-up modem connection, consider entering your bid a little earlier. If you have a broadband connection, try entering bids closer to the auction's close.

More Options!

If you are willing to pay more than the minimum allowable bid to win an item, try entering a bid that is a few dollars more than the minimum allowable. The current high bidder may already have a higher proxy bid set, and bidding a single dollar more than the current bid may be insufficient.

Try This!

Look for auctions that sellers schedule to close at off hours, such as early morning, when fewer buyers are likely to bid on the item.

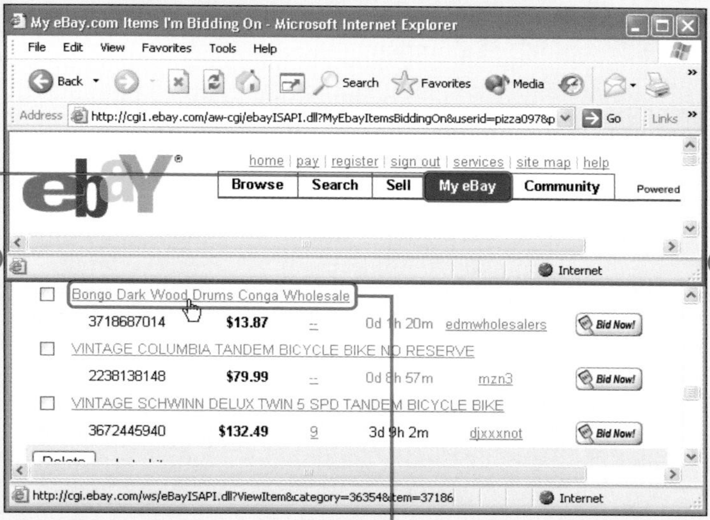

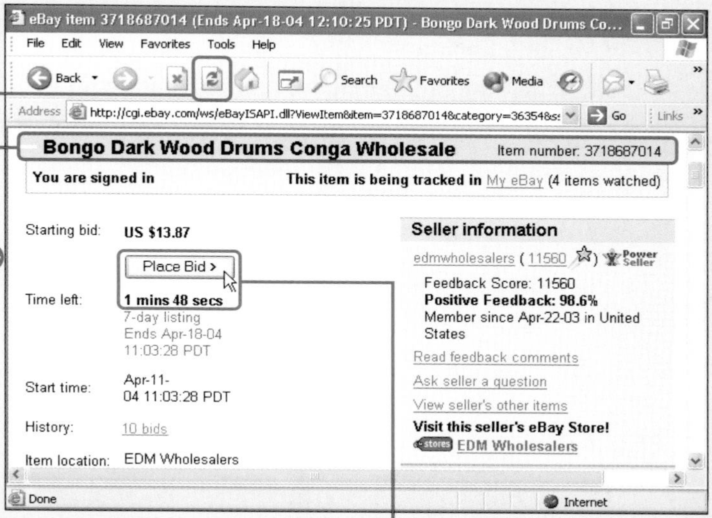

④ Click My eBay.

⑤ Click the link for the item you are watching.

○ eBay displays the item's listing.

⑥ Click the Refresh button every five to ten seconds to check for new bids.

⑦ One or two minutes from closing, click Place Bid, type the lowest allowable bid amount, and then click the Continue button.

○ eBay accepts your bid, and you can check back in a couple minutes to determine if you won.

AUTOMATE
your bidding

When you enter a maximum bid, eBay's proxy bidding feature automates your bidding for you, increasing the bid incrementally, as needed, to outbid other potential buyers up to the maximum bid you typed. However, eBay's proxy bidding might not be the most effective tool for sniping. Other programs and online services provide tools that can help you snipe more effectively.

The most responsive tools are available through online services. The sniping software resides on a fast Internet server that is capable of entering a series of bids and checking incoming bids much faster than you can on your computer. You simply specify your maximum bid and let the service wage the bidding war on your behalf. These services are most useful for people who have a relatively slow dial-up modem connection.

If you have a broadband connection, consider installing sniping software on your computer. The sniping software uses your existing connection to carry on the bidding war, so you avoid any service fees. This task shows you where to obtain and how to use Auction Sentry.

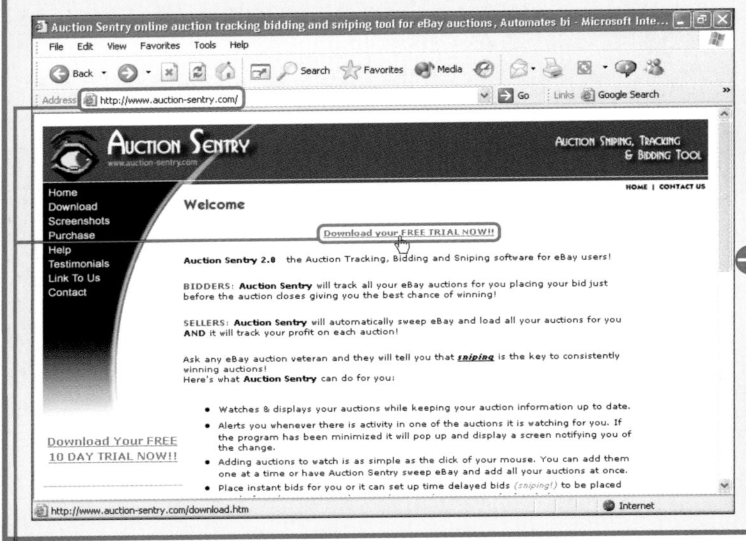

① Type **www.auction-sentry.com/download.htm** and press Enter.

② Click Download your FREE TRIAL NOW!! and follow the onscreen instructions to save the installation file and install the program on your computer.

Note: Before using Auction Sentry, add any items you want to bid on to your eBay watch list, so you can easily add them to Auction Sentry.

○ The installation routine places a shortcut for Auction Sentry on the desktop.

③ Double-click the Auction Sentry shortcut.

○ The Auction Sentry program window appears.

DIFFICULTY LEVEL

Did You Know?

On eBay, when you enter a bid, you cannot cancel it under most conditions. By scheduling a bid with Auction Sentry, you can cancel the bid any time before the scheduled time.

More Options!

For a good sniping service, check out BidRobot at www.bidrobot.com. This service, created by eBay guru Chuck Eglinton, costs about $4 per week or $35 for an entire year and boasts a 70 percent success rate. AuctionSniper.com at www.auctionsniper.com is also an excellent service — you pay 1 percent of the transaction price only if you win an auction.

Important!

Click the Synchronize PC's clock with eBay's button ( ) to make sure that your computer and eBay are on the same time.

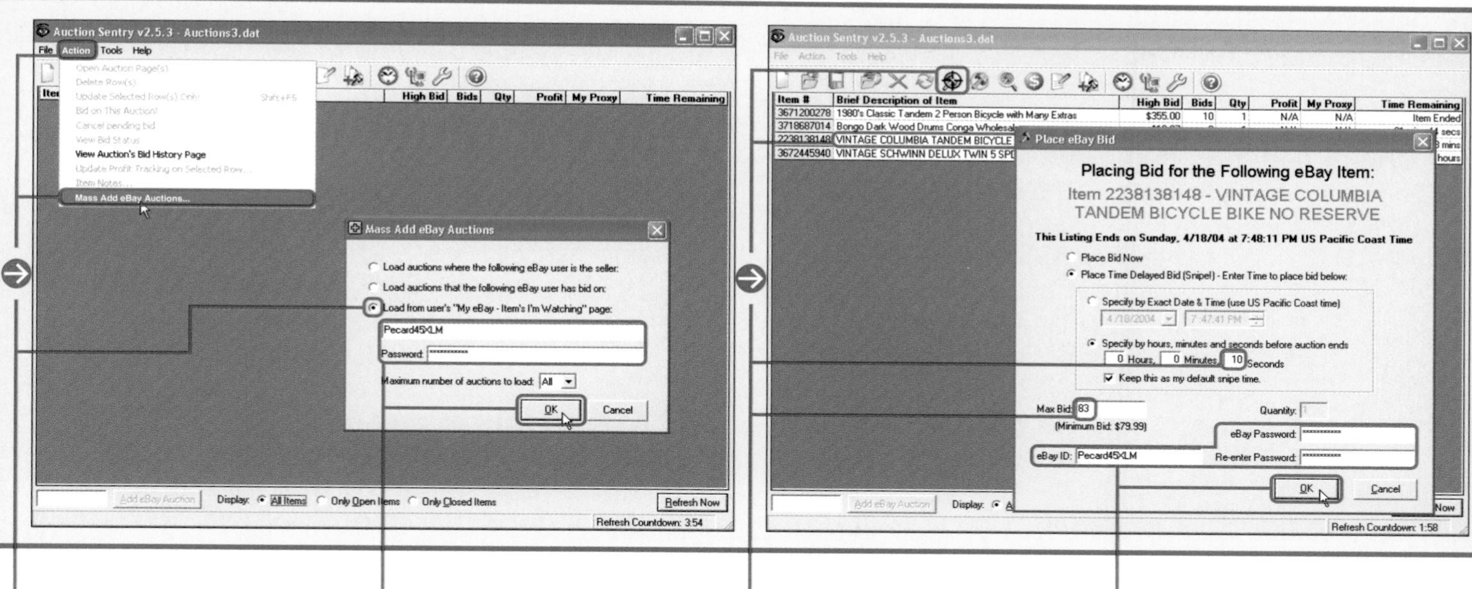

4 To add the items on your eBay watch list to Auction Sentry, click Action.

5 Click Mass Add eBay Auctions.

6 Click Load from user's "My eBay – Item's I'm Watching" page.

7 Type your eBay user ID and password.

8 Click OK and click Yes, if prompted to confirm.

○ Auction Sentry retrieves and displays the items on your Watch List.

9 Click an item on which you want to bid.

10 Click the Bid on This Auction button.

11 Type the number of seconds before the auction close that you want Auction Sentry to place your bid and type your maximum bid.

12 Type your eBay user ID and password.

13 Click OK.

○ At the time you specified, Auction Sentry begins bidding on your behalf up to your maximum bid.

Master Your E-mail

Most computer users quickly master basic e-mail tasks: how to check for incoming e-mail messages, respond to them, and compose and send e-mail messages to friends, relatives, and business associates. If you are a slightly more advanced user, you know how to attach files to outgoing messages and open files attached to the messages you receive. However, few users go beyond these basic tasks.

In this chapter, you learn ten additional tips and techniques to take control of your e-mail and manage your messages more efficiently. The first two tasks in this chapter focus on making your e-mail more accessible by taking advantage of free Web-based e-mail accounts. A Web-based account enables you to send and receive e-mail from any computer in the world with an Internet connection and a Web browser. Additional tasks show you how to keep your e-mail messages small so they travel faster and require less storage space; avoid viruses that might be attached to messages; and manage your e-mail boxes to prevent clutter. If, like most e-mail users, you receive a daily dose of unsolicited messages, called *spam*, this chapter introduces you to tools and techniques that can help you reduce the amount of spam you receive.

By using the e-mail options described here and practicing the techniques as directed in these tasks, you can begin to use e-mail more efficiently, effectively, and securely from anywhere in the world.

TOP 100

Get a FREE HOTMAIL account

Many companies, including Yahoo!, MSN, and Netzero, offer free e-mail accounts, many of which are Web-based; that is, you can check and send e-mail messages by logging in to the company's Web site rather than using an e-mail program. This is useful if you need to access e-mail when you are on a trip and cannot dial in to your local Internet service provider.

Many users also sign up for free e-mail accounts to give themselves an alternate e-mail address when they need to register to use a particular Web site. By typing this alternate e-mail address rather than their primary e-mail address, they keep their primary address safe from spammers.

One of the most popular free, Web-based e-mail services is MSN Hotmail. In this task, you learn how to connect to Hotmail and set up your free account and use it to send and receive e-mail. In the next task, you learn how to access your Hotmail account from your e-mail program.

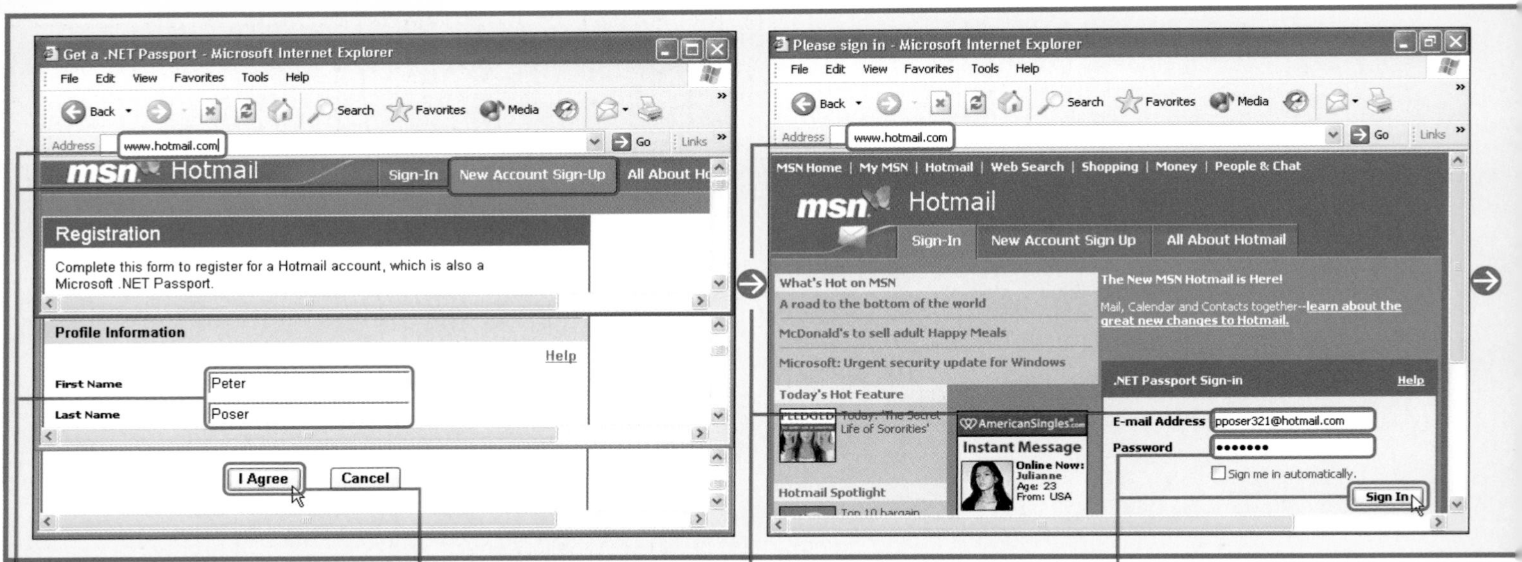

1. Type **www.hotmail.com** and press Enter.
2. Click the New Account Sign-Up tab.
3. Type the requested profile and account information.
4. Scroll down the page, read the license agreement, click I Agree, and follow the onscreen instructions to specify any additional preferences.
5. To check your e-mail, type **www.hotmail.com** and press Enter.
6. Type your Hotmail e-mail address here.
7. Type your password here.
8. Click Sign In.

More Options!

The screen that displays your list of incoming messages contains a toolbar for managing those messages. Before you can take an action on a message, you must click its check box to select it. You can then click the appropriate button to delete (Delete), block (Block), or junk (Junk) the selected messages. Junking a message reports it to Hotmail as spam, so the mail server can screen it out in the future.

More Options!

You can choose to receive e-mail messages only from specified contacts, essentially screening out any and all junk mail. After signing in, click the Today tab and click the Junk E-mail folder link to display your options.

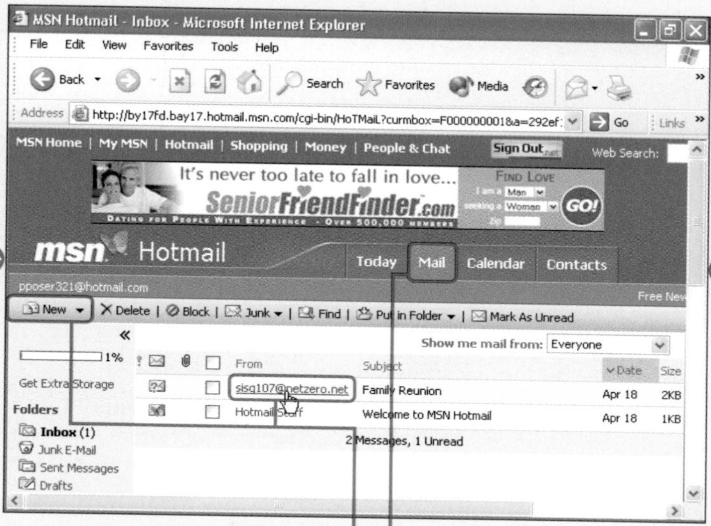

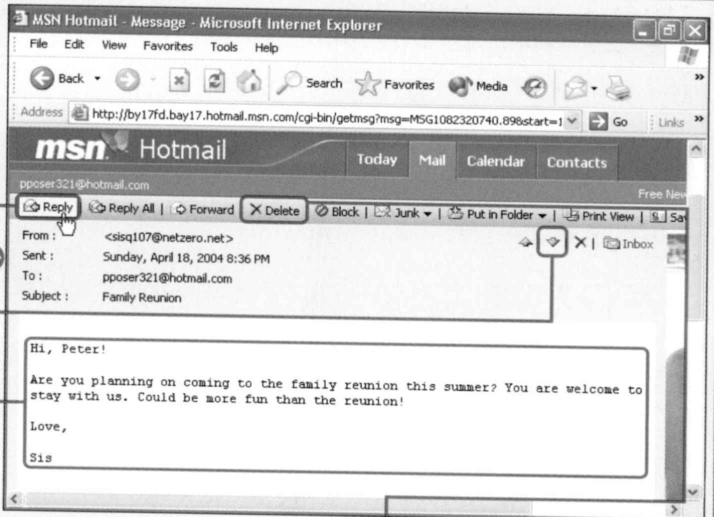

- Hotmail signs you in and displays Hotmail's Today tab.

Note: The first time you sign in, you must fill out a form specifying your preferences, such as which MSN newsletters you would like to receive.

9 Click the Mail tab.

10 To read a message, click its link.

- To compose a new message, click the New button.

- Hotmail displays the contents of the selected message.
- To reply to the message, click Reply.
- Click here to view the contents of the next message.
- To delete the message, click Delete.
- To disconnect at any time, click the Sign Out button.

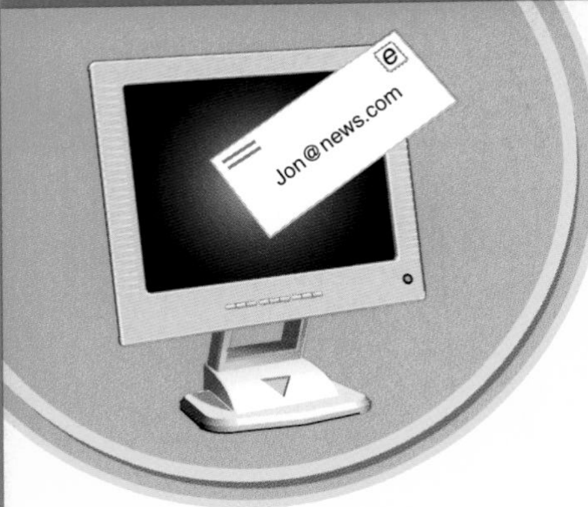

ACCESS HOTMAIL from Outlook Express

When you are on the road, accessing your Hotmail account via the Web usually is the preferred method. However, if you are at home or work and typically use a dedicated e-mail program, such as Outlook Express, to access another e-mail account, you probably want your e-mail program to check your Hotmail account for messages, as well. Your e-mail program can then check any and all e-mail accounts for incoming messages and display them in one convenient location.

In Outlook Express, you can add an account for Hotmail along with your user ID and password, so Outlook Express has the information it needs to connect to Hotmail and retrieve any messages. When you connect to the Internet and choose to send and receive mail, Outlook Express can then check your Hotmail account for incoming mail and send any mail you chose to send from your Hotmail account. This task shows you how to set up a Hotmail account in Outlook Express.

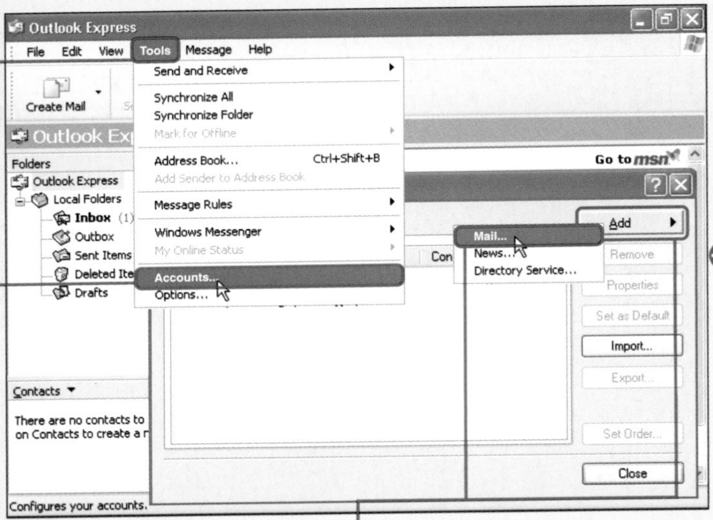

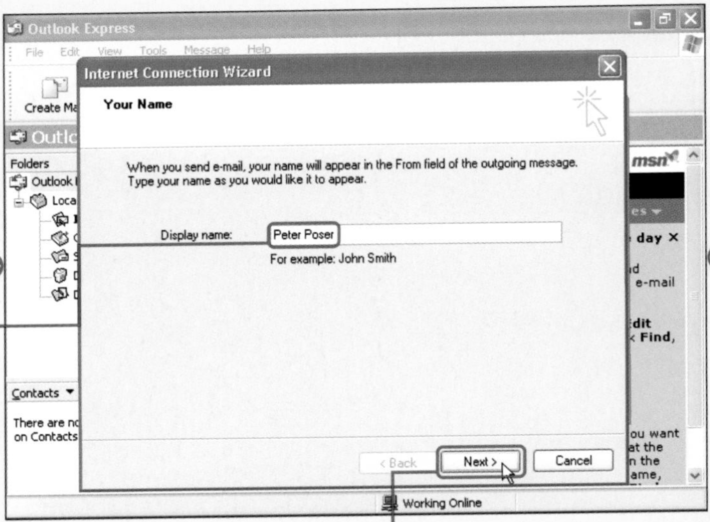

1 In Outlook Express, click Tools.

2 Click Accounts.

○ The Accounts dialog box appears.

3 Click Add.

4 Click Mail.

○ The Internet Connection Wizard appears.

5 Type your name as you want it to appear in messages you send.

6 Click Next, type your Hotmail address, and click Next.

Customize It!

You can change your Hotmail account settings at any time. Click Tools, click Accounts, click the Mail tab, and then double-click your Hotmail account to display the account settings. To set your Hotmail account as the default for sending and receiving e-mail, click its name and click the Set as Default button.

More Options!

If you do not use Outlook Express for e-mail, consider using a program called Hotmail Popper to manage your Hotmail account without having to access the Web. Learn more about this handy program at www.boolean.ca/hotpop/.

Did You Know?

Some Internet service providers feature Web-based e-mail access for their subscribers. Go to your ISP's Web site to see if it has a way for you to log in and check your e-mail.

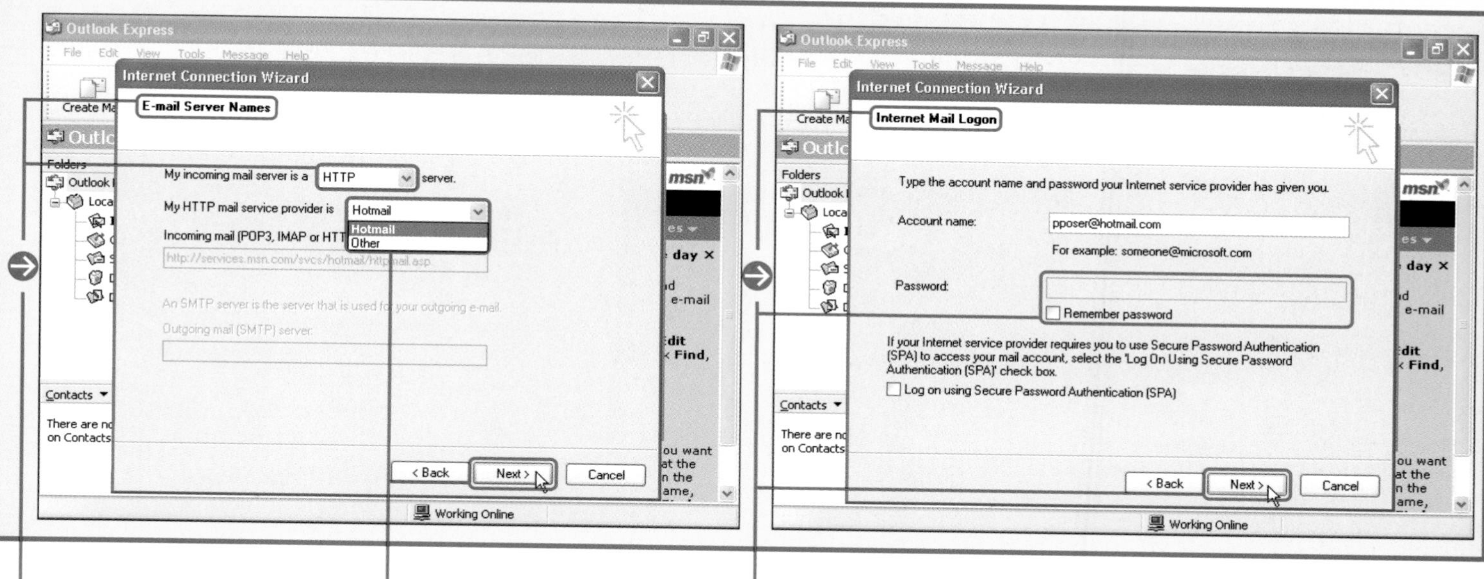

- The Internet Connection Wizard prompts you to specify e-mail server names.

7. Click here and click HTTP.
8. Click here and select Hotmail.
9. Click Next.

- The Internet Connection Wizard prompts you to enter your logon information.

10. If you share this computer with others, leave the Password box blank and click this check box to remove the check mark.
11. Click Next.

- The Wizard displays a message indicating that you have successfully entered the information required to set up your account.

12. Click Finish.

- The Internet Connection Wizard saves your settings and returns you to the Internet Accounts dialog box.

SEND PLAIN TEXT messages

DIFFICULTY LEVEL

Many computer users like to send messages with colored text, graphics, and fancy backgrounds. But all of these enhancements add to the size of the message and slow down its transmission speed. It travels more slowly from your computer to the recipient's mail server and from the mail server to the recipient's computer. In addition, it consumes more storage space. To trim the size of the messages you send, consider sending plain text messages, as shown here.

More Options!

This task shows how to enter a setting for sending all messages as plain text. You can leave the setting as is and choose the plain text or HTML option for individual messages. Before sending a message, click Format and then click either Plain Text for text-only messages or Rich Text for HTML enhancements, such as graphics and text formatting.

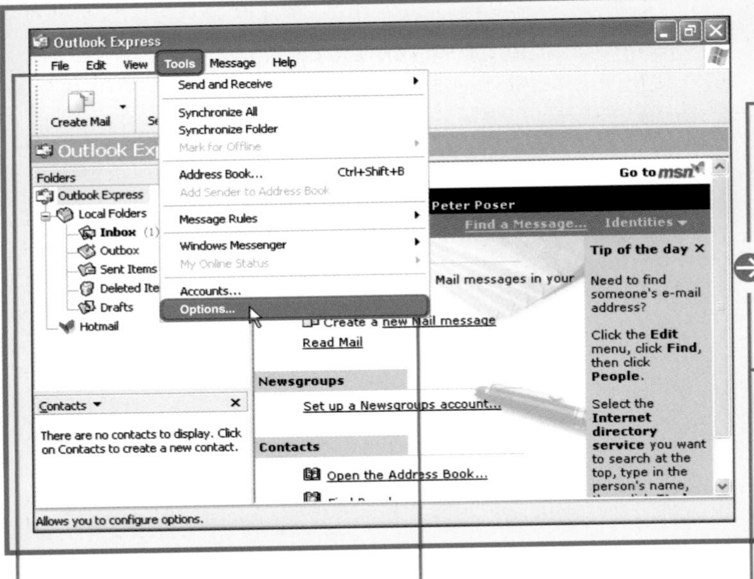

① In Outlook Express, click Tools.

② Click Options.

○ The Options dialog box appears.

③ Click the Send tab.

④ Click Plain Text.

⑤ Click OK.

○ Outlook Express saves the setting and now sends all messages in the plain text format.

RECEIVE PLAIN TEXT messages

DIFFICULTY LEVEL

Many e-mail messages, especially spam messages, contain fancy text, background graphics, animations, and sometimes even programming code that spammers can use to verify your e-mail address and perform other activities without your approval. To keep the messages you receive free of this additional content, consider choosing to receive only the text portion of a message, as shown here. By choosing to receive plain text messages, you instruct your e-mail program to strip out any enhancements.

More Options!

If you are concerned about e-mail viruses in Outlook Express, click Tools, click Options, and click the Security tab to check and/or change the security settings for incoming messages. Also, consider installing an anti-virus program that scans all incoming and outgoing e-mail messages, as explained in task #95 and task #96.

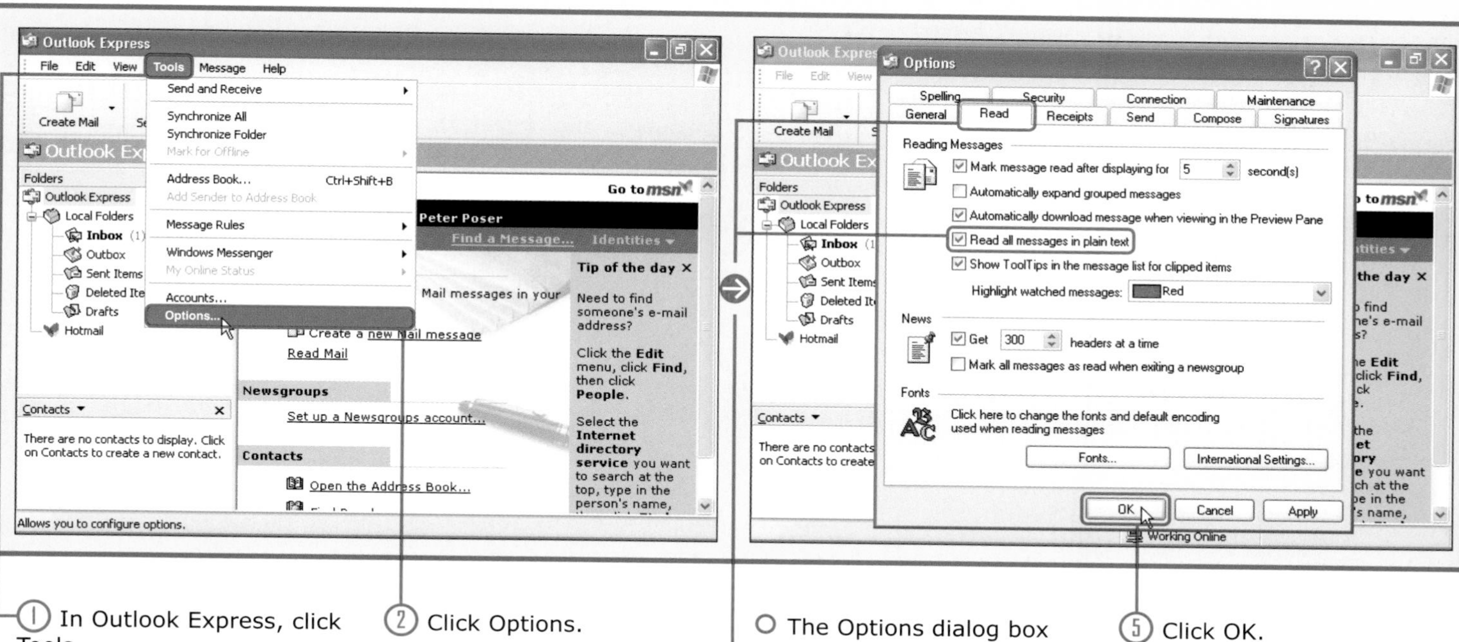

1. In Outlook Express, click Tools.
2. Click Options.

- The Options dialog box appears.

3. Click the Read tab.
4. Click Read all messages in plain text.
5. Click OK.

- Outlook Express saves your changes. When you receive a message Outlook Express displays only the text, using placeholders for any other content.

Hide the preview pane for INCREASED SECURITY

Your Outlook Express preview pane can give you a quick look at the contents of a message, but it can also enable a message to breach your system's security. Some messages can contain computer code that automatically sends a reply to the sender indicating that you read the message. This helps spammers verify that your e-mail account is active, so they continue sending you unsolicited messages and perhaps even sell your e-mail address to other spammers.

If you receive spam regularly, consider turning off the preview pane. With the pane hidden, you can select a message without opening or reading the message, and then you can choose to delete the message, if it appears to originate from a suspicious source. Of course, you can always choose to read a message by double-clicking its Subject line and opening the message in its own window. This task shows you how to turn off the preview pane in Outlook Express. Other e-mail programs offer similar options.

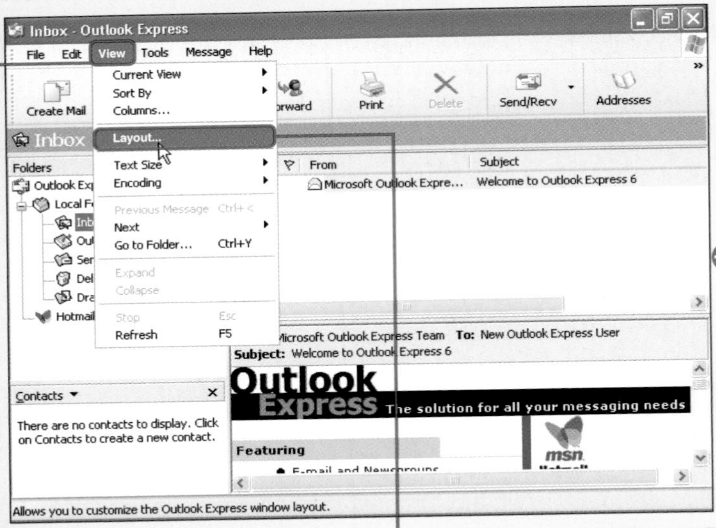

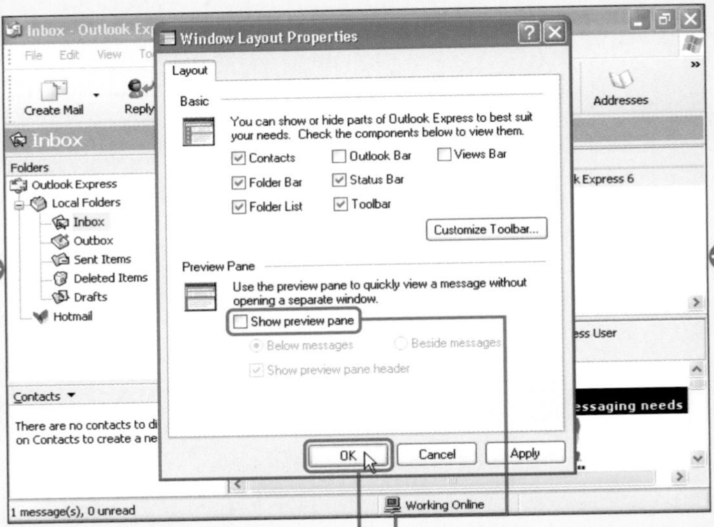

1. Click View.
2. Click Layout.

- The Window Layout Properties dialog box appears.

3. Click Show preview pane to clear the check mark from the box.
4. Click OK.

Caution!

Viruses transmitted through e-mail typically hide in e-mail attachments. You should scan any attached files for viruses, as explained in task #98, before opening or running the file.

More Options!

The Outlook Express window is completely customizable. Click View and then click Layout. In the Window Layout Properties dialog box, you can turn any of the window elements on or off, including the Outlook Bar and the contacts list, or click the Customize button for more options.

More Options!

Some e-mail programs are less vulnerable to viruses than others. If you are willing to change e-mail programs, check out Mozilla Thunderbird at www.mozilla.org/projects/thunderbird/ and The Bat! at www.ritlabs.com.

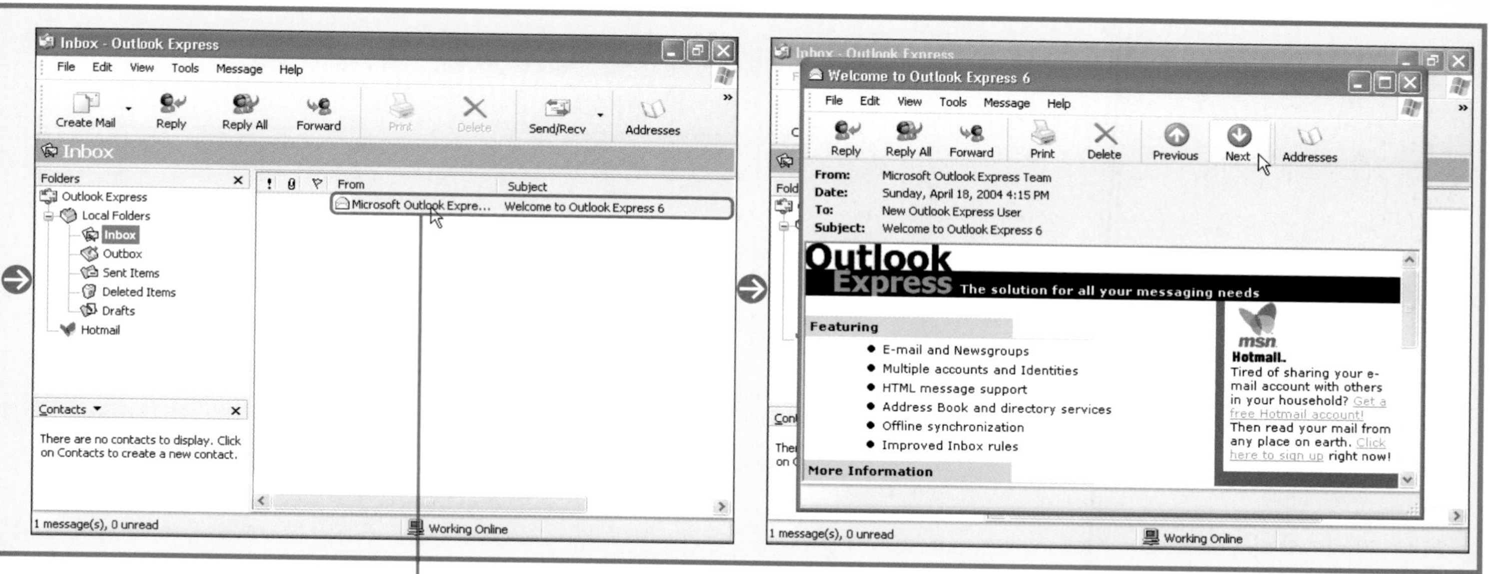

- The preview pane disappears.

5. To read a message, double-click its description.

- The message appears in its own window.

Block SPAM

Spam is unsolicited e-mail — computerized junk mail — and it is a very costly and time-consuming annoyance. Some anti-spam groups estimate that more than 40 percent of all e-mail is spam, and the percentage is growing. Businesses report that they spend more than $10 billion a year combating spam and lose more than $4 billion a year in productivity. Spam also afflicts home users, stuffing their e-mail boxes with ads for pornography, sexual enhancements, low-interest mortgages, and a host of other sometimes fraudulent products and services.

People typically become targets of spam when they enter their e-mail addresses to register at a particular Web site or enter a contest. But even if you do not give out your e-mail addresses, spammers can track you down with mass mailings to random addresses. Merely opening one of these messages can send a confirmation that your e-mail address is valid and active, thus making you a prime target. This task shows you how to download and install Spam Bully for Outlook or Outlook Express to reduce the amount of spam you receive.

BLOCK A SENDER'S E-MAIL

1. Type **www.spambully.com** and press Enter.

2. Click the Download link and follow the onscreen instructions to download and install Spam Bully.

   ○ Spam Bully installs its components as part of Outlook or Outlook Express.

3. Run Outlook or Outlook Express.

   ○ Spam Bully adds its toolbar to Outlook or Outlook Express and displays its setup wizard.

4. Follow the wizard's instructions to specify your preferences.

DIFFICULTY LEVEL

More Options!

If you have a folder full of good mail or of spam, click the folder and then click the arrow to the right of the Train Filter button and click Learn this folder as spam or Learn this folder as good mail. This helps Spam Bully block spam and allow acceptable messages automatically.

More Options!

Outlook Express has a Block Senders list that blocks all e-mail that originates from a specific e-mail address. To add an e-mail address to the list, click the description of a message you received from the sender, click Message, and then click Block Sender.

More Options!

Spam Bully features an option to punish the spammer, but the punishment is mild. Spam Bully loads any Web pages recommended in the e-mail message several times without purchasing anything, theoretically increasing the cost of bandwidth to the spammer.

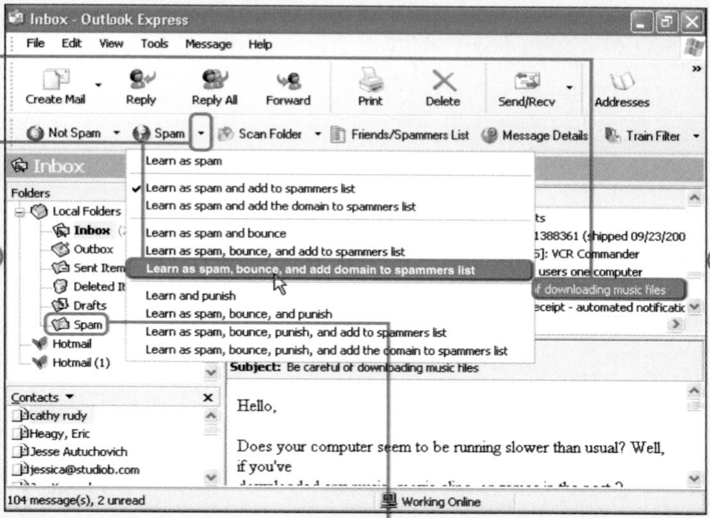

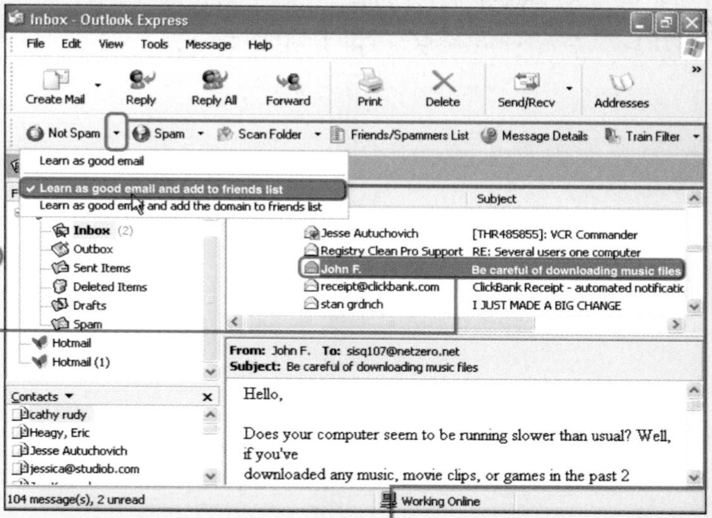

5 Click a message that you know is spam.

6 Click here and select the way you want Spam Bully to treat this message.

- Spam Bully moves all messages that it considers to be spam to the Spam folder.

ACCEPT A SENDER'S MAIL

7 To always accept mail from a particular sender, click a message from the sender.

8 Click here and select how you want Spam Bully to treat messages from this sender.

AUTOMATICALLY FILTER

incoming mail

If you prefer to keep your business and family correspondence separate or even place messages from every sender in a separate folder, you can create a folder for each group of messages and then drag messages from your inbox and drop them into their designated folders. You can also choose to have your e-mail program filter and sort the messages for you automatically. For example, you can have all messages from pzone317@illiterati.org automatically placed in a Relatives folder and have all messages from billiejoe421@coop324.com placed in a Business folder. You might even consider instructing your e-mail program to place all messages from a particular domain into the Deleted Items folder.

Most e-mail programs contain a filtering option that enables the program to filter and sort messages based on something in the sender's address, the message description, or the subject line. This task shows you how to set up a filter in Outlook Express. If you use a different e-mail program, check its help system for options.

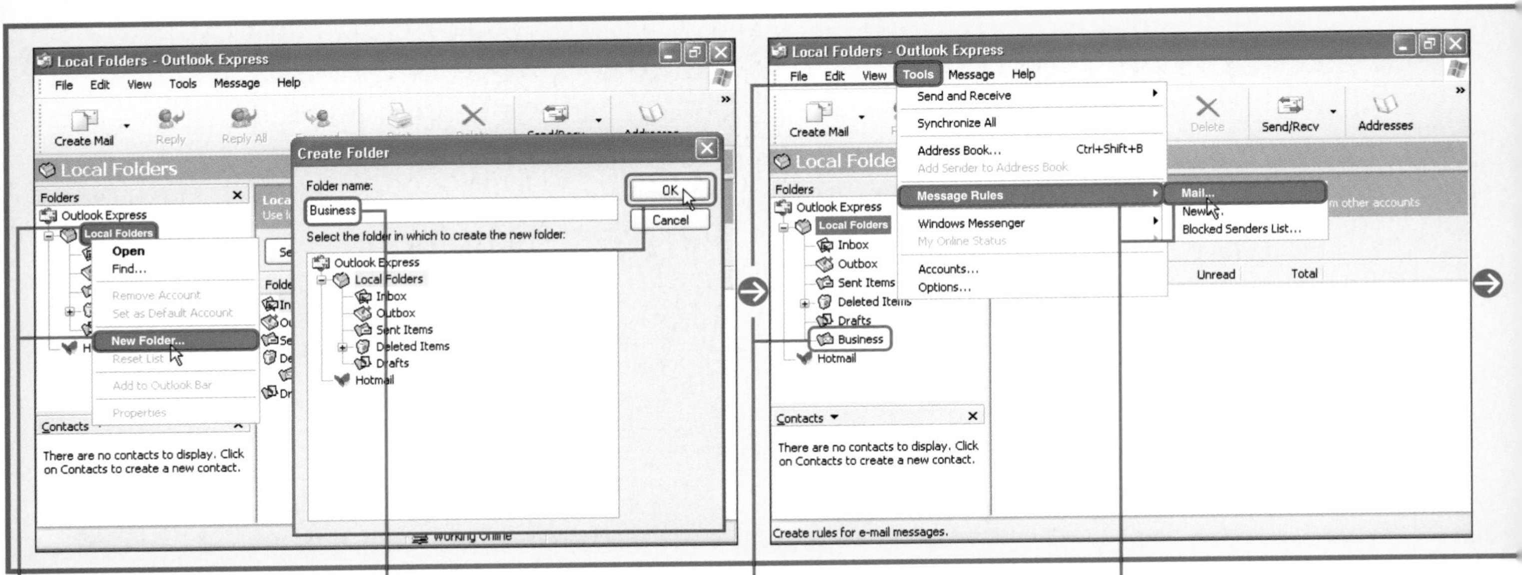

1. To create a new folder in Outlook Express, right-click the Local Folders folder.
2. Click New Folder.
3. Type a name for the folder.
4. Click OK.

- The new folder appears.

5. Click Tools.
6. Click Message Rules.
7. Click Mail.

DIFFICULTY LEVEL

More Options!

Scroll down through the list of conditions and actions and check out all of the available options. Near the end of the Actions list is the option Delete it from server, which is an excellent option to choose for known spammers. Outlook Express can delete the message from the server without your ever seeing it.

Caution!

Many users set a filter when they go on vacation that automatically notifies a sender that the recipient is on vacation. This is a bad idea. If you receive spam, your automatic reply confirms your e-mail address to the spammer. It also notifies potential crooks that you are not home. Consider sending a notification to only those people who need to know and whom you trust.

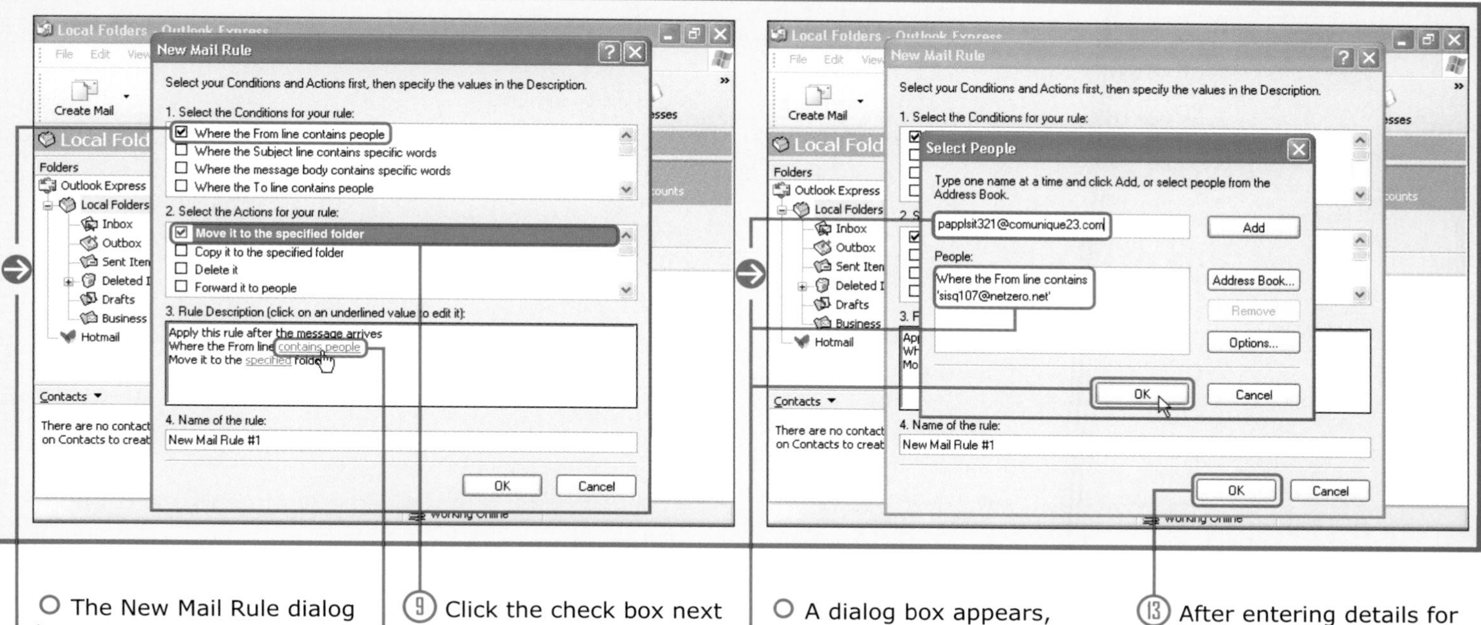

- The New Mail Rule dialog box appears.

8 Click the check box next to each option you want the filter to consider.

9 Click the check box next to each action you want the filter to perform on the message.

10 Click the link for the condition or action you specified.

- A dialog box appears, prompting you to specify details about the condition or action.

11 Enter the requested details.

12 Click OK.

13 After entering details for all conditions and actions you set, click OK.

- When Outlook Express receives a message that meets the specified condition, it performs the specified actions on that message.

Compress
FILE ATTACHMENTS

If you attach files to your outgoing messages, try to limit the size of the file attachments to 1 to 3 megabytes (MB), especially if you send the file over a dial-up modem connection or the recipient receives the message over a dial-up modem connection. Otherwise, the message can take several minutes to send or receive, or your mail server or the recipient's mail server might reject the message because it exceeds its size limit. Many e-mail servers limit the size of e-mails to prevent system overloads.

If you have a large file or several files that you want to attach to an outgoing message, consider using WinZip to compress the file or files before sending them. Depending on the type of file, WinZip might be able to compress it down to as much as one-tenth of its original size. The compressed file not only travels much more quickly to its destination, but it takes less storage space on your computer, the recipient's computer, and the mail servers.

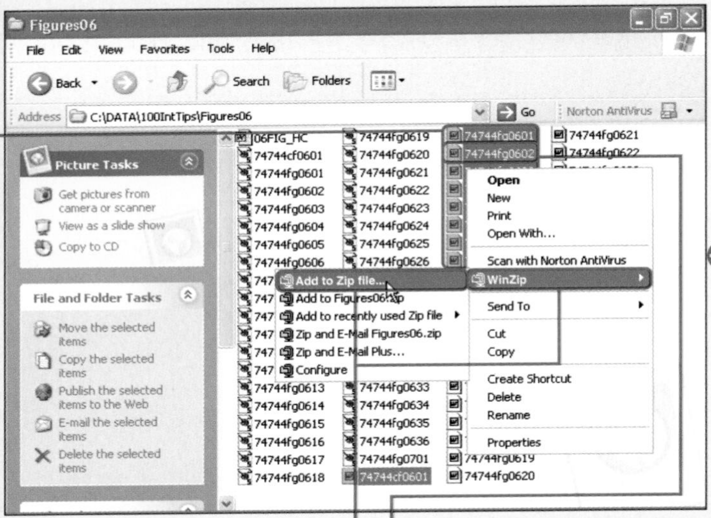

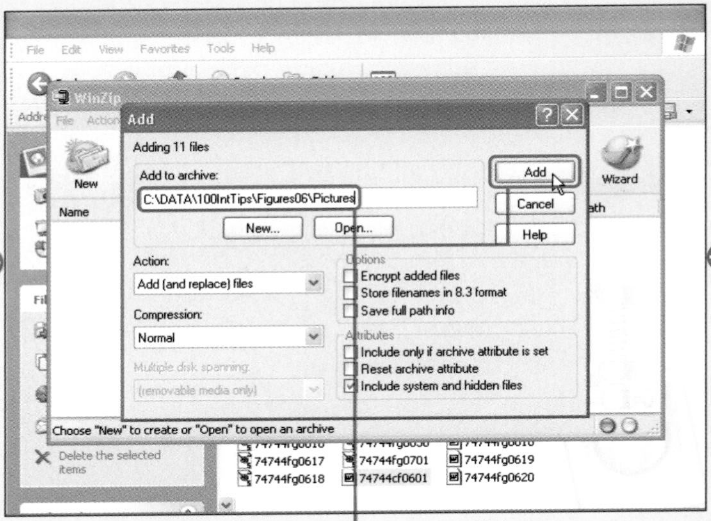

Note: You can obtain WinZip from www.winzip.com, as explained in task #22.

1. In My Computer, highlight the file or files you want to compress.
2. Right-click one of the selected files.
3. Click WinZip.
4. Click Add to Zip File.

- The Add dialog box appears.

5. Click at the end of the entry in the Add to archive box and type a name for the new Zip file.
6. Click the Add button.

DIFFICULTY LEVEL

Try This!

If you need to send a large file, consider using an instant messaging program to exchange the file, as explained in task #77. If you are sending the file to a business, it might have an FTP (File Transfer Protocol) server that enables you to upload files to it using an FTP program.

More Options!

WinZip's Add dialog box features a Compression drop-down list with options that enable you to choose the desired amount of compression. Choose the highest compression available to create the smallest Zip file.

Important!

For the recipient to access the compressed file or files, he or she must have WinZip or another program that can extract files from a WinZip file. In recent versions of Windows, including ME and XP, you can right-click a Zip file, click Open With, and click Compressed (zipped) Folders to access a Zip file's contents.

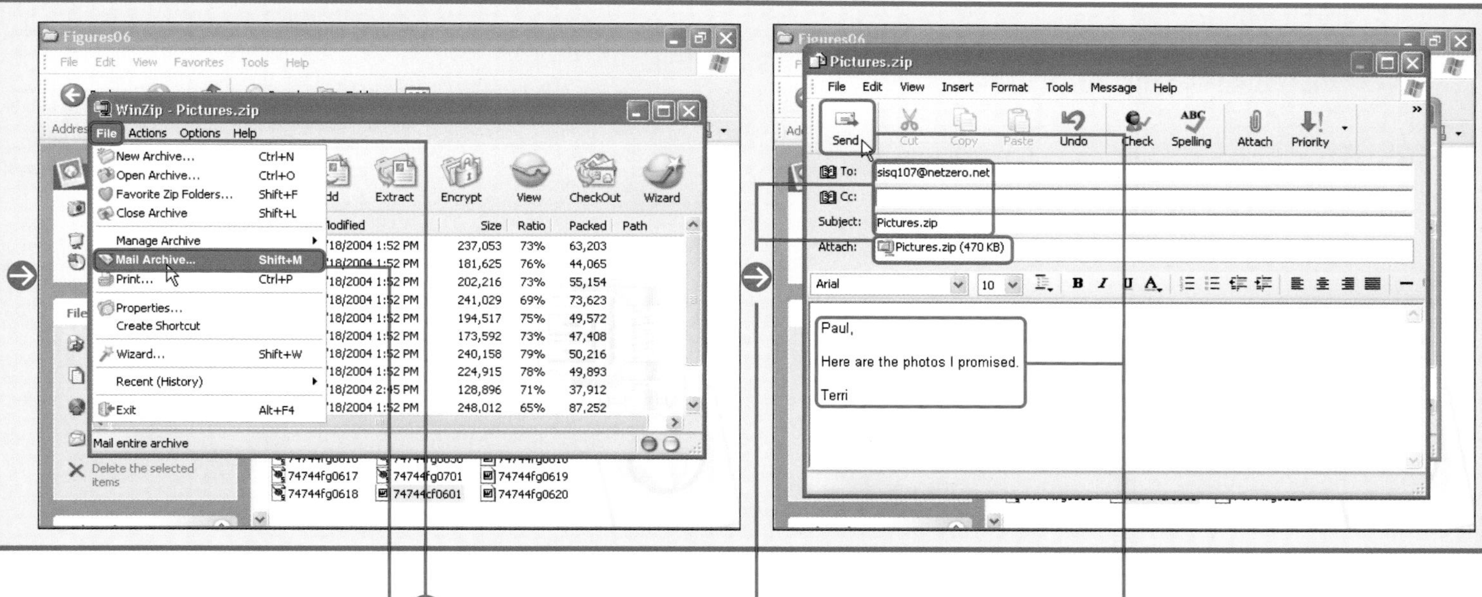

- The WinZip window shows the compressed files that the new Zip file contains.

7. Click File.
8. Click Mail Archive.

- WinZip starts your e-mail program and adds the Zip file as an attachment to a new message.

9. Specify message recipients and message description.

Note: See your e-mail program's documentation for details.

10. Type your message.
11. Click the Send button.

- Your e-mail program sends the message and attachment.

Keep PHOTOS SMALL

A single high-resolution photo taken with a relatively new digital camera typically results in a file that exceeds 1 megabyte. Higher resolution photos or scans saved as TIF files can be several megabytes in size. These files are suitable for producing high-quality photo prints, but many users never send photos intending the recipient to create photo prints. Most people send photos expecting the recipient to view the photo onscreen, and these high-resolution photos far exceed the quality needed for onscreen viewing. A smaller photo that has a lower resolution usually serves the purpose, and these files can be one-twentieth the size of the originals.

To make your photos suitable for online viewing and keep size to a minimum, consider resizing the photo. Most screens are set to display at 800 pixels by 600 pixels (800 x 600), so a photo resized to 640 x 480 takes up most of the screen. This task demonstrates the change in file size that results when you change the physical size of the image in Paint Shop Pro. Most digital image editors feature similar commands.

1. Open the original picture in your digital image-editing program.
2. Note the file's original size.

Note: If the file's size does not appear, right-click the file in My Computer and click Properties.

3. Click Image.
4. Click Resize.

Note: See your image-editing program's documentation for equivalent commands.

Try This!

Decrease the color depth or number of colors used to render the image onscreen. Decreasing the color depth from 16 million colors to 32 thousand or even 256 colors can render a decent looking photo and trim the file size down to a third of the original size.

More Options!

If a photo has a great deal of extraneous background, consider cropping out the background to focus in on the subject.

More Options!

Some digital cameras include a "small pictures" or "TV screen" mode to snap pictures at 640 x 480 pixels. Or, they may include software that can automatically resize images for you depending on the intended use.

Did You Know?

TIF image files save all the details needed to render a photo print, resulting in relatively large files. You can try to compress them, but compression often results in a file that is only slightly smaller than the original.

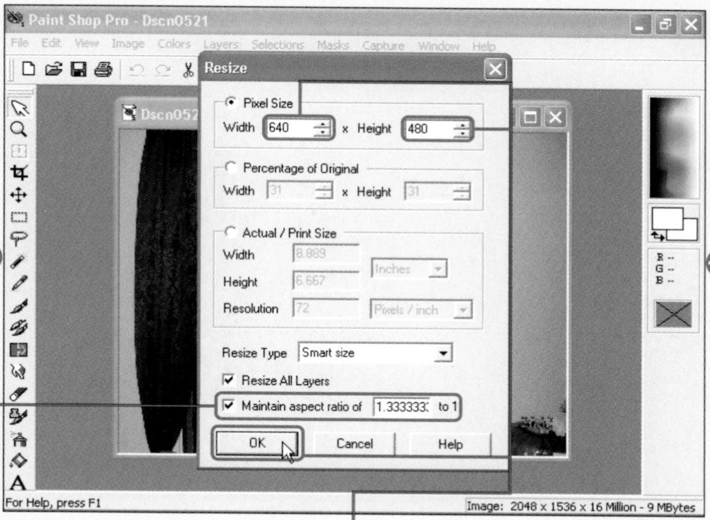

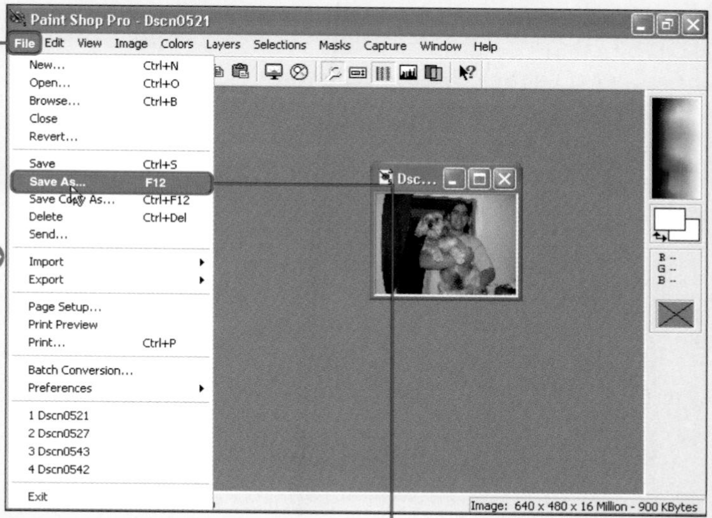

- The Resize dialog box appears.
- (5) Make sure you select the option to maintain the aspect ratio.
- (6) Click in the Width box and type 640.
- The entry in the Height box changes to 480.
- (7) Click OK.
- The digital image editor resizes the photo.
- (8) Click File.
- (9) Click Save As, and use the Save As dialog box to save the file using a different name.

Maintain your MAILBOXES

As you send, receive, and even delete e-mail messages, they can begin to stack up in your mailboxes and consume valuable storage space on your computer's hard drive. When you begin to notice a build-up or, better yet, on a regular basis, you should do some maintenance to permanently remove any messages you no longer need and then compact your e-mail folders to eliminate any unused space left by the deletions. E-mail maintenance not only frees up storage space but can also enhance the speed of your e-mail program and make it much easier for you to track down the messages you really need.

When you delete a message in most e-mail programs, the program dumps the message in a Deleted Items folder as a safety net, so as you work through this task, check the Deleted Items folder for any items you may want to permanently dispose of. When you delete items from the Deleted Items folder, the program typically deletes those items permanently. This task shows you how to removed deleted messages in Outlook Express.

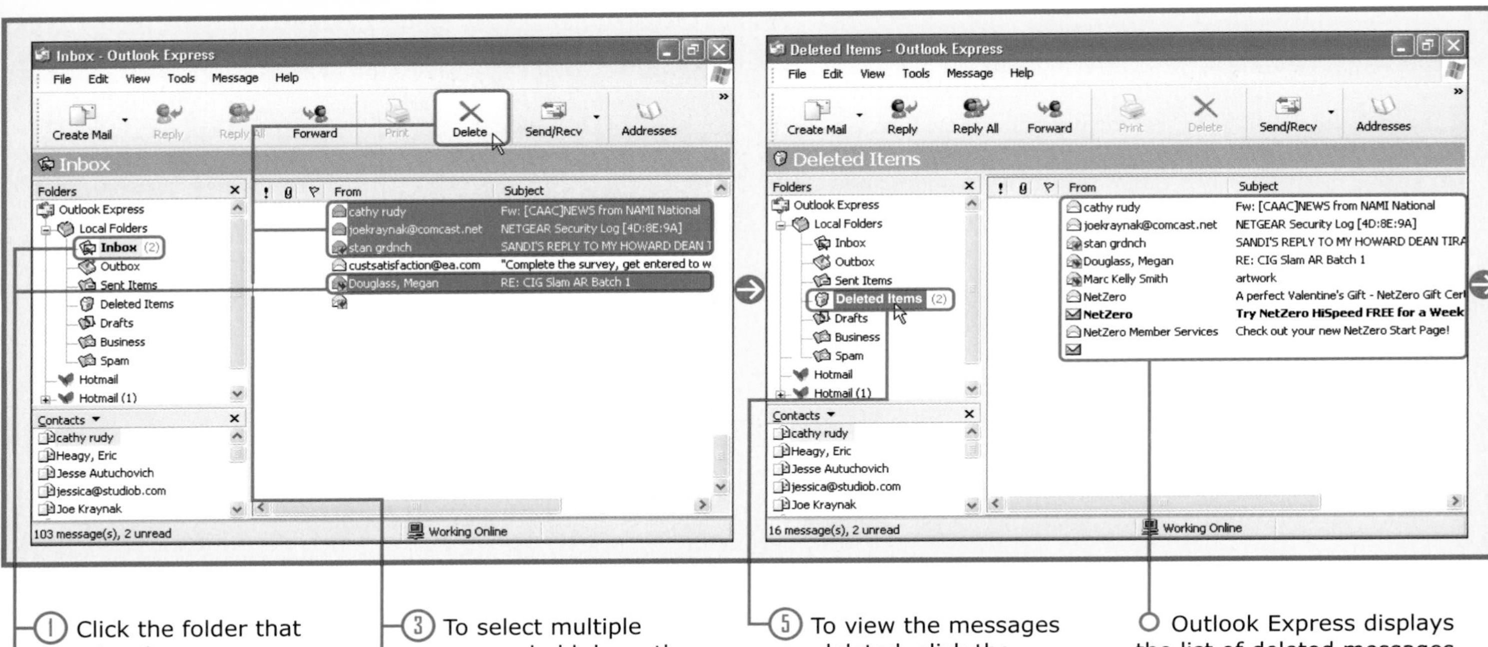

1. Click the folder that contains the messages you want to delete.
2. Click the message you want to delete.
3. To select multiple messages, hold down the Ctrl key while clicking the descriptions of additional messages.
4. Click the Delete button.

- The messages are moved to the Deleted Items folder.

5. To view the messages you deleted, click the Deleted Items folder.

- Outlook Express displays the list of deleted messages.

Try This!

When selecting messages to delete, press Ctrl+A to select all messages and then Ctrl+click the messages you do not want to delete.

More Options!

Outlook Express can automatically remove messages from the Deleted Items folder when you exit the program. Click Tools, click Options, and click the Maintenance tab. Click Empty messages from the 'Deleted Items' folder on exit (☐ changes to ☑). Click OK.

Caution!

The Maintenance tab in the Options dialog box has a Clean Up Now button that can automate e-mail maintenance for you, but it can be too thorough. It features an option for deleting the message bodies of all downloaded messages, which you may not be able to retrieve again.

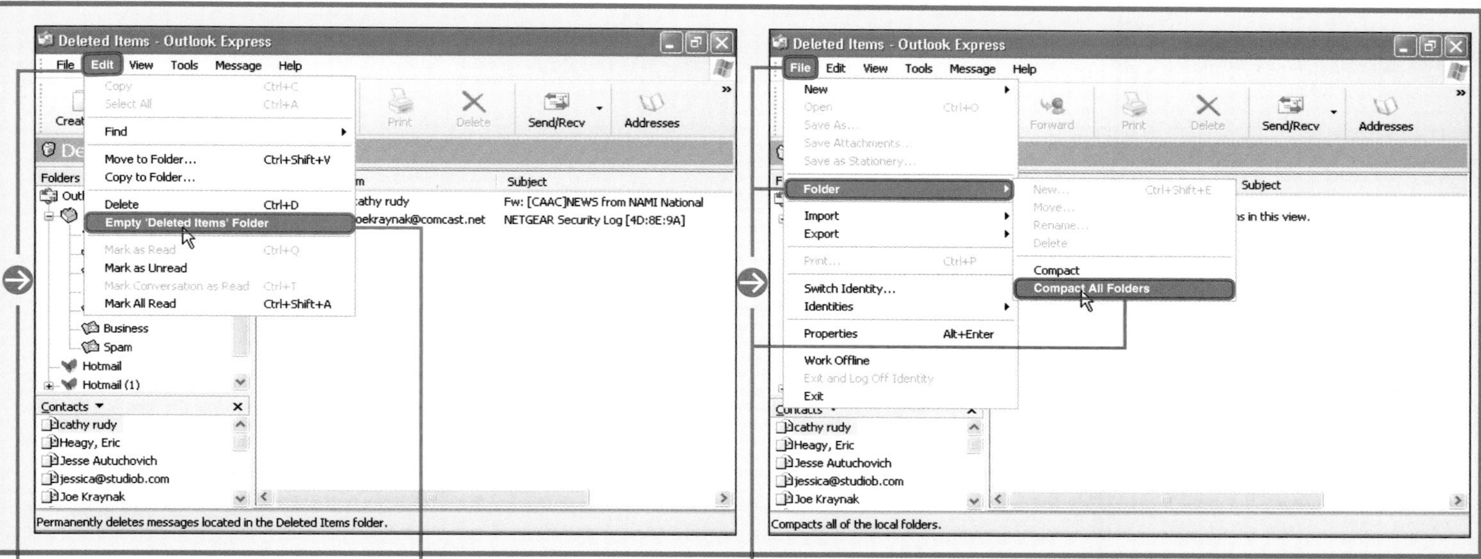

6 To permanently delete the messages, click Edit.

7 Click Empty 'Deleted Items' Folder.

- If asked to confirm, click Yes.

8 Click File.

9 Click Folder.

10 Click Compact All Folders.

- Outlook Express compacts the folders. This can take several minutes, depending on the number of messages you deleted and the size of the folders.

Keep in Touch with Instant Messaging

America Online Instant Messenger, or AIM, has always been one of America Online's most popular features. With instant messaging, you type a message to a friend, relative, or acquaintance who is also online and is running an instant messaging program, and then you click a button to send the message. The message pops up on the other user's screen and typically initiates a conversation. Most instant messaging programs also support voice chat; on a system equipped with a sound card and a headset, complete with earphone(s) and a close-talk microphone (for clarity), you can carry on a voice conversation, just as if you were talking on the phone.

Many Internet users take advantage of instant messaging to keep in touch with friends and family without running up a huge phone bill, and most users know the basics. However, you can learn additional techniques and tips to tap the full power of instant messaging. In this chapter, you learn where to obtain an instant messaging program that can talk to a wide variety of other instant messaging programs, including AIM and MSN Messenger. You learn how to save conversation transcripts, use voice features, videoconference, play two-player games, exchange large files that might be too large for e-mail, check stock alerts, and protect your privacy and system security.

With the right instant messaging programs and the tasks in this chapter, you have everything you need to communicate effectively, inexpensively, and securely with friends, family, acquaintances, and business associates all around the world.

TOP 100

TOP 100

Install a universal INSTANT MESSAGING CLIENT

America Online's instant messaging feature is so popular that it naturally migrated to the Internet and inspired a host of companies to develop their own instant messaging programs. Some of the more popular choices are MSN Messenger, Yahoo! Messenger, and ICQ ("I seek you"). AIM and these other instant messaging programs can connect you with others to chat live online, but each program uses a distinct protocol to communicate. If you have some friends who use MSN Messenger and others who use AIM, for example, you need to have both programs running on your computer. When you add Yahoo! Messenger and ICQ to the mix, you now need to run at least three programs — ICQ supports AIM.

Fortunately, you can find programs on the Internet that support multiple instant messaging protocols, enabling you to communicate with all of your friends and family using a single program. This task introduces one of the better universal instant messaging programs, Trillian, and shows you where to download a free copy of it.

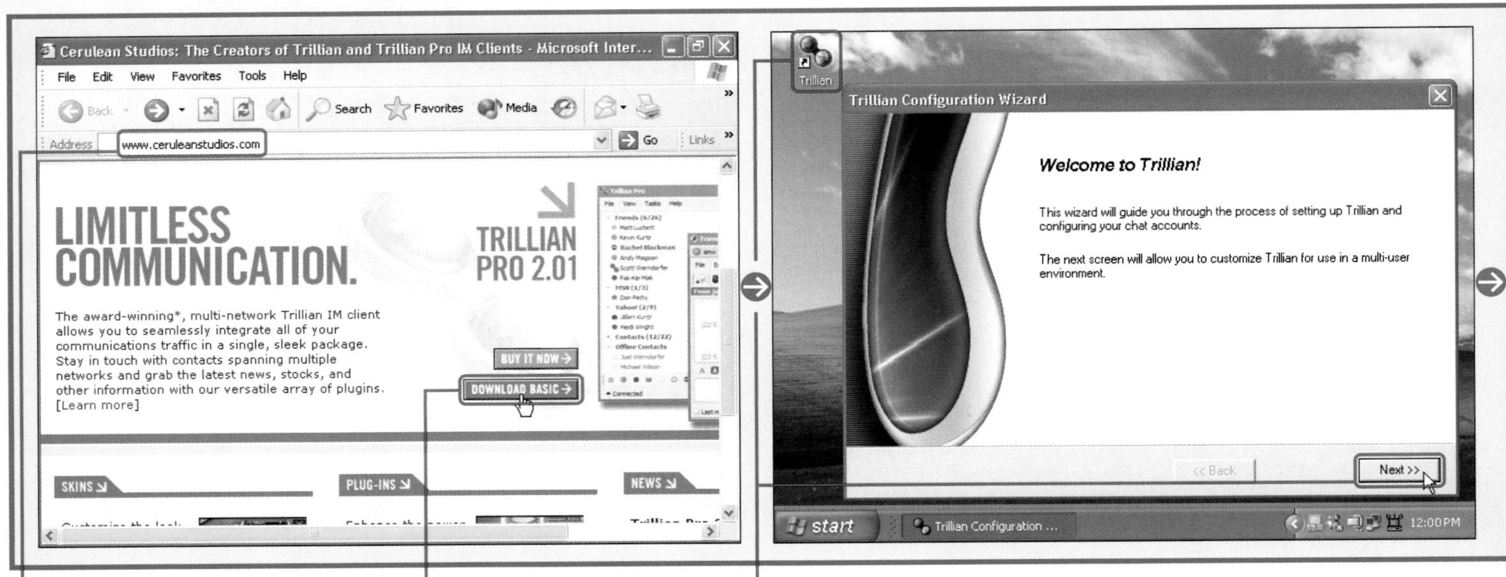

1. Type **www.ceruleanstudios.com** and press Enter.

2. Click the Download Basic button and follow the onscreen instructions to download and install Trillian Basic.

- The installation routine places an icon for Trillian on the desktop.

3. Double-click the Trillian desktop shortcut.

- The first time you run Trillian, it displays the Trillian Configuration Wizard.

4. Click Next and follow the setup wizard's instructions to enter the requested settings and preferences.

Note: You must register for an AIM, MSN Messenger, Yahoo! Messenger, or ICQ account before setting up the service in Trillian, but once you have a screen name, the wizard helps you enter the information to connect to those services.

#71

DIFFICULTY LEVEL

Did You Know?

Trillian works best for users who already use two or more instant messaging programs. Trillian's Configuration Wizard not only helps you establish connections with various networks, but also retrieves your buddy lists from those networks.

Attention!

As of this writing, Trillian supports only basic features of AIM and MSN Messenger, including text-based instant messaging and file sharing. It does not support voice transmissions or videoconferencing, so keep AIM and MSN Messenger installed on your computer if you plan to use those features.

More Options!

Integrity Messenger, which you can download from www.integritymessenger.com, is another fine multi-network instant messaging program.

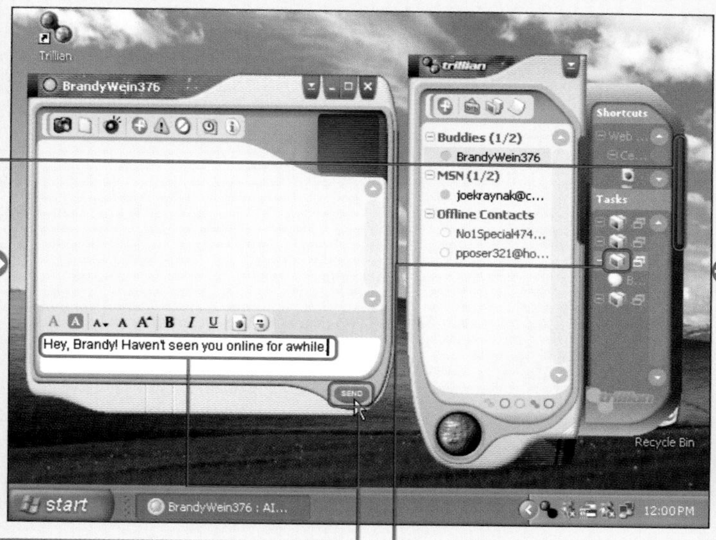

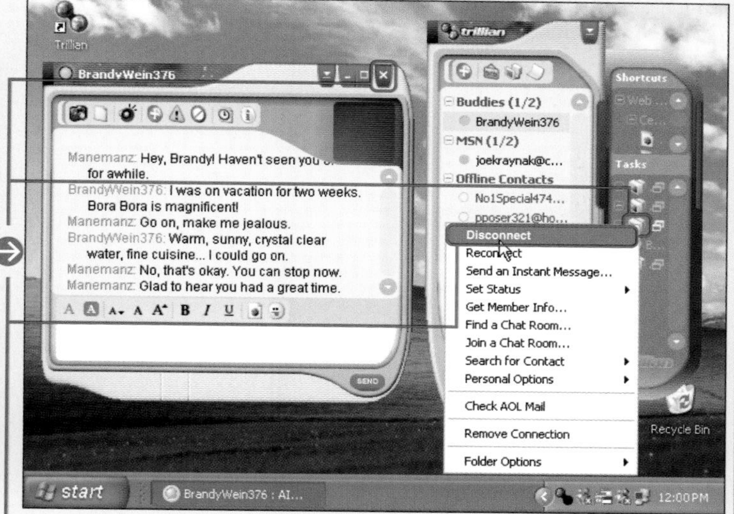

- Trillian appears.
5. Click the drawer bar.
- Clicking the drawer bar toggles the drawer open and closed.
6. Rest the mouse pointer on an icon to view the account name, and then click the account you want to use.
- An instant message window appears.
7. Type your message here.
8. Click Send.
9. To disconnect from an instant messaging network, click Close.
10. Right-click the connection.
11. Click Disconnect.
- Trillian disconnects from the instant messaging network and grays out the icon for the connection. To reconnect, right-click the icon and click Reconnect.

View conversation TRANSCRIPTS

If most of your conversations consist of small talk, you might have no need or desire to save your discussions for future reference. However, if you have intimate conversations with friends or intriguing discussions with colleagues and confidants, then you may want to save your conversations and view them later. This is especially useful if you are using instant messaging to obtain answers or technical support.

All instant messaging programs provide a way of capturing and saving a conversation *transcript*. The program typically saves the transcript as a text-only file that you can open in any word processor or a text editor such as Windows Notepad. Trillian automatically records every instant messaging session you have with a particular person and stores a complete transcription history in a separate text file. You can choose to view the message history, or transcript, at any time during or after your current session. If you are using a different instant messaging program, check its help system for instructions on how to save and view conversation transcripts.

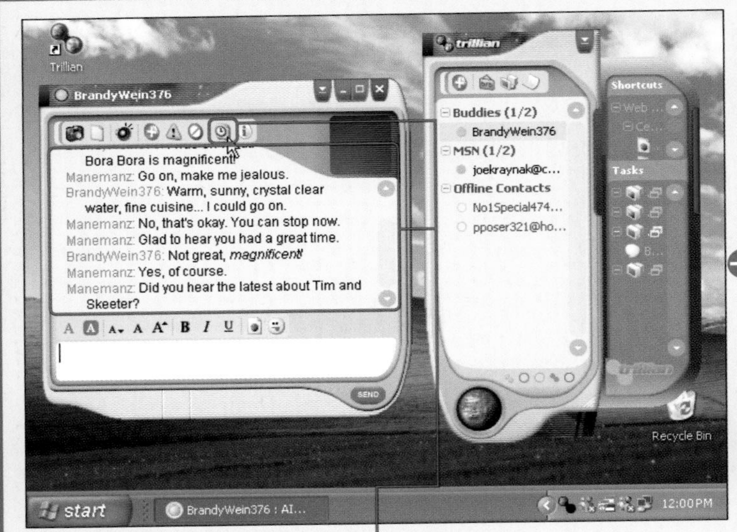

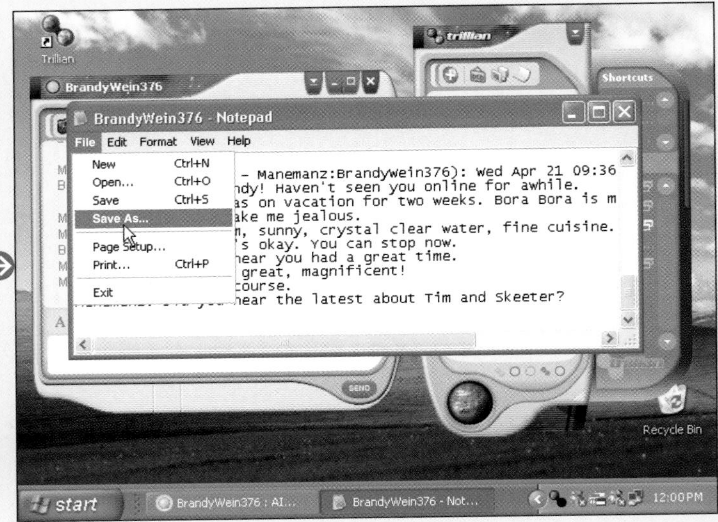

VIEW TRANSCRIPT FROM TRILLIAN

Note: This example requires the use of Trillian software. To obtain and install Trillian, see task # 71.

① Carry on your instant messaging discussion as you normally do.

② To view a transcript of your conversations with this person, click the Message History button.

○ Notepad runs and displays the transcript of conversations you have had with this person, including the current conversation.

Try This!

Go to www.ceruleanstudios.com and check out the available skins and plug-ins you can download and install to customize Trillian. Skins enhance the Trillian interface with decorative borders and color schemes. Some of these skins can actually enhance usability by making the controls seem more user-friendly.

More Options!

To enter preferences for Trillian, get help, access the Connection Manager, or change the settings for your instant messaging programs, click the Options button ( ) and select the desired command.

Remove It!

If other people have access to your computer, your private chats with other users might not be so private. You can disable automatic logging. Click the Options button ( ), click Preferences, click Message History, open the Automatically Log drop-down list, and then select None. Click OK to finish.

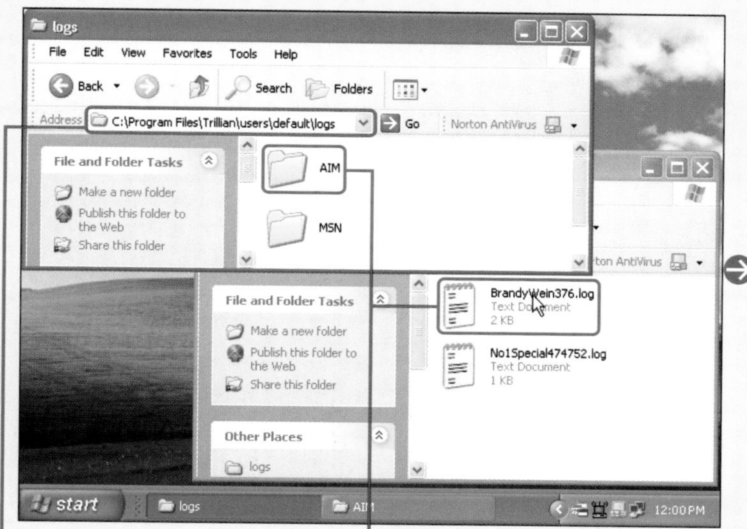

BrandyWein376.log - Notepad

File Edit Format View Help

Session Start (AIM - Manemanz:BrandyWein376): Wed May 19 17:12:55 2004
BrandyWein376: Hey, Mark! What's up?
Manemanz: Hi, Brandy. Boy, am I glad to hear from you.
BrandyWein376: Of course, everyone is.
Manemanz: No, really, I'm having serious computer problems at work.
BrandyWein376: You, too, huh? What's your computer doing?
Manemanz: It runs slow all the time and then keeps giving me messages that I'm running low on memory.
BrandyWein376: Did you install any new software?
Manemanz: Nope, that's what's so weird.
BrandyWein376: And you probably did a virus scan, so I won't even ask.
Manemanz: Yep, did the virus scan... came out clean.
BrandyWein376: Did you try disabling memory resident programs?
Manemanz: I wouldn't know where to start. How do you do that?
BrandyWein376: Do Start/Run, type msconfig, and press Enter.
BrandyWein376: Click the Services tab, click Hide All Microsoft Services, and click Disable All.
BrandyWein376: Then, click the Startup tab and click Disable All.
BrandyWein376: Click OK, restart your computer, and see what happens.
Manemanz: Okay, I'll give that a shot.
BrandyWein376: If the problem's gone, go back and enable whatever you disabled until you find the bugger that's causing the problem.
Manemanz: Sounds tedious.

OPEN OTHER TRANSCRIPTS

1. Run My Computer.
2. Navigate to the Program Files\Trillian\users\default\logs folder.
3. Double-click the folder for the desired IM service you used for the conversation.
4. Double-click the name of the user you conversed with.

- Notepad displays a transcript of all the conversations you have had with this person listed by date and time.

Place free PHONE CALLS

The four main instant messaging programs — AIM, MSN Messenger, Yahoo! Messenger, and ICQ — all support voice chat. With voice chat, you and the person with whom you are chatting establish a direct connection between your two computers and talk as if you were speaking on the telephone. Of course, each computer needs standard audio hardware, including a sound card and a headset — or speakers and a microphone.

To use voice chat, you must connect using the instant messaging service's software. In other words, to carry on a voice conversation with a friend who uses AIM, you must run AIM, as well. This task shows you how to initiate a voice conversation using AIM. The other three instant messaging programs require very similar steps. Expect a slight delay in the time it takes your voice to travel to its destination, especially if you have a dial-up modem connection.

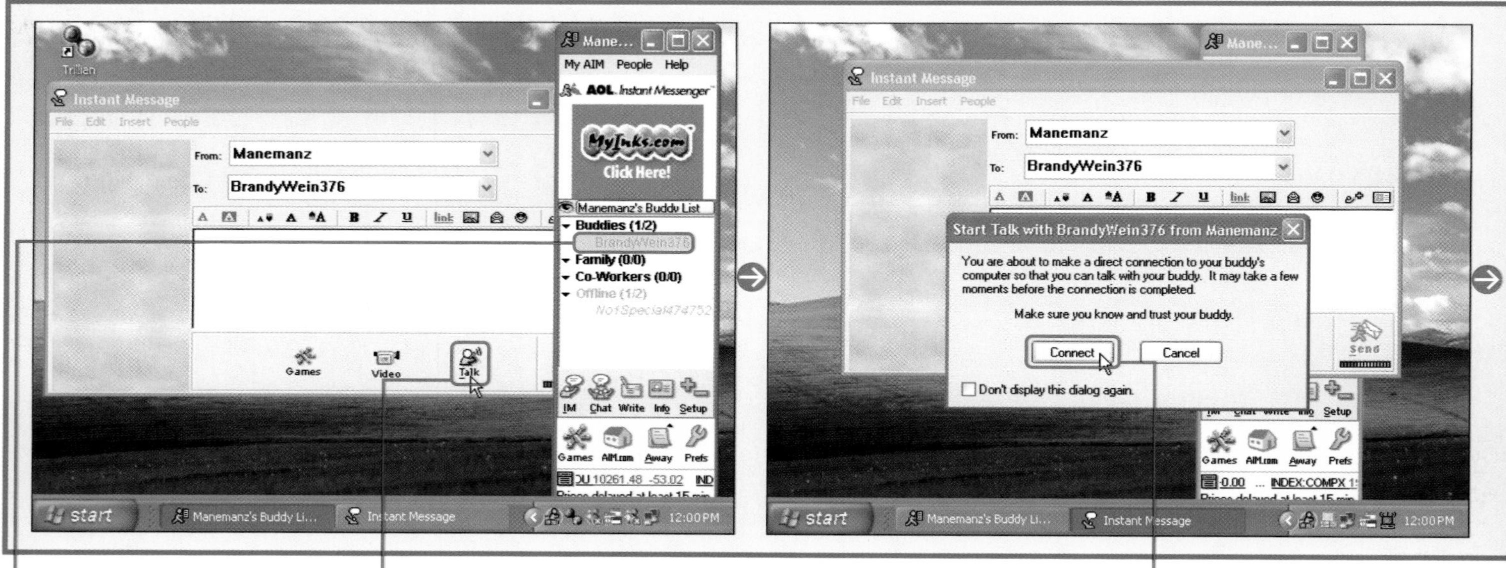

① In AIM, double-click the name of a buddy who is currently online.

○ The Instant Message window appears.

② Click the Talk button.

○ The Start Talk with dialog box appears, indicating that voice talk requires a direct connection that could make your computer vulnerable.

③ Click the Connect button.

Caution!

Establish a direct connection only with people you know and trust. A direct connection can open your system to another user, giving him or her access to files on your computer.

More Options!

You do not actually call a phone when you use instant messaging for voice chat, but recent versions of AIM and MSN Messenger do enable you to dial a phone over the Internet for a few cents per minute. In AIM, click People and click Contact using AIM Phone. In MSN, click Actions and click Make a Phone Call.

Attention!

Talking over the Internet is more like talking on a walkie-talkie than on a phone. Learn to wait until your buddy is finished talking before you begin talking. If you talk while your buddy's voice is arriving, your sound card can muddle the signal, making it incomprehensible.

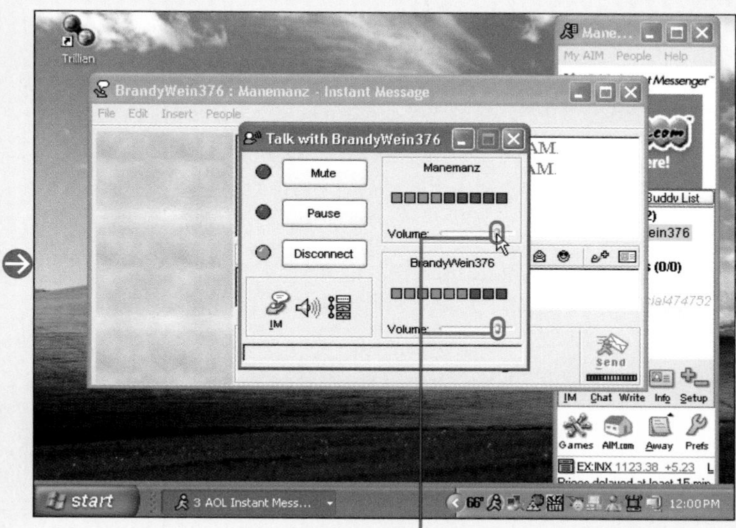

○ The Talk with dialog box appears, indicating that you are now connected.

④ Drag the sliders to control the speaker and microphone volumes.

⑤ To end a conversation, click Disconnect.

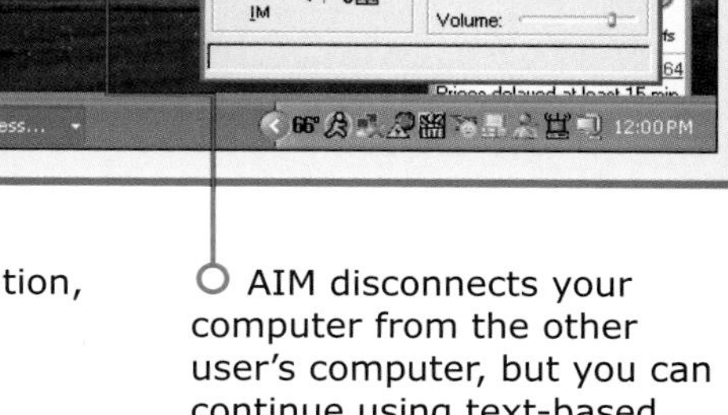

○ AIM disconnects your computer from the other user's computer, but you can continue using text-based instant messaging.

VIDEOCONFERENCE

via instant messaging

Although most phones do not enable you to see the person on the other phone, most instant messaging programs do support videoconferencing. To take advantage of this feature, you must equip your computer with a video camera, commonly called a *Webcam*. You can purchase a Webcam at most electronics or computer stores, including Best Buy. Most Webcams include a built-in microphone and plug into the USB or FireWire port on your computer, making installation very easy. In most cases, you can plug in the camera and start videoconferencing immediately. Of course, for you to see the other person, he or she must install a Webcam, as well.

After you equip your system with a Webcam, you can videoconference with others who use a compatible videoconferencing program. You have the best chance of connecting with people who use the same instant messaging program. As with voice chat, when you videoconference, your computer establishes a direct connection with the other user's computer, so choose to videoconference only with users whom you trust.

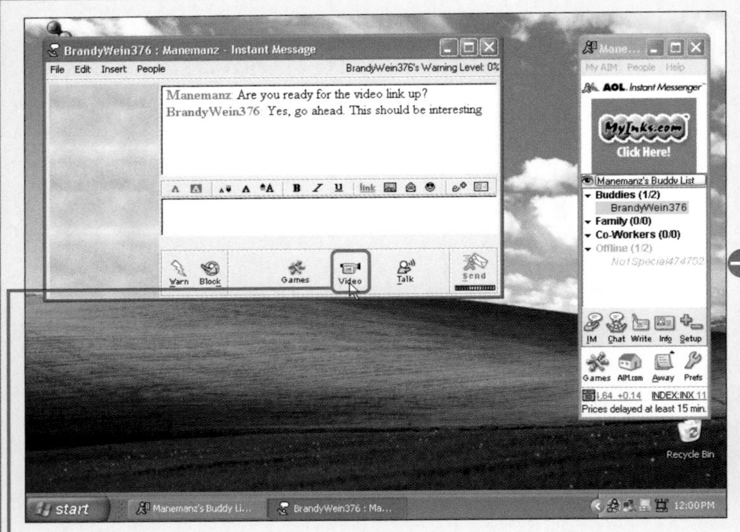

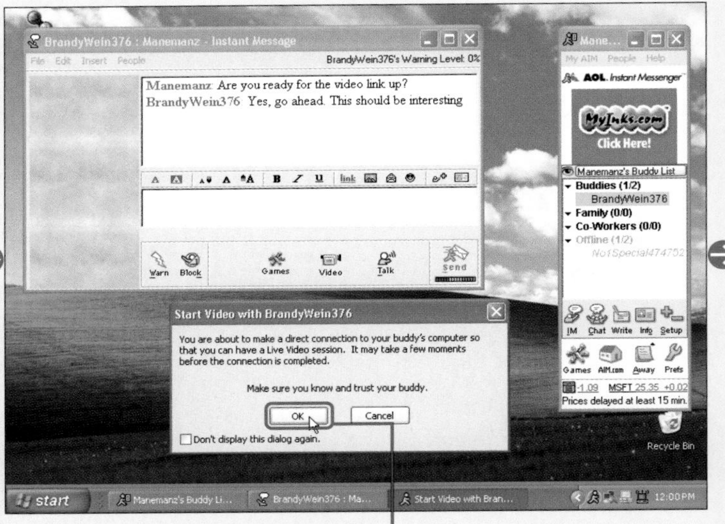

1 After connecting with another AIM user, click the Video button.

○ The Start Video dialog box appears, indicating that you are about to make a direct connection with the other person's computer.

2 If you trust the other person, click OK.

○ AIM triggers a dialog box on the other person's computer inviting the person to establish a video connection.

DIFFICULTY LEVEL

More Options!

To test and adjust your camera, click File, IM Preferences. The AOL Instant Messenger Preferences dialog box appears. Scroll down the Category list and click Live Video. Click the Video/Audio Tuning button, and follow the onscreen instructions.

Attention!

Various problems can prevent you from establishing a video hookup with another person. If you have problems, go to AIM's Web site at www.aim.com and click the Video IM link.

Try This!

To enhance image quality, place your video camera directly in front of you and make sure your face is sufficiently illuminated with light from behind the camera. Most digital Webcams allow you to adjust the focus by rotating the ring around the lens.

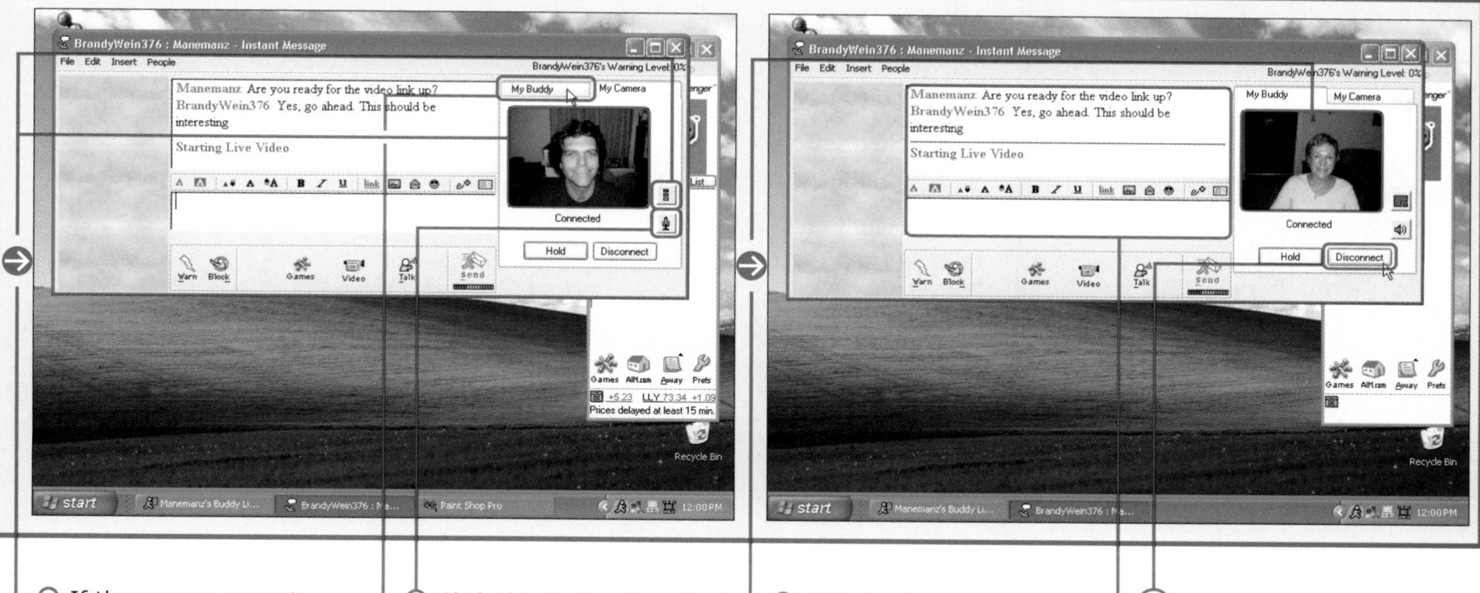

- If the person accepts, AIM displays the My Camera tab with your video input.
- Click this button to adjust the video quality.
- Click this button to adjust the volume.
- ③ Click the My Buddy tab.
- AIM displays the video input from the other person's computer.
- ④ When you are done talking, click Disconnect.
- After disconnecting, you can still carry on text-based instant messaging.

PLAY GAMES
with your buddies

Instant messaging can be very entertaining, but many instant messaging programs feature interactive video games to further enhance your experience. AIM is one of the best instant messaging services for playing games. It features more than a dozen board games, puzzles, and arcade games that you can play alone or with a buddy online. These games can keep you and your buddies entertained for hours, especially if you experience any lulls in the conversation. You can access all of the games directly from the AIM window, as shown in this task.

MSN Messenger, Yahoo! Messenger, and ICQ all feature games, as well, although the steps you use to access the games vary greatly, especially the steps to access multiplayer games. The tips on the next page explain how to access the games features of these other instant messaging programs. If you need additional information, check out the instant messaging program's home page on the Web.

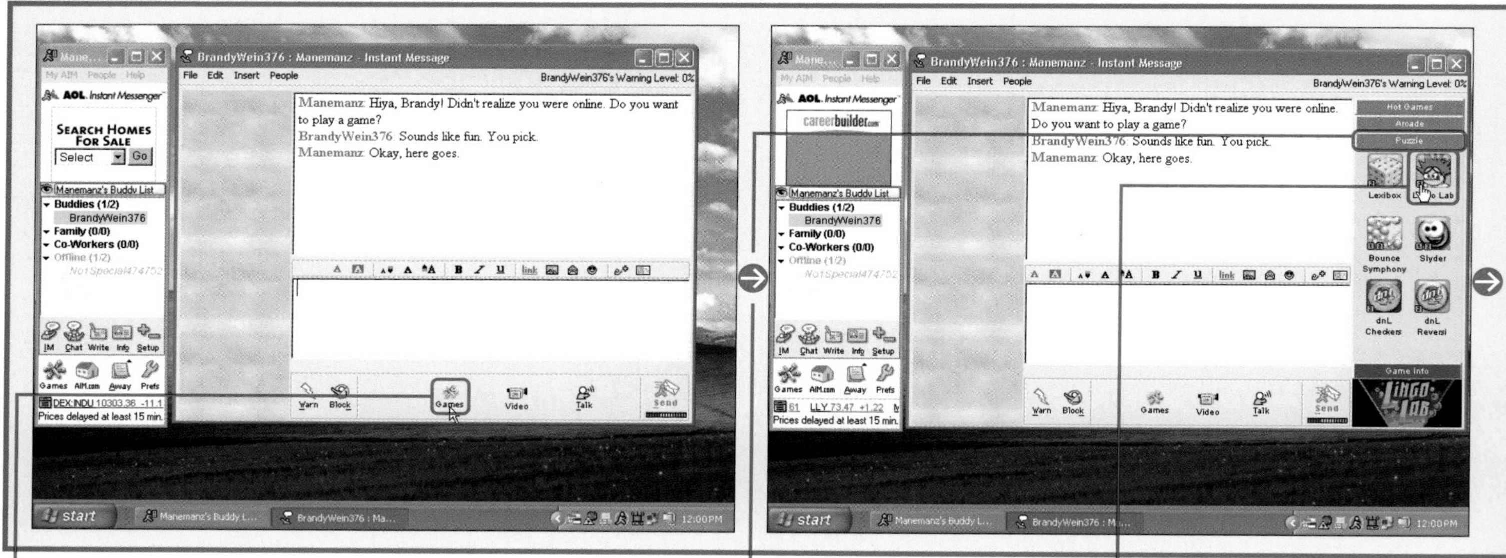

1. In AIM's Instant Message window, click the Games button.

Note: If you are not already using AIM, you can download a free copy from www.aim.com.

- The Games panel appears.

2. Click the tab for the type of game you want to play.

- AIM displays icons for the games in the selected group. The number indicates the 1-player or 2-player version.

3. Click the icon for the game you want to play or click the number to specify the 1- or 2-player version.

DIFFICULTY LEVEL

Check It Out!

Yahoo! Messenger also features games through its IMVironments add-ons. Type **messenger.yahoo.com** in your browser's Address bar, press Enter, and then click the link for IMVironments to check out and optionally download IMVironments.

Apply It!

Like AIM, MSN Messenger provides access to its games directly from the Messenger window. Click the MSN Games tab, which connects you to MSN Games by Zone.com, where you can click the link for the free game you want to play.

Apply It!

ICQ features online games, as well. To access the games area, click the Main button (), click Xtraz Center, and click the Games button. Click Single Player or Multiplayer, and click the GO link for the desired game.

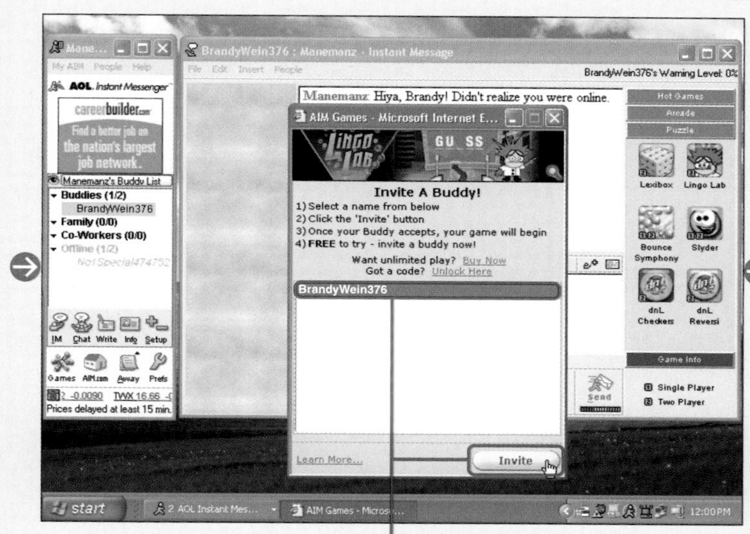

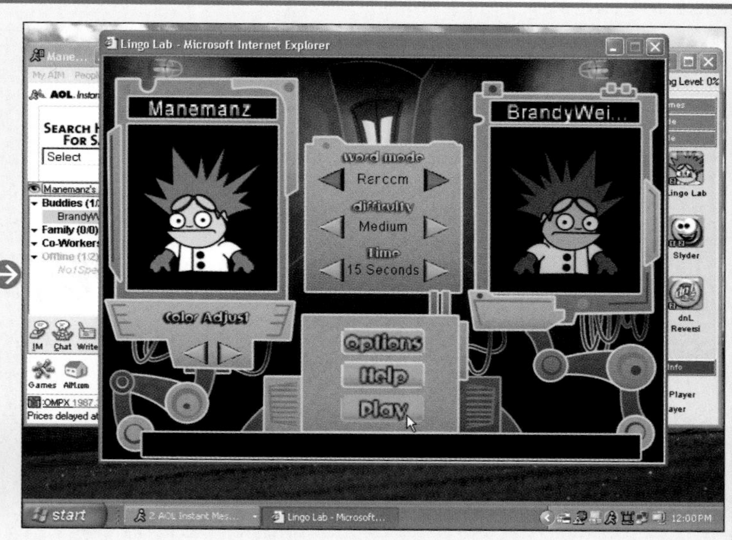

○ If you selected a 2-player version, the AIM Games dialog box appears, prompting you to invite a buddy.

4. Click your buddy's name.
5. Click the Invite button.

○ Assuming that your buddy accepts your invitation, the game starts in its own window, and you can begin to play.

Filter UNWANTED MESSAGES

You can meet many polite and interesting individuals through instant messaging services, but you can meet some very annoying people, as well. If someone becomes particularly annoying or starts to harass you during an instant messaging session, you can choose to block the person, preventing him or her from sending you additional instant messages.

AIM also features a somewhat more serious punishment for those who annoy you — warnings. When you send a warning, the warning level of the recipient increases by 5 percent, negatively affecting the user's ability to send and receive messages. If the user receives enough warnings, the service bumps the person off for a limited "cooling off period," after which the person can return.

This task shows you how to use both features to make someone back off in AIM. It also shows you how to unblock a person you blocked and how to choose to accept messages from only those people who are on your buddy list. The tips on the next page explain how to access similar features in ICQ, Yahoo! Messenger, and MSN Messenger.

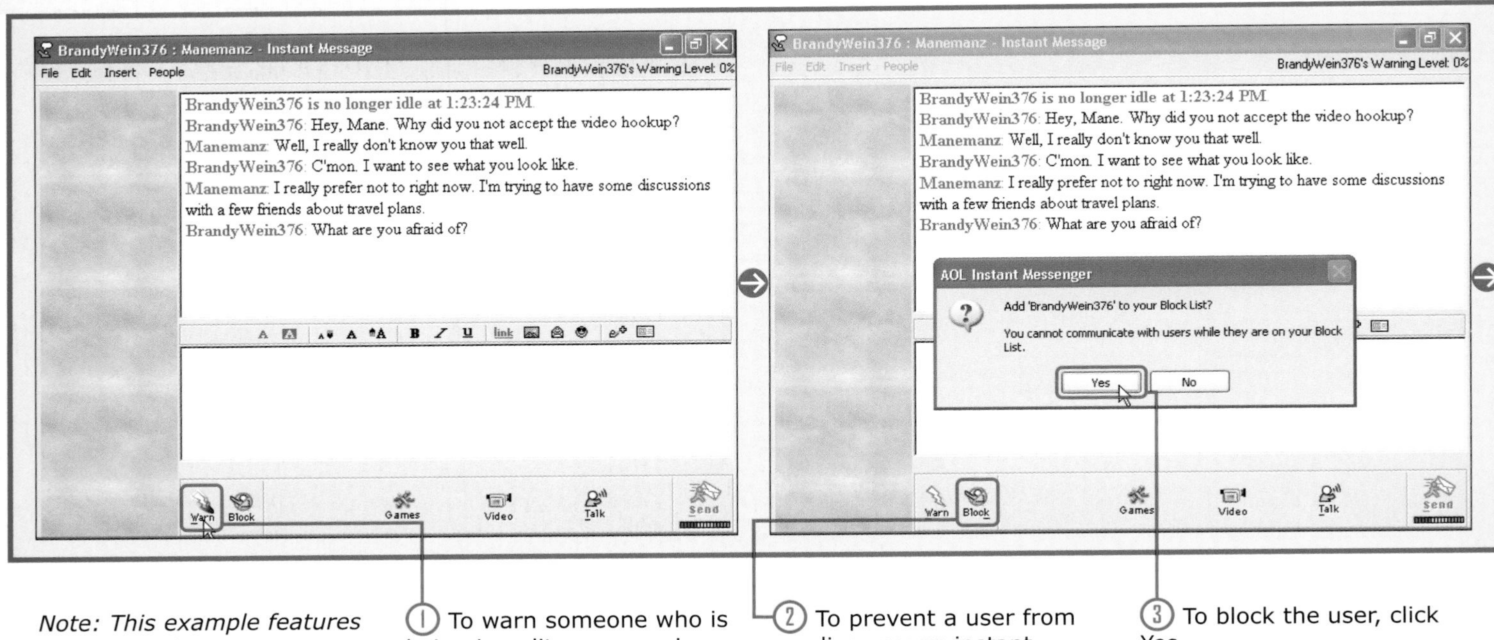

Note: This example features America Online Instant Messenger. If you use a different instant messaging program check its help system for information about similar features.

1. To warn someone who is being impolite or annoying, click the Warn button.

   ○ AIM sends a warning message to the user and increases his or her warning level by 5 percent.

2. To prevent a user from sending you an instant message, click the Block button.

   ○ The AOL Instant Messenger dialog box appears, prompting you to confirm.

3. To block the user, click Yes.

   ○ AIM blocks the user and shows him or her as "signed off."

#76

DIFFICULTY LEVEL

Apply It!

To block an MSN Messenger user who is currently annoying you, display the instant messaging window for that user and click the Block User button ( ).

Apply It!

To block a Yahoo! Messenger user who is currently annoying you, display the instant messaging window for that user and click the Ignore button ( ).

Apply It!

In ICQ, you can prevent specific users from sending you instant messages by choosing to ignore them. In ICQ's opening window, click the Main button ( ) and click Preferences and Security. Click Ignore List and then click the Add To Ignore List button to add the name of a user.

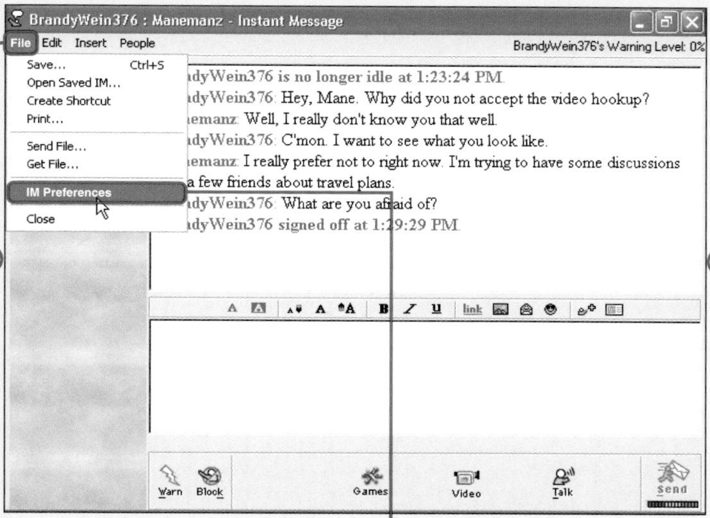

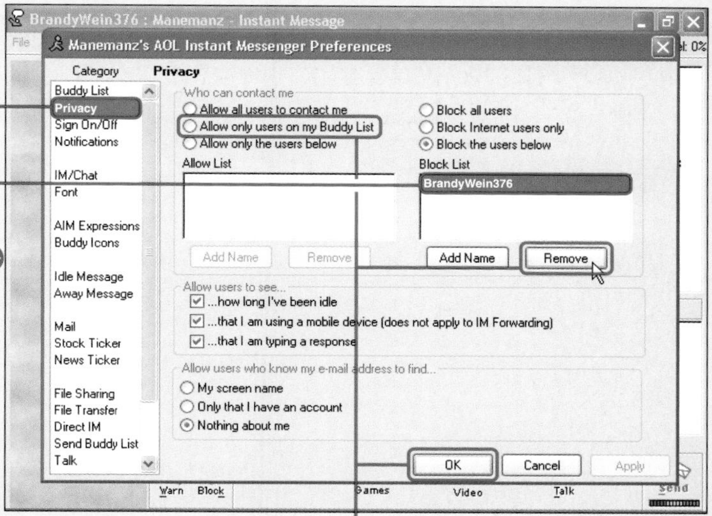

4 To check your Blocked list, click File.

5 Click IM Preferences.

- The AOL Instant Messenger Preferences dialog box appears.

6 Click Privacy.

7 To remove a name from the Block List, click the name.

8 Click the Remove button.

- To enable instant messaging for only those people on your buddy list, click here.

9 Click OK.

Share LARGE FILES

Many e-mail servers limit the size of file attachments to only a few megabytes to conserve storage space on the server and prevent system overload. If you try to send an attachment that exceeds the limit of your e-mail server or the recipient's e-mail server, the server bounces the message back to you, which is one reason why many businesses resort to sharing files with their customers and clients over the Web or by using FTP file servers. Users can connect using their Web browsers or an FTP program and download files of any size to their computers. When you need to share a large file with a friend or colleague, however, and neither of you has access to an FTP file server, your options are limited.

Fortunately, the latest batch of instant messaging programs feature file-sharing capabilities that enable users to exchange files directly between their two computers. A large file transfer over a dial-up modem connection can take some time, but whatever your connection speed, you can accomplish the transfer. This task demonstrates the basic procedure using AIM.

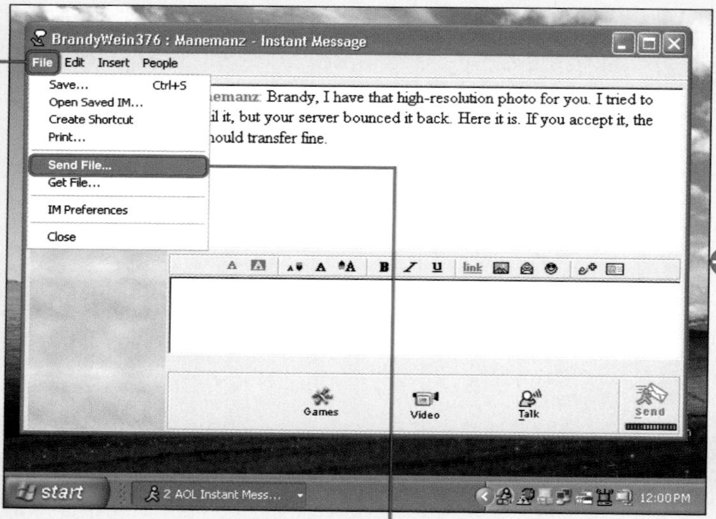

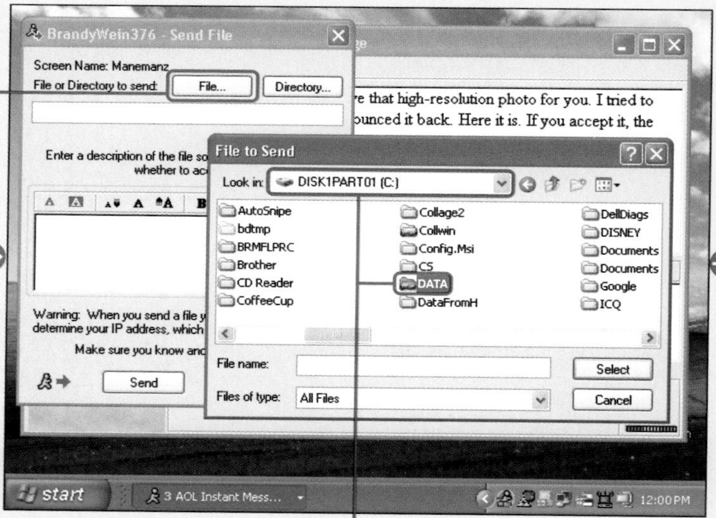

1. In the Instant Message window, click File.
2. Click Send File.

- The Send File window appears.

3. Click the File button.

- The File to Send dialog box appears.

4. Click here and select the drive that stores the file.
5. Double-click the folder that stores the file and double-click any subfolders until the folder that contains the file opens.

Put It Together!

Before sending a large file, use WinZip to compress it, as explained in task #22.

More Options!

You can choose to send an entire folder full of files to your buddy. Click File, click Send File, click the Directory button, select the folder you want to send, click OK, and then click the Send button.

More Options!

You can make your computer more open to file sharing, allowing your buddies to get files off of your computer without your having to send them. Click File, click IM Preferences, click File Sharing, and then enter your preferences.

Apply It!

MSN Messenger, Yahoo! Messenger, and Trillian all include a button in the instant messaging window for sending a file or photo.

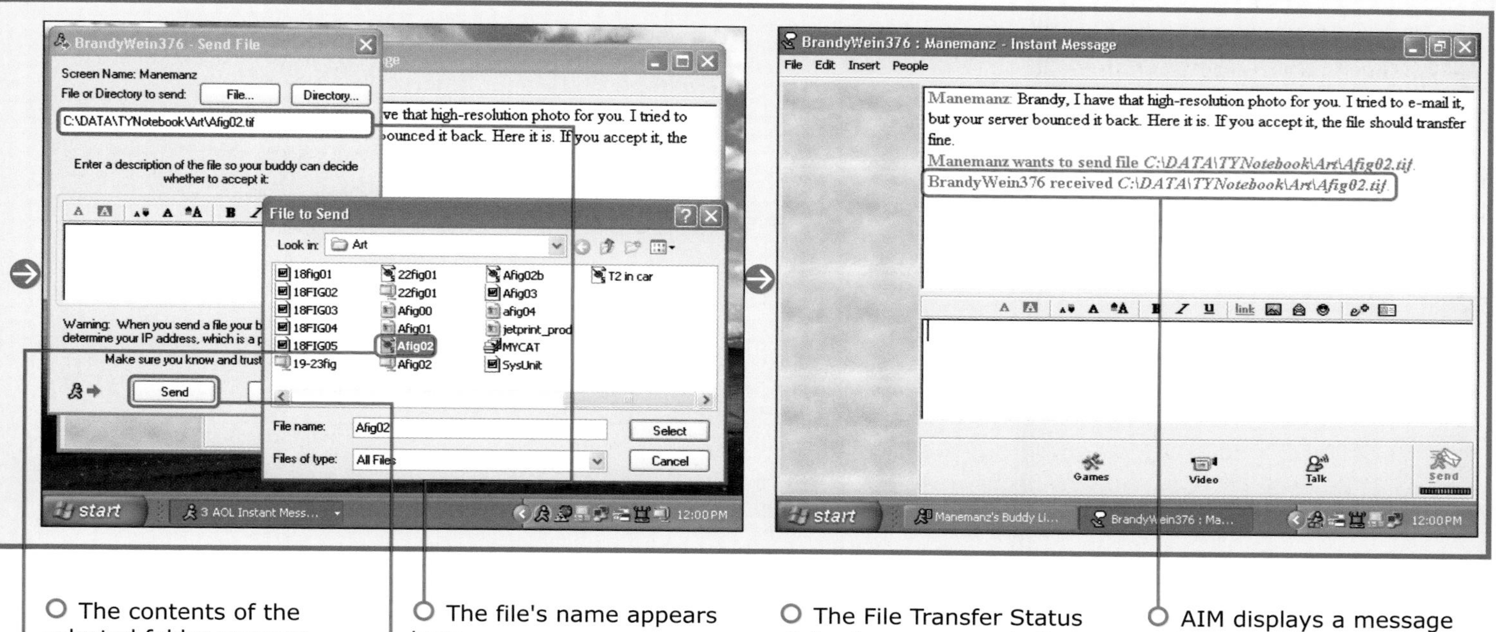

- The contents of the selected folder appears.

6 Double-click the name of the file you want to send.

- The file's name appears here.

7 Click Send.

- The File Transfer Status dialog box appears, indicating that AIM is waiting for your buddy to accept the file.

- AIM displays a message indicating that your buddy received the file.

Check for INCOMING E-MAIL

DIFFICULTY LEVEL

When you register to use a particular instant messaging service, the service creates an e-mail account for you, and the instant messaging program checks for incoming mail whenever you sign in. When you receive a message, the program plays a sound and/or displays an icon that indicates you have mail waiting. With a click of the mouse, as shown here, you can check your e-mail or send an e-mail message. This task shows you how to access e-mail from AIM.

More Options!

To have AIM check other e-mail accounts, click My AIM, click Edit Options, and click Edit Preferences. Click Mail, click the Add Mailbox button, and then enter the settings required to log in to your e-mail account. Include the account type, your e-mail address, and your password.

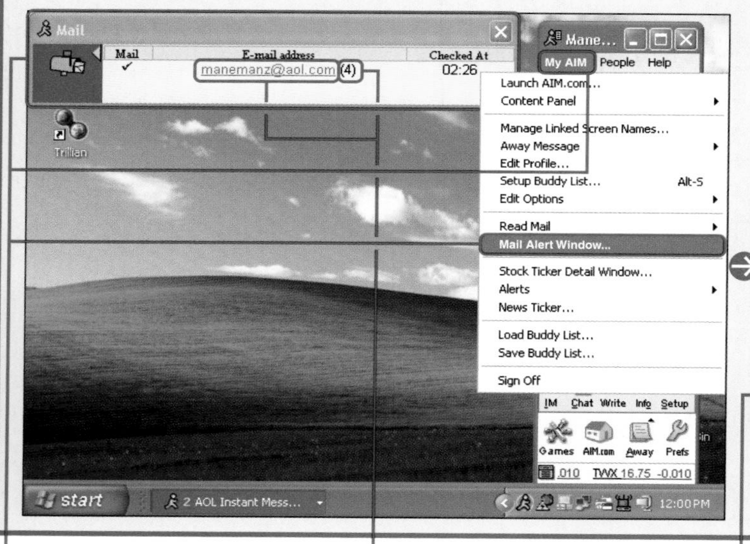

1. In AIM's Instant Message window, click My AIM.
2. Click Mail Alert Window.

- The Mail alert window appears for your screen name.
- The Mail window displays the number of e-mail messages you received.

3. Click this link to read your messages.

- AIM connects you to the America Online Web site for checking mail.

4. To read a message, double-click its description.

- The message opens in its own window.

Receive STOCK ALERTS

DIFFICULTY LEVEL

Yahoo! Messenger includes tabs for stocks, a personal calendar, an address book, news, and weather. MSN Messenger features tabs for MSN Money, Expedia travel services, local traffic forecasts, MSN Shopping, MSN Games, and MSNBC News. Even AIM, which has remained focused on instant messaging, displays a stock ticker and a content panel where you can choose to display Sports, What's New with AIM, featured chats, and AIM for Fun. This task shows you how to enter stock ticker symbols for your portfolio in AIM.

Check It Out!

To access stock quotes in MSN Messenger, click the CNBC on MSN Money tab ( ). To enter stock ticker symbols in Yahoo! Messenger, click the Stock tab ( ).

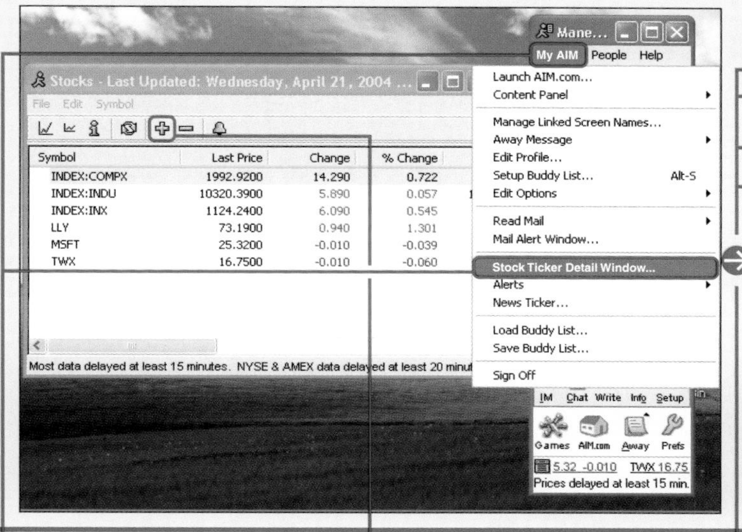

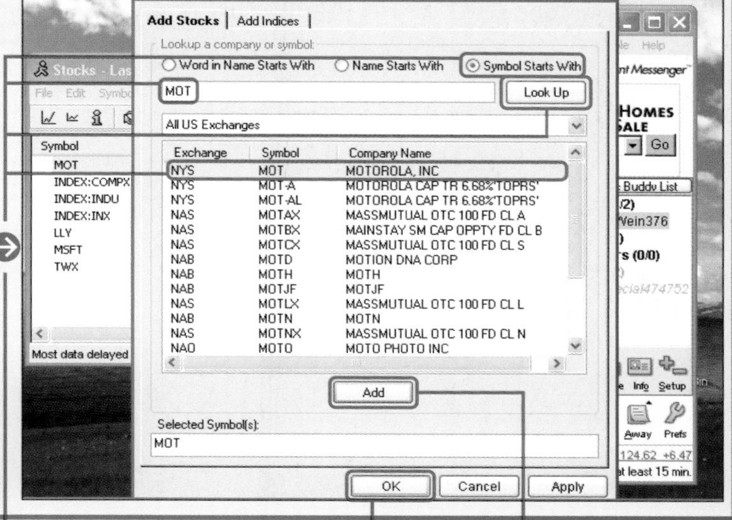

① In AIM's opening window, click My AIM.

② Click Stock Ticker Detail Window.

○ The Stocks window shows a list of ticker symbols it tracks.

③ Click the Add Symbol(s) button.

○ The Add Stocks window appears.

④ Click Symbol Starts With.

⑤ Type the stock symbol.

⑥ Click the Look Up button.

⑦ Click the stock symbol.

⑧ Click Add.

⑨ Click OK.

○ AIM adds the stock to the list.

Secure YOUR PRIVACY

Whenever you engage in online chat or instant messaging with anyone you do not know and trust, be careful when composing a profile or passing along sensitive information. Most people know that they should not use their real last names when conversing with strangers and that they should never divulge their passwords or any credit card information. However, even mentioning where you work, live, or attend school can provide a stranger with too much information.

In addition to being careful when entering any personal information, you can take advantage of privacy settings in your instant messaging program to restrict other users from accessing your personal information. Allowing only the users on your buddy list to contact you, for instance, can protect your personal information from anyone you do not know. You can also prevent other users from viewing your profile, your screen name, and other details about you. This task shows you how to enter privacy settings in AIM. The tips on the next page show how to protect your personal information in other instant messaging programs.

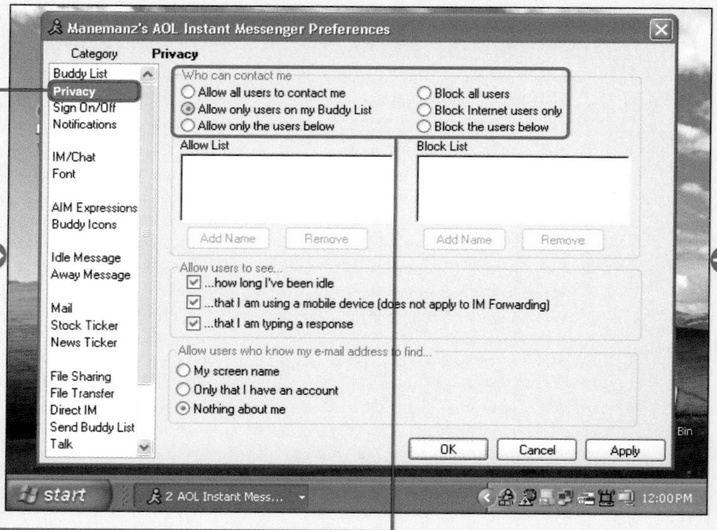

1. In the opening AIM window, click My AIM.
2. Click Edit Options.
3. Click Edit Preferences.

- The AOL Instant Messenger Preferences dialog box appears.

4. Click Privacy.
5. Click the option to specify which users can contact you and which users cannot.

DIFFICULTY LEVEL

Apply It!

MSN Messenger's privacy settings enable you to manage your Block list and hide information from any other people who share your computer. Click Tools, click Options, and click the Privacy tab to access your options.

Apply It!

Yahoo! Messenger's security settings are very similar to AIM's. You can choose to ignore other users, hide your online status, and prevent other people from knowing that you are online. To access the settings, click Login and then click Privacy Settings.

Apply It!

ICQ features several security categories for protecting your personal information, blocking potential spam messages, blocking users, and making your presence invisible. To access the settings, click the Main button and then click Preferences and Security.

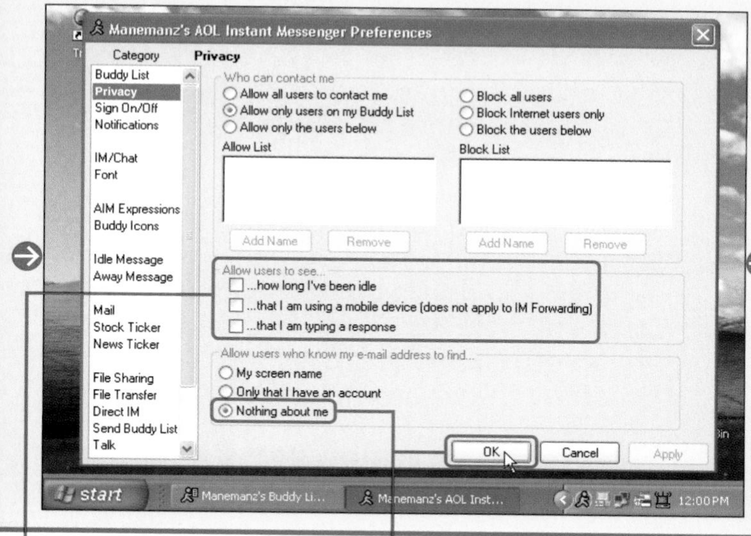

⑥ Click the check box next to anything you do not want other users to see.

○ Clicking a check box removes the check mark and prevents other users from viewing the information.

⑦ Click Nothing About Me to prevent other users from viewing your screen name or other information.

⑧ Click OK.

○ AIM saves your settings and closes the dialog box.

⑨ To edit your profile, click My AIM.

⑩ Click Edit Profile.

○ The Create a Profile dialog box appears.

⑪ For additional privacy, enter your first name, but omit your last name, maiden name, and street address.

⑫ Click Next and follow the onscreen instructions to complete your profile.

Establish Your Web Presence with a Blog

A *blog*, short for *Web log*, is a personal Web site that people often create to express their observations and opinions, maintain a journal of their experiences, and/or keep in touch with friends and family members. Unlike a Web page, which usually requires some knowledge of HTML coding, blogs require very little technical know-how. To update a blog, the *blogger* — the person who creates and maintains the blog — types an entry or comment and clicks a button to post it to the blog. Almost immediately, the blog software posts the entry, and it appears online, where visitors can view it in their Web browsers. Blogs typically display entries in the order in which the blogger enters them, presenting the most recent entry first. Blogs often encourage visitors to add their opinions and insights.

This chapter provides a brief overview of blogging, showing you how to locate blogs that might interest you, add comments to existing blogs, and start your own blog using Google's Blogger. The chapter then offers techniques and tips to enhance your blog, link it to other sources of news and information, make it more interactive, and promote it so more people can find it and contribute to it. With the tasks in this chapter, you can create and maintain a blog that draws visitors from all over the world and fosters a community in which you can share your life, your opinions, your art, or whatever else you have to offer.

TOP 100

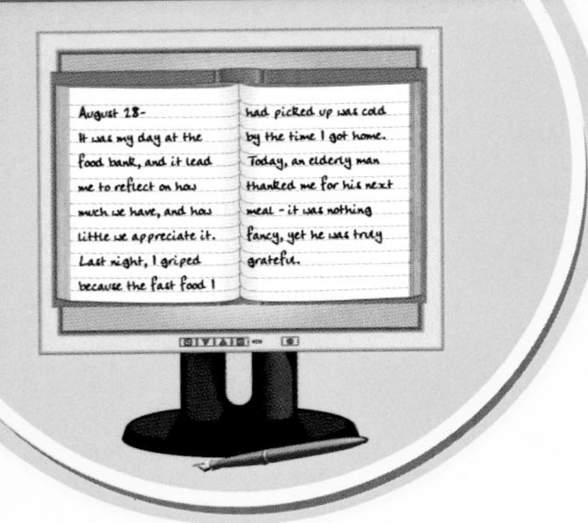

Search for SPECIFIC BLOGS

Thousands of blogs covering every topic from art to war to the art of war populate the Web, so tracking down blogs that interest you can pose a daunting challenge. Where can you find a blog about Middle East politics? Do any independent filmmakers have their own blogs? Which of your favorite celebrities maintain their own blogs? Blogs might turn up in a general Google search, but Google usually mixes them in with standard Web sites that often appear first in the list of found sites. If you want to limit your search to blogs, you need to take a different approach.

Fortunately, the Web features several blog directories that can help you track down the best blogs in any given category. These blog directories function just like Web site directories, enabling you to browse through categories or search for specific blogs by name. This task shows you how to connect to a blog directory called Blogarama and use it to locate specific blogs that you might find interesting.

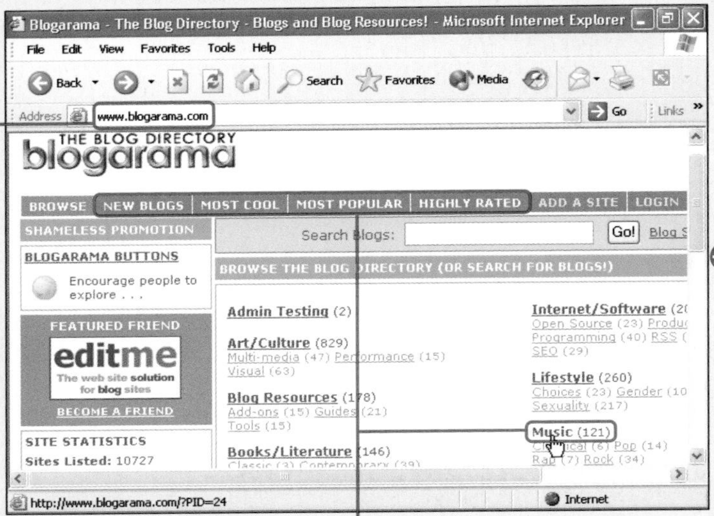

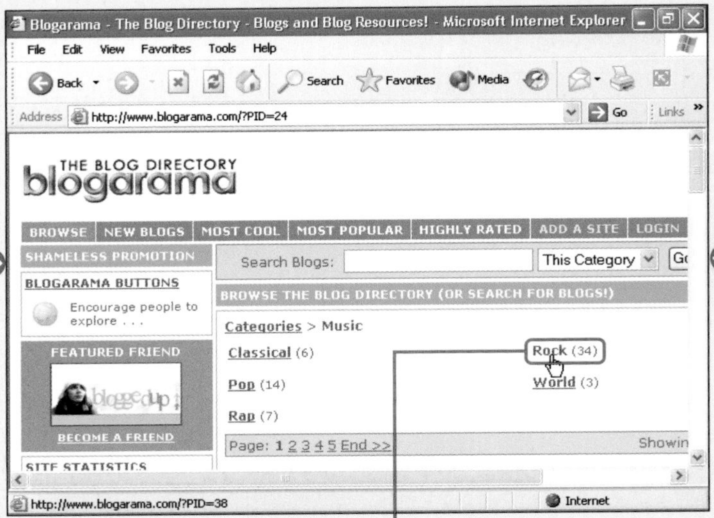

① Type **www.blogarama.com** and press Enter.

○ Your browser displays the Blogarama blog directory.

○ You can search by New Blogs, Most Cool, Most Popular, or Highly Rated.

② Click the desired blog category.

○ Blogarama displays a list of the selected category's subcategories.

③ Click the desired subcategory.

More Options!

The Web has several excellent blog directories, including BlogWise at www.blogwise.com, Globe of Blogs at www.globeofblogs.com, Root Blog at www.rootblog.com, and BlogSearchEngine at www.blogsearchengine.com.

Try This!

When searching for a specific blog, type your search phrase in quotation marks to limit your search to blogs that have that exact search phrase in their title or description.

Check It Out!

Blogarama allows you to review the blogs it lists. To submit a review, find the blog at Blogarama, click the Reviews link next to the blog's description, and click the Submit a Review for this Site button. Complete the form and assign a rating of 1 to 5.

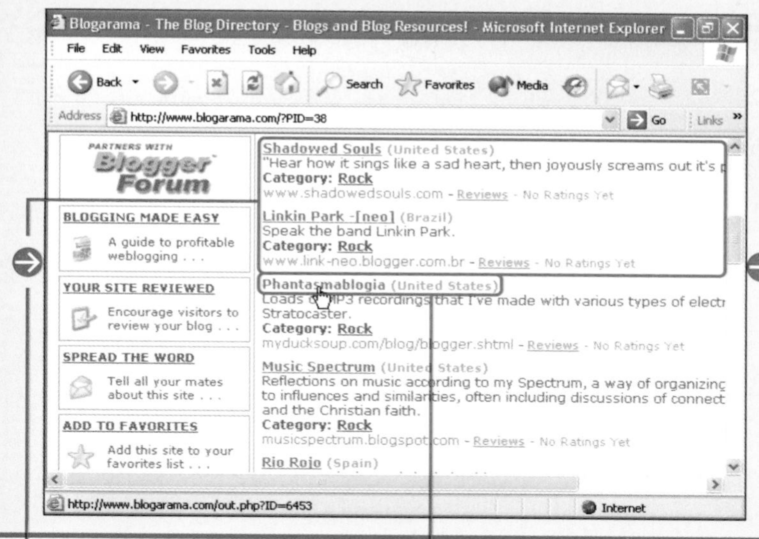

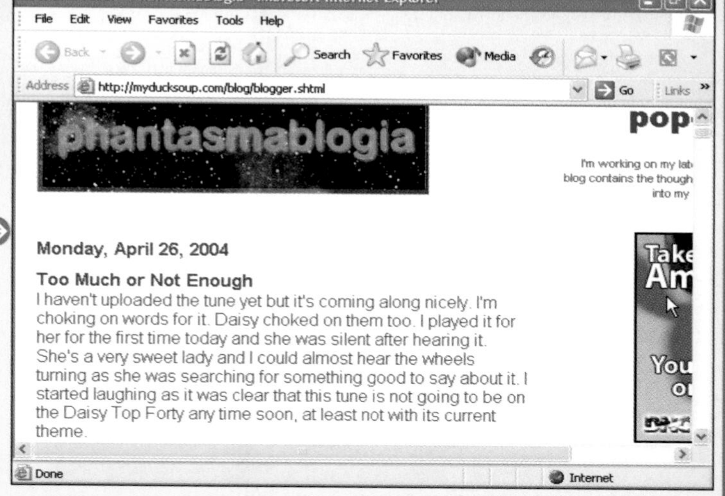

- Blogarama displays a list of sites in the selected subcategory.

4. Scroll down the list of sites and read their descriptions.

5. When you see a site that you want to visit, click its link.

- Internet Explorer displays the blog.

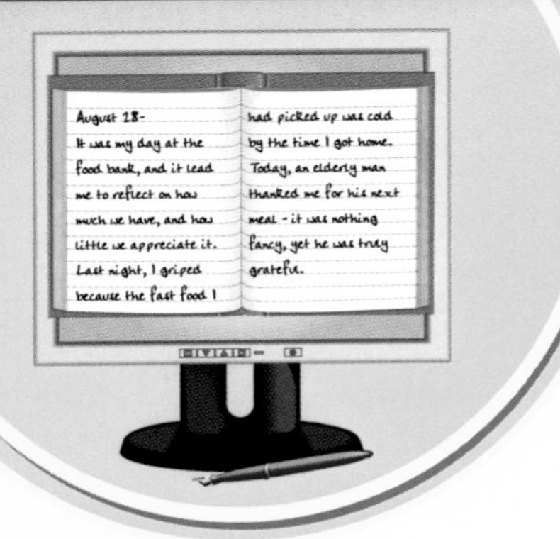

Join a GROUP BLOG

A single individual typically creates and manages his or her own blog, posting updates daily and responding to any comments that visitors post. However, two or more people can create and maintain a *group blog*. With a group blog, all members of the blog can log on and make changes to the blog, turning it into a collaborative creation. Joining an existing group blog is often a great way to acclimate yourself to the world of blogging without having to take the full responsibility for creating your own blog and keeping it up to date.

Most blogs encourage visitors to contribute feedback and comments, but they do not allow others to change the overall structure and content of the blog. Group blogs provide some degree of control to all members, but membership is typically by invitation only. To join a group blog, you must contact the blogger in charge and request an invitation. This task shows you how to request an invitation and demonstrates what to do when you receive an invitation.

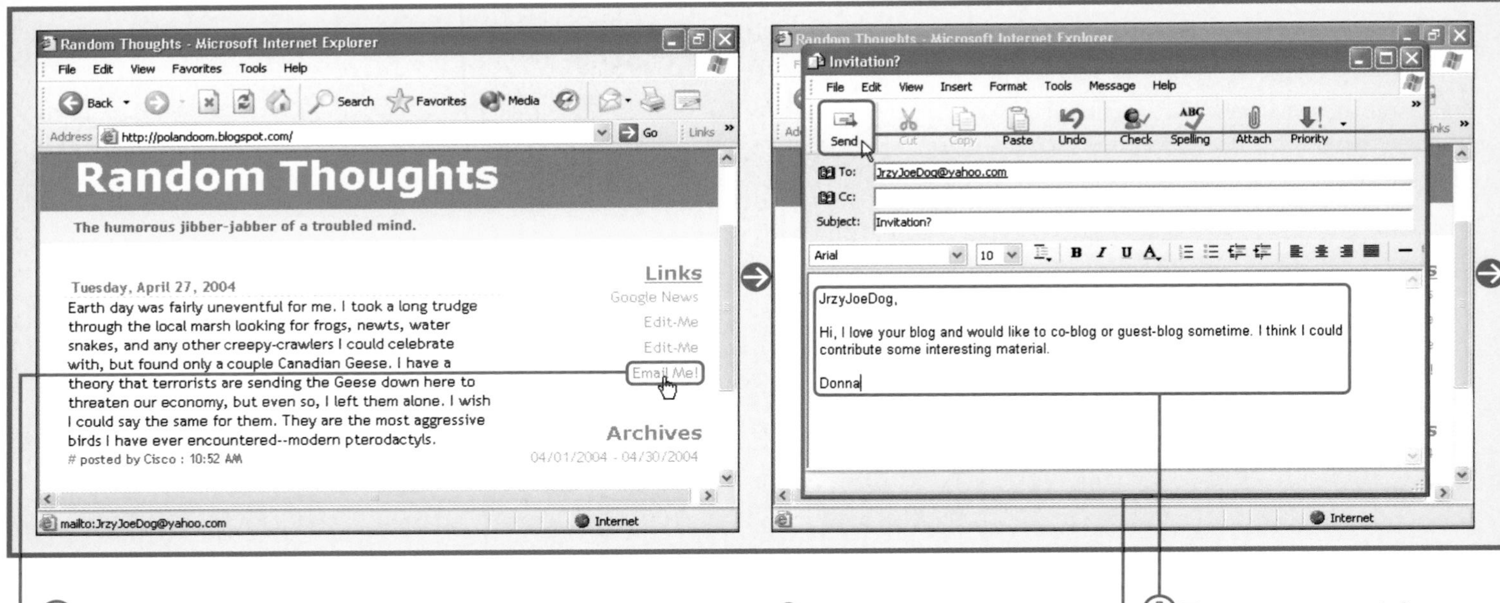

1. Click the link for contacting the blog's creator.

- Your e-mail program opens a new message window addressed to the blog's creator.

2. Type your request for an invitation to the group blog.
3. Click Send.

Attention!

Many blog hosting services require you to be a member of the service before you can join a group blog. This typically requires you to enter a user name, e-mail address, and password. After you have an account, you can click a special button or link to access any invitations you might receive.

Did You Know?

Free blog hosting services typically restrict the number of group blogs you can join. Many services provide you with one free group blog, whether you choose to create your own or join someone else's, so pick your group blog carefully.

Apply It!

Consider creating your own group blog to use for a club, classmates site, or family meeting place. You can share photos, post announcements and invitations, and even share contact information.

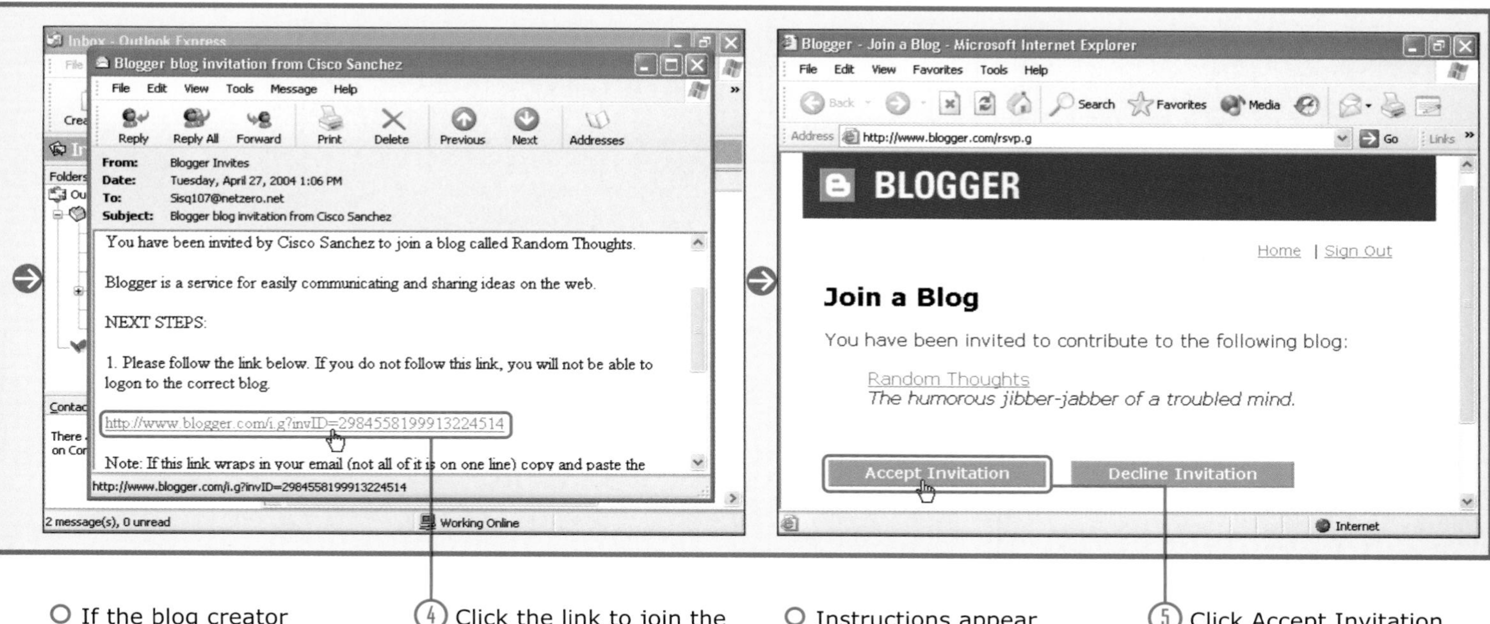

- If the blog creator decides to invite you, he or she e-mails you an invitation.

4. Click the link to join the blog.

- Instructions appear explaining how to proceed.

5. Click Accept Invitation.

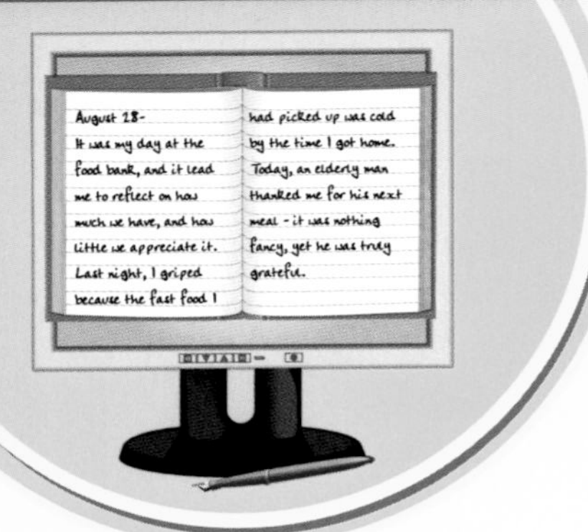

Start your OWN BLOG

Many users avoid trying to establish a presence on the Web because the mere thought of creating a Web page and managing a site seems overwhelming. They think that they need to learn HTML or master a Web page editor in order to create a site that looks somewhat attractive. And once they create the site, they need to learn to use other software to transfer the Web page to a Web server. Of course, some Web hosts, such as Yahoo!, provide tools to simplify the process, but using those tools daily to keep the pages up to date can be more work than most users want to invest.

Several blog hosting services on the Web provide users with simplified tools for creating and maintaining a presence on the Web via a personal blog. In most cases, creating a blog consists of answering a few questions and completing an online form. This task shows you how to connect to Blogger, one of the more popular blog hosting services, and use its tools to create your own custom blog.

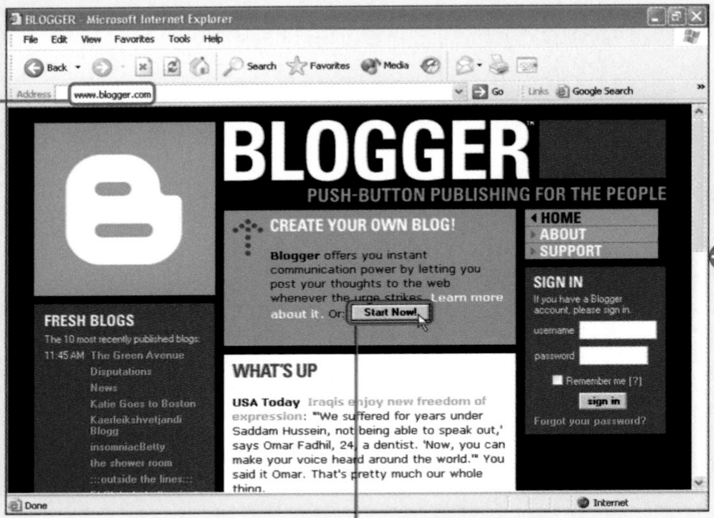

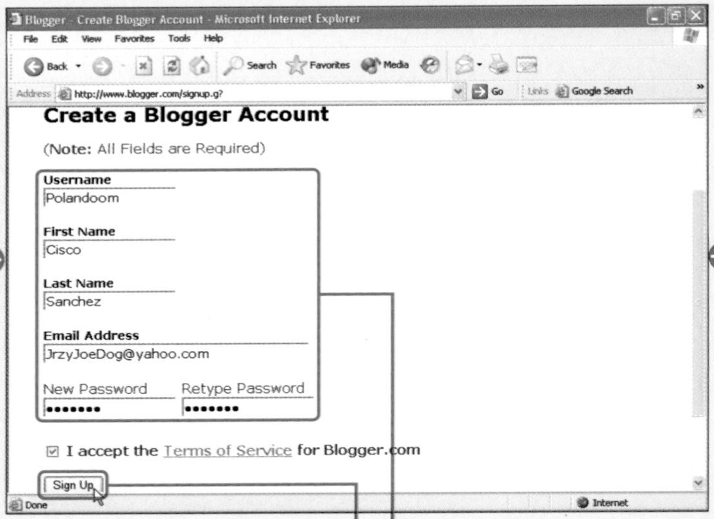

1. Type **www.blogger.com** and press Enter.

- Blogger's home page appears.

2. Click the Start Now! button.

- Blogger prompts you to enter the information required to register for a new account.

3. Type the requested information.
4. Click the Sign Up button.

DIFFICULTY LEVEL

Important!

When blogging, realize that most blogs are public. An unflattering picture of a coworker or acquaintance that you post on a public blog might cause problems for you later. Even messages posted to a private blog can be made public, if one of the people in your blog chooses to make it public. Be discreet.

More Options!

Several other companies offer free blog hosting, including Blog-City at www.blog-city.com Blogging Network at www.bloggingnetwork.com, Live Journal at www.livejournal.com, eBloggy at www.ebloggy.com, and Xanga at www.xanga.com.

Did You Know?

If you have a Web server where you would like to store your blog, you can download and install a program, such as Moveable Type, on the Web server, which enables you to edit your blog right on your Web server. You can download a copy of Moveable Type from www.moveabletype.org.

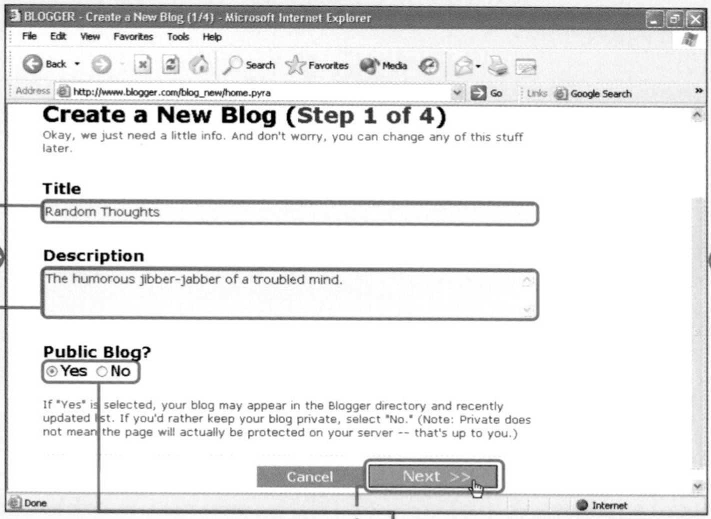

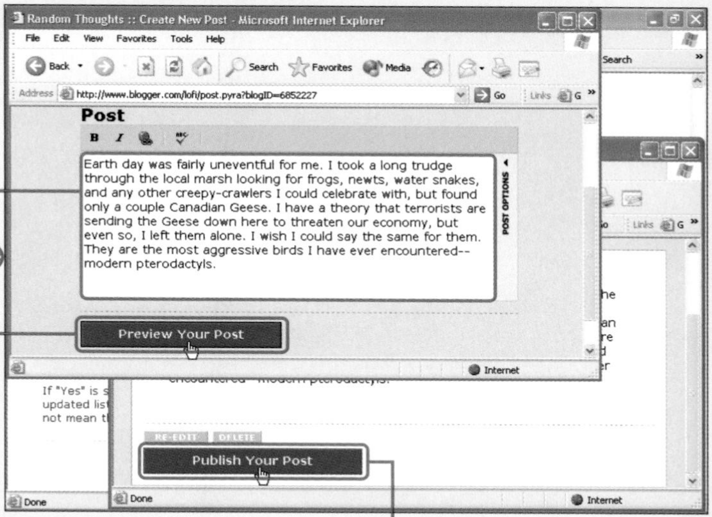

- Blogger prompts you to type a title and brief description of your blog.
- 5 Type a title for your blog.
- 6 Type a description of your blog.
- 7 Click the option to specify whether you want your blog to be public or private.
- 8 Click Next and follow the onscreen instructions to create your blog.
- After Blogger creates your blog, it displays a screen where you can type your first entry.
- 9 Type your entry here.
- You can preview your post before publishing it.
- 10 Click Publish Your Post.
- Blogger publishes your entry on your blog, where visitors can view it.

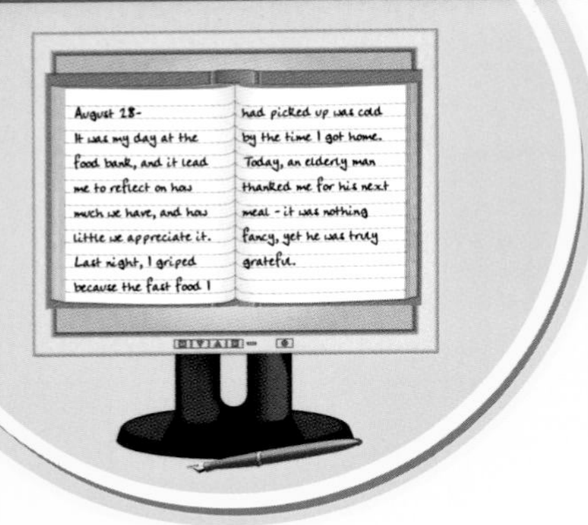

Access the LATEST HEADLINES

Many blogs feature the creator's response to the latest news and information around the world. If your blog focuses on late-breaking news, consider having the latest news and information delivered to your desktop via RSS feed. RSS, short for Rich Site Summary, is a technology that enables sites to freely share updated information with any other sites that want to broadcast it as syndicated content. For example, CNN provides a news feed that other news and information sites around the world can choose to display on their sites.

Many sites that feature RSS feeds allow users to subscribe, often for free, to obtain up-to-the-minute news and information. With an RSS feed from ESPN, for example, a baseball fan can have the latest sports scores and information delivered to the desktop. This task explains how to download and install a popular news reader, called Awasu, and shows you how to use it to display the latest news, sports, weather, and information.

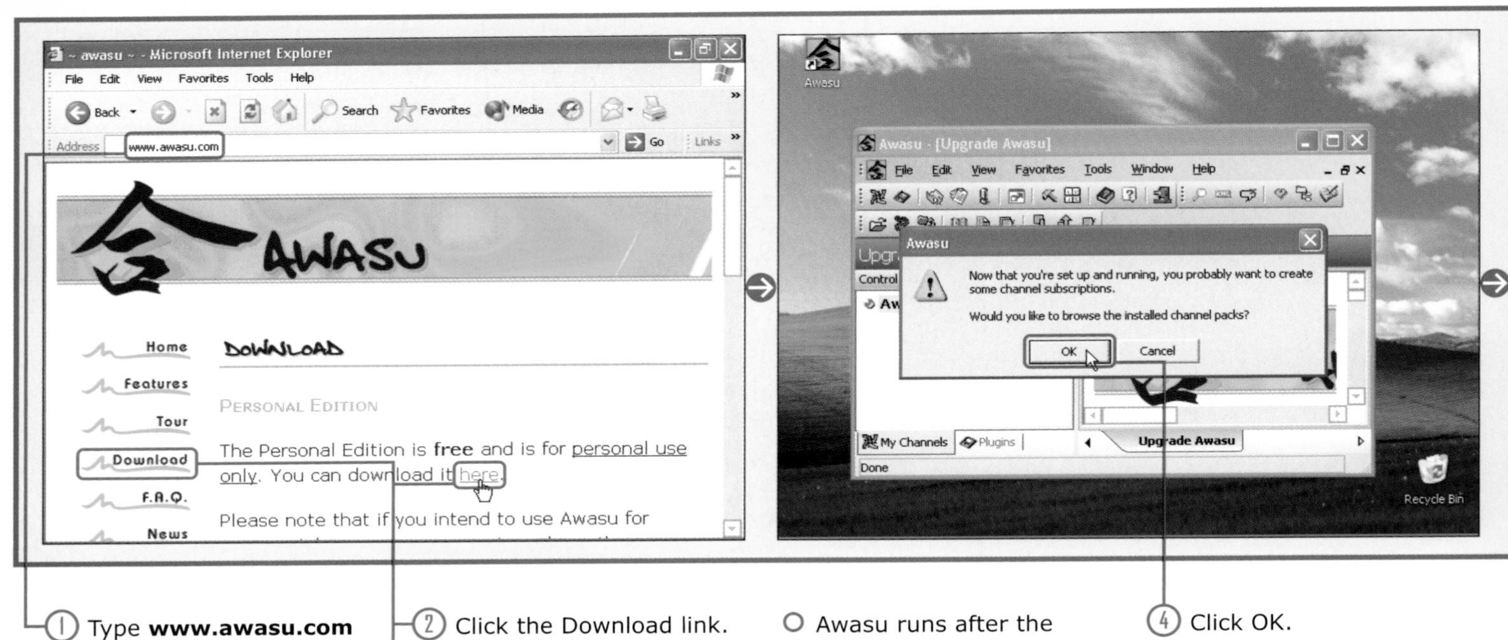

1. Type **www.awasu.com** and press Enter.

- Awasu's home page appears.

2. Click the Download link.

3. Click here to download the current version of the Awasu news reader, and install it on your computer.

- Awasu runs after the installation, and displays the Awasu dialog box asking if you want to browse the available channel packs.

4. Click OK.

Remove It!

To delete a channel you subscribed to, click the channel in the Control Center list, click File, and then click Delete channel. When Awasu prompts you to confirm the deletion, click OK.

More Options!

By default, Awasu updates each channel's content daily. To have Awasu update a channel now, right-click the channel and click Update now. When Awasu displays a channel's content, its Web page, you can right-click the Web page, as you can in Internet Explorer, for additional options, such as saving the page to your desktop. Be aware that some sites might ban you from their RSS feed if you check for updates too frequently.

Did You Know?

By default, any Blogger Pro blog includes a site feed that others can use to subscribe to your site.

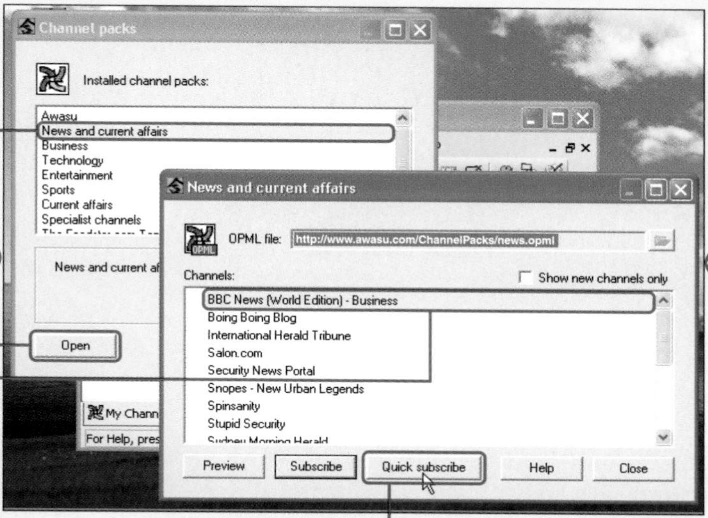

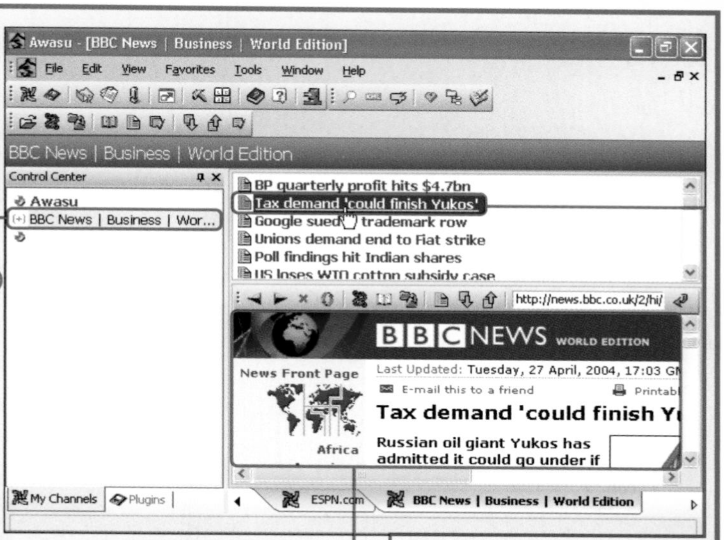

- Awasu displays the channel pack categories.
- 5 Click the desired category.
- 6 Click Open.
- 7 Click the desired channel.
- 8 Click the Quick Subscribe button and click OK.
- The Subscribe button lets you change settings, including how often Awasu checks for updated content.
- Channels you subscribed to appear here.
- 9 Click the desired channel.
- 10 Click the desired headline.
- The selected story appears here.

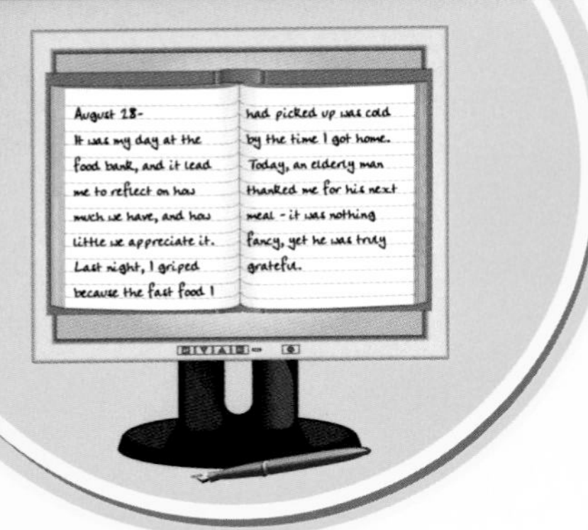

UPDATE
your blog often

Unlike a Web site that can continue to draw visitors for many months after the Web master stops updating it, blogs call for daily updates to keep visitors coming back. In many ways, blogs are more like news media than like personal Web sites. Visitors depend on the changing nature of your blog and on your fresh insights and observations to keep them engaged. In addition, if a visitor posts a comment to your blog, and you do not respond in a timely manner, the person probably will not return any time soon.

Your blog's success depends on returning visitors and "word of mouth," so if you want it to succeed, update it often — at least daily — and make sure you include some interesting tidbits. Updating a blog is a fairly simple process, as shown in this task. Of course, the process varies depending on which blog host or software you use, but in most cases, the process consists of publishing a daily post.

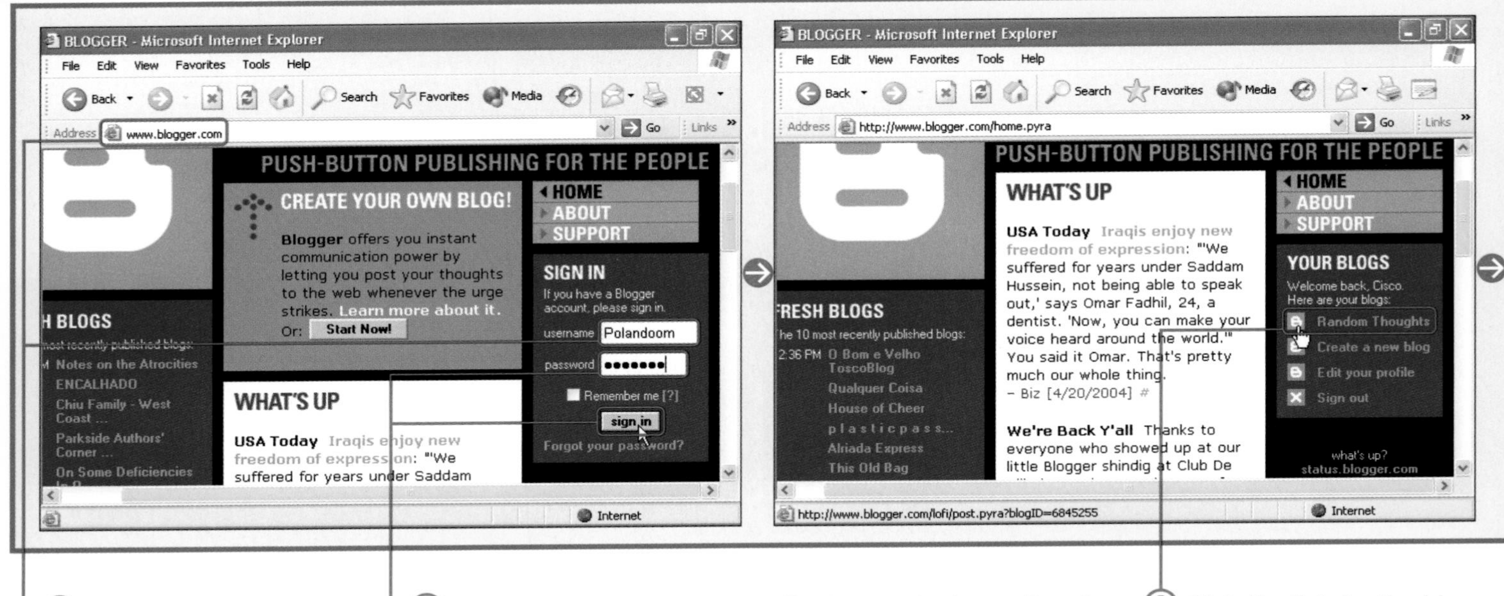

1. Type **www.blogger.com** and press Enter.

○ Blogger's home page appears.

2. Type your user name here.

3. Type your password here.

4. Click the sign in button.

Note: See task #83 to start up a Blogger account.

○ Blogger displays a list of your blogs.

5. Click the link for the blog you want to update.

DIFFICULTY LEVEL

Important!

If you are going on vacation or are too busy to update your blog daily, publish a post indicating the date on which you will return. Otherwise, visitors might worry about you or assume that you no longer maintain your blog.

More Options!

At the top of the screen you use to compose your posts are three tabs — Posting, Settings, and Template. These tabs contain options for updating your blog, changing its title and description, modifying its template, and controlling other features of your blog's appearance and function.

More Options!

Before publishing a post, click Blogger's Spellcheck button ( ) to check for any misspellings or typos.

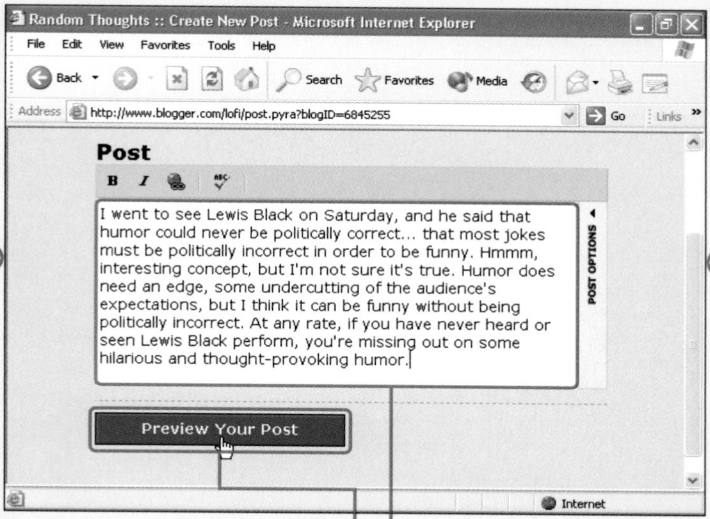

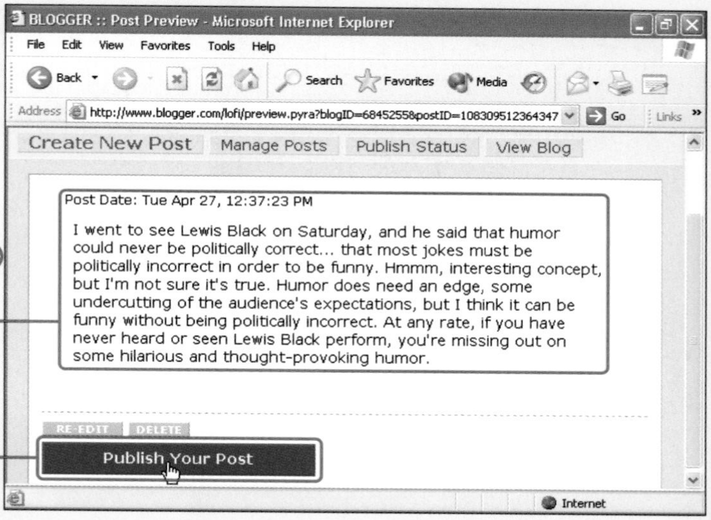

○ Blogger displays a blank text box for typing your message.

⑥ Type the message you want to post.

○ You can preview your post before publishing it.

○ Blogger displays your message as it will appear on your blog.

⑦ Click Publish Your Post.

○ Your post appears on your blog.

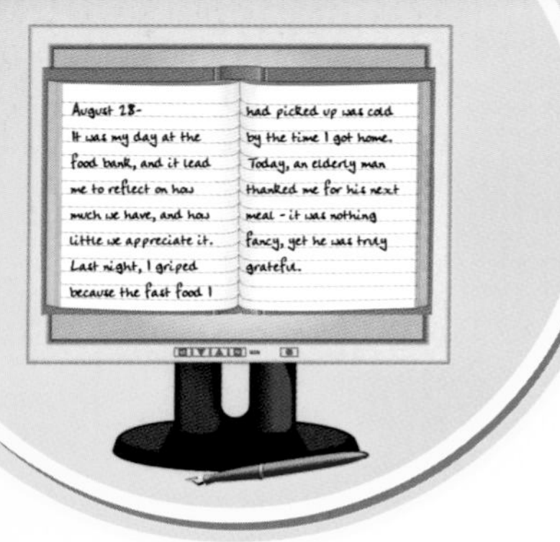

LINK YOUR BLOG

to other sources

If you use your blog to present other sources of information on the Web or to comment on information and reports from other Web sites or blogs, you might want to link your blog to those sites. In many cases, you can simply copy a site's URL and paste it as a link into one of your posts. If you are using Blogger as your blog host, an easier way to add a link to another site is to use the BlogThis! button in the Google toolbar, introduced in task #36.

This task assumes that you have installed the Google toolbar and activated it in Internet Explorer. It also assumes that you use Blogger as your blog host. If you use Blogger and the Google bar is turned on in Internet Explorer, you can turn on the BlogThis! button and use it to add a link for any Web page or blog displayed in Internet Explorer to your blog.

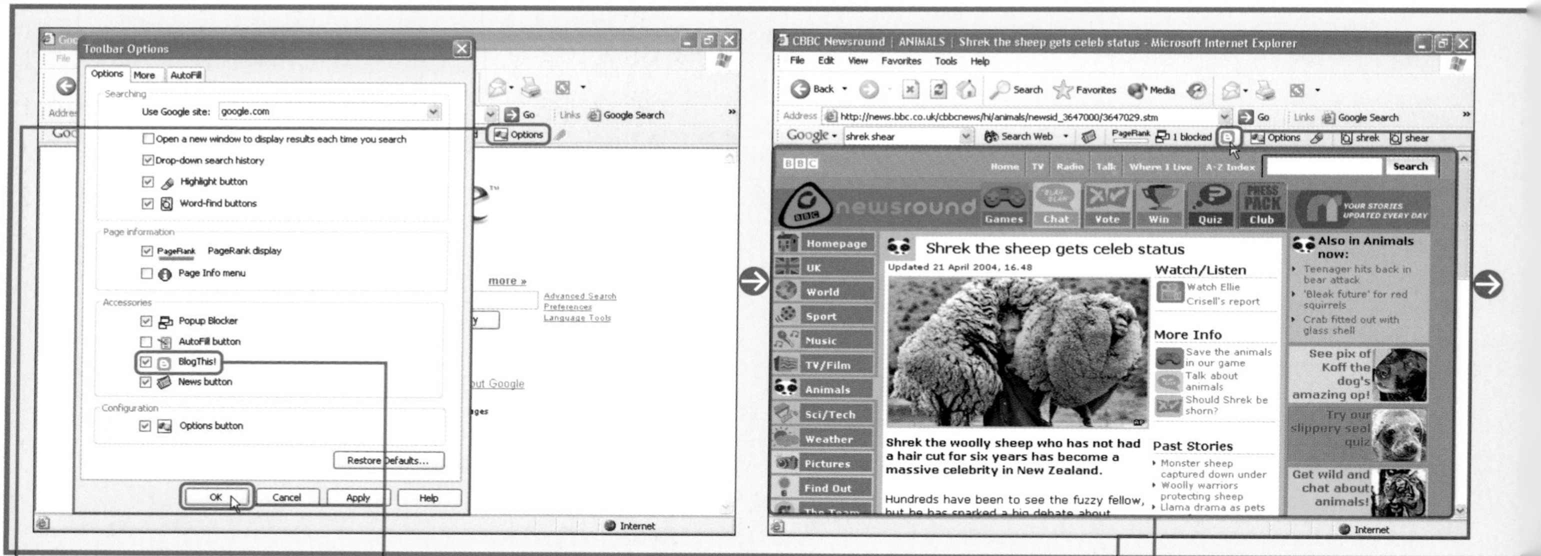

① In the Google toolbar, click the Options button.

○ The Options dialog box appears.

② Click BlogThis! to checkmark the box.

③ Click OK.

○ The BlogThis! button appears in the Google toolbar.

④ In Internet Explorer, display the page you want to connect to your blog.

⑤ Click the BlogThis! button.

Did You Know?

You can add a link to a post without using the BlogThis! button. Highlight the address in your browser and press Ctrl+C. When typing your message to post, click the insert link button ( ), and press Ctrl+V to insert the address. Click OK. Just before the </a> code, type the link's name as you want it to appear on your blog. For example, a link to Google's home page would look like this: <a href="http://www.google.com/">Google</a>

More Options!

To have the BlogThis! feature include text from a Web page or blog you are linking to, highlight the text before clicking the BlogThis! button. BlogThis! inserts the text as a quote.

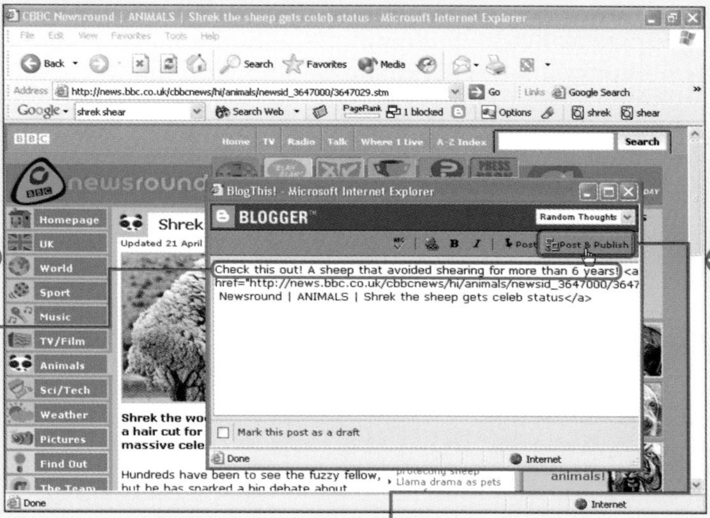

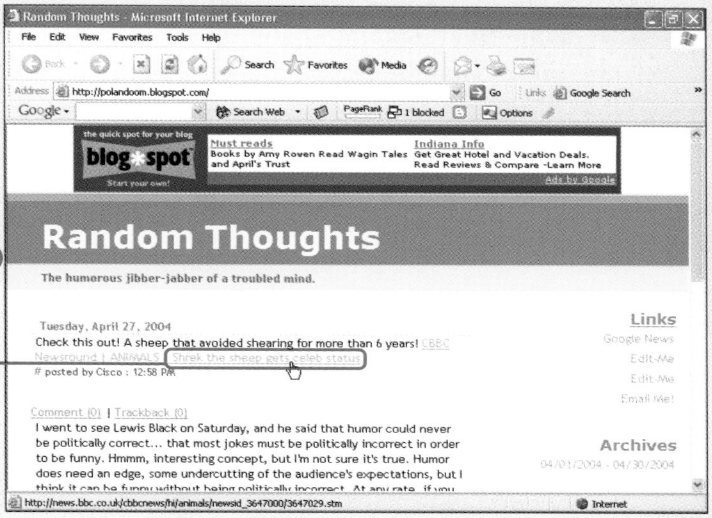

- Blogger appears and displays the HTML code for creating a link to the selected page.

6. Type any additional text before and/or after the HTML code.

7. Click the Post & Publish button.

- Blogger publishes your comment, along with a link to the site.

- When you view your blog, it displays a link to the specified site.

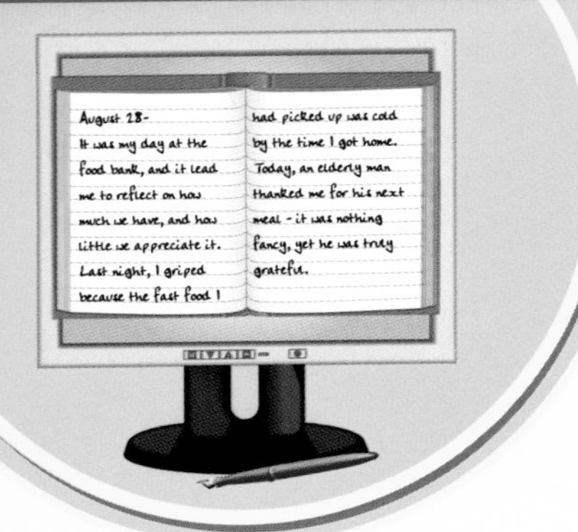

Make your blog interactive with a COMMENTS AREA

Interactive blogs — blogs that encourage visitors to post their own comments — are typically the most active blogs, as well. A comments area gives visitors a sense that they have a voice at your site, provides you with different perspectives, and can enrich your site with other observations and insights. To make your blog interactive, you can add comments capability. With comments, your posts appear as they normally do, but preceding or following each post is a Comments link that visitors can click to display a text box for typing their own observations and insights.

At the time of this writing, Blogger has no comments feature built into it. However, several third-party services offer comments hosting that you can use along with most blog hosting services, including Blogger. This task shows you one such third-party service, called HaloScan.

After your register for HaloScan, it typically supplies you with three codes that you can paste into your blog's template to add Comments links.

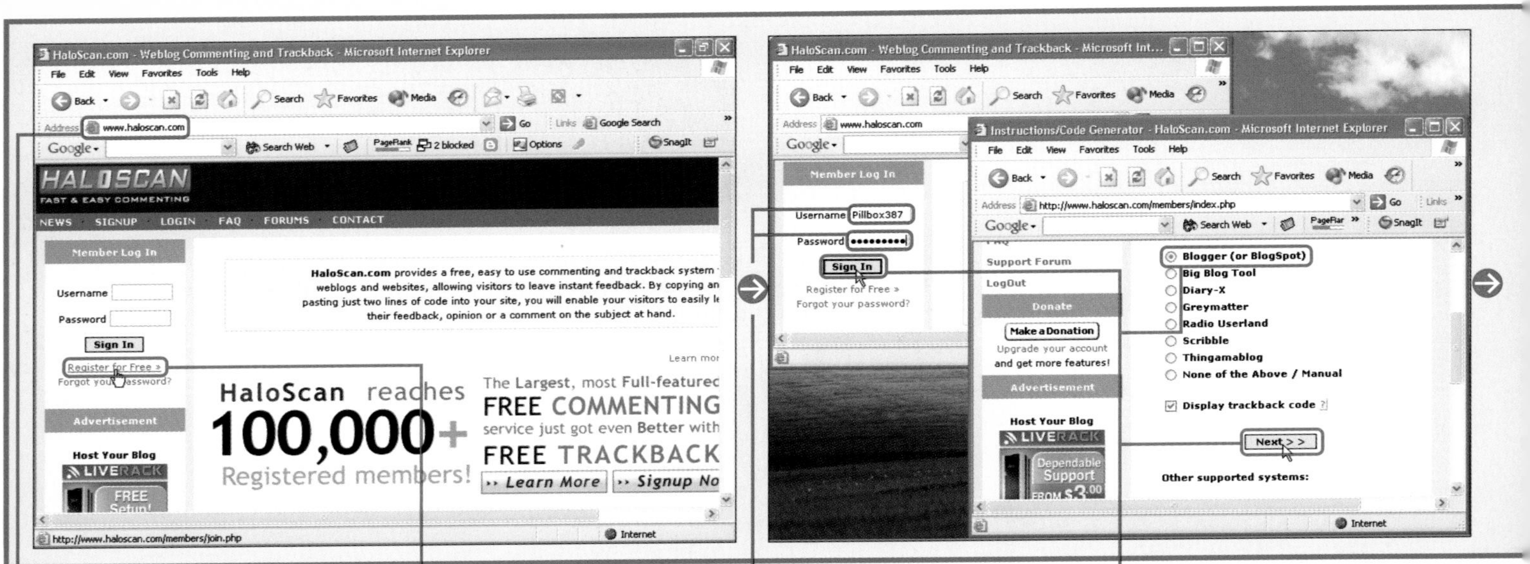

1. Type **www.haloscan.com** and press Enter.
   - HaloScan's home page appears.
2. Click the Register for Free link.
   - Follow the onscreen instructions to register for a free account.
   - After you register, HaloScan prompts you to log in.
3. Type your user name.
4. Type your password.
5. Click Sign In.
6. Click Blogger (or Blogspot).
7. Click Next.

DIFFICULTY LEVEL

Important!

If you choose to add a comments feature to your blog, make sure you update your blog regularly and reply to any comments that call for replies. Otherwise, a user might feel ignored and choose not to revisit your blog.

Attention!

If you click the Preview button and are not satisfied with the changes, close the preview window and click the Clear Edits button to start over.

More Options!

Other comment hosting services include YACCS at rateyourmusic.com/yaccs/, BlogOut at www.klinkfamily.com/BlogOut/blogout.html, and CommentThis! at commentthis.com.

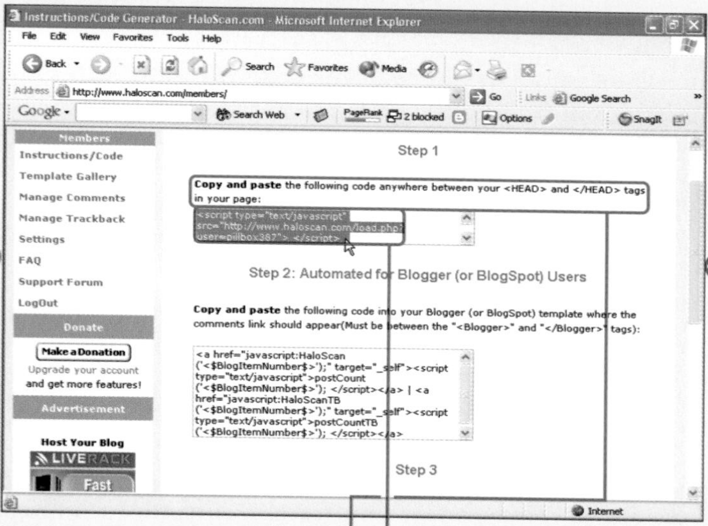

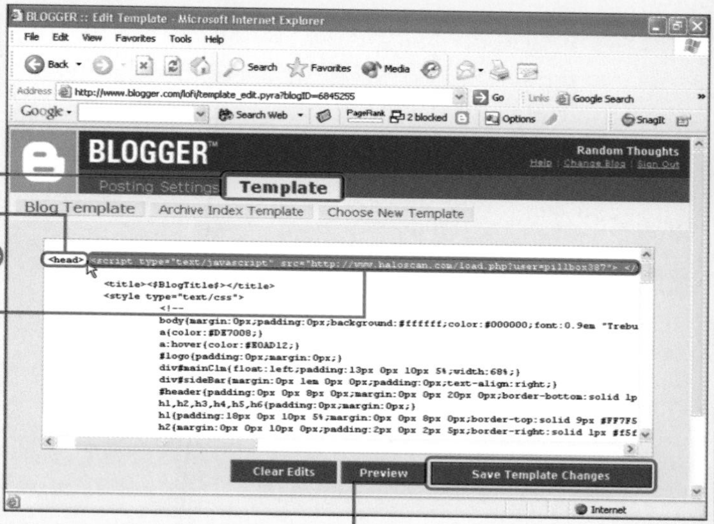

- HaloScan displays the required codes along with instructions on where to paste them into your blog template.

8. Highlight the code and press Ctrl+C to copy it.
9. Follow the onscreen instructions to determine where to paste the code.
10. In Blogger, click the Template tab.
11. Click where HaloScan instructed you to insert the copied code and press Ctrl+V.

- The first HaloScan code is inserted in your template.

12. Repeat steps 8 to 11 to insert the other two codes.
13. When you are satisfied with the changes, click Save Template Changes.

- Blogger saves the changes to your template.

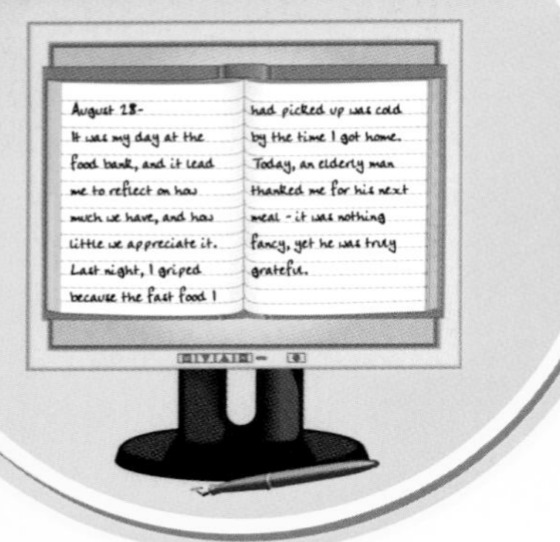

Hide YOUR E-MAIL ADDRESS from spammers

Most users add their e-mail addresses to their blogs to enable visitors to e-mail them to note problems with the blog, to offer corrections to posted information, or to establish personal contact. However, some automated Web search engines, called *e-mail spiders*, roam the Web for the sole purpose of collecting e-mail addresses from various Internet sources, including blogs, to add them to spam mailing lists. Most Web spiders benefit you by adding your blog to Web directories, such as Google, to attract more visitors to your site.

However, e-mail spiders are dedicated to helping spammers deliver unsolicited e-mail to unsuspecting victims.

To prevent e-mail spiders from adding your e-mail address to a mailing list, you can format your address in such a way that it does not look like an e-mail address but still functions as one. This task shows you how to enter your e-mail address in your Blogger template, but you can use the same trick in any HTML-coded blog template.

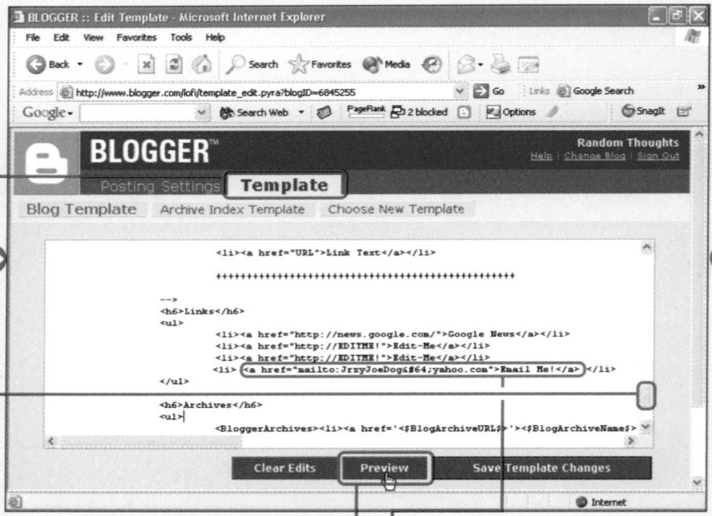

1. Log on to Blogger.
2. Click the link for the blog in which you want to add your e-mail address.

Note: See task #83 to set up a Blogger account.

- Blogger displays the text box for typing a new post.

3. Click the Template tab.
4. Scroll down to where you want to type your e-mail address.
5. Type **<a href="mailto:*myname@mailserver.com*">Email Me!</a>** replacing the italicized text with your e-mail address.

Note: @ functions as an @ sign, but most Web spiders do not recognize it as an @ sign.

6. Click Preview.

Did You Know?

The code used to insert the e-mail link includes the text "Email Me!" This is the actual link text that the user clicks to send you a message. You can type anything in place of it.

Important!

Disguising the @ sign as @ is not foolproof. Someone visiting your site can obtain your e-mail address and add it to a mailing list manually. Other more secure options are available; consult your blog hosting service for advice.

More Options!

When you first start blogging, consider setting up a separate e-mail account for registering your blog and managing e-mail you receive regarding the blog. Task #61 shows you how to sign up for a free Hotmail account.

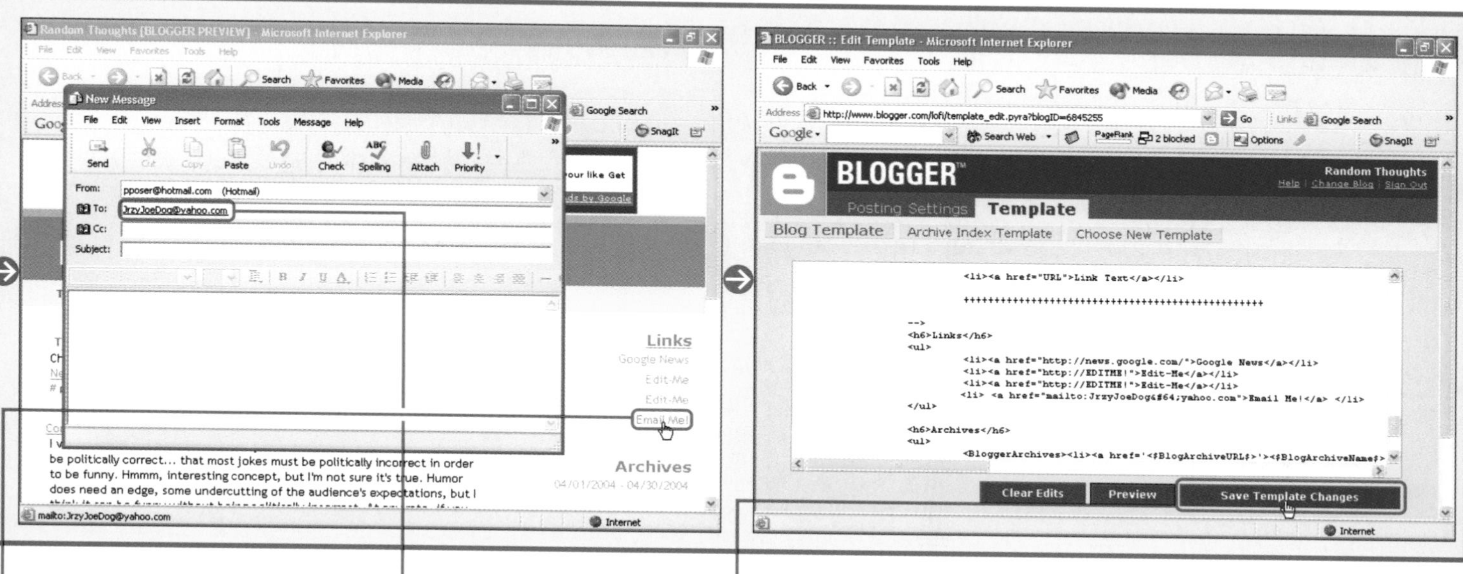

- Your blog displays a link that visitors can click to send you e-mail.

7. Click the link.

- Your e-mail program displays a new message window addressed to your e-mail address.

8. Close the preview window and click the Save Template Changes button.

- Blogger applies your changes to the template.

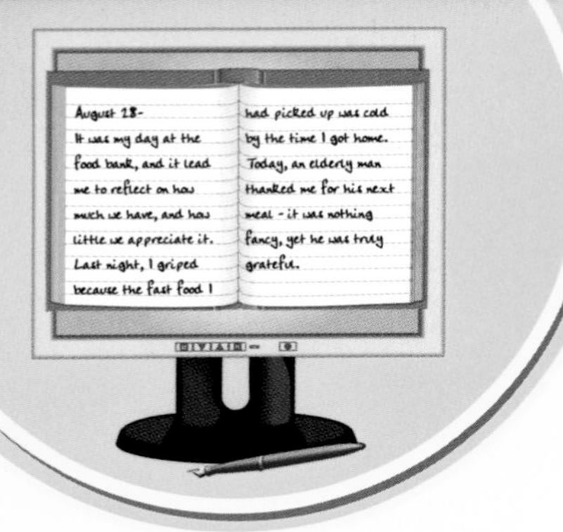

ATTRACT READERS
to your blog

Your blog might turn up in a Google or Yahoo! search, but search engines and directories are not the avenues that most blogs travel to earn their fame. Bloggers use more of a word-of-mouth, grassroots marketing strategy that consists of letting friends, family, colleagues, and various Internet communities know that they have a blog and that they want people to visit it.

To attract visitors to your blog, take one or more of the following approaches: add a link to your blog to all of your e-mail messages; add a link to your blog to any messages you post in forums that cover topics relating to your blog; tell all of your friends, family, and colleagues about your blog; trade links with other bloggers — place links to their blogs on your blog in exchange for them linking their blogs to yours; keep your blog up-to-date and interesting to encourage visitors to return and recommend your blog to their friends.

This task shows you how to add a link to your blog to your outgoing e-mail messages.

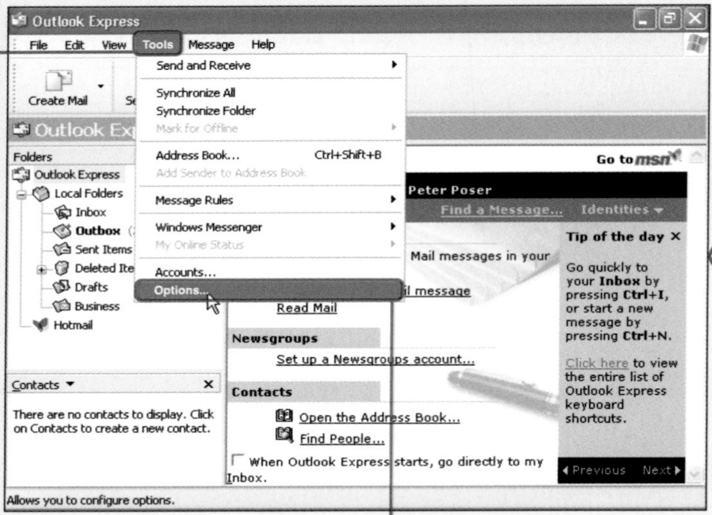

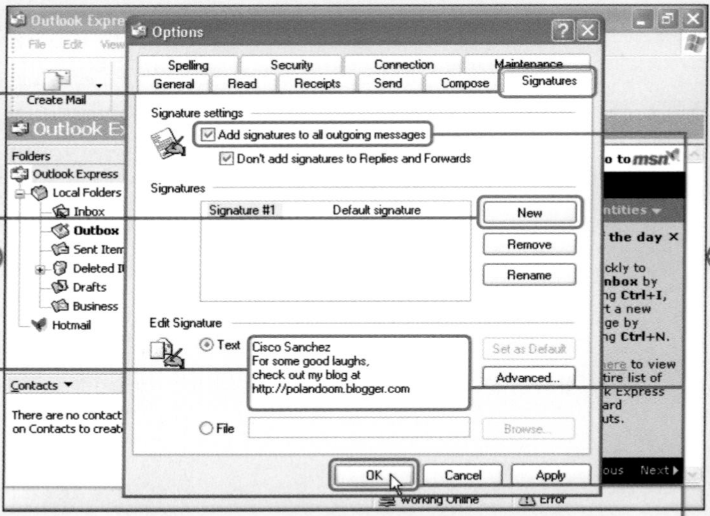

1. In Outlook Express, click Tools.
2. Click Options.

- The Options dialog box appears.

3. Click the Signatures tab.
4. Click New.
5. Click in the Edit Signature text box.
6. Type your signature, including your blog's address.
7. Click here.
8. Click OK.

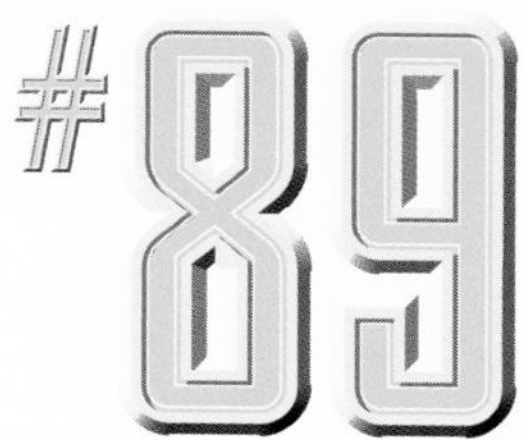

Attention!

Many forums allow users to add a signature file to their profiles for posting messages to the forum. You can add a link to your signature file by typing in your blog's address. However, some forums might discourage this type of advertising, especially if you are promoting a commercial blog.

Try This!

If you have business cards, add your blog's address to your business card.

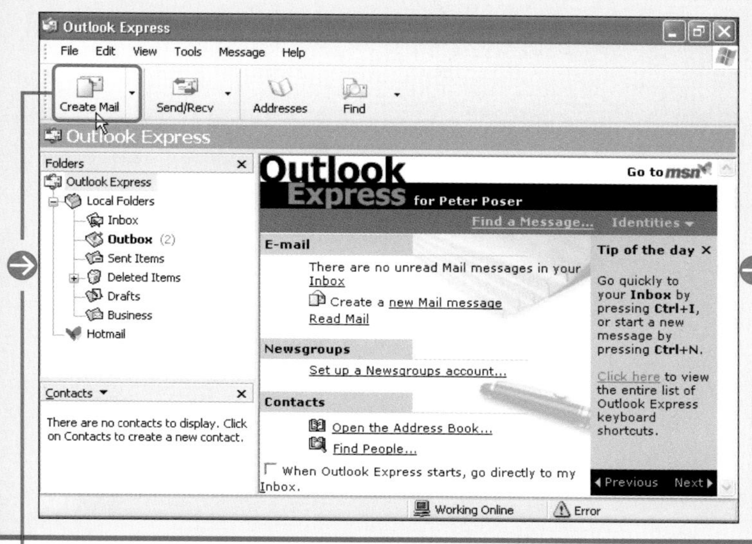

9 Click the Create Mail button.

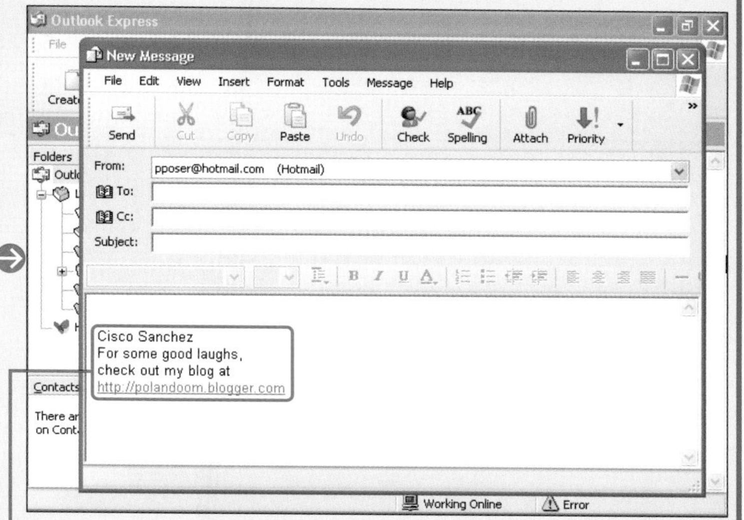

○ Outlook Express opens a new message window displaying the signature you added, along with the link to your blog.

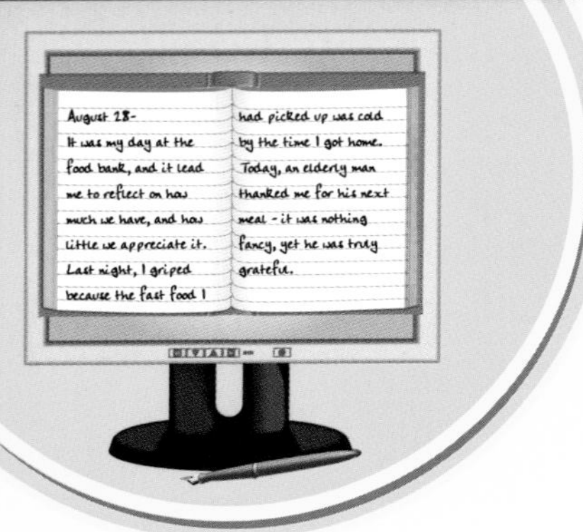

List your blog with BLOG DIRECTORIES

Given that the Internet accommodates millions of active blogs, visitors are unlikely to stumble upon yours. Of course, automated search engines, such as Google, may add your blog to their search directories, but even so, if someone searches Google for a word or phrase that your blog contains, the list of returned sites might be in the millions, and your blog might end up on page 10 of the search results.

To more effectively publicize your blog, list it with various blog directories. Most blog directories encourage blog creators to add their sites. Some of these directories contain only a few thousand blogs, increasing the chances that somebody looking for your blog will find it. This task shows you how to list your blog on Blogarama. The Web has several other blog directories, as mentioned in task #81, so when you are done at Blogarama, list your blog at these other directories, as well.

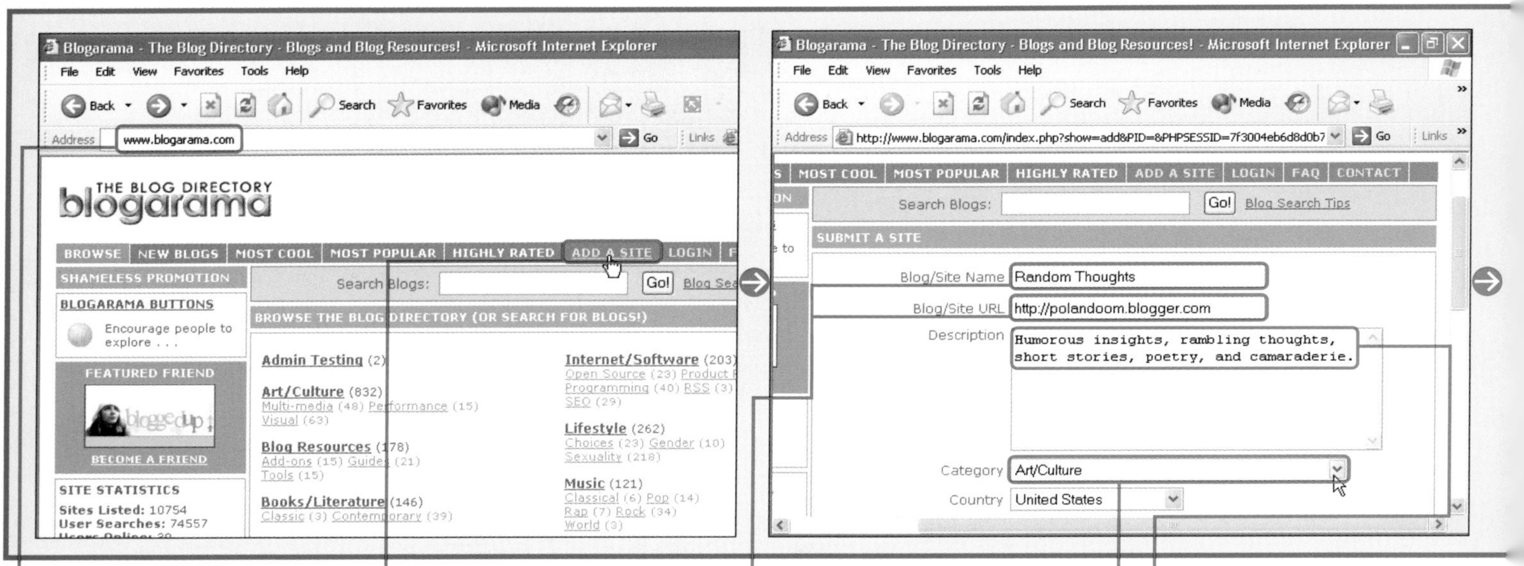

1. Type **www.blogarama.com** and press Enter.

- Internet Explorer opens Blogarama's home page.

2. Click the ADD A SITE tab.

- The SUBMIT A SITE form appears.

3. Type your blog's name.
4. Type your blog's address.
5. Type an accurate description of your blog, using as many key words as you can think of that can help a user find it.
6. Click here and select the Blogarama category in which you want Blogarama to list your blog.

DIFFICULTY LEVEL

Did You Know?

The username and password you enter at Blogarama is for logging on to Blogarama; it is not the username and password you use to log on to your blog hosting service.

More Options!

When you find other blogs you like, consider contacting the blog's creator and asking if he or she is willing to link his or her blog to your blog. To add a link to someone else's blog, insert the following code in your blog template, replacing the italicized text with text that points to the correct destination:
<a href="http://*www.sitename.com/*">*Site Title*</a>

More Options!

Forums that address topics related to your blog can be a great place to advertise your blog. Make sure you include a link to your blog in your posts to the forum.

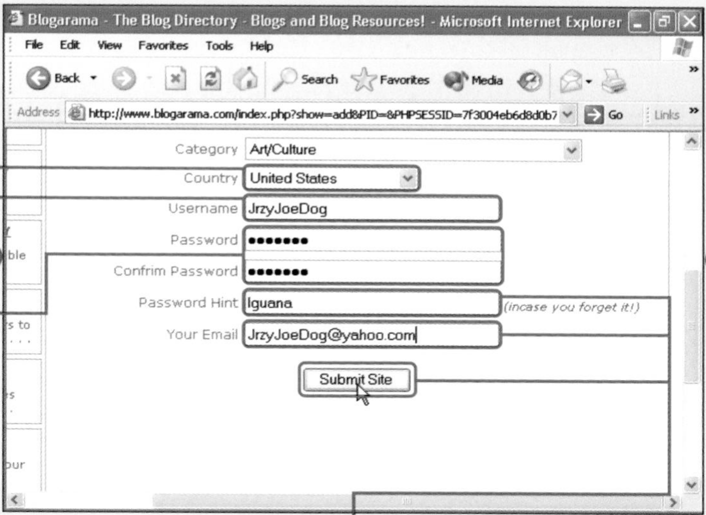

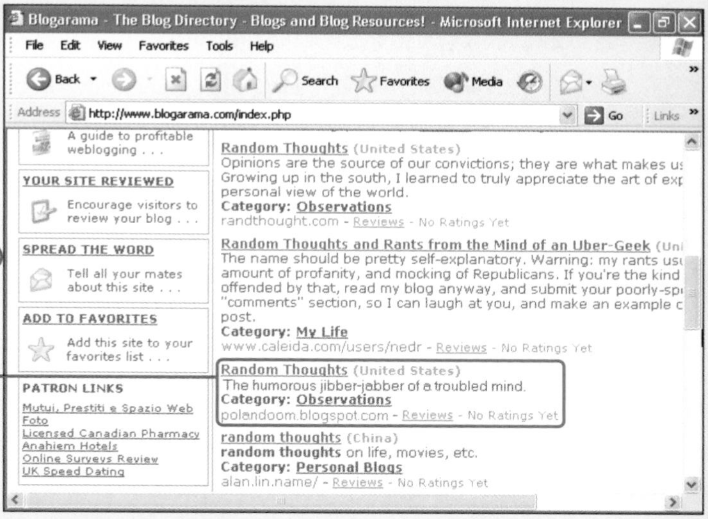

7 Click here and select the country in which you live.

8 Type a username to identify yourself.

9 Type a password in both of these boxes.

10 Type a password hint, if desired.

11 Type your e-mail address.

12 Click Submit Site.

- After Blogarama verifies your site, which can take several days, and adds it to the directory, the site appears in the directory.

Protect Your System from Viruses and Crackers

Whenever your computer connects to the Internet, it opens itself to attacks from viruses and *crackers* — meddlesome computer hackers who often use their computer expertise to break into networked computers. Viruses can hide in nearly any program you download from the Web or receive as a file attachment to an e-mail message. They can even hide in documents you receive. Crackers can break into your computer, often just for the fun of it, but sometimes to use your computer resources, vandalize files, or steal important data.

Is your computer at risk? If your computer remains connected to the Internet at all times, such as through a cable modem connection, it is more vulnerable to crackers. If you download and install programs, including games, or you receive and open file attachments you receive via e-mail, your system has a higher risk of picking up a virus. However, any computer that connects to a network, including the Internet, is susceptible to virus infections and break-ins. You can make your computer less vulnerable by learning about the threats and by installing and running software designed to protect your system.

This chapter introduces you to various tools and techniques for protecting your computer's security and preventing virus infections. Here, you learn how to install security patches, scan incoming files for viruses, install a *firewall* to prevent break-ins, and make sure your instant messaging software is not providing unauthorized access to your computer.

TOP 100

Test your computer's SECURITY ONLINE

The only computers that are completely secure are computers that never connect to the Internet or use files from other computers. That means that most computers are vulnerable to break-ins and/or virus infections. Still, many users give little thought to online security, often assuming that their Internet service provider is responsible for keeping the connection safe and secure. However, you really do not know how vulnerable your system is until you test your Internet connection. You just might discover that your system is wide open to break-ins and viruses.

Several software companies on the Internet provide free diagnostics to test your computer's vulnerabilities. These diagnostics typically determine whether or not your computer is running an anti-virus program and how visible your computer is on the Internet. If your computer is highly visible — that is, if it has a port number that a cracker can identify — then your computer is very vulnerable to break-ins. In this task, you run Symantec's security check to determine your computer's vulnerability.

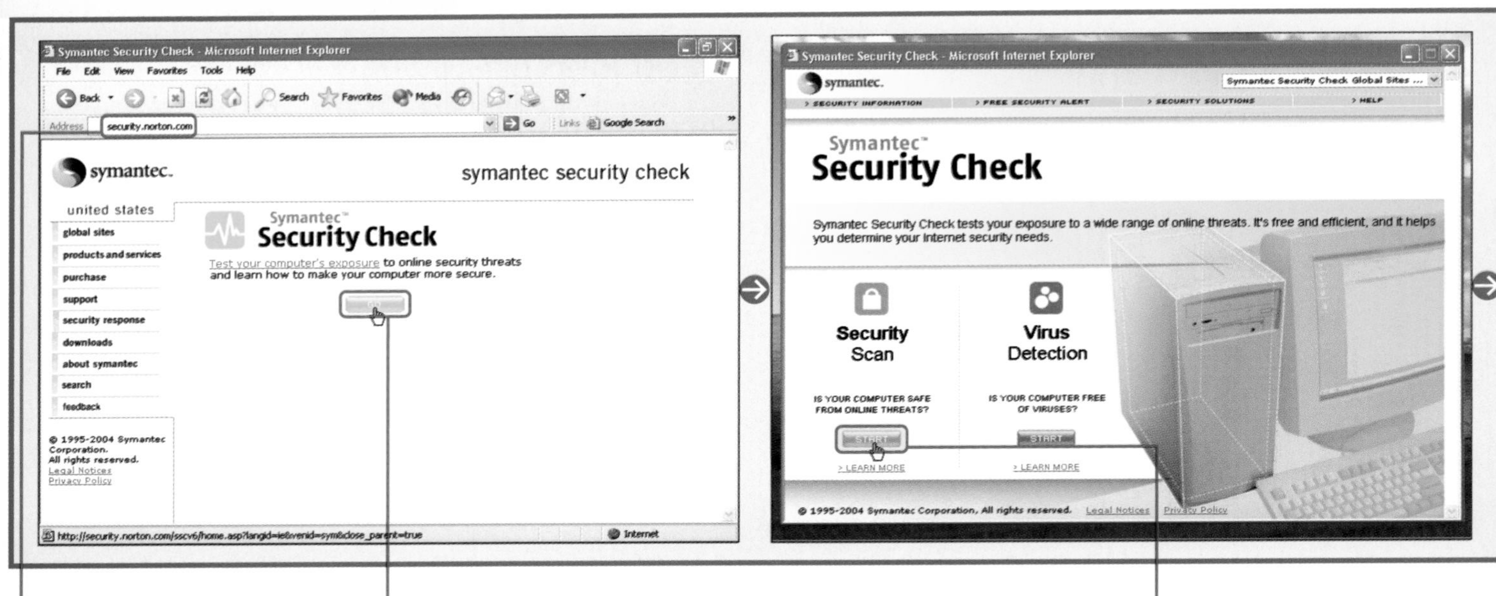

1. Type **security.norton.com** and press Enter.

○ Your browser opens the Symantec Security Check page.

2. Click Go.

○ The Symantec Security Check page appears.

3. Under Security Scan, click the START button.

More Options!

After the scan is complete, you can click the Virus Detection tab and click the Start button to have Symantec Security Check scan your computer for known viruses and *Trojan horses*. A Trojan horse is a program that pretends to be useful but carries out activities that a user does not authorize, such as collecting or destroying data. Unlike viruses, Trojan horses do not replicate.

Important!

As you browse the Web, some sites display pop-ups with exaggerated security warnings to sell you unnecessary software or services. The most suspect ads appear in windows that have no obvious way to close them. By responding to the ad, you reward the advertiser, so press Alt+F4 to close the window, and refer to tasks #6 and #7 to learn how to remove adware and block pop-ups.

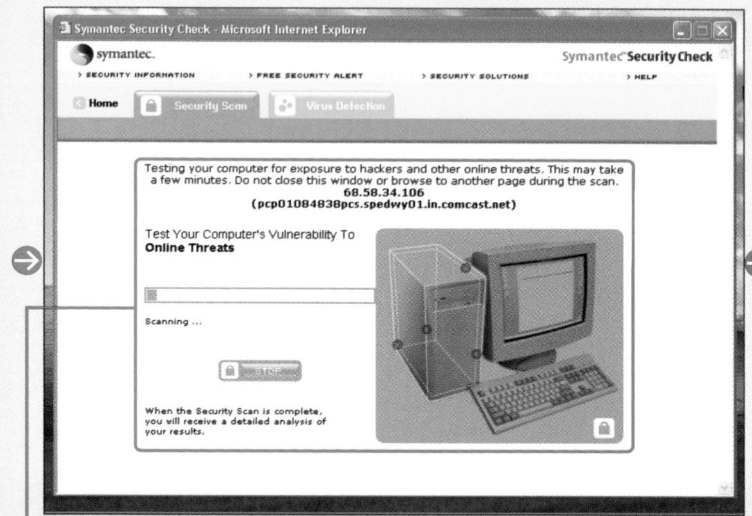

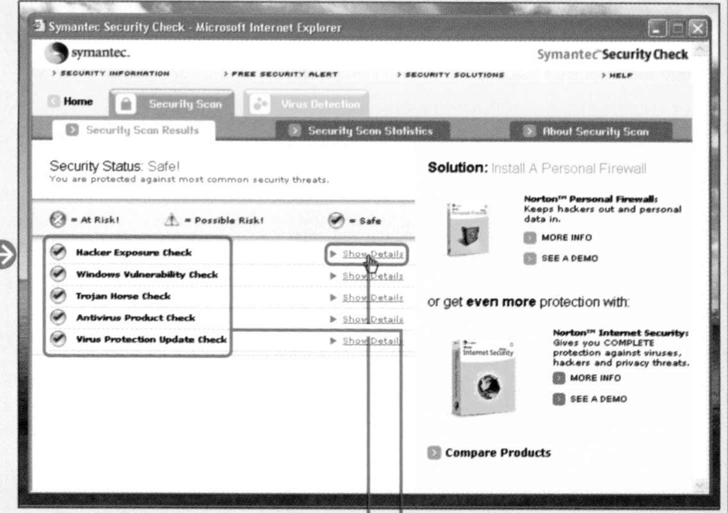

- Symantec Security Check displays its progress as it scans your computer and Internet connection.

- When the scan is complete, Symantec Security Check displays its results.

4. Note any insecure areas that require attention.

- This computer is secure.
- You can click the Show Details link to view additional information.

Install software
SECURITY PATCHES

Crackers constantly search for security vulnerabilities in software that they can exploit to break into systems. They focus especially on security flaws in the operating system, such as Windows; in browsers, including Internet Explorer; and in e-mail programs, such as Outlook Express. When they find and exploit a security flaw in a program, the program developer typically creates a *security patch* to fix the problem. In order to maintain your computer's security, you should check for and install any security patches on a regular basis.

If your computer runs Windows ME or a more recent version of Windows, installing security patches is relatively easy. Windows includes a utility called Windows Update that can determine whether your computer has the latest security patches and, if your computer does not have the patches installed, lead you through the process of installing them. If you have a different version of Windows or use programs other than Internet Explorer and Outlook Express to access the Internet, then check the help systems of those programs to determine how to install any available security patches.

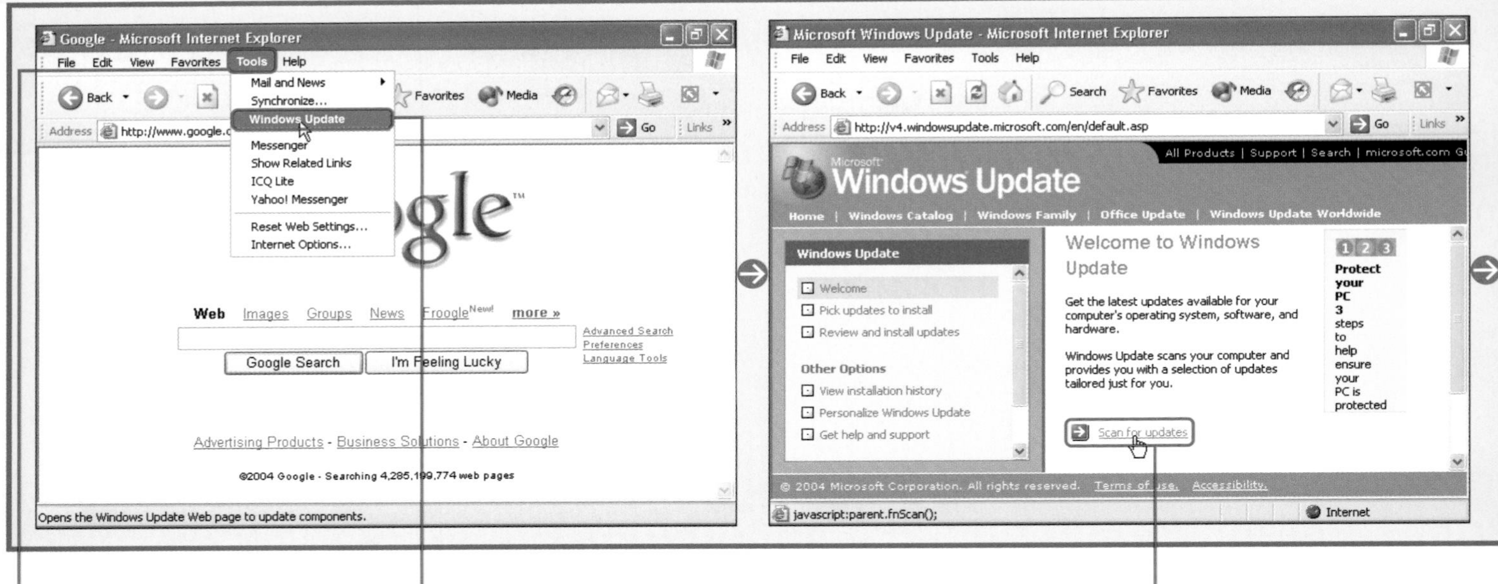

1. In Internet Explorer, click Tools.
2. Click Windows Update.

○ Internet Explorer opens Microsoft's Windows Update page.

3. Click the Scan for updates link.

Add It Automatically!

To enable or disable Windows automatic updating, right-click My Computer, click Properties, and then click the Automatic Updates tab. Click the check box next to Keep my computer up to date. This toggles the option on or off. Click OK.

More Options!

To have Windows automatically download and install updates without prompting you to confirm, enter your preferences in the System Properties dialog box. Right-click My Computer, click Properties, and then click the Automatic Updates tab. Under Settings, click Automatically download the updates, and install them on the schedule that I specify (○ changes to ◉). Select the day and time you want Windows to check for and install updates and click OK.

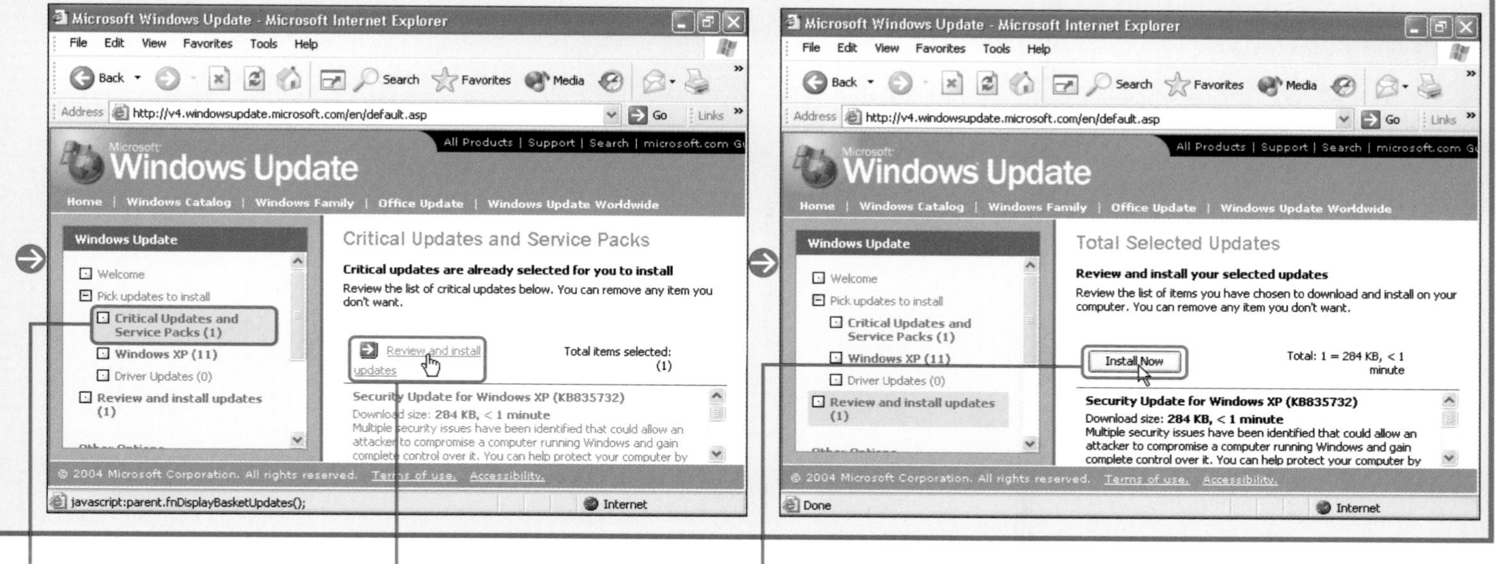

○ Windows Update scans for updates and displays a list of available updates.

4 Click the Critical Updates and Service Packs link.

○ Windows Update displays the critical updates, which include all security patches, and selects all of them for installation.

5 Click the Review and install updates link.

○ Windows Update displays a list of the updates it is ready to install.

6 Click the Install Now button.

○ Windows installs the updates. If an update requires you to restart Windows, a dialog box appears prompting you to restart.

Check your browser's SECURITY SETTINGS

As you browse the Web, some Web sites attempt to install ActiveX controls or Java applets on your computer with or without your permission. In most cases, these small programs add functionality to the Web pages or browser, enhancing Web sites with forms, animations, and interactive content. However, they can also place adware on your computer, change your browser's home page, steal or delete data, and cause other problems.

To prevent ActiveX controls or Java applets from installing on your computer without your knowledge, you can tighten the security settings in your Web browser. Most browsers, including Internet Explorer, provide settings for completely blocking ActiveX controls and Java applets or for displaying a dialog box that requires your confirmation before installing them.

Because so many Web sites use ActiveX controls and Java applets to add functionality to their sites, you usually do not want to disable them altogether, but you should make sure your browser can warn you of any potentially dangerous controls or applets. This task shows you how to check and adjust the security settings in Internet Explorer.

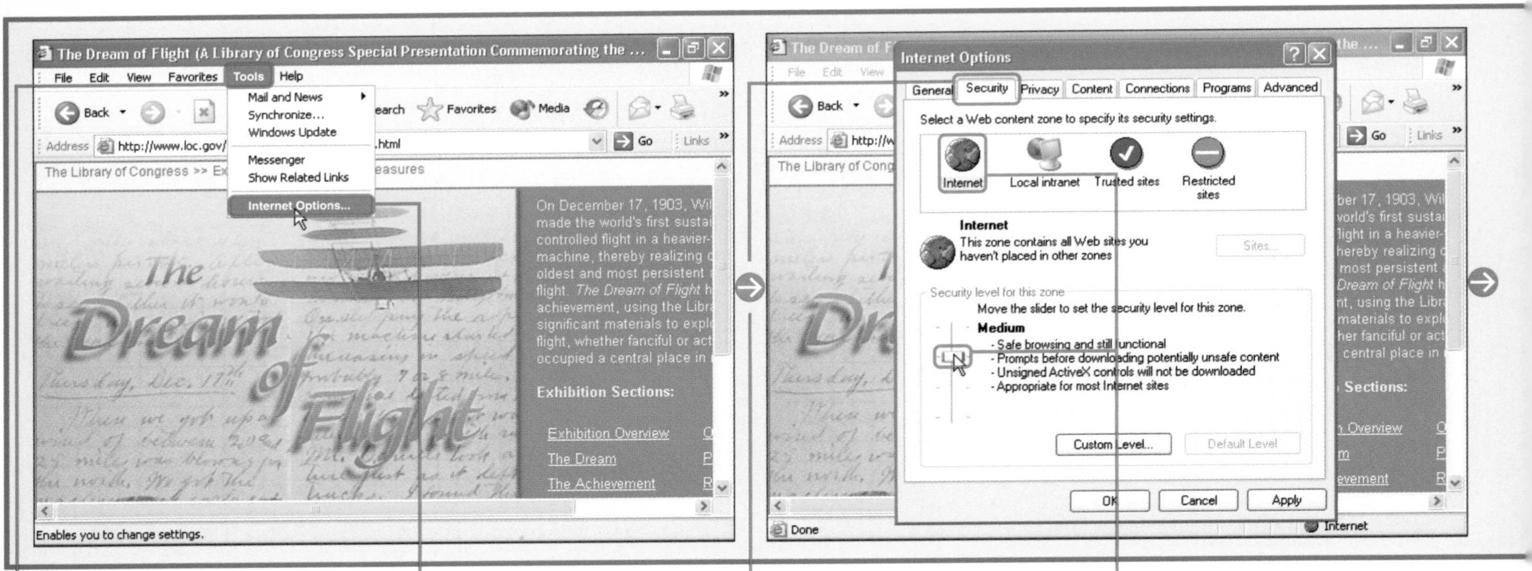

1. In Internet Explorer, click Tools.
2. Click Internet Options.

- The Internet Options dialog box appears.

3. Click the Security tab.
4. Click Internet.
5. Drag the slider to the desired setting.

DIFFICULTY LEVEL

More Options!

The Security tab features a Trusted Sites icon and a Restricted Sites icon. Click one of the icons and then click the Sites button to add sites to a trusted or restricted sites list. Internet Explorer relaxes security for trusted sites and prevents cookies and ActiveX content for any restricted sites.

More Options!

To determine what Internet Explorer blocks and what it permits, click the Custom Level button. This displays a list of items you can enable or disable individually.

Important!

Heightening security to the strictest level prevents some sites from functioning at all. To access the site, either relax the security level for the Internet zone or add the site's address to your list of trusted sites.

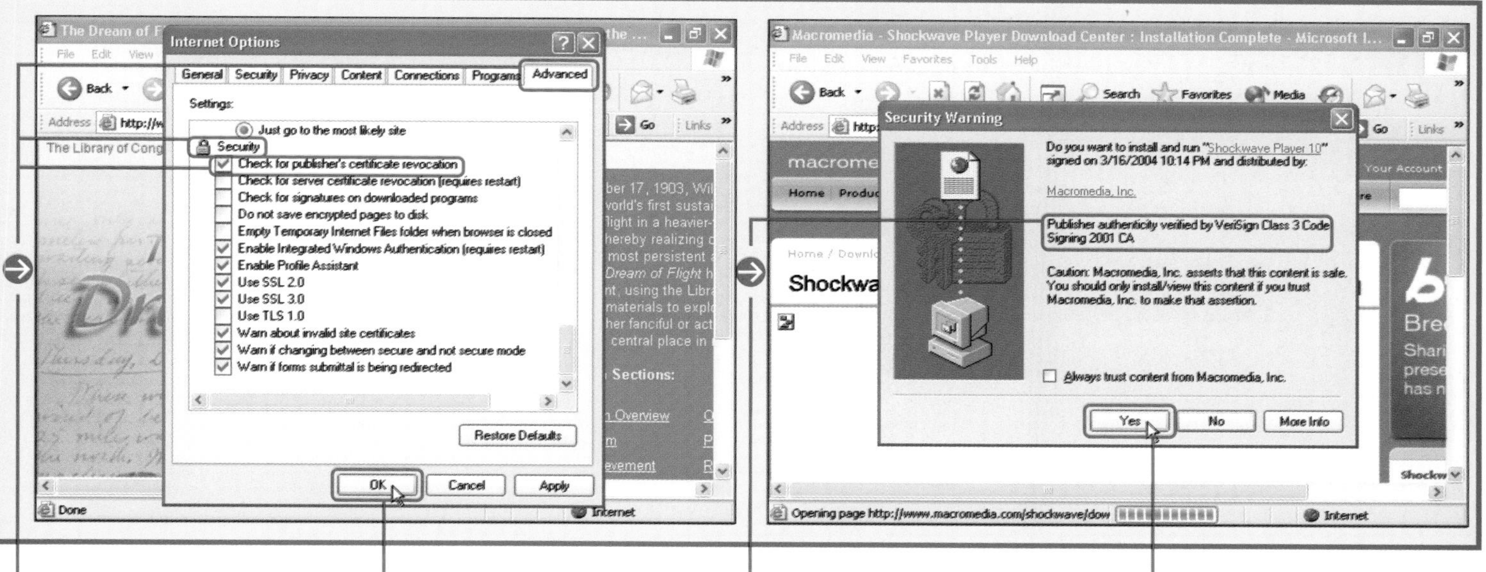

6 Click the Advanced tab.

7 Scroll down to the Security options.

8 Click Check for publisher's security revocation

9 Click OK.

- Internet Explorer saves the security settings and closes the Internet Options dialog box.

- With a medium or high security level, Internet Explorer asks for confirmation before installing an ActiveX control.

10 Make sure the company's certificate is valid.

11 To install the control, click Yes.

- That ActiveX control installs and adds functionality to the browser so it can play the selected file type.

Disable file and printer SHARING

If your computer is part of a network and other computers need access to it, you must have file and printer sharing enabled. This allows your computer to share its disk storage, folders, files, and printer with other computers in the network. However, it also makes it more open to crackers. If you mark disks or folders as shared, any computer connected to the network has access to everything on those disks and folders. So if a cracker breaks into your network, he or she can copy and delete files and folders, rearrange them, and even install and run programs on your computer.

If your computer is part of a network and it is the computer that connects directly to the Internet, you should disable file and printer sharing for the network connection that your computer uses to connect to the Internet. For example, if your computer uses dial-up networking to connect to the Internet via modem, you should disable file and printer sharing for your dial-up networking connection. This task shows how to disable file and printer sharing in Windows XP.

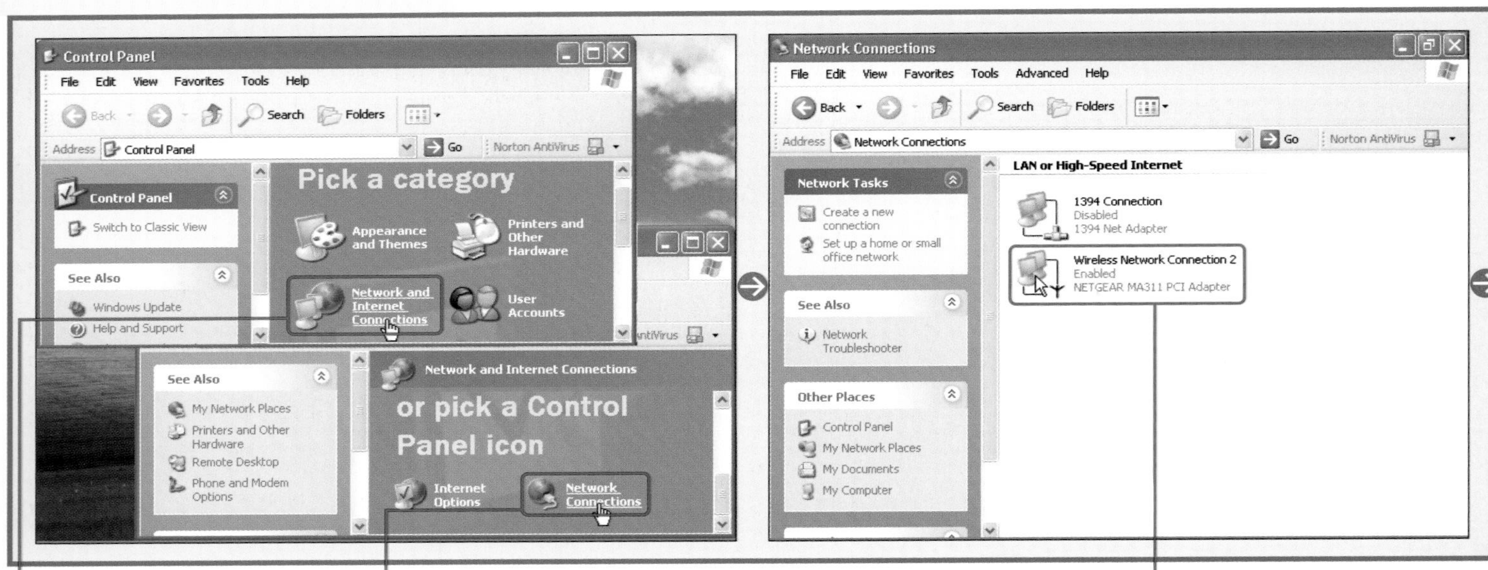

1. Open the Windows control panel and click the Network and Internet Connections link.

- The Network and Internet Connections icons appear.

2. Scroll down and click the Network Connections link.

- The Network Connections icons appear.

3. Double-click the icon for your Internet network connection.

DIFFICULTY LEVEL

Important!

You do not need to disable file and printer sharing for all of your network connections. Disable file and printer sharing only for your Internet connection. Otherwise, other computers on the network cannot share the resources on your computer.

More Options!

Turning off file and printer sharing for the computer that connects to the Internet is only one precaution. You should also install a firewall on the computer, as explained in task #99. In addition, be selective in marking which folders to share on your computer; you do not need to share everything.

More Options!

If your computer is not part of a network and you see, in the Network Connection Properties dialog box, that Client for Microsoft Networks is installed, click it and click the Uninstall button to remove it from your system. This removes file and printer sharing for Microsoft Networks, as well.

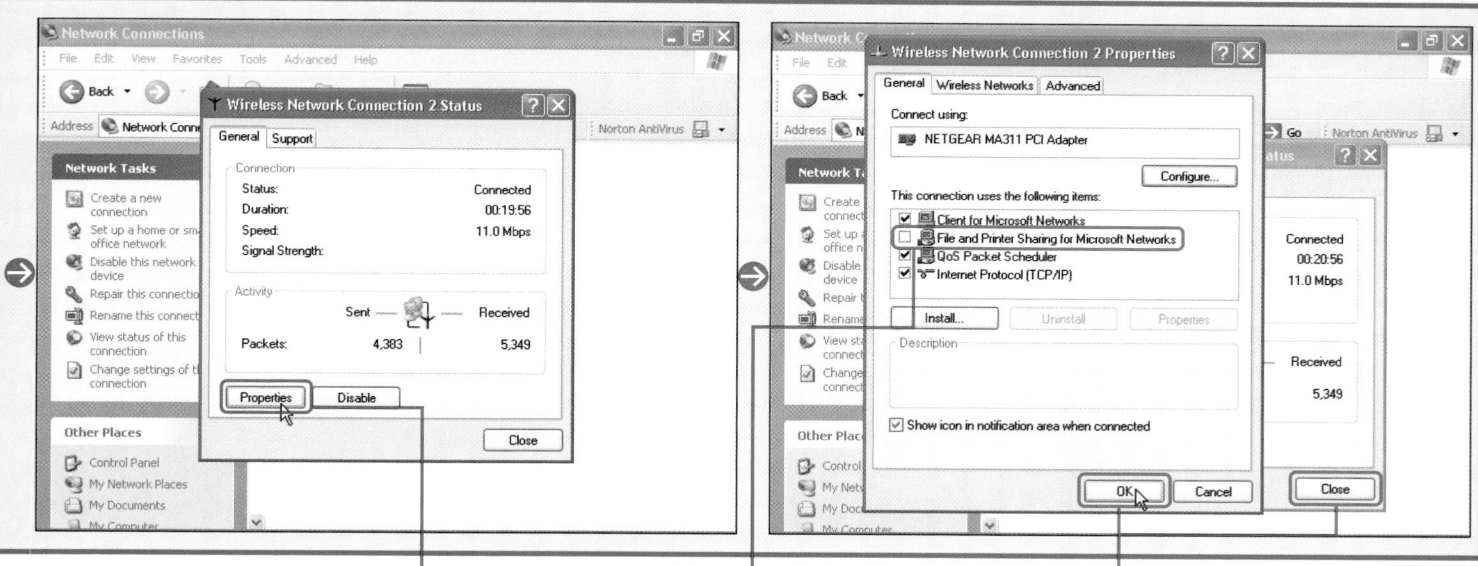

- The Network Connection Status dialog box appears.

4. Click the Properties button.

- The Network Connection Properties dialog box appears.

5. If the check box next to File and printer sharing for Microsoft Networks is checked, click the box to remove the check mark.

6. Click OK.

- Windows saves your change.

7. Click Close.

- The Network Connection Status dialog box closes.

Install an ANTI-VIRUS PROGRAM

The Internet is a dangerous place for a computer, especially when it comes to viruses and Trojan horses. Any program you download and install can carry a virus. Nearly any e-mail attachment can infect your computer. Even ActiveX controls embedded in Web pages can carry destructive computer code. And once a virus infects your system, it usually acts as a tenacious bug, making it extremely difficult to remove.

Before you connect to the Internet, you should install an anti-virus program on your computer and learn how to use it. An anti-virus program protects your system in two ways: it scans incoming files to prevent infection, and it scans files already on your computer to rid your computer of any infection it might already have. Most anti-virus programs also scan outgoing messages to prevent spreading viruses.

If you have never checked your computer for viruses, go back to task #91, and run Symantec System Check for Viruses on your computer. Then, return to this task to download and install Norton AntiVirus on your computer.

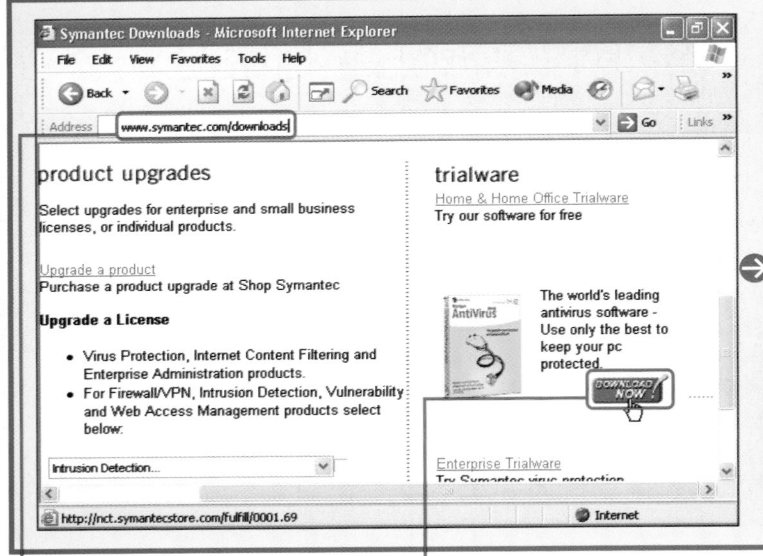

1. Type **www.symantec.com/downloads** and press Enter.

- Internet Explorer opens Symantec's downloads page.

2. Scroll down and click the Download NOW! button for Norton AntiVirus.

- Follow the onscreen instructions to download and install Norton AntiVirus.

- After installation, Norton AntiVirus runs on your computer, and its icon appears in the system tray.

3. Double-click the icon for running Norton AntiVirus.

DIFFICULTY LEVEL

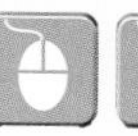

Attention!

The Norton AntiVirus trialware works for only 15 days. After that, you need to pay for the program to continue using it.

More Options!

Another excellent anti-virus program is McAfee VirusScan. Go to download.mcafee.com to download a 15-day free trial of the program.

Important!

Anti-virus programs have a database of virus signatures that they use to identify potential viruses. Because viruses constantly change, you need to keep your virus signatures up-to-date. Most anti-virus programs automatically check for and download updates on a regular basis, but check to make sure. Your anti-virus program is only as effective as it is up-to-date.

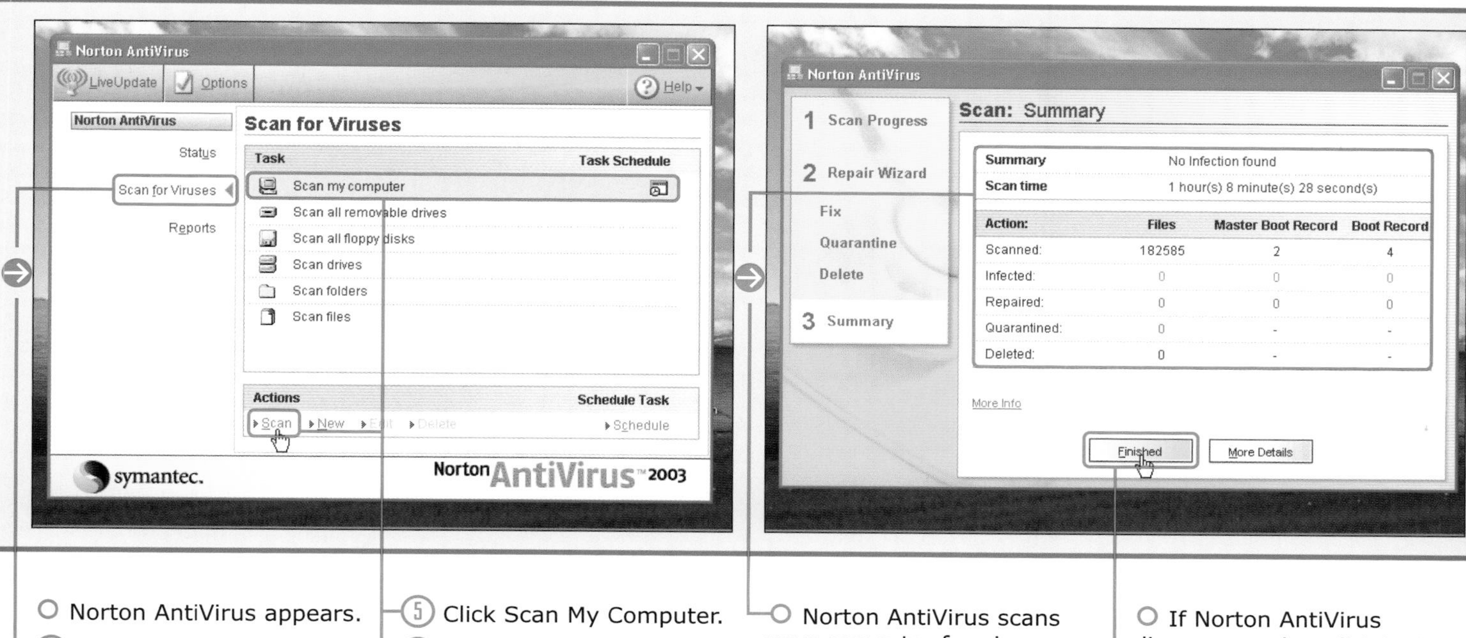

- Norton AntiVirus appears.
4. Click Scan for Viruses.
5. Click Scan My Computer.
6. Click Scan.

- Norton AntiVirus scans your computer for viruses and displays its results here. This scan found no virus infection.
- If Norton AntiVirus discovers a virus, it tries to isolate it and then provides you with instructions for removing it.

7. Click the Finished button.

Enable AUTO-PROTECT

Most anti-virus programs have an auto-protect feature that runs automatically whenever you start your computer and continues to run as you use your computer to perform various tasks. On startup, the auto-protect feature scans your computer's boot directory for viruses, a common point of attack. Whenever you download a file from the Internet, auto-protect scans it and reports any potential viruses, so you can take immediate action before you open or run the file. In addition, auto-protect can scan incoming and outgoing e-mail messages and attachments for known viruses.

When you install most anti-virus programs, the program enables the auto-protect feature by default. However, you should make sure auto-protect is on and configured to provide your system with optimum protection. This task shows you how to enable auto-protect in Norton AntiVirus for Windows and enter your protection preferences.

You can also follow the steps in this task to disable auto-protect for times when you install a program that cannot install properly when an anti-virus program runs in the background.

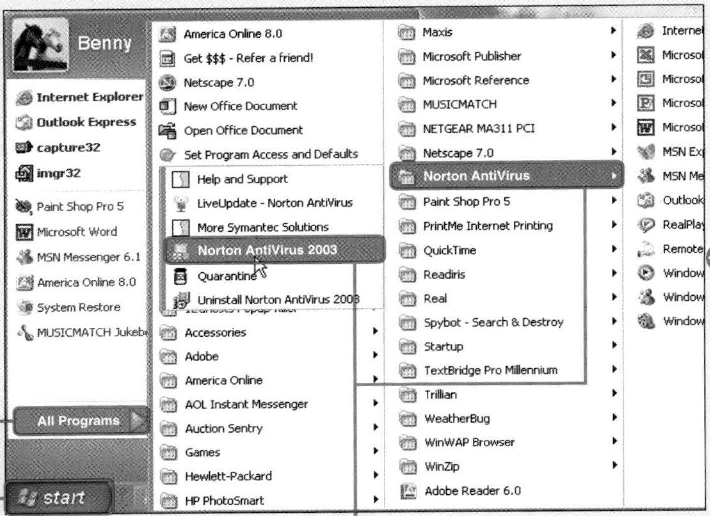

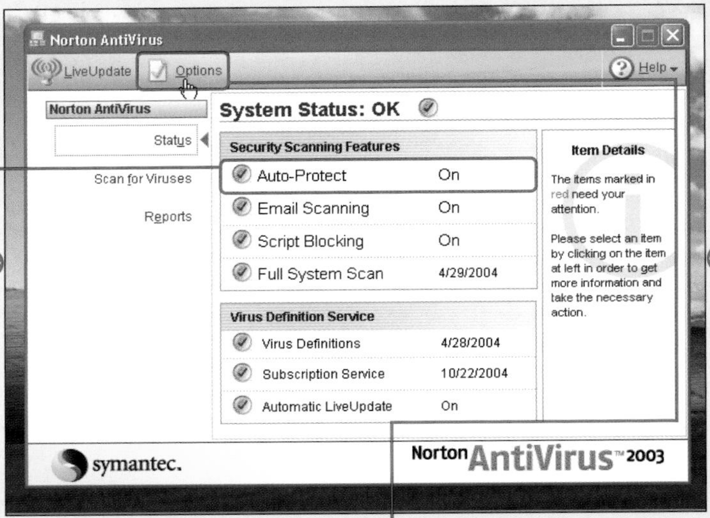

1. Click the Windows Start button.
2. Depending on which version of Windows you use, click either Programs or All Programs.
3. Click Norton AntiVirus.
4. Click Norton AntiVirus.

- Norton AntiVirus appears and indicates whether auto-protect is on or off.

5. Click the Options button.

Try This!

When Norton AntiVirus is running, its icon appears in the Windows system tray at the right end of the toolbar. You can double-click the Norton AntiVirus icon ( ) to run the program.

DIFFICULTY LEVEL

More Options!

You can enable Norton AntiVirus to update itself automatically. In the Norton AntiVirus Options dialog box, click LiveUpdate. Click each check box to place a check mark in each. Enable automatic LiveUpdate (☐ changes to ☑), Enable virus protection updates (☐ changes to ☑), and Notify me of Norton AntiVirus program updates (☐ changes to ☑).

Customize It!

To schedule Norton AntiVirus to scan your computer for viruses, run Norton AntiVirus, click Scan for Viruses, click the Schedule link, and enter the scheduled frequency and time.

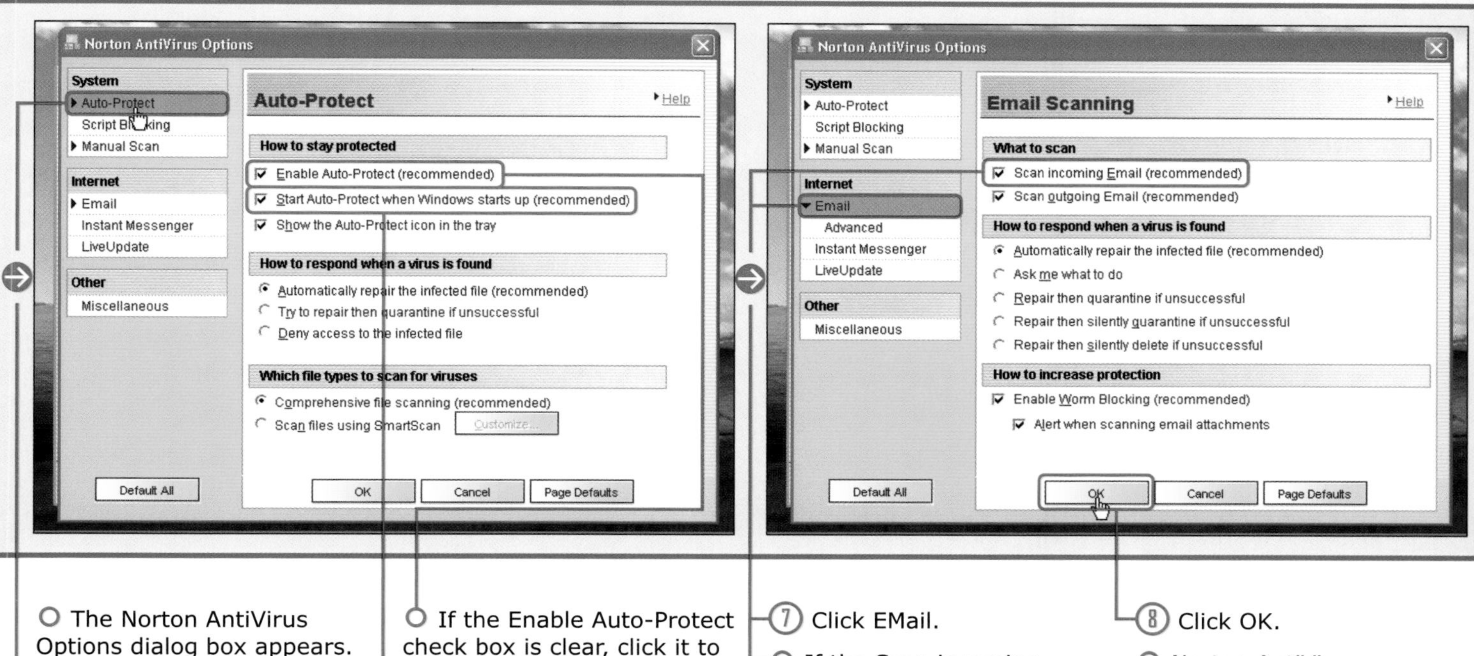

- The Norton AntiVirus Options dialog box appears.

6. Click Auto-Protect.

- If the Enable Auto-Protect check box is clear, click it to enable auto-protect.
- If the Start Auto-Protect when Windows starts up check box is clear, click it to have Windows run Auto-Protect at startup.

7. Click EMail.

- If the Scan incoming Email check box is clear, click it to have Norton AntiVirus scan e-mail you receive for viruses.

8. Click OK.

- Norton AntiVirus saves your settings and returns you to its main program window, which you can now exit.

Avoid sources of RISKY SOFTWARE

As games, applications, and other software travel around the Internet, they commonly contract viruses that then pass from one computer to the next. Here's the scenario: A virus infects your friend's computer without his or her knowledge. Your friend downloads a cool game that has no virus and installs it. The installation file becomes infected. The friend then e-mails you the infected file to install on your computer to keep you from missing out on the fun. You install it, infecting your computer. If the virus is relatively new and your anti-virus program does not have the virus's signature in its database, even your anti-virus program cannot protect you.

To prevent this scenario from happening, take two precautions. First, as shown in this task, never install or run a program that someone sent you. Find out where the person obtained the file — usually at a Web site — and download it from there. Most Web servers scan their files for viruses regularly. Also, scan any file attachments before opening them, as explained in task #98.

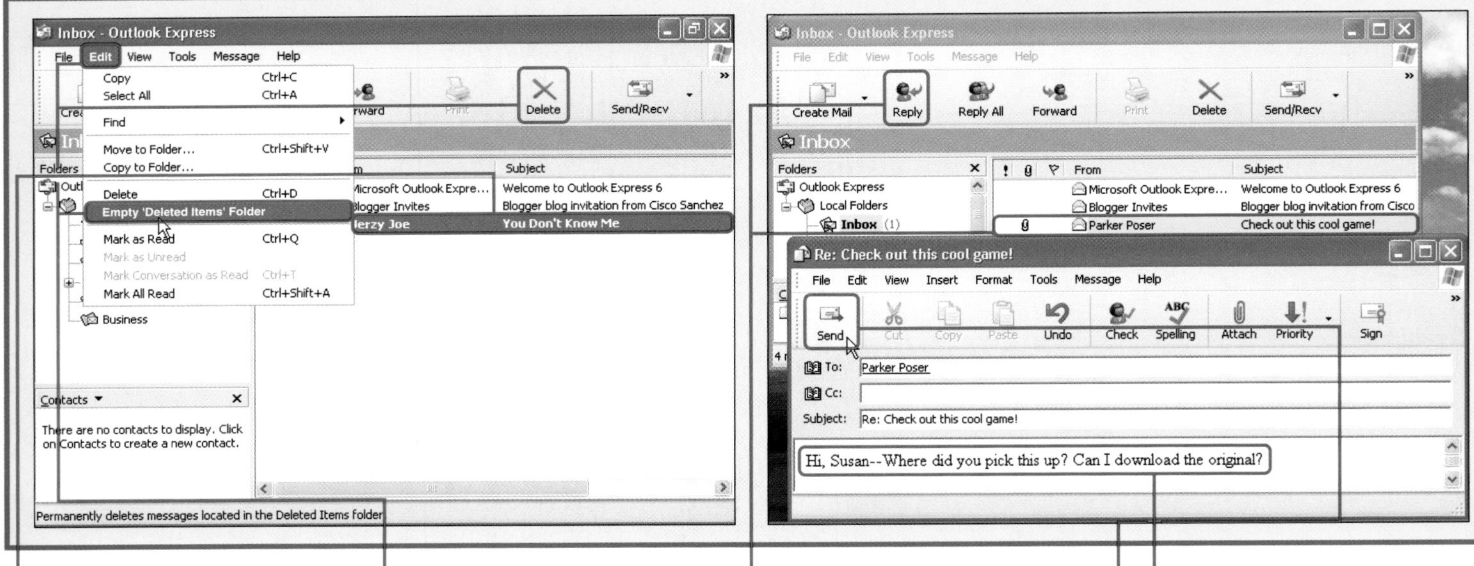

DELETE AN ATTACHMENT FROM AN UNKNOWN SENDER

① Click the message.

② Click Delete.

③ Click Edit.

④ Click Empty 'Deleted Items' Folder.

VERIFY THE SOURCE OF AN ATTACHED FILE

① If you receive an e-mail message that has an attached program file from a friend, click the message.

② Click Reply.

③ Type a message asking your friend to specify the file's source.

④ Click Send.

○ When your friend replies, go to the source and download the file from there.

DIFFICULTY LEVEL

Caution!

After you download a program file but before you install it, scan it for viruses as instructed in task #98.

Did You Know?

Although program files carry most viruses, macro viruses can travel in document files as well. Although most word processing programs have settings to protect against macro viruses, the settings usually disable macros, which is not something most users want to do. Scan any document files you receive for viruses before opening them.

Did You Know?

Viruses can also travel on floppy disks, CDs, and DVDs, so before you use any files on a disk you receive, scan the disk for viruses.

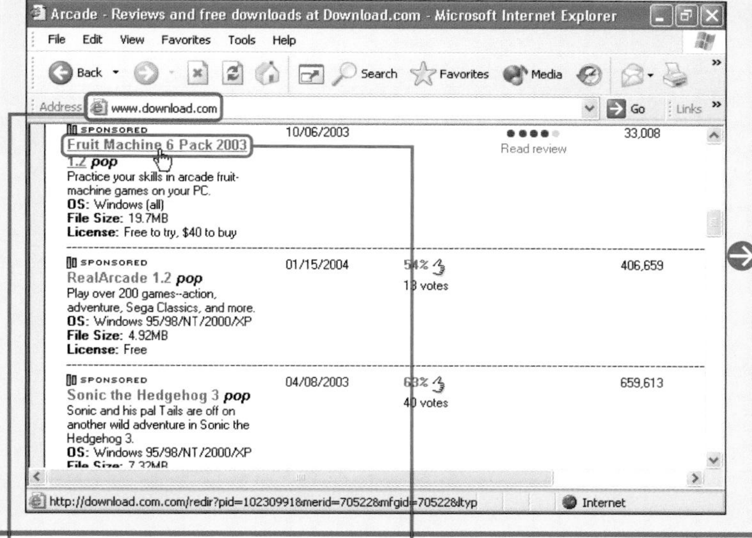

Fruit Machine 6 Pack 2003 - Reviews and free downloads at Download.com - Microsof...

Download.com Review of Fruit Machine 6 Pack 2003

Download Now
Free download 19.7MB

CNET User Opinions

Read user opinions of Fruit Machine 6 Pack 2003

DOWNLOAD SAFER PROGRAMS

1. To locate safer program files, type **www.download.com** and press Enter.
2. Follow the trail of links to the desired file.

Note: In most cases, download now redirects you to the company Web site, from which you download the original file.

3. Click the Download Now link and use the resulting dialog box to save the file.

- Your browser downloads the file and stores it in the selected folder.

Scan disks and files for VIRUSES

Whenever you receive a file — via e-mail, by downloading it from a Web site, or on a disk or CD from a friend — the first impulse is to open it. Resist the urge. The file might seem innocent enough, but it could carry a virus. If the file is a program file, whose name typically ends in .com or .exe, be especially careful, as explained in task #97. But even file formats considered safe in the past, such as JPEG and MP3, can carry viruses, although this is rare.

Instead of opening a file or running a program right away, scan it for viruses to make sure no known virus attached itself to the file. If you have Norton AntiVirus Auto-Protect enabled, it scans incoming e-mail and any attachments, but if you receive files on disk from a friend or colleague or had auto-protect disabled when you downloaded a file, scanning the file before opening or running it is a good safety precaution. This task shows you how to use Norton AntiVirus for Windows to scan disks, folders, and individual files for viruses.

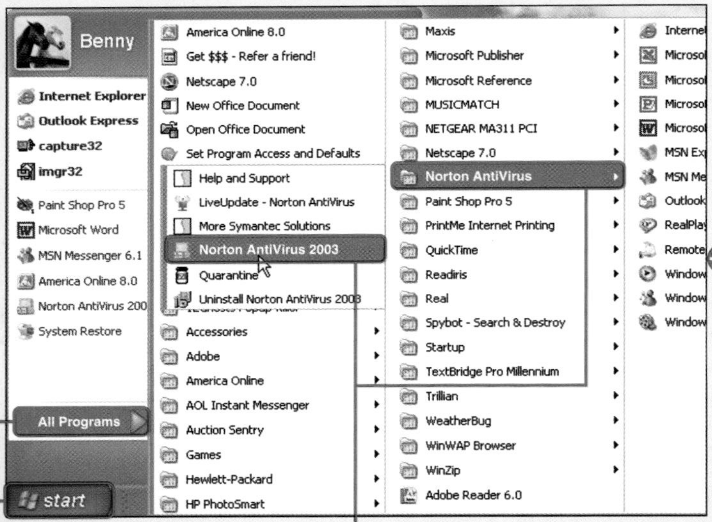

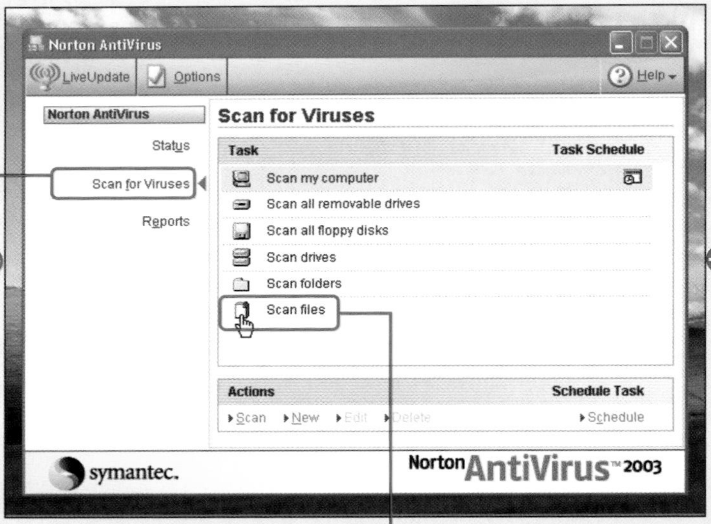

1. Click Start.
2. Click either Programs or All Programs.
3. Click Norton AntiVirus.
4. Click Norton AntiVirus.

- Norton AntiVirus appears.

5. Click Scan for Viruses.
6. Double-click Scan Drives, Scan Folders, or Scan Files.

Try This!

In My Computer, right-click a disk, folder, or file you want to scan for viruses and click Scan with Norton AntiVirus. Norton AntiVirus automatically scans the selected item and displays its results.

DIFFICULTY LEVEL

Did You Know?

Outlook Express has a feature that can block incoming mail attachments that might carry viruses, but it can block more than you want it to. If you see that many of your e-mail attachments are not arriving, disable this feature in Outlook Express. Click Tools, click Options, click the Security tab, and click the check box next to Do not allow attachments to be saved or opened that could potentially be a virus (☑ changes to ☐). Click OK.

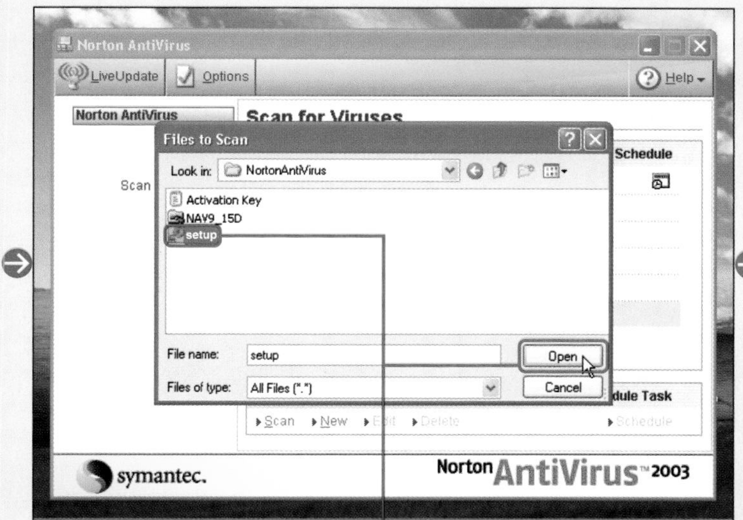

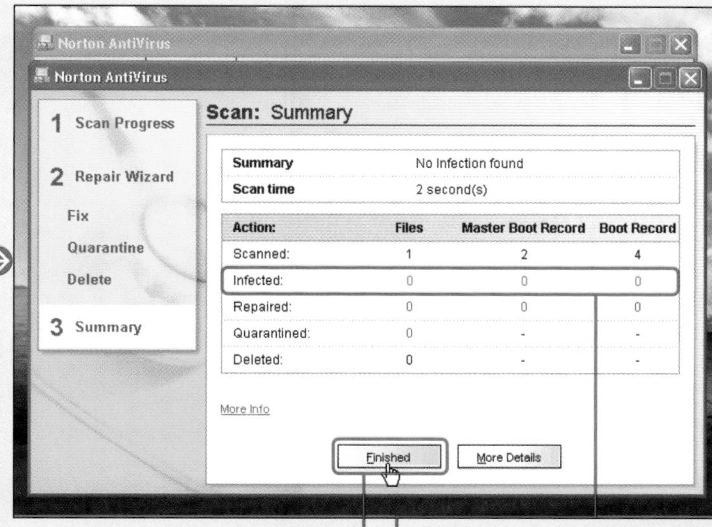

- A dialog box appears, prompting you to select the files, folders, or drives you want to scan.

Note: The dialog box differs depending on the selected option.

7. Select the drive or drives, folders, or files you want to scan.
8. Click the Open button in the Files to Scan dialog box, or click the Scan button in the Scan Folders or Scan Drives dialog box.

- Norton AntiVirus displays a window showing the scanning operation's progress and then displays the results.
- If Norton AntiVirus discovers a virus, it displays the virus name here and shows any corrective action it took. This scan found no virus infection.

9. Click Finished.

Enable the Windows FIREWALL

When you connect your computer to the Internet, you place it on a network connected to millions of other computers. To help your computer navigate on this information superhighway, your Internet service provider assigns it a number that identifies it. With this number, anyone with a moderate amount of knowledge and desire can follow your every move on the Internet and even break into your computer to use your computer's resources, steal or destroy data, or perform other malicious activity without your knowledge.

If you connect to the Internet using a dial-up modem, your computer faces less risk than if it has an *always on* connection, such as a DSL or a cable modem. If you connect to the Internet, check your e-mail, browse the Web, and then disconnect, your system is not very vulnerable. However, if your computer remains on and connected, you should install and enable a firewall for protection.

A firewall stands between your computer and the Internet, hiding its address from other users, and preventing unauthorized access. This task shows you how to enable the firewall included with Windows XP.

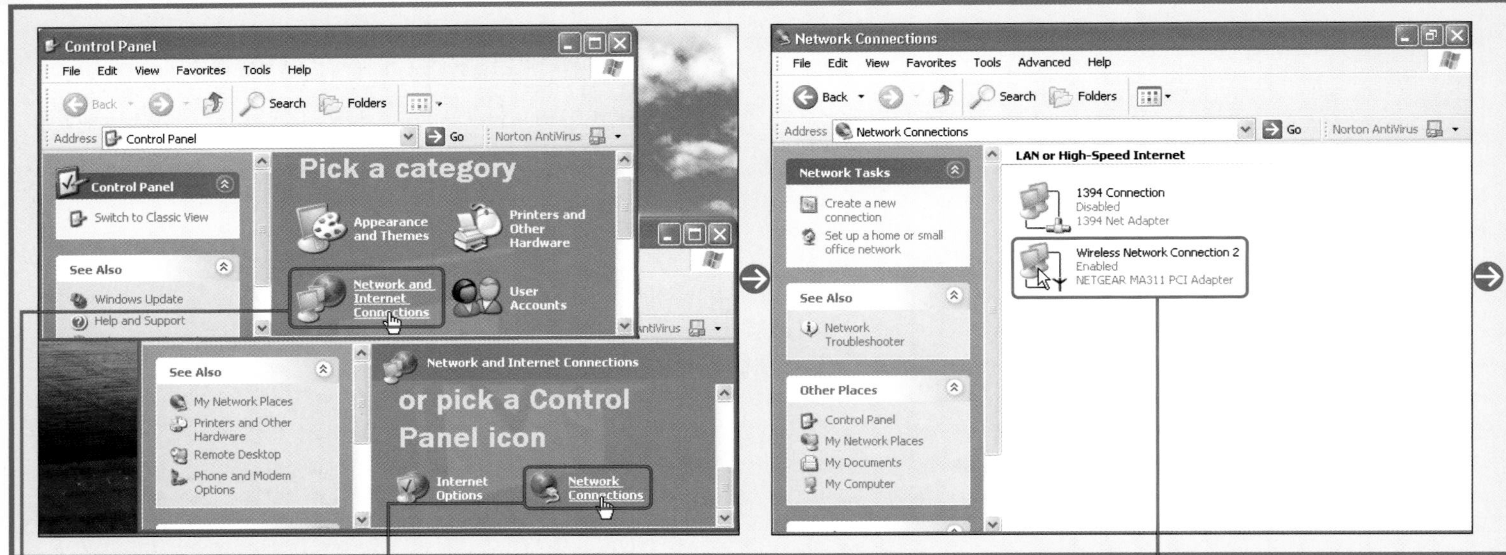

1. Open the Windows control panel and click the Network and Internet Connections link.

- The Network and Internet Connections icons appear.

2. Scroll down and click the Network Connections link.

- The Network Connections icons appear.

3. Double-click the icon for your Internet network connection.

DIFFICULTY LEVEL

Cross-Platform

If your computer runs a version of Windows that does not feature firewall protection, you can obtain freeware or shareware firewalls. ZoneLabs has a great reputation and offers a free firewall, called ZoneAlarm, which you can download from www.zonelabs.com. Scroll down the page and click the ZoneAlarm (free) link.

Did You Know?

Many networks are equipped with a router, which directs packets of data between two networks. Although the router is not a firewall, it acts as a buffer between the Internet and the local network, helping to secure the network.

Did You Know?

In the past, Microsoft recommended that you enable firewall protection only on the computer that connects directly to the Internet. Now, Microsoft recommends that you enable the firewall on all computers on your network.

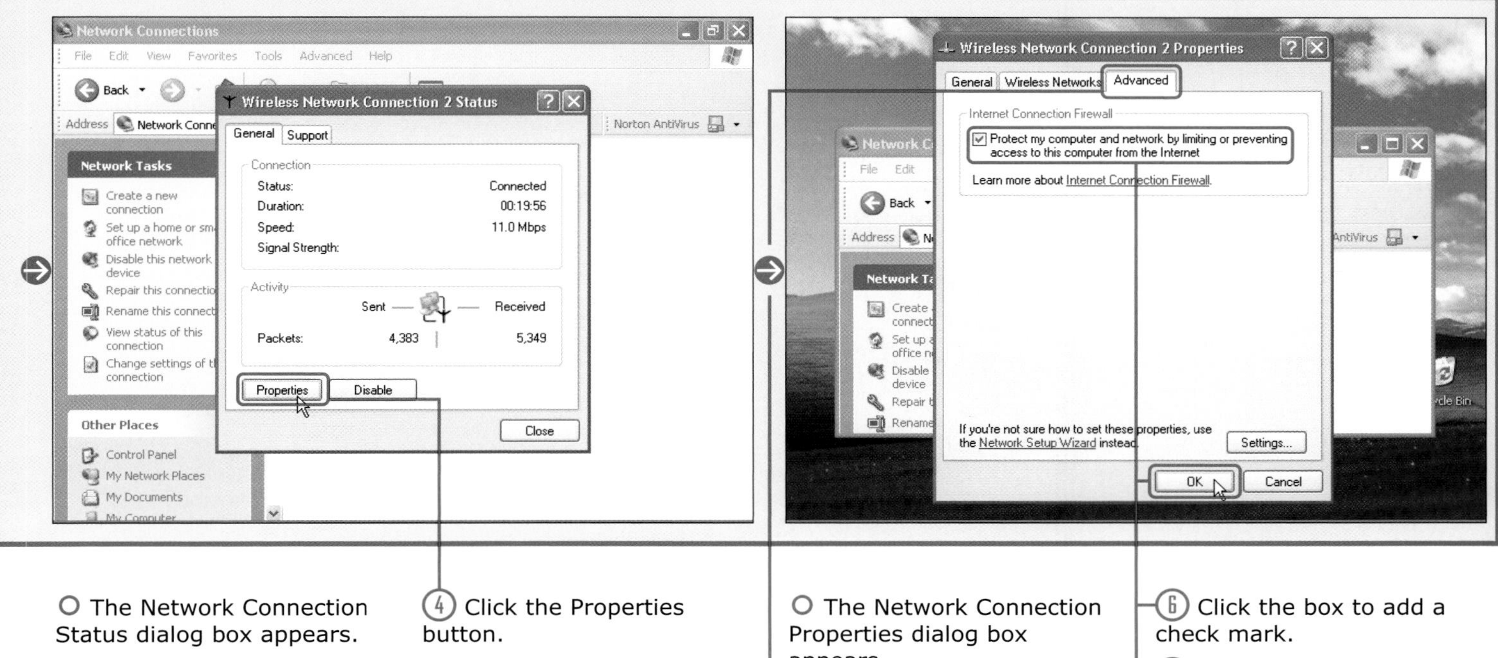

- The Network Connection Status dialog box appears.

4. Click the Properties button.

- The Network Connection Properties dialog box appears.

5. Click the Advanced tab.

6. Click the box to add a check mark.

7. Click OK.

- Windows XP enables the firewall.

Check your INSTANT MESSENGER SETTINGS

Norton AntiVirus and other anti-virus programs feature options to scan any incoming files that you might receive via your instant messaging program. However, many instant messaging programs such as AOL Instant Messenger (AIM) have built-in computer sharing capabilities that make it possible for someone to connect to your computer, access its files, and even run programs on it. You can adjust the settings in your instant messaging program to disable computer sharing, file sharing, and other features that make your computer vulnerable.

This task shows you how to adjust your preferences in AIM for optimum security. Here, you learn how to disable file sharing, file transfer, and direct instant messaging, which all make your computer more open to potential threats. If you want to use these capabilities, take these steps, but examine your options more closely. You can, for instance, allow file sharing for only those people on your buddy list, and you can specify which folder users can access. Likewise, you can specify which people you want to allow to connect to your computer for direct instant messaging.

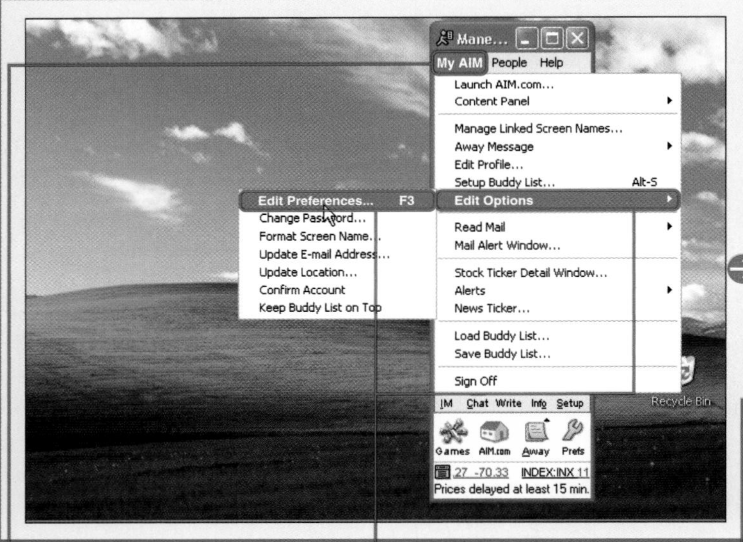

Note: This task requires the AOL Instant Messenger

① In AIM, click My AIM.

② Click Edit Options.

③ Click Edit Preferences.

○ The AOL Instant Messenger Preferences dialog box appears.

④ Click File Sharing.

⑤ Click Don't Allow under For users on my Buddy list.

○ When you select Don't Allow for your buddies, the AIM automatically selects Don't Allow under For users not on my Buddy list.

More Options!

To access file transfer settings in Yahoo! Messenger, click Login, click Preferences, and click File Transfer. You can then choose global settings that instruct Messenger whether or not to accept files from people who send them and whether to allow people who try to obtain files from you to get them.

More Options!

Both MSN Messenger and Yahoo! Messenger have options for checking incoming files for viruses. If you choose to accept files from other users, enable this option and type the path to your anti-virus program's utility for checking IMs. If you are using Norton AntiVirus, check C:\Program Files\Norton AntiVirus for a file named ccIMScan.exe.

Attention!

MSN Messenger has no options for disabling file sharing or application sharing. If someone invites you to share an application or accept a file, you can refuse.

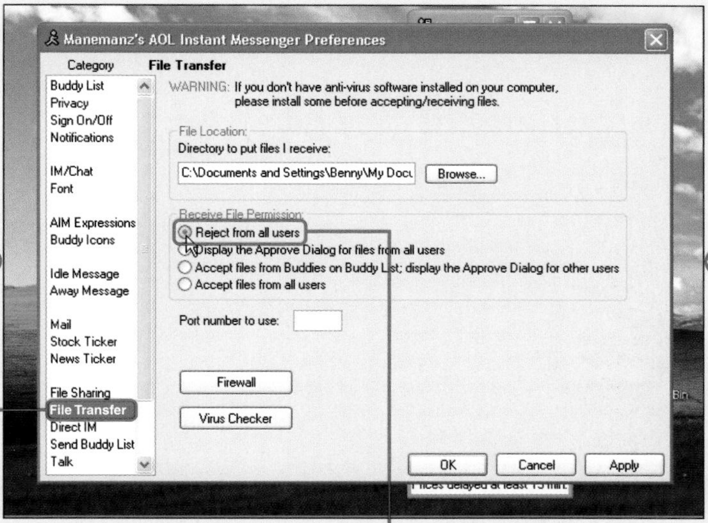

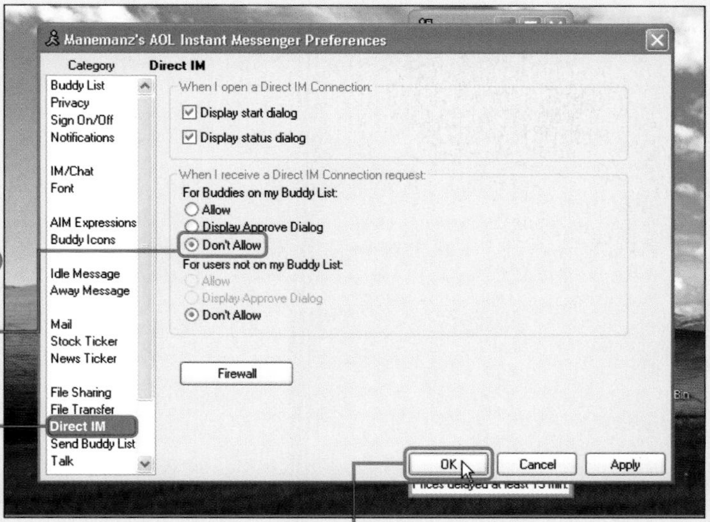

⑥ Click File Transfer.

- AIM displays the File Transfer settings.

⑦ Click Reject from all users.

⑧ Click Direct IM.

- AIM displays the Direct IM options.

⑨ Click Don't Allow under For Buddies on my Buddy list.

- When you select Don't Allow for your buddies, AIM automatically selects Don't Allow under For users not on my Buddy list.

⑩ Click OK.

- AIM applies your new preferences.

INDEX

Numbers

A

B

C

D

E

F

INDEX

J

K

L

M

N

O

INDEX

INDEX